# TEACHING PUBLIC BUDGETING AND FINANCE

Many universities offer the Master of Public Administration (MPA) or other public affairs degree, which includes at least one course in public budgeting or public financial management. The faculty who teach these courses can however sometimes struggle to cover the breadth of material required and to fully engage students in what can be a technical subject. *Teaching Public Budgeting and Finance: A Practical Guide* addresses this challenge by sharing hands-on classroom expertise from leading scholars and creative instructors in the field. Drawing on their extensive experiences with teaching, researching, and engaging in service, each contributor reflects on how their area of expertise can be taught most effectively, providing a discussion of student learning outcomes, pedagogical approaches, relevant resources, and appropriate course assignments.

While no one book can provide a final say on classroom instruction, this first-of-its kind primer on teaching public budgeting and financial management courses is a detailed, indispensable guide for all faculty looking to improve the learning experience of students in the classroom. *Teaching Public Budgeting and Finance: A Practical Guide* is required reading for early career faculty as they prepare to teach the course for what may be the first time, as well as for more senior faculty looking to update their course, complement their own teaching strengths, or teaching the course for the first time in several years.

**Bruce D. McDonald III, Ph.D.**, is Associate Professor of Public Budgeting and Finance at NC State University. He also serves as the Editor-in-chief of *Public Administration*, Co-editor-in-chief of the *Journal of Public Affairs Education*, Co-editor of *Routledge's Public Affairs Education Book Series*, and President of the North Carolina Public Administration Alliance.

**Meagan M. Jordan, Ph.D.**, is Associate Professor of Public Budgeting and Finance in the School of Public Service at Old Dominion University. She previously served as the Secretary of the Association for Budgeting and Financial Management and is the Chair of the Budget and Finance Management Section of the Network of Schools of Public Policy, Affairs, and Administration. She serves on the editorial board of the *Journal of Public Affairs Education*.

# ROUTLEDGE PUBLIC AFFAIRS EDUCATION

EDITORS

**BRUCE D. MCDONALD III**
*Associate Professor of Public Budgeting and Finance*
*North Carolina State University, Raleigh NC*

**WILLIAM HATCHER**
*Associate Professor of Public Administration*
*Augusta University, Augusta GA*

The Routledge Public Affairs Education series, edited by William Hatcher and Bruce D. McDonald III, publishes books designed to assist faculty in the classroom and in the management of public administration, public affairs, and public policy programs. To accomplish this, the book series explores evidence-based practices, commentary about the state of public administration education, and pedagogical perspectives. The Routledge Public Affairs Education series examines the future of public administration education, teaching practices, international public administration education, undergraduate public administration programming, and other relevant topics to advance the field's knowledge. For more information about the series, or to submit a book proposal, please contact series editors William Hatcher at wihatcher@augusta.edu and Bruce D. McDonald III at bmcdona@ncsu.edu.

## RECENTLY PUBLISHED BOOKS

**The Public Affairs Faculty Manual**,
*Bruce D. McDonald III and William Hatcher*

**Undergraduate Public Affairs Education**,
*Madinah F. Hamidullah*

**Teaching Public Budgeting and Finance**,
*Bruce D. McDonald III and Meagan M. Jordan*

# TEACHING PUBLIC BUDGETING AND FINANCE

## A Practical Guide

*Edited by Bruce D. McDonald III*
*and Meagan M. Jordan*

Routledge
Taylor & Francis Group

NEW YORK AND LONDON

Cover image: Getty Images

First published 2022
by Routledge
605 Third Avenue, New York, NY 10158

and by Routledge
2 Park Square, Milton Park, Abingdon, Oxon OX14 4RN

*Routledge is an imprint of the Taylor & Francis Group, an informa business*

*Library of Congress Cataloging-in-Publication Data*
A catalog record for this title has been requested

ISBN: 978-1-032-14670-6 (hbk)
ISBN: 978-1-032-14668-3 (pbk)
ISBN: 978-1-003-24044-0 (ebk)

DOI: 10.4324/9781003240440

Typeset in Bembo
by Newgen Publishing UK

2: 41036 2953 33497 44788 71 222 15337
–BDM

To my great instructors and mentors, and to the many practitioners
that have contributed to my classes.
–Meagan

# CONTENTS

*List of Figures*                                                      *ix*

*List of Tables*                                                        *xi*

*Editor Biographies*                                                  *xiii*

*Contributor Biographies*                                              *xv*

*Acknowledgments*                                                     *xix*


1  Teaching Public Budgeting and Finance                                1
   *Bruce D. McDonald III and Meagan M. Jordan*

2  Public Budgeting and Finance in Context                              9
   *Meagan M. Jordan and Merl Hackbart*

3  Revenue                                                             30
   *Justin M. Ross and Denvil R. Duncan*

4  Public Budgeting Mechanics                                          51
   *Katherine G. Willoughby and Colt Jensen*

5  Capital Budgeting and Debt Financing                                75
   *W. Bartley Hildreth*

6  Financial Management                                               109
   *Craig L. Johnson and Yulianti Abbas*

7  Auditing and Internal Controls                                          155
   *Carl J. Gabrini*

8  Financial Condition Analysis                                            171
   *Craig S. Maher*

9  Pensions                                                                201
   *Kenneth A. Kriz*

10 Nonprofit Budgeting and Financial Management                           219
   *Carol Ebdon*

11 Incorporating Social Equity                                            236
   *Bruce D. McDonald III and Sean McCandless*

12 Case Studies and Service Learning in Public Budgeting
   and Finance                                                            257
   *Meagan M. Jordan and Bruce D. McDonald III*

*Index*                                                                   277

# FIGURES

| | | |
|---|---|---|
| 2.1 | Interdisciplinary roots of public budgeting and finance | 11 |
| 4.1 | An enterprise framework | 64 |
| 4.2 | State of Virginia budget documents | 67 |
| 4.3 | City of Charlotte, budget for community relations, FY 2021 | 68 |
| 4.4 | City of Charlotte, budget for community relations with performance measures and FTE count, FY 2021 | 69 |
| 4.5 | State of Wyoming budget appropriation bill, FY 2021–2022 | 70 |
| 5.1 | Annuities | 88 |
| 6.1 | Statement of Net Position, State of California, June 30, 2019 | 121 |
| 6.2 | Statement of Activities, State of California, June 30, 2019 | 124 |
| 6.3 | Balance Sheet – Governmental Funds, State of California, June 30, 2019 | 129 |
| 6.4 | Schedule of Fund Balances by Function, State of California, June 30, 2019 | 131 |
| 6.5 | Statement of Revenues, Expenditures, and Changes in Fund Balances – Governmental Funds, State of California, June 30, 2019 | 132 |
| 6.A1 | Statement of Net Position – Proprietary Funds, State of California, June 30, 2019 | 143 |
| 6.A2 | Statement of Revenues, Expenditures, and Changes in Fund Balances – Proprietary Funds, State of California, June 30, 2019 | 147 |
| 6.A3 | Statement of Cash Flows – Proprietary Funds, State of California, June 30, 2019 | 149 |
| 6.A4 | Statement of Fiduciary Net Position, State of California, June 30, 2019 | 153 |

| | | |
|---|---|---|
| 6.A5 | Statement of Changes in Fiduciary Net Position, State of California, June 30, 2019 | 154 |
| 8.1 | Structure of Comprehensive Annual Financial Reports | 175 |
| 8.2 | Brown's dimensions of fiscal condition | 178 |
| 8.A1 | Sources of Brown's 10-Point Test: Balance Sheet | 187 |
| 8.A2 | Sources of Brown's 10-Point Test: Statement of Revenues, Expenditures, and Changes in Fund Balances | 188 |
| 8.A3 | Brown's 10-Point Test: Detroit, MI | 189 |
| 8.A4 | Sources of Maher's ratios: Statement of Net Position | 194 |
| 8.A5 | Sources of Maher's ratios: Statement of Activities | 195 |
| 8.A6 | Maher's ratios: Detroit, MI | 197 |
| 9.1 | Basic structure of pensions | 206 |
| 9.2 | Relationship among the key measures of the funded status | 209 |
| 9.3 | Average funded ratio of pension plans by 2019 funded status | 209 |
| 11.1 | The budget cycle | 242 |
| 12.1 | Bloom's taxonomy of learning | 267 |

# TABLES

2.1    Federal revenues and expenditures, 2019 and 2018    13
2.2    Federal nondefense discretionary spending by selected
      functions, 2018    13
2.3    State and local government finances, 2018 (thousands)    14
3.1    Marginal benefit/price ratio of consumer goods to hypothetical
      buyer    37
3.2    Buyer's utility maximizing choices from Table 3.1 under a
      $7 budget constraint    38
3.3    Marginal benefit/price ratio of consumer goods to hypothet-
      ical buyer    38
3.4    Buyer's utility maximizing choices from Table 3.3 under a
      $7 budget constraint    39
3.5    Marginal benefit/price ratio of consumer goods to hypothetical
      buyer    39
3.6    Buyer's utility maximizing choices from Table 3.5 under a $7
      budget constraint    39
3.7    Comparison of efficiency outcomes for different policy choices    40
4.1    Budget timelines of United States governments    54
4.2    Exercise 1—governance, development, and budget mechanics    59
4.3    Exercise 2—making calculations and comparisons    61
4.4    Exercise 3—local strategies to boost resiliency following disaster    63
4.5    Exercise 4—research report: budgeting in a pandemic    65
4.6    Outline of public budgeting: theories and practice    71
5.1    Establishing capital budgeting and debt management policies    78
5.2    Sample capital facilities inventory    82
5.3    Bloomberg assignment    83

| | | |
|---|---|---|
| 5.4 | Capital improvement project detail sheet | 86 |
| 5.5 | Ranking method | 87 |
| 5.6 | Time value of money calculations | 89 |
| 5.7 | Using excel functions | 90 |
| 5.8 | Model financial plan | 91 |
| 5.9 | Fiscal impact analysis – projecting revenue from new development | 92 |
| 5.10 | Fiscal impact analysis exercise | 93 |
| 5.11 | Relationship of fixed coupon and current year | 94 |
| 5.12 | Model debt plan | 95 |
| 5.13 | Revenue coverage capacity example | 96 |
| 5.14 | Debt project assignment | 96 |
| 5.15 | Basis for determining cost of capital | 97 |
| 5.16 | Valuing a bond with annual coupon | 98 |
| 5.17 | Financial structure and debt service analysis | 99 |
| 5.18 | Secondary market pricing | 100 |
| 5.19 | Quick reading of the official market disclosure document | 103 |
| 5.20 | Case analysis of a revenue bond financing | 103 |
| 5.21 | Enterprise revenue bond analysis: bond covenants and project financing | 104 |
| 5.22 | State GO credit quality analysis | 105 |
| 7.1 | Suggested learning outcomes | 157 |
| 7.2 | Federal websites | 158 |
| 7.3 | State, local, and professional websites | 159 |
| 7.4 | Example websites, Florida | 159 |
| 7.5 | Topics in governmental and not-for-profit auditing | 160 |
| 8.1 | Brown's 10-Point Test for Detroit, MI, FY 2017 | 179 |
| 8.2 | Maher's measuring financial condition for Detroit, MI, FY 2017 | 182 |
| 8.3 | Discussion questions | 184 |
| 9.1 | Primary characteristics of pension plans | 207 |
| 9.2 | Sample assignment questions | 213 |
| 9.A1 | Individual plan funded status | 216 |
| 9.A2 | Actuarial contribution rate by plan | 217 |
| 10.1 | Resources for teaching | 231 |
| 11.1 | Suggested learning outcomes | 244 |
| 11.2 | Pedagogical strategies to incorporate social equity into budgeting classes | 246 |
| 12.1 | Case cycle for a course | 261 |
| 12.2 | Types of case study presentations | 262 |

# EDITOR BIOGRAPHIES

**Bruce D. McDonald III, Ph.D.**, is Associate Professor of Public Budgeting and Finance at NC State University. He also serves as the Editor-in-chief of *Public Administration*, Co-editor-in-chief of the *Journal of Public Affairs Education*, Co-editor of *Routledge's Public Affairs Education Book Series*, and President of the North Carolina Public Administration Alliance. He received a BA in Communications from Mercer University, MA in International Peace and Conflict Resolution from American Military University, M.Sc. in Economic History from the London School of Economics, MEd in Training and Instructional Design from NC State University, and Ph.D. in Public Administration and Policy from Florida State University. His research focuses on public budgeting and finance in the context of the fiscal health of local governments. His research has appeared in journals such as the *Journal of Public Administration Research and Theory*, *Public Administration Review*, and the *American Review of Public Administration*.

**Meagan M. Jordan, Ph.D.**, is Associate Professor of Public Budgeting and Finance in the School of Public Service at Old Dominion University. She previously served as the Secretary of the Association for Budgeting and Financial Management and is the Chair of the Budget and Finance Management Section of the Network of Schools of Public Policy, Affairs, and Administration. She serves on the editorial board of the *Journal of Public Affairs Education*. She received her BA in Economics from Austin College, an MPA from the University of Arkansas at Little Rock, and a Ph.D. in Public Administration from the University of Kentucky. She has taught, consulted, and trained in the areas of performance budgeting, budget process, ethical management, and strategic planning. Her research focuses on state and local government budget theory and process, revenue policy, and popular financial reporting and transparency. Her research has appeared in journals such as *Public Budgeting and Finance*, *Public Finance and Management*, the *Journal of Government Financial Management*, the *Journal of Public Budgeting, Accounting, and Financial Management*, *American Review of Public Administration*, *Public Administration Quarterly*, and the *Journal of Policy Analysis and Management*.

# CONTRIBUTOR BIOGRAPHIES

**Yulianti Abbas, Ph.D.**, is a faculty member and the Director of Graduate Program in Accounting at the Faculty of Economics and Business, Universitas Indonesia. She is also a founding member and researcher at the Tax Education and Research Center, the Institute for Economic and Social Research Universitas Indonesia. She received her Ph.D. in Public Affairs from Indiana University under a Fulbright Fellowship.

**Denvil R. Duncan, Ph.D.**, is Associate Professor of Public Economics in the Paul H. O'Neill School of Public and Environmental Affairs at Indiana University. He received both a B.Sc. and M.Sc. from the University of the West Indies, Mona and his Ph.D. from Georgia State University. He teaches public finance and microeconomics courses in the undergraduate, MPA, and doctoral program. His primary research focuses on economic agents' responses to taxation.

**Carol Ebdon, Ph.D.**, is Professor of Public Administration in the School of Public Administration at the University of Nebraska at Omaha. She was previously the Finance Director for the City of Omaha, and has served as a board member for a variety of nonprofit organizations. Her research interests are primarily in the areas of local government budgeting and financial management.

**Carl J. Gabrini, Ph.D.**, is Assistant Professor of Accounting in the Wright School of Business at Dalton State College. Prior to his academic career, Dr. Gabrini served as the Lead Senior Auditor for the Florida Auditor General. He received a BA in political science and government from State University of New York at Stony Broke, an MBA Dowling College, M.Sc. in Taxation from the University of Central Florida, and his Ph.D. in public administration and policy from Florida

State University. His research focuses on auditing, accounting information systems, and governmental and nonprofit accounting. His research has appeared in the *Journal of Public Administration Research and Theory*, *State and Local Government Review*, and the *Journal of Applied Business and Economics*.

**Merl Hackbart, Ph.D.**, is Emeritus Professor of Finance and Public Policy in the Martin School of Public Policy and Administration at the University of Kentucky. He has served twice as Kentucky's State Budget Director and has held several administrative positions at the University of Kentucky. He received a BS in Economics from South Dakota State University and his Ph.D. in Economics from Kansas State University. His research has focused on various aspects of public financial management. His research has appeared in *Public Administration Review*, *Public Budgeting and Finance*, the *Journal of Public Affairs Education*, and *Public Finance Review*, among others.

**W. Bartley Hildreth, Ph.D.**, is Professor of Public Management and Policy, and former Dean, in the Andrew Young School of Policy Studies at Georgia State University. He is also a Fulbright Scholar, a Fellow of the National Academy of Public Administration and a recipient of the Aaron B. Wildavsky Award for lifetime scholarly achievement in the field of public budgeting and financial management. He has served as a city CFO, on the boards of state and city bond issuing authorities, and as a public member of the Municipal Securities Rulemaking Board. He received a BA in political science from the University of Alabama, an MPA from Auburn University at Montgomery, and a Ph.D. in public administration from the University of Georgia.

**Colt Jensen** is a Ph.D. student in the Department of Public Administration and Policy at the University of Georgia. He received an MPA and MA in Political Science from Appalachian State University. His research focuses on intergovernmental collaboration and local government administration.

**Craig L. Johnson, Ph.D.**, is Associate Professor at the O'Neill School of Public and Environmental Affairs at Indiana University. He received a BA in Social Science and Government from Hartnell College and an MPA and Ph.D. in Public Administration from the State University of New York at Albany. His research focuses on public financial management, municipal finance, capital markets and financial intermediation, public budgeting and finance, economic development, and tax increment finance. His latest book is the 2nd edition of his co-edited volume, *Tax Increment Financing and Economic Development: Uses, Structures and Impact* (co-edited with Kenneth A. Kriz).

**Kenneth A. Kriz, Ph.D.**, is University Distinguished Professor of Public Administration in the Department of Public Administration at the University of Illinois at Springfield. He served as Vice-chairperson of the City of Omaha,

Nebraska Civilian Employees Retirement System from 2006 to 2011 and on the Board of Trustees of the Wichita, Kansas Police & Fire Retirement System and the Joint Investment Committee for the city's pension funds from 2014 to 2018. He was a Fulbright Scholar in the Republic of Estonia during academic year 2004–2005 and a Fulbright Senior Specialist in the Czech Republic in 2008. His research focuses on subnational debt policy and administration, public pension fund management, government financial risk management, economic and revenue forecasting, and behavioral public finance. His research has appeared in *Public Budgeting and Finance*, the *Municipal Finance Journal*, *Quarterly Review of Economics and Finance*, and the *Journal of Public Budgeting, Accounting, and Financial Management*.

**Craig S. Maher, Ph.D.**, is Professor of Public Budgeting and Finance and Director of the School of Public Administration at the University of Nebraska at Omaha. He is also a Research Fellow at the Center for Great Plains Studies and he has served on the board of directors for the American Society of Public Administration's Section on Public Performance and Management, the National League of Cities and Urban Institute's Legislating-for-Results Advisory Committee, and the Government Accounting Standards Board Service Efforts and Accomplishments Task Force. He received his Ph.D. in Political Science from the University of Wisconsin-Milwaukee. His research focuses on public finance with an emphasis on revenue policy, fiscal federalism, and financial condition analysis. His research has appeared in *Public Administration Review*, the *Journal of Public Affairs Education*, the *Journal of Public and Nonprofit Affairs*, and *Public Budgeting and Finance*.

**Sean McCandless, Ph.D.**, is Assistant Professor of Public Administration and Associate Director of the Doctorate in Public Administration program at the University of Illinois Springfield. He also serves as the Case Study Editor of the *Journal of Public Affairs Education*. He received a BA in History, Political Science, and Psychology from Colorado State University – Pueblo and an MA in Political Science and Ph.D. in Public Affairs from the University of Colorado Denver. His research focuses on social equity, diversity, and inclusion. His research has appeared in *Public Administration Review*, the *Journal of Public Affairs Education*, *Public Integrity*, and *Administrative Theory and Praxis*.

**Justin M. Ross, Ph.D.**, is Professor of Public Economics in the Paul H. O'Neill School of Public and Environmental Affairs at Indiana University. He received his BS in Business Economics from Wright State University and a Ph.D. in Economics from West Virginia University. He teaches public revenue, managerial economics, and cost-benefit analysis in the MPA program, as well as the doctoral seminar in revenue theory.

**Katherine G. Willoughby, Ph.D.**, is the Margaret Hughes and Robert T. Golembiewski Professor of Public Administration in the Department of Public

Administration and Policy at the University of Georgia in Athens. She is also a Fellow of the National Academy of Public Administration. She received her BS in Psychology from Duke University, MPA from NC State University, and her Ph.D. in Public Administration from the University of Georgia. She has spent over 30 years teaching, conducting research, and consulting about public budgeting, finance, and management. She is an internationally recognized expert on subnational government budgeting and regarding public budgeting reforms, particularly performance budgeting. She is the author of several books, including *Public Budgeting in Context: Structure, Law, Reform and Results* and her research has been published in outlets such as *Public Administration Research*, *Public Budgeting and Finance*, and *Public Performance and Management Review*.

# ACKNOWLEDGMENTS

We acknowledge all of the great instructors of public budgeting and finance courses.

# 1

# TEACHING PUBLIC BUDGETING AND FINANCE

*Bruce D. McDonald III and Meagan M. Jordan*

Teaching is challenging, and it is a task that is complicated by the lack of preparation and training. While doctoral programs train students to engage in research and become subject matter experts, few doctoral programs in public administration provide any dedicated focus to preparing students to teach. However, the role of teaching can be stressful and cause difficulty in finding a work-life balance amongst scholars (Schwoerer, Antony, & Willis, 2021). What to teach, how to teach, what book to assign, and how to write learning objectives can all be new experiences for an early career faculty member. To help in their role as teachers, some faculty seek out new methodologies (Jones, 2020; Witkowski, Reyes, & Padilla, 2021) and tools (Rinfret, 2020) to improve the pedagogical structure of the course. Others seek innovative ways to enhance their experience and engagement with students' material (Dolamore, 2020; Meyer, 2020; White, 2020; Yu & Campbell, 2020).

When it comes to teaching courses related to public budgeting and finance, the need for good teaching is clear. Currently, there are more than 90,000 governments and 1.6 million nonprofits in the United States. It is the responsibility of Master of Public Administration (MPA) programs to prepare their students to go into these organizations and take leadership positions. A core component of this preparation is coursework in public budgeting and finance. Public budgeting and finance is an essential area of knowledge for our students to acquire, yet how the material should be taught remains an issue of much discussion. Evidence of this discussion can be seen at the annual conferences of the Network of Schools of Public Policy, Analysis, and Administration and the Association for Budgeting and Financial Management in recent years, as both conferences have frequently included panels on the issue of pedagogy and program management related to public budgeting

DOI: 10.4324/9781003240440-1

and finance courses. While these conversations have been a good start, help and guidance are still needed for faculty in the trenches of teaching.

With the development of this, we have aimed to provide that help and guidance. To address the concerns and challenges of teaching public budgeting and finance, we have sought out the experience of leading scholars from critical areas in the field. Drawing on their extensive experiences with teaching, researching, and engaging in service, we asked them to reflect on how their area of expertise can be taught effectively. These reflections took a number of forms with each scholar providing a discussion of their student learning outcomes, pedagogical approaches, relevant resources, and appropriate course assignments. While the book does not propose to be the final say in teaching public budgeting and finance, we believe that the result is an aide that faculty can use to improve the quality of their teaching, as well as to improve the experience of students in the classroom and their overall learning of the material.

The audience for this book is fourfold. For early career faculty, the book is a useful resource as they prepare to teach their assigned courses. The first few years of a tenure track position are rough as early career faculty work to establish their research agenda while balancing the need to be effective in the classroom. The experiences of the scholars discussed in this book provide a pathway that eases the transition from student to faculty member by giving guidance on what and how they to teach. For senior faculty, how we teach a class can become relatively fixed over time. The approaches utilized by the scholars in this book are a resource for faculty that have made the decision to update the classes. Through the experiences of their colleagues, senior faculty can find new ideas about the pedagogy of public budgeting and finance. We also believe that there is an audience among the faculty whose expertise is narrowly focused on certain public budgeting and finance topics. In this case, faculty can use this book to complement their areas of strengths. Finally, sometimes the public budget and finance course is assigned to faculty with public management expertise that is outside of public budgeting and finance. The breadth of material that can be covered in a public budgeting and finance-related course may leave faculty unsure of how to best teach a particular focus, but the experience of scholars from that focus can help to fill the void.

## Our Experiences

Our experiences teaching in MPA programs led us to edit this book. Both of us have worked in different academic institutions. We both worked in MPA programs housed in regional teaching universities, and now we both work for research-orientated institutions. And we have taught a variety of courses in public budgeting, financial management, and public finance, among others. As we have gone about our careers, we have experienced the challenges of teaching firsthand, and we have seen students struggle to understand and apply the material. As we have looked to improve our students' classroom experiences, we have found little help. While many of the textbooks in the field include PowerPoint slides and practice questions that can be used in the classroom, there has been a lack of resources on *how* best to teach the material. This is a problem within all subfields of public administration, but it is particularly important for public budgeting and finance. After all, like Constand, Pace, and Clarke (2016) note, courses involving finance and accounting components are inherently harder for students. To have successful student outcomes in these courses, a more targeted focus on pedagogy is needed.

## Pedagogical Challenges

As scholars who focus on public budgeting and finance, we care deeply about our teaching material. Yet, the very characteristics that make public budgeting and finance a dynamic and critical field of study create pedagogical challenges. The field is exceedingly broad, with numerous areas of research and practice. Therefore, there are issues of what material to cover in a course and students' preparedness for technical material. Yet, public budgeting and finance is essential to the MPA curriculum because public programs and policies require funding for their creation and implementation. These courses are critical to the MPA curriculum as they provide the necessary grounding for leadership positions in public organizations.

### *What to Teach?*

The topics covered in a public budgeting and finance course vary greatly across MPA programs regardless of the course title. The focus and geography of the MPA program influence course content and which material to emphasize. For instance, a program in a state capital and within a college of arts and studies may focus more on state budgets and the political process of budgeting, whereas a program located in the Washington, DC area may concentrate more on the federal budget and fiscal policy implications.

While the subject area is ubiquitous in MPA curricula, the number of required and elective courses on the topic varies, influencing the content and depth of coverage. Many MPA programs have one required course that focuses heavily on the budget process and types of revenue. Other MPA programs may have two required courses, one class that focuses more on budgeting and a second course that focuses on revenue policy. Yet, another program with a second required course may focus more on accounting and reporting or financial management more broadly.

Of course, covered topics are also decided by the faculty members. For programs large enough to have faculty training in public budgeting and finance, the faculty are often highly specialized, like capital debt or state sales tax policy. For most programs, however, the faculty who teach these courses are often generalists who teach a variety of courses in their departments. In both cases, they often lack the expertise needed in all areas of public budgeting and finance.

## *Who Is Learning?*

MPA students come from a range of academic backgrounds and many are mid-career students. Therefore, prior training in finance, accounting, economics, or political science cannot be assumed. A city librarian, national park service ranger, or state highway department engineer may not have prior training or education in any of the previously listed areas. Yet, basic competency in the subject matter requires understanding the political process and some technical aspects. Some students' math phobia further hampers this understanding of the course material. Even mid-career students often have the perception that the topic is not relevant to them since they are not one of the "bean counters" working in the budget office.

## *How to Teach?*

Teaching public budgeting and finance requires balancing soft skills like managing and leading people and hard skills like budget analysis and other financial calculations. However, this is particularly challenging since the expertise of the instructor is usually not evenly balanced across all the skills of the field. So, the instructor has the task of winnowing down the material and presenting it so that the students, with their varied backgrounds, learn practical application to public programs and policies. Decision-making and policy impact are the common denominators to the various topics. Even a mid-career budget analyst student needs to learn how revenue policy may impact economic activity, the importance of financial transparency and citizen participation, or the consequences of defaulting on a revenue bond. It is the instructor's task to take siloed sections of the field and bring them together into one or two courses that illustrate relevance to the management of programs and policies.

## Synopsis of Chapters

The chapters in this teaching guide provide the teaching insights from the authors' years of experience. Each topical chapter offers learning objectives, assignment ideas, and other resources for public budgeting and finance that are developed out of the teaching, research, and service experience of leading scholars in the field. The authors often provide alternative approaches or suggestions for asynchronous online, synchronous online, and in-person instruction. Included in the book are chapters on core topics, such as the mechanics of budgeting, financial management, and revenue. There is also a chapter dedicated to budgeting and finance for the nonprofit sector, and a couple of chapters provide pedagogical guidance on incorporating conversations about social equity and experiential learning tools.

After this introductory chapter, Merl Hackbart and Meagan Jordan instruct on the "big picture" of public budgeting and finance and how to place it into context for MPA students. Chapter 2 discusses public budgeting and finance as a multidisciplinary field with a breadth of topics areas that can be viewed as separate areas of study. Therefore, the authors discuss the importance of teaching students the environment that these various topics within the discipline share. They stress the importance of keeping the political process and economic condition in the foreground. The chapter also discusses the roles of the different levels of governments and their influence on budgeting, revenue, and capital budgeting and debt financing, and accountability.

The book begins to dive into key topical areas of public budgeting and finance with Chapter 3. Focusing on revenue policy, Justin Ross and Denvil Duncan explain their approach to teaching the assessment of revenue policy and applying that assessment to revenue instruments. The authors also discuss the philosophical views that may contribute to decision-making. Finally, Ross and Duncan provide an outline of their teaching approach, which organizes the presentation of the revenue material into an easy-to-apply process for the novice teacher.

Katherine Willoughby and Colt Jensen address teaching the mechanics of public budgeting in Chapter 4. As the most ubiquitous topic in MPA programs within the public budgeting and finance field, Willoughby and Jensen discuss the importance of focusing on the ability of students to read and interpret a budget. Included in the discussion is a pathway for teaching the basic concepts of budget cycles and format and emphasizing the development of the practical skills that successful budgeters will need in their careers.

Chapter 5 details how Bartley Hildreth teaches capital budgeting and debt. Hildreth emphasizes the principles of good management of capital budgeting and debt financing. He organizes his course material with his REMIT framework (respect, environment, methods, interpret, and transparently). After explaining the five parts of the framework, he illustrates the application of each portion of the framework.

Next, in Chapter 6, Craig Johnson and Yulianti Abbas, respectively, provide an overview of their teaching approach to financial management. The chapter reviews the accounting principles and accounting standards. The authors offer instruction on the accounting equation and all parts of the comprehensive financial report. The discussion of the updates and purpose of accounting standards and the use of the financial statements place the material in a managerial context.

Chapter 7 covers the teaching of auditing and internal controls by Carl Gabrini. Gabrini brings his extensive experience as a government auditor and his experience teaching auditing to discuss how to integrate the auditing and internal controls subject matter into an MPA course. The chapter focuses on explaining the types of audits and the auditing process. He illustrates the audit and internal control role in monitoring strategic, operational, and financial condition and performance.

Teaching financial condition analysis is Chapter 8. Craig Maher addresses the mechanics of producing a financial condition analysis. Included in the discussion of mechanics is how fiscal health can be measured using different tools and approaches. He simplifies the mechanics by identifying the key ratios to calculate and interpreting their meaning. He also provides help on finding data necessary for the calculations within a Comprehensive Annual Financial Report. His discussion on his approach to teaching financial condition analysis goes beyond the measures to guide students to learn about government finances' political, demographic, and economic context.

In Chapter 9, Kenneth Kriz addresses the unique challenges of teaching pensions in a traditional MPA program. The author addresses where to discuss pensions in a public budgeting and finance course and how to prepare students for the pension material. Kriz also discusses the issue of how to teach the characteristics of pension plans and pension policies and provides an alternative approach to the material based on the course.

Carol Ebdon covers the teaching of nonprofit budgeting and financial management in Chapter 10. She starts by placing the subject in the context of most MPA public budget and finance courses. While highlighting the distinction between budgeting in the government and nonprofit sectors, she introduces the nature of organizational structure for nonprofits. Ebdon guides teaching the material effectively through a discussion of what the structure means for budgeting, financial reporting and analysis, and internal controls.

Chapter 11 is not about a traditional budget and finance topic. Instead, Bruce McDonald and Sean McCandless address the emerging issue of integrating social equity into a public budgeting and finance course. The authors explain the real-world concerns regarding social equity and its relevance to public administration and public budgeting and then provide guidance and strategies on integrating social equity into teaching the budget process. They also provide tangible examples of the integration in practice. Finally, McDonald and McCandless suggest learning outcomes for this new approach to teaching public budgeting.

The final chapter also focuses on a pedagogical approach. Jordan and McDonald discuss case studies and service learning as forms of experiential learning for public budgeting and finance in Chapter 12. Regarding case studies, they address how to select a case, incorporate it into the class (including a discussion of using case studies in different class modalities), and the challenges of case discussions. Next, we define service learning and discuss the benefits of incorporating service learning into a public budgeting and finance course. Finally, we outline the necessary conditions for incorporating service learning, teaching with a service learning project, and service learning challenges.

## Conclusion

Teaching and training the next generation of public administrators and leaders are tremendous responsibilities that come with an incredible reward. But teaching can also be difficult. Every semester brings a new set of challenges to address, whether it be challenges related to pedagogy, content, or student concerns. As faculty who teach in MPA programs, we signed on for the task. The desire to improve the public organizations that surrounds us by raising up new leaders and strengthening current leaders is what motivates us, and we owe it our students, our communities, and ourselves to prepare them as best as we possibly can.

As we work to prepare students for the future, it is important to remember that how we teach can have a significant effect on how well our students learn the material (see Bolyard, 2021; Slagle, 2020). Our aim with this book is to help faculty in the field succeed in the classroom. By bringing together some of the leading scholars and faculty from the field, we can learn from their experience, better understand what our students should be learning in class, and how we can enhance that learning experience. Effective teaching is a skill that must be practiced and honed, and we are excited to support you on that journey.

## References

Bolyard, W. L. (2020). Get flipped: Using learning technologies to engage student learning. *Journal of Public Affairs Education, 27*(2), 257–259.

Constand, R. L., Pace, R. D., & Clarke, N. (2016). Accounting faculty teaching ratings: Are they lower because accounting classes are more difficult? *Journal of Accounting and Finance, 16*(4), 70–86.

Dolamore, S. (2020). Written communication by public servants: A case study on responding with the right words amid challenging contexts at the Housing Authority of Baltimore City. *Journal of Public Affairs Education, 27*(1), 96–109.

Ebdon, C. E. (2021). Nonprofit budgeting and financial management. In B. D. McDonald & M. M. Jordan (Eds.), *Teaching public budgeting and finance: A guide for teaching professional competencies* (pp. 214–230). Routledge.

Gabrini, C. J. (2021). Auditing and internal controls. In B. D. McDonald & M. M. Jordan (Eds.), *Teaching public budgeting and finance: A guide for teaching professional competencies* (pp. 150–165). Routledge.

Hildreth, W. B. (2021). Capital budgeting and debt financing. In B. D. McDonald & M. M. Jordan (Eds.), *Teaching public budgeting and finance: A guide for teaching professional competencies* (pp. 75–108). Routledge.

Johnson, C. L., & Abbas, Y. (2021). Financial management. In B. D. McDonald & M. M. Jordan (Eds.), *Teaching public budgeting and finance: A guide for teaching professional competencies* (pp. 109–149). Routledge.

Jones, P. A. (2020). Implementing specifications grading in MPA courses: A potential strategy for better work-life balance. *Journal of Public Affairs Education, 26*(4), 531–547.

Jordan, M. M., & Hackbart, M. (2021). Public budgeting and finance in context. In B. D. McDonald & M. M. Jordan (Eds.), *Teaching public budgeting and finance: A guide for teaching professional competencies* (pp. 9–29). Routledge.

Jordan, M. M., & McDonald, B. D. (2021). Case studies and service learning in public budgeting and finance. In B. D. McDonald & M. M. Jordan (Eds.), *Teaching public budgeting and finance: A guide for teaching professional competencies* (pp. 252–271). Routledge.

Kriz, K. A. (2021). Pensions. In B. D. McDonald & M. M. Jordan (Eds.), *Teaching public budgeting and finance: A guide for teaching professional competencies* (pp. 196–213). Routledge.

Maher, C. S. (2021). Financial condition analysis. In B. D. McDonald & M. M. Jordan (Eds.), *Teaching public budgeting and finance: A guide for teaching professional competencies* (pp. 166–195). Routledge.

McDonald, B. D., & McCandless, S. (2021). Incorporating social equity. In B. D. McDonald & M. M. Jordan (Eds.), *Teaching public budgeting and finance: A guide for teaching professional competencies* (pp. 231–251). Routledge.

Meyer, S. J. (2020). Everything is fine? Using "The Good Place" to teach administrative ethics. *Journal of Public Affairs Education, 27*(2), 126–140.

Rinfret, S. R. (2020). Telepresence robots: A new model for public administration course delivery. *Journal of Public Affairs Education, 26*(3), 380–390.

Ross, J. M., & Duncan, D. R. (2021). Revenue. In B. D. McDonald & M. M. Jordan (Eds.), *Teaching public budgeting and finance: A guide for teaching professional competencies* (pp. 30–74). Routledge.

Schwoerer, K., Antony, M., & Willis, K. (2021). #PhDlife: The effect of stress and sources of support on perceptions of balance among public administration doctoral students. *Journal of Public Affairs Education, 27*(3), 326–347.

Slagle, D. R. (2020). Online education: Practical, theory-based advice for the instructor. *Journal of Public Affairs Education, 27*(3), 380–382.

White, S. S. (2020). In memoriam: H. George Frederickson. *Journal of Public Affairs Education, 26*(3), 255.

Willoughby, K. G., & Jensen, C. (2021). Public budgeting mechanics. In B. D. McDonald & M. M. Jordan (Eds.), *Teaching public budgeting and finance: A guide for teaching professional competencies* (pp. 51–74). Routledge.

Witkowski, K., Reyes, A. M., & Padilla, M. (2021). Teaching diversity in public participation through participatory research: A case study of the PhotoVoice methodology. *Journal of Public Affairs Education, 27*(2), 218–237.

Yu. H. H., & Campbell, T. M. (2020). Teaching leadership theory with television: Useful lessons from *Game of Thrones*. *Journal of Public Affairs Education, 27*(2), 141–175.

# 2

# PUBLIC BUDGETING AND FINANCE IN CONTEXT

*Meagan M. Jordan and Merl Hackbart*

Oftentimes, public budgeting and finance (here forth "public finance") classes focus on the source and use of public funds and budgeting processes. While revenue policies and budgeting processes are the major components of governments' financial management systems, accounting, auditing, and capital budgeting systems, as well as legacy liability management strategies (i.e., health benefits and pension funds) are also important components a government's financial management structure and system. It is critically important, in a public budgeting and financial management course, that students gain an understanding of the complexities and interrelationships of a government's financial management and budget decision-making systems.

Such complexities and interrelationships are fostered by both the internal environment of the government organization as well as external factors beyond the control of that government, such as the economy and constituent values and political factors. Combined, those complexities and interrelationships establish the context within which administrative officials and policymakers arrive at budget and other related financial policy decisions. It is important to stress to students that whether one pursues a career as a financial manager, program administrator, or policy analyst, a public administrator's ability to carry out his or her responsibilities effectively will be enhanced or limited by a person's understanding of and ability to work with the constraints and opportunities associated with an organization's financial management and budgeting system.

The public, including public administration students, are generally aware of government budgeting or government funding from the evening news. Federal budget issues are also highlighted when Congress is in a budgetary deadlock due to issues that may be directly, or often, indirectly related to budget decisions.

DOI: 10.4324/9781003240440-2

Political arguments or debates regarding taxes levied by the federal or state government are in the limelight during election season. Unfortunately, this extent of public finance exposure is mainly superficial.

Public finance students need to appreciate that budget decisions are determined by the resolution of conflicting policy priorities, values, current and future economic conditions, or by the impact of external and intergovernmental issues. Most budget processes are designed to facilitate such conflict resolutions, compromises, and ultimately budget decisions. The need to resolve policy and priority conflicts through transparency and clarification of facts via a government's formalized budget process adds to the complexity of government budgeting and financial management.

Students must understand that political, intergovernmental, and economic conditions may constrain and influence budget decisions and understand the government's statutory and constitutional mandated budget processes, which establish the specific budget preparation, approval, and execution processes. Such budget processes vary from state to state but share standard process components. With an understanding of such components and relationships, students may conclude that budgeting is the culmination and resolution of differences in opinion regarding the availability of public resources and the best use of those resources to the maximized benefit of citizens.

This chapter aims to provide areas and opportunities for instructors to highlight the big picture of public finance. The following two sections address the environment in which public finance operates. Then, the chapter addresses the components and activities of public finance systems, and ends with public finance challenges facing public managers. At the end of each chapter section are summary highlights to emphasize key teaching points.

## The Role of Government and the Federal System

Public administration (and public policy) is a multi-disciplinary field, and public finance reflects that multi-disciplinary nature. In public administration, public finance is concerned with government funds from raising, collecting, borrowing, accounting, spending, and investing. As such, public finance encompasses policy, political, managerial, and technical skills and knowledge from accounting, political science, economics, management, and finance. Figure 2.1 illustrates the breadth of public finance within public administration and how public finance professionals utilize knowledge, skills, and practices derived from or shared with other disciplines. For instance, within a government's public finance system, the program planning (business) and budget decisions are determined with input from several public stakeholders and officials (political science). Forecasting techniques are often used to determine the likely future availability of funds and the impact of reliance on certain revenue sources (economics). The influx of revenue must be accounted for, reported (accounting), and invested (finance). The evaluation of the

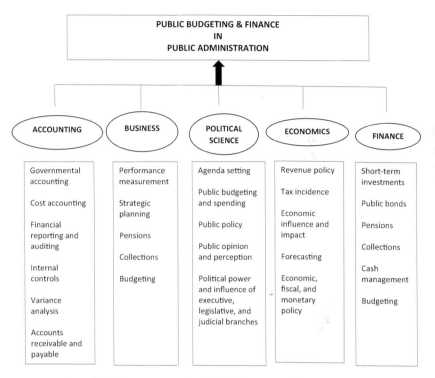

**FIGURE 2.1** Interdisciplinary roots of public budgeting and finance

effective use of those funds (business) in implementing public programs and policies is another aspect of public finance.

The financing of government functions is critical to the existence of government. Therefore, it is appropriate to begin the discussion of public finance with a discussion of the role of government. All aspects of the role or functions of government require funding from the public coffers. Different levels of government take on different roles, which affects their revenue-raising and spending choices. The role of government is to provide a place for "the market" to exist. Governments provide a mechanism for the enforcement of laws, contracts, and property rights. However, the role of government goes beyond allowing markets to operate.

Market failure is the economic explanation for government provisions. Businesses within the marketplace have a clear profit motive and cannot always sustain "desirable" activities or stop "undesirable" activities while maximizing their profits. Keep in mind that the economic ideal of the marketplace, equilibrium, is where supply equals demand. This is the most efficient point. The market will supply what the consumer demands at the equilibrium quantity and equilibrium price. Market failure is disequilibrium. The idea is that the government provision also occurs because the private sector would not supply a product otherwise or at least in the desired quality or quantity.

From that perspective, economists have broadly defined goods and services which need to be provided by the public sector as public goods and services, as opposed to private goods and services. This division is based on the ability and willingness of the market economy to deliver such goods and services. Public goods are goods that the private market economy cannot allocate due to their characteristic of joint consumption. Examples include national defense, police and fire protection, parks, and similar services and goods that allocation by the market fails to work.

Government intervention is not always through government provision; it may also lead to regulation. The private sector may not be *willing* to sustain "desirable" activities or stop "undesirable" activities if it conflicts with their profit motive. Governments encourage positive externalities (i.e., vaccines, green space) and discourage negative externalities (i.e., water contamination, noise pollution). Encouragement or discouragement of private-sector marketplace activity may be in the form of taxes, fines, taxes subsidies, or tax credits. Government regulation also takes place to correct market failures such as imperfect information (i.e., consumer protection) and costly business entry requiring a monopoly (i.e., utilities).

With the U.S. multi-level federal system, budget and finance staff of federal, state, and local governments must understand the roles of all the three levels of government regarding program development, funding, and implementation responsibilities. Such an understanding is critical for efficient and effective planning, authorizing, approving, and implementing programs, and assuring accountability for public expenditures. While the need for such understanding is clear, insuring and coordinating the roles of the three levels of government adds complexity. This federal system requires intergovernmental coordination and management to ensure that public programs meet citizen needs in the most efficient and effective manner. Consequently, it is important to provide students with an overall view of the financial and programmatic relationships to provide the "context" of state and local budgeting and financial management.

The provision of uniquely federal public goods and services (i.e., defense and social security) ensures consistency of services across the nation. However, the division between state and local government responsibilities tends to be less distinctive, and, consequently, states and localities often share responsibilities for several functions. As a result, there is significant variability across the states regarding financing education, public protection, and other local and quasi-state level goods and services. It is also necessary to note that "local" in public finance does not always refer to cities, towns, and counties. Special purpose governments are often included in the "local" designation, including school districts, airport authorities, utility districts, and other special revenue-raising districts and authorities.

Tables 2.1 and 2.2 provide a perspective of the relative role of the federal in providing and financing various categories of public goods and services. The federal

**TABLE 2.1** Federal revenues and expenditures, 2019 and 2018

*REVENUES*

| Sources | Dollars (Billions) | |
|---|---|---|
| | *2019* | *2018* |
| Individual Income Taxes | 1,718 | 1,684 |
| Payroll Taxes | 1,243 | 1,171 |
| Corporate Income Taxes | 230 | 205 |
| Other | 272 | 269 |
| **TOTAL RECEIPTS** | **3463** | **3329** |

*EXPENDITURES*

| | 2019 | 2018 |
|---|---|---|
| Social Security | 1,038 | 982 |
| Medicare | 775 | 704 |
| Medicaid | 409 | 389 |
| Income Security Programs | 303 | 286 |
| Other | 485 | 418 |
| Offsetting Receipts | -276 | -259 |
| **Total Mandatory** | **2,734** | **2,520** |
| Defense | 676 | 622 |
| Nondefense | 661 | 642 |
| **Total Discretionary** | **1,338** | **1,263** |
| Net Interest | 375 | 383 |
| **TOTAL OUTLAYS** | **4,447** | **4,108** |
| **(% of GDP)** | **(21%)** | **(20.3%)** |

Source: Congressional Budget Office (2019, 2020)

**TABLE 2.2** Federal nondefense discretionary spending by selected functions, 2018

| Budget Function | In Billions |
|---|---|
| Transportation | 104 |
| Education, Training, Employment, and Social Services | 102 |
| Community and Regional Development | 94 |
| Income Security | 74 |
| Health | 70 |
| Administration of Justice | 61 |
| Natural Resources and Environment | 59 |
| International Affairs | 56 |
| Agriculture | 9 |

Source: Congressional Budget Office (2019)

government focuses on social policy areas, with about 60 percent of its spending going to Medicare, Medicaid, Social Security, and other public welfare programs. These are the "entitlement" programs that the government obligates itself to fund based on formulas calculated for the recipients. The remaining spending is spending on net interest (less than 10 percent) and discretionary spending (about 30 percent), with about half of discretionary spending going to defense. Meanwhile, as shown in Table 2.3, local governments are the primary level for the provision of public safety, but local government is not solely responsible for law enforcement. All levels of government have a role in funding transportation, with the transportation burden being a much more significant proportion of local government spending. Therefore, shared and overlapping responsibilities across levels of governments further illustrate the complexity of government roles. For instance, education funding is predominantly local, but as most state constitutions mandate, states have funding responsibility as well. Furthermore, the federal government provides additional education funding in the form of grants. States have a dominant role in the function area of public welfare; however, the federal government

**TABLE 2.3** State and local government finances, 2018 (thousands)

|  | *State Government* | *Local Government* |
| --- | --- | --- |
| Intergovernmental Revenue | 688,153,027 | 612,133,355 |
| Individual Income Taxes | 390,002,949 | 35,712,920 |
| Property Taxes | 17,457,845 | 529,580,698 |
| General Sales Taxes | 315,929,835 | 95,082,008 |
| Current Charges | 235,935,966 | 311,597,025 |
| Other | 982,741,780 | 427,550,646 |
| **TOTAL REVENUE** | **2,630,221,402** | **2,011,656,652** |
| Education | 322,250,848 | 724,011,015 |
| Public Welfare | 658,766,759 | 59,362,193 |
| Transportation | 116,397,678 | 107,557,530 |
| Police | 16,099,464 | 102,700,567 |
| Fire | 0 | 52,044,155 |
| Hospitals | 88,563,497 | 110,748,271 |
| Health | 44,225,184 | 57,615,705 |
| Correction | 50,718,809 | 30,552,812 |
| Capital Outlay | 135,313,220 | 243,209,426 |
| Other | 666,499,313 | 149,699,339 |
| **Total Direct Expenditure** | **1,849,648,413** | **1,960,984,073** |
| Intergovernmental Expenditure | 562,398,270 | 16,802,386 |
| **TOTAL EXPENDITURE** | **2,412,046,683** | **1,977,786,460** |
| **(% of GDP)** | **(11.7%)** | **(9.6%)** |

Source: U.S. Census Bureau (2020).

also provides funding in this area and often requires a certain level of funding from the states. Looking more closely at detailed budgets will reveal the role that local, state, and federal governments have in transportation and other areas. Altogether, government spending on the provision of goods and services constitutes about 40 percent of the United States' economic activity as measured by gross domestic product (GDP). The roles of the various levels of government, especially the shared program responsibilities across levels of government, not only creates financial complexity but also increases managerial complexity.

## *Big Picture Points*

1. The federal system of financing public programs adds additional complexity to state and local budgeting systems.
2. The federal fiscal system of shared program and financing responsibility requires budget and finance staff to analyze funding responsibilities and the impact of changing policies at other levels of government.
3. The role of the government determines the provisions of public goods, regulatory activities, and fiscal policy to fund them.

## The Economy and Politics

At the beginning of a public finance class, it is important to indicate to the students that public budgets and financial management plans and decisions are made in an environment influenced and limited by constituent values, political positions and attitudes, and economic conditions. Of these context factors, economic conditions, present and future, establish program needs and public budgetary response limitations. While economic conditions are major decision influencing factors for all levels of government, current and future economic conditions and trends are especially important for state and local governments due to the requirement for state and local governments to balance their budgets financially. Unconstrained by such requirements, the federal government has major responsibility for policy initiatives and policy-related budget and appropriation decisions to mitigate the impact of economic downturns throughout countercyclical fiscal policy.

While the status of the economy and its impact on revenue generation is a critical factor in determining the affordable size and focus of public budgets, political factors and citizen values and priorities also establish constraints to public budget decision making. Combined, these external factors play major roles in determining what is programmatically desired by constituents and what is fiscally feasible. These external facts and factors also impact the nature and content of policy initiatives for which budgets represent the government's policy and program decisions.

Because of the importance of current and future economic conditions in determining public budgeting environments, it is helpful to include a review of basic macroeconomics and the role of government in an economy in the initial public budgeting classes. This review and discussion can include a discussion of the economic role of government in the economy and the impact of government fiscal policy. It may also include the types of government expenditures such as public capital and infrastructure investment, income assistance, as well as other public good expenditures and how fiscal policy can impact the status of the economy. The students' understanding of the role of government in the economy will assist them as they study budget planning and policy as well as budget processes.

The efforts of governments to impact the economy or economic activity with their spending and tax policies is merged with politics. The economic environment is also a political environment. Interest groups, elected officials, and political parties navigate the political process and set the political agenda. The political agenda is where the decisions are formally made. It is also where philosophical views and preferences about the government's role in the economy (i.e., economic development, jobs stimulus, zoning) are battling for influence. The political process determines what spending and tax policies are considered and implemented. Therefore, a basic understanding of political processes and activity at all levels of government is expected and necessary. All of the technical knowledge shared by accountants, budget analysts, economic forecasters, and other public finance technicians are subjected to the political decision-making process that ultimately funds policies and programs. With government spending making up approximately 40 percent of the GDP, the importance of that political process cannot be overstated. Government spending responds to the economy or influences economic activity, but the government is also a chief economic actor.

In addition to the role of fiscal policy, monetary policy also plays a role in the economy; therefore, exposure to the FED (Federal Reserve System) role in the economy is also valuable. As the central banking of the U.S., the FED influences the economy through the adjustments to interest rates and bank rules and regulations that impact the availability and security of capital. The FED website has several videos which provide clear and concise discussions of the roles and responsibilities of the FED, including monetary policy and its relationship to the economy. It is also useful for students to understand the impact of FED policy on the financial markets. This understanding is important as state and local governments fund public pensions and increasingly rely on bonds for financing infrastructure.

The following sections address various activities within the public finance system. Some of these activities are very technical and require specialized skills. However, students must always be aware that a significant shift in the economic or political environment can sometimes upend the technical activities or results of the public finance system.

## *Big Picture Points*

1. Public finance operates in an economic and political environment.
2. The government acts to influence the economy via monetary and fiscal policy.
3. The political agenda is where fiscal policy (spending and taxing) decisions are formalized.

## Budgeting and Revenue Issues and Processes

As noted earlier, effective budgeting and related revenue issues comprise the basic components of a state or local governments public financial management system. The preparation and execution of a government's budget reflect debt management, legacy costs, and other financial management issues and their implications. Consequently, the major challenge faced by a government's financial management team is that finance staff must be simultaneously and equally focused on preparing and executing its budget while continually monitoring the government's current and future revenue situation. While projected revenues are important for preparing budgets at all levels of government, the requirement of states and local governments to balance their budgets requires continuous monitoring of receipts throughout the fiscal year.

Budgeting for all levels of government involves four elements of the budget cycle which include the (1) budget preparation by the executive branch, (2) budget review and approval by the legislative branch, (3) budget execution by the executive branch, and (4) budget performance review and accountability assessment. In carrying out each element of the budget cycle, elected officials and budget staffs acquire, review, and analyze past, current, and future program needs and resource availability. Such analysis and reviews can highlight the need for program adjustments and the adequacy of the current revenue base to support budget initiatives. While the specific processes and activities involved in each of the elements of the budget cycle vary for the federal, state, and local governments, the responsibilities of the branches of government are similar for the elements of the budget cycle while varying in complexity, time frames, and interaction with the other levels of government. For example, since the creation of the executive budget and budget process in the 1920s, the President, Governor, or Mayor has the responsibility to initiate the budget preparation process while working cooperatively with the legislative branch for other elements of the budget cycle.

Because the budget planning and preparation process is a responsibility of the executive branch of government, the chief executive budget office typically issues budget guidelines to agencies or departments to follow in preparing their budget requests. Past or current data and information regarding program needs, program performance, and prior funding levels assist in establishing the basis for budget requests for what is often referred to as the current services budget (unless the government uses an alternative budgeting system such as zero-base budgeting). The analysis of past program performance relative to program needs and goals highlights the previous fiscal year's budget adequacies or inadequacies. Such agency-based requests, supplemented by policy initiatives of the chief executive, establish the initial framework for budget preparation.

Agencies or departments are typically required to build their budget requests based on their assessment of the "current services" budget or the funding needs for operating its programs at their current levels (adjusted for cost of service). Program or agency budget requests above or below the current services cost-adjusted budget are justified based on program goals or policy changes from executive (Governor or Mayor) guidance or the judgment of program managers resulting from program performance assessments.

Regardless of the type of budgeting system used by a government (line item, program, zero base, performance, etc.), agency personnel and central budget staffs are challenged to build budget requests or budget recommendations on information and data regarding needs, financial feasibility, and best assessments of future citizen needs, tax revenues, and emerging longer-term issues as well as program priorities. Agency staff typically build their requests based on past data and knowledge (the known) coupled with assessments of the current program needs and status (the knowable) and best assessments of future needs and conditions. Assessing future conditions and needs (the unknowable) provides a significant challenge for effective and efficient government budgeting. A similar challenge is faced by the central budget office and legislative staff, and presidents, governors, and mayors, as the future is subject to changes due to current trends, unanticipated events, and the availability of tax and other revenue sources finance programs and activities included in the final approved budget.

The executive branch's finance and budget staff's responsibility to monitor revenue receipts and changes in program needs are critically important for state and local governments due to their constitutional or statutory responsibility to end the fiscal year with a financially balanced budget. Such a challenging responsibility is particularly important during periods of economic downturns. Such economic fluctuations and their revenue implications pose challenges in ensuring a balanced budget. When revenue shortfalls are anticipated during the budget execution phase of the budget cycle, state and local governments must take action. Available actions include reducing appropriations, using rainy day or budget stabilization funds, and increasing revenues, including tax increases or the receipt of federal funds, such as occurred during the COVID-19 pandemic or the recession of 2008–2009. The federal government does not face the challenge of a balanced budget requirement; therefore, monitoring of spending is focused on accountability and assessment of changes in programmatic needs.

## *Big Picture Points*

1. Budgeting and revenue policy and revenue performance are the main elements of public financial management systems.
2. The budgeting process for all levels of government involve four elements of the budget cycle which clarifies the role of the executive and legislative branch in the preparation, approval, and execution process.
3. Unlike the federal government, which can approve and execute an unbalanced budget, the balanced budget requirement for state and local governments necessitates that finance officials continually monitor revenue receipts during the execution phase of the budget cycle and take action if revenue receipts fail to meet revenue expectations.
4. Uncertainty regarding program needs and future revenues are major challenges to effective budget formation and execution.
5. Because of uncertainty about future revenues and unforeseen spending needs, rainy day and/or budget stabilization funds have become standard components of state and local government financial management systems and policies.

## The Longer Term: Capital Budgeting, Debt, and Legacy Issues

The key to students understanding capital budgeting and its relationship to debt financing is their awareness of the vast difference between the federal government and state and local governments. The federal budget merges expenditures for operating programs and capital or infrastructure investments into a single appropriation. State and local governments prepare both an operating budget as well as a capital budget.

The operating budget preparation tends to focus on the assessment of current or near-term needs for current programs and their funding levels. Conversely, state and local budget preparers must also analyze longer-term funding needs such as funding for infrastructure, which is primarily funded by the selling or issuance of bonds. Yet, the current year's operating budget includes the current year's annual debt service payment for outstanding bond issues.

For state and local governments, the separate capital budget process involves a forward assessment of the need for new, rebuilt, and expanded infrastructure. That assessment must determine and meet the demands of a changing population and economy. Infrastructure financed by debt has a pre-determined schedule of debt service payments on the existing stock of outstanding bonds. The debt financing of capital or infrastructure investments (roads, bridges, streets, public buildings, and educational facilities) occurs because the large expenditures may be beyond the government's financial capacity to fund them in a single fiscal year. The *benefits received* principle suggests that payment of the infrastructure should spread over the project's useful life. Those who benefit from the infrastructure in the future will also contribute to paying for it. Therefore, capital budgets must create and reflect the long-term commitment to provide the funds to meet the interest and principal payments on the bonds.

Partially at the encouragement of rating agencies, state and local governments are beginning to assess their long-term debt capacity. In other words, they must determine how much of their budget is going to debt service each year. With estimates of future debt capacity, budget staff and policymakers must balance between capital or infrastructure needs and the future ability to support the associated debt service without significantly impacting operating program funding.

At the federal level, debt does not involve a long-term spending plan. The federal government issues debt to cover current expenses. However, students need to understand the difference between the federal debt and the federal deficit. The deficit reflects a structural imbalance, meaning that there is more spending than revenue coming in. Debt occurs when the federal government borrows by issuing Treasury securities to cover the deficit. The size of the debt reflects the accumulation of deficits minus the rare surplus.

An additional long-term commitment on the state and local operating budget is legacy costs, which primarily refer to the long-term liabilities to fund retirement and health care benefits for state and local employees. The current year's funding of pension benefits or legacy costs is based on the actuarially required or recommended contribution for a state or local government's pension system. Pension plans are typically designed to provide retirement benefits based on an employee's salary history and years of employment. In most cases, the employee also contributes a portion of his or her salary to the pension fund. Therefore, the operating budget has pre-determined costs associated with debt service and legacy costs, representing relatively "fixed" budget requirements as opposed to the variable budget costs for most operating programs.

## *Big Picture Points*

1.  The federal government's budgeting of infrastructure and use of debt is vastly different from state and local governments' use of debt and capital budgets.
2.  Due to the cost of infrastructure or capital projects, state and local governments prepare both operating and capital budgets.
3.  Most capital projects are funded by bonds which create future debt service requirements which must be included in budget appropriations.
4.  As the funding for capital projects for state and local governments increasingly involves debt funding, assessment of current and future debt capacity is an integral part of the budgeting for the capital and infrastructure process.
5.  Legacy and pension benefits for government employees establish future payment liabilities.

## Accountability, Assessment, and Transparency

The public financial management system provides the means to administer public programs and policies; therefore, accountability and outcomes assessment are important components of a government's financial management system. Such a system is critical in ensuring transparency and building public confidence that their government is operating in a manner that attempts to ensure efficiency, legality, and effectiveness of public programs and government operations. Such accountability involves two major types of activities.

It is critical that state and local governments ensure public confidence regarding the legality and appropriateness of financial transactions via annual audits of department and agency financial transactions. Such audit processes and procedures include continuous reviews of financial transactions by state or local government agencies (normally by accounting and internal audit offices) and periodic audits by external or third-party audit reviews. Government accounting guidelines or standards are developed by the Government Accounting Standards Board, which reviews and analyzes various types of financial transactions and issues accounting system standards and processes referred to as Generally Accepted Accounting Principles or GAAP.

The standards provide detailed guidance for how transactions are to be recorded and recognized and establishes a basis for comparisons of program and agency financial activities. The rating agencies place great emphasis on the comparability of financial data across similar governments. Compliance with GAAP assures the rating agencies, and the public, of comparability of state and local government data. Financial audits involve periodic reviews of accounting systems to ensure that transactions are appropriately recorded and reported and whether the government's account system is GAAP compliant. With "clean" audits, the public is assured that a government is appropriately reporting on government transactions and ensures transparency of government operations.

The second component of accountability and assessment is the program evaluation. Determining if programs effectively and efficiently provided the service or product as intended by the funding is the evaluation's purpose. Such program assessment activities may be internal to an agency, or governments might have independent offices that provide such assessments. For example, the U.S. Government Accountability Office provides Congressional committees with program performance or effectiveness reviews. States may house such performance reviews in a state audit office, or the state legislature may have a committee or staff whose role it is to conduct program reviews and assessments. While the performance review structure varies across the federal, state, or local governments, the information gathered from such reviews can assist the executive branch in budget preparation and execution. The performance reviews can also provide information to legislative leaders or legislative committees as they review budgets or pursue legislation to enhance program efficiency and effectiveness.

Providing relevant financial data and program performance assessments for the public is an important responsibility of public organizations. Effective press relationships can enhance the public's understanding of financial information regarding budget proposals and budget enactments. Such information is important in ensuring the public is informed about public policy purposes and initiatives. It is also a critical mechanism for meeting transparency goals, gaining the support of program initiatives, and helping to ensure public confidence in governmental operations.

While effective communication and transparency of public financial information are important goals, governments continue to struggle to determine what data or information should be routinely or periodically provided. The challenge of informing the public is magnified by the complexity of governmental operations, including the shared funding of some programs across different governments. Furthermore, the public may not know what data or information they would like to know about the programs and activities they care about. Therefore, governments are reacting to the need for transparency with a multi-medium approach. The publicly accessible traditional budget hearings and "town halls" still exist along with the more innovative efforts at citizen outreach and participation. For instance, a growing trend is to provide popular financial reports that focus on communicating comprehensive financial information to the non-expert public. Such reports are increasingly available on government websites along with traditional financial reports. Also increasingly available are budget simulation tools that allow residents to share their budget preferences. In addition to the traditional media tools like press briefings, public officials are using social media to assist the public's understanding of the nature, operation, and financial implications of programs and activities.

## Big Picture Points

1. Standards for public funds accounting are critical to ensuring transparency and public confidence in the integrity of public sector financial reports and reporting.
2. National accounting standards for governments are established by the Government Accounting Standards Board (GASB).
3. There are two major types of audits which are financial and performance audits. Financial audits focus on the integrity and accuracy of government financial reporting, and performance audits focus on the outcomes of governmental programs.
4. Completed audits often provide suggestions for improved transparency and accountability for the audited jurisdiction or entity.
5. Transparent communication with the public involves a multi-medium approach, such as budget simulations, popular financial reports, social media, and the traditional use of press briefings and public hearings.

## Information and Data

Information and data are important factors in effective public financial management. Dealing with uncertainty is one of the major challenges students will face in their careers as public servants. Consequently, it is useful to provide students with an understanding of how the existence or absence of information may impact their ability to administer programs or prepare budgets and financial plans. Information can be classified as known, knowable, and unknown data or information and provide the basis for determining financing responsibilities, revenue sharing, and expenditure needs.

Fortunately, the U.S. Department of Commerce, the Department of Labor, the Internal Revenue Service, and the various federal agencies compile and make available a broad array of data regarding program, funding, program needs, regional comparisons, and the like to provide the known information. Such data provide the basis for program design, budget preparation, and funding decisions. While historical or known data are useful in establishing the base for budgets (whether at the federal, state, or local level of government), knowable data varies across government divisions. For example, states and local governments have access to current tax receipts and program participants; therefore, they incorporate such data in developing budgets that meet current needs and, often, in the short-term future.

However, the unknowable data, which is important in the design of programs and the development of future financing plans, is the most difficult to obtain. For example, revenue forecasting and forecasting models are normally based on past relationships and data and are supplemented by current observations of revenue receipts. The major challenge is that revenue forecasting involves predicting the "unknowable" data regarding the future performance of the economy, political changes, changes in federal, state, and local tax structures and modifications in funding responsibilities for the programs that are financially shared among the levels of government.

Similarly, while data and information regarding citizen demands and preferences may be available from past indicators, it is more challenging to assess current and future preferences and needs to design and plan programs. Surveys, polls, group discussions, and public hearings are strategies often used to assess such citizen preferences. Of course, the effective and transparent dissemination of information to the non-finance expert citizen also requires assembling and synthesizing data in a meaningful and comprehensible manner.

Public financial managers are users and providers of financial data. Therefore, students must practice synthesizing financial data as providers and analyzing financial data as users so that they are prepared to deal with unanticipated events. Effectively managing the known, knowable, and unknown data is essential for creating valuable and contextual data for decision making and policymaking. As noted earlier, budget proposals and appropriations are dependent on an assessment of past conditions, current conditions, and expected future conditions (the unknowable). At the same time, knowable conditions (the current fiscal year conditions) and the unknowable conditions can and will impact the preparation of budgets and will foster adjustments to previously approved budgets.

## *Big Picture Points*

1. Public finance decisions are made with some degree of uncertainty because data is either known, knowable, or unknowable. Unknowable data are the future conditions regarding performance, the economy, elections, funding responsibilities, and citizen preferences.
2. Public managers are both users and providers of information and data essential for decision making and policymaking.

## Emerging Issues and Challenges

Governments are simultaneously involved in several overlapping budget cycles. While budget staff and policymakers may be involved in preparing budgets, they may have to respond to unanticipated events and adjust the current fiscal year budget. Such events may include changing economic conditions, changes in federal support of programs, natural disasters, and the like. In other words, while state and local government officials are preparing or approving future budgets, they are also involved in the budget execution of the current fiscal year. They may also be involved in the budget accountability and performance assessments of previous budgets. The major point to pass to students of public finance is that they should be alert to the fact that budgeting cycles are interactive and, therefore, budget processes may be disrupted by changing program needs or economic and other conditions.

So, it is important for students to understand the interaction of budget cycles and that unanticipated events may necessitate adjustments to both budget preparation and execution processes. They should also be aware of various strategies used in adapting to changing budget conditions. Depending on the nature of the government (economic, political, or statutory), different budget impacts will elicit different response strategies. For example, it was not possible to anticipate the COVID-19 pandemic and its impact on the federal, state, and local governments. The response by states has varied considerably as they address increased unemployment compensation and the cost of providing vaccines amidst a decline in state revenue. The states' budget maneuvers were mandatory operating budget expenditure reductions, delaying pension payments, delaying capital projects, and terminating programs.

Emerging and unanticipated events such as COVID-19, natural disasters, federal program changes, and other economic disruptions have different budget and financial impacts that vary in length and magnitude. Therefore, budget staff and policymakers need to consider the nature of the issue (i.e., length of time, area of government), its probable impact on program needs, and the expenditure impacts as they prepare a response. The challenge is that they must be responsive to the unique moment that required the budget adjustment while also fulfilling the constitutional or statutory requirements to provide certain services (i.e., education and prisons) and balance their budget. These challenges are expected to grow exponentially as the consequences of environmental changes and infrastructure decline accumulate.

As suggested, the response strategy to unanticipated events depends on the nature of the budget cycle disruption. Fortunately, there are sources of strategy options that budget staff can use. Sources of budget adjustment strategies from peers are available through professional associations such as the National Association of State Budget Officers, the National League of Cities, the Government Finance Officers Association (see Appendix for list and description of resources), and other organizations. These organizations also assist state and local government officials by informing them of potential changes in federal legislation, impacting program structures, funding options, and strategies used by other states or localities for similar situations. Furthermore, academic research has extensively covered approaches to budget adjustments based on the nature of the unanticipated event. For instance, academic scholars provided insight into the use and effectiveness of budgetary strategies in response to the Great Recession (Arapis, Reitano, & Bruck, 2017; Gorina, Maher, & Joffe, 2018; Jimenez, 2017; Marlowe, 2013; Miller & Smith, 2011) and the COVID-19 pandemic (Joyce & Prabowo, 2020; Smith-Walter & Snow, 2020).

Another growing trend in budgeting is the attention to social equity concerns. There's an increasing realization that sincere efforts at social equity must be addressed at the planning and finance stage. Since budgets are a statement of priorities, governments are increasingly being expected by constituents to prioritize social equity in the budget process. Prioritizing equity means considering the budgetary impact on groups during the budget planning process and evaluating budget outcomes. Public participation and/or input throughout the budget process is part of the incorporation process. Bringing the commitment to social equity into the budgeting process and as part of the budget cycle ensures the formalization of that commitment on the political agenda. Incorporating social equity is addressed in more detail in Chapter 11.

## *Big Picture Points*

1. Most all governmental policies and activities have budget and financial implications.
2. Emerging or unforeseen issues impacting governmental budgets have both short-term and long-term implications and impacts. For example, natural disasters impact businesses and employment leading to revenue reductions

in the short term. However, such disasters may permanently eliminate some businesses which have long-term employment and revenue implications.

3. It is important for students to understand that there are various budget response strategies to unanticipated events that can be employed to sustain programs during an economic downturn or another type of government operations disturbance.

4. There are multiple "support groups," such as national professional associations, that provide updates on possible budget impacts (changes in federal programs and finances), as well as strategies employed by other states and local governments to mitigate the impact of unanticipated events.

5. A commitment to formalizing social equity means merging the effort with the public budgeting process and cycles.

## Summary and Observations

Public administration and public policy graduate students have a vast array of backgrounds, from the arts to the sciences to the social sciences. So, spurred by the fear of math or money, students often express a hesitancy toward public finance. However, that hesitancy usually subsides once they understand the role of public finance systems in making the implementation of public programs and public policies possible. In other words, students need a big-picture view of public finance to understand its implications fully.

Except for small cities and special purpose governments where public finance professionals take on multiple roles, most jurisdictions have staff dedicated to each of the technical areas. For instance, a director of budgeting is often separate from or subordinate to the director of finance. If the jurisdiction is large enough, the budget director will supervise several budget analysts assigned to different departments within the government. Many MPA students move on to a career as a budget analyst while staff degreed in accounting are more likely to hold the positions involved in recording transactions and creating financial statements. An economist may serve as the state forecaster, and a more traditional business finance staffer may be responsible for making short-term investment decisions for liquidity purposes and long-term investment decisions to manage the pension fund.

Furthermore, a forward-looking and effective department manager must understand the influence of the political and economic environment and shifts in the environment that impact spending and funding. Optimal planning for the attainment and maintenance of technology, space, supplies, and infrastructure requires revenue awareness and budget planning. This is also required to recruit and retain personnel and the responsiveness to changes in stakeholders' demand for services.

The vastness of the public budgeting and financial management discipline within public administration and policy is necessary to fully account for the responsibilities and impact of public finance on creating and executing public programs, public services, and public policies. Revenue-raising and spending decisions occur in a political environment within economic conditions with the expectation of accountability and transparency. Those decisions reflect the role of government and likely interact with the roles of other governments. While past conditions influence the planning of future conditions, future conditions are unknown, but unforeseen events will unquestionably take place, making for an exceptionally dynamic system. Each substantive area of public administration and policy (i.e., education, social services, human resources, defense, public transportation, criminal justice) is a recipient of public financial resources. The existence of each area has public financial implications. The most effective leaders in public administration appreciate the breadth of knowledge, skills, and ability employed to fund public policies and programs.

Finally, because public finance within public administration is such a vast field of study, there are research opportunities regarding each of the topics identified in Figure 2.1. As a result, students need the flexibility to go beyond the public administration academic journals that specialize in public finance research. It is best to encourage a combination. For instance, a student's research on popular financial reporting may utilize accounting journals in addition to public budgeting and financial management journals. Similarly, students' research on the impact of sales taxes may lead them to supplement their resources with economics journals. Additionally, there are an array of professional reports, databases, and academic quality resources via government and professional association websites (see Appendix). The forthcoming chapters will provide more resources for instructors and students to delve into specific areas of public finance.

## References

Arapis, T., Reitano, V., & Bruck, E. (2017). The fiscal savings behavior of Pennsylvania school districts through the Great Recession. *Public Budgeting & Finance, 37*(3), 47–70.

Congressional Budget Office. (2019). *The budget and economic outlook: 2019–2029.* Congressional Budget Office.

Congressional Budget Office. (2020). *The budget and economic outlook: 2020–2030.* Congressional Budget Office.

Gorina, E., Maher, C., & Joffe, M. (2018). Local fiscal distress: Measurement and prediction. *Public Budgeting & Finance, 38*(1), 72–94.

Jimenez, B. S. (2017). Institutional constraints, rule-following, and circumvention: Tax and expenditure limits and the choice of fiscal tools during a budget crisis. *Public Budgeting & Finance, 37*(2), 5–34.

Joyce, P. G., & Prabowo, A. S. (2020). Government responses to the Coronavirus in the United States: Immediate remedial actions, rising debt levels and budgetary hangovers. *Journal of Public Budgeting, Accounting & Financial Management, 32*(5), 745–758.

Marlow, J. (2013). Strategy, priority-setting, and municipal capital budget reform: Three cases from the Great Recession. *Journal of Public Budgeting, Accounting & Financial Management, 25*(4), 693–718.

Miller, L. J., & Smith, D. L. (2011). The Great Recession's impact on New York City's budget. *Municipal Finance Journal*, *32*(1), 89–113.

Smith-Walter, A., & Snow, D. (2020). Making budget decisions in the shadow of the COVID-19 pandemic: The Massachusetts case. *Municipal Finance Journal*, *41*(2/3), 61–73.

U.S. Census Bureau. (2020). Annual survey of state and local government finances: 2018 data release. Retrieved from www.census.gov/programs-surveys/gov-finances/newsroom/updates/2018released-data.html

## Appendix: Sources of Studies in Public Budgeting and Financial Management

**Association of Government Accountants:** Professional Association. Citizen-centric reports from state and local governments. Restricted access to most research e-reporting, performance management and accountability research.

**Congressional Budget Office:** Supports Congress with analyses on budget and economic issues. Cost estimates. Research on a wide range of issues pertaining to the budget, finance, the economy, taxes, social security, and several policy areas. Data on budget and economic projections.

**CSPAN:** Extensive collection of videos of public policy hearings, especially U.S. Senate and House of Representatives. Searchable by committee name (i.e., Ways and Means Committee and Appropriations Committee).

**Governmental Accounting Standards Board:** Establishes accounting and reporting standards for state and local government. GASB sponsored research related to reporting and accounting standards and practices. Videos are also available.

**Government Finance Officers Association:** Professional association of federal, state, and local officials. Reports on government surveys. Reports on topics including budgeting, bonds, and implementation of federal policies. Reports on best practices. Several "elected official's guides" plainly explain finance topics such as internal control and financial reports.

**International City/County Management Association:** Professional association of local government management and employees. Research, reports, and databases on a broad area of local government issues, including finance, budget, and economic development.

**National Association of State Budget Officers:** Professional organization. Advances state budget practices. Reports and data on state budget process, expenditures, capital budgeting. Annual fiscal survey of states. Videos also are available.

**National Conference of State Legislatures:** Represents legislatures and provides research relevant to state legislative staff. Research, reports, and data on state fiscal policies.

**National League of Cities:** Represents local government leaders. Reports on various local government issues, including finance, economic development, and budget-related concerns.

**Office of Management and Budget:** The government's central budget office for the federal government. Houses current and past executive budgets include the executive memos that outline the President's budget priorities and conditions. (Similar websites exist for state and local governments and have budget process information, budgets, and other financial reports.)

**U.S. Census – Government Finances:** Has public sector section with data on state and local government finances, government employment, building permits, tax collections. Research on economic conditions, labor, housing, and demographic-related topics.

**U.S. Department of Commerce:** Promotes job creation and economic growth. Research on jobs, employment, trade. Houses the Census Bureau.

**U.S. Federal Reserve:** The central bank. Oversees monetary policy. Publishes relevant research, data, speeches, and videos. Research topics include economic conditions, economic cycles, tax policy impact, the economic impact of various policies. Numerous videos on the economy available.

**U.S. Government Accountability Office:** Lead by U.S. Comptroller General. Provides information, research, and reports focused on performance and accountability at the request of Congressional committees and subcommittees or as statutorily required. Research topics include tax policy, the economy, tax administration, budgets, financial audits, economic development, and performance audits of various agencies and programs. Videos of hearings are also posted.

# 3

# REVENUE

*Justin M. Ross and Denvil R. Duncan*

The question of how to pay for government may be the most triggering subject in public finance. One is as likely to hear "taxation is theft" as "taxes are the price we pay for a civilized society." Taxation has been the basis of political revolutions all around the world, particularly those that feature a transition to the establishment of individual rights, and is a reoccurring character in the Abrahamic religions. As Martin, Mehrotra, and Prasad (2009, p. 1) write:

> Taxes formalize our obligations to each other. They define the inequalities we accept and those that we collectively seek to redress. They signify who is a member of our political community, how wide we draw the circle of "we." They set the boundaries of what our governments can do. In the modern world, taxation is the social contract.

Consequently, far from being a strictly technical subject, the study of public revenues is tied up extensively with philosophy and politics. Without this context, students can be derailed from understanding how revenue systems "work" when it conflicts with deeply embedded presuppositions of how they think "it should work." For those who can treat it as a purely technical problem to be solved, they risk being unable to communicate with decision makers and citizens.

For the instructor who is up for the challenge, teaching public revenue is a deeply rewarding experience. It combines the "wonkiness" of fiscal analysis with the contradictions of philosophy. Many steadfast students who take to it initially with prescribed views on what is right will have this aspect of their views melt away under the sheer weight of pragmatic challenges and empirical uncertainties. This chapter provides a strategy for realizing this experience.

DOI: 10.4324/9781003240440-3

## Objectives

The heart of revenue policy is in the analysis and weighing of trade-offs among revenue instruments. The students' end goal should be to achieve competence in this task, familiarity with the revenue instruments they are likely to confront, acquire the associated technical skills, and communicate effectively on information relevant to the concerns of the decision makers. Although most variations of revenue policy are minor variations on a set of common instruments, nevertheless the possibilities they can be confronted with is vast. The technical skills such as estimation and valuation, a necessity in any revenue course, are also highly fluid and atrophy quickly in our era of rapid data revolutions and shifting employer demands.

In order to prepare to face innumerable revenue instruments and challenges unforeseen, there are three instrumental objectives for teaching the principles of revenue policy analysis that allow them to identify and communicate the trade-offs. For these instrumental objectives, students should be able to:

1.  Identify the possible goals of revenue policy;
2.  Apply the revenue policy criteria in the evaluation of instruments; and
3.  Communicate with decision makers from a diverse set of views and philosophies on taxation in society.

Scoring revenue policy according to different criteria within these objectives provides the bread-and-butter of tax policy analysis, so the remainder of this section will elaborate on these objectives.

### *Identify the Possible Goals of Revenue Policy*

Students should be able to identify the goals of revenue policy, which are:

1.  Raise revenues to finance the production of government;
2.  Allocate the cost of government across stakeholders;
3.  Change behaviors of economic actors;
4.  Redistribution of economic resources; and,
5.  Macroeconomic stabilization.

The ability of a revenue policy to produce revenues, whether for general expenditures or special funds, is perhaps the most self-evident goal. It is also the goal most likely to be at odds with the others, including the list's second goal of allocating the cost of government across stakeholders. Should a bridge be paid for by tolls, so that the users of the infrastructure be the source of funds? From general purpose taxation? Perhaps local sales taxes on businesses where the bridge facilitated additional commerce? If general purpose, what tax structure represents a proportional sacrifice from taxpayers?

A third goal of revenue policy can be to influence the behavior of economic actors. It is mostly assured that a tax policy will have the consequence of influencing actor behavior, but altering the incentives of economic actors may be the outright goal. The most classic examples are found in "sin" taxes such as those on alcohol and cigarettes in which there is a preference for diminishing the activity through taxation rather than banning it outright. The correction of externalities, or third-party spillover effects from private decision making that result in a misallocation of resources, is another example where behavioral change is sought. The taxation of gasoline may be desirable because its consumption induces pollution that we would like to discourage and because some may wish the cost of infrastructure to be borne by those directly benefiting from it, but the pollution reduction motivation is in conflict with the goal of producing revenues from gasoline consumers. In states that have proposed carbon taxes, operationalized as fuel taxes, with the proceeds to be distributed to households or to offset other tax reductions, will likely find that it has some potential to diminish their funds for infrastructure coming from general motor fuel taxes.

Because revenue policies like taxes seek to extract from the private economy, redistribution of economic resources is another prominent goal. Wealth taxes, consumption taxes, and income taxes are likely to burden different taxpayers based on the actions they take at different points in their work-life cycle. That comparing the pre- and post-tax distribution of resources to gauge how systems affect income and wealth inequality is a common exercise in revenue estimation is an indicator of how important this goal is to the public.

Macroeconomic stabilization is the smoothing of business cycles that experience expansions and recessions, with the most widely recognized tool of revenue policy being the Keynesian idea that tax burdens should be reduced during recessions and increased during expansions. The goal of macroeconomic stabilization is most widely recognized at the federal level by automatic stabilizers, such as the progressive schedule of tax rates that imply lower average tax rates for taxpayers whose incomes decline. However, subnational business cycles can and do deviate from national counterparts, and both state and local governments endlessly consider the impact of tax systems on their general economic conditions. Furthermore, taxes differ in their distortionary effects, and more government expenditure projects are likely to improve well-being if they are financed by taxes with less costly distortions.

These goals partially inform a common set of criteria for evaluating revenue instruments, which assists in determining their fit amongst the alternative goals.

## Apply the Revenue Policy Criteria in the Evaluation of Instruments

The following criteria is adopted from Mikesell (2011, pp. 350–353), where a tax revenue instrument can be evaluated according to[1]:

1.  Revenue adequacy;
2.  Efficiency;
3.  Equity (horizontal and vertical);
4.  Collectability; and
5.  Transparency.

For taxes, revenue adequacy could be defined as the ability to produce revenues at socially acceptable rates. A tax with low revenue potential may not be worthwhile in the face of substantive administration costs or high degrees of evasion and avoidance. Furthermore, the relationship between revenues and rates is not strictly positive. This conjures a demand for a variety of technocratic skills related to revenue estimation to produce measures of tax base elasticities, tax elasticities, and tax buoyancy.

In the hierarchy of behavioral responses (evasion, avoidance, and real), efficient revenue instruments minimize distortionary effects through the real responses. Taxes, for instance, that have little impact on economic decision making are efficient, whereas an inefficient tax induces actors to recalculate their choices on the basis of the impact. An exception to this is where the economic behavior itself has undesirable spillover effects on non-participating parties. Evasion and avoidance response, by contrast, diminish revenue production but otherwise have no effects on efficiency.[2] The key exercise in determining tax distortions is to identify *substitution margins*, or instances where the tax has made an economic decision more expensive relative to alternatives, causing actors to choose alternatives. A substitute to food prepared at dine-in restaurants would include food prepared at home if the two forms are taxed at different rates. A tax levied on the fluid ounces of sugary beverages might induce consumers to substitute toward drinks with higher sugar concentration per fluid ounce. A business property tax may distort firms into choosing more labor-intensive practices or raise the cost of production sufficiently to avoid producing altogether. Cataloging opportunities for substitution as a consequence of tax rate differentials across geographic regions, consumer products, and business inputs represent bread-and-butter tax policy analysis.

Imposing the obligation to pay implies a sacrifice in well-being across people, but there are seemingly unlimited dimensions under which the distribution of this sacrifice can resemble: income groups, household composition, geographic regions, age, race, sex, and so on. One of the more central issues to teach is that politics and law can describe only theoretical incidence of taxation, whereas the true economic incidence is determined through market forces on prices, and this can only be estimated. A tax on a business entity, for example, can be shifted forward (onto consumers through higher prices), backward (onto suppliers and employees through lower prices), or absorbed by the business owners as lost profit. Partially because of unknown economic incidence, statutory measures of incidence remain extremely common, expressing measures of taxes paid by various groups. Statutory equity in taxation can arise from similar taxpayers receiving similar tax bills (horizontal), and whether the amount of the tax changes with the ability of the taxpayer to bear the burden of taxation (vertical). The estate tax is applied to taxpayers with a large stock of accrued wealth, in the multiple millions for US federal taxes. The estate tax lacks horizontal equity when comparing two households of identical lifetime earnings but differ in their choices between consuming and saving. This may be regarded by many as vertically equitable for taking a progressive structure since it does not apply to lower income households.

Collectability: Minimizing the burden of public and private resources devoted to administering the tax and collecting the revenue. Efficient collection generally avoids complex provisions and regulations as well as multiple filing and reporting requirements. Collection efficiency is often a motive for third party remittance issuance, such as requiring retailers to collect and remit the sales tax their customers statutorily owe when completing the purchase, saving households the cost of learning what is taxable at what rate while limiting the potential audit points for revenue departments.

A transparent system is one in which people can predict their tax bills. There should be design consistency such that the government can provide clear guidance on rules to tax authorities, taxpayers, and third parties in defining how a tax will be calculated. The US Treasury Inspector General for Audit, for example, has at times reported IRS agents to answer customer tax law questions incorrectly as often as 27 percent of the time (Milbourn, 2002). Nor should the system be a private negotiation between payer and government if transparency is the goal. In some communities, developers negotiate impact fees and other side payments in exchange for accommodating code changes, which aid in permitting flexibility and dealing with customized situations, but is at the same time low in transparency.

### Communicate with Decision Makers from a Diverse Set of Views and Philosophies on Taxation in Society

Almost nobody adopts explicit philosophical systems, and even less so for those specific to taxation. Nevertheless, people behave in ways that can be described as favoring particular appeals to taxation.

1. Utilitarians: Taxes should be allocated in a manner that maximizes social welfare according to some notion of collective well-being, usually according to an ability to pay concept. "Equal proportional sacrifice" or "Equal marginal sacrifice" are tax theories in the ability to pay perspectives that is frequently used to justify progressive or proportional taxation.
2. Beneficiarians: Tax burdens should fall on those who benefit from the spending, with public services levied on a willingness-to-pay principle. A perfectly developed benefit principle system is one where taxes function like prices in the allocation of resources across markets. Common examples of benefit principle thinking include user fees for government services, property taxes for local schools, and gasoline taxes to fund highway maintenance.

3. Contractarians: Those who prefer tax systems that would be acceptable or otherwise emerge from a socially acceptable process that respects individual rights are coming from a contractarian tradition. A Rawlesian tax system would be a tax system that everyone would agree to if they stood behind a "veil of ignorance" of their actual social position, which is popular among many progressives under banners like "tax justice." Libertarians similarly favor an approach under which the tax system implies the use of police powers of the state to deprive loss of liberty or property for the non-compliant, and accordingly such the purpose of the government expenditures must justify these rights' violations.

These positions may place different weights on the goals and criteria most relevant to them. Recognizing these differing perspectives can help analysts anticipate questions and pressing points of evaluation.

## Suggested Approach

With so much potential conflict in goals, criteria, and philosophical perspectives, a by-product of a competent analysis is it provides sufficient ammunition for every group to wage their political battles. A steady application of the criteria and how it fits into alternative goals requires practice, and working in deliberative groups is a rewarding approach that mimics the environments in which fiscal analysts often work. An approach to teaching a course deep on revenue could organize in the following way:

- The concepts and tools for the goals, criteria, and perspectives are front-loaded and instructor led. This is the "framework" for future analysis of individual instruments. Supplementary readings reinforce the lecture concepts and acclimate students to the jargon of the discipline.
- After the opening weeks of the instructor-led overview of the framework, the course shifts into more student-led discussion oriented around questions of policy debate around revenue instruments. Organizing around the series of broad classes of revenue instruments (e.g., income taxes, consumption taxes, fines and fees). The goal should be to take an applied problem, and have the students evaluate a given policy proposal's merits according to elements in the framework. For this, it is recommended to have a couple of assigned readings as part of their research on how to evaluate each proposal, but turnover the discussion to the students for the practice.
- Applied tools (e.g., calculating tax elasticities, forecasts, buoyancy, fiscal capacity, etc.) can be delegated to stand-alone assignments. The resulting products should likely emphasize written communication as well as data presentation in the form of tables and visuals.
- A culminating analytical report and presentation.

For a shorter class, or one where revenue represents just a few weeks of a broader public finance course, the goals are of course less ambitious as they introduce terminology and broad stylized facts (e.g., "how do we pay for government?") and the likely approach, a quick introduction of goals and philosophy followed by introducing major revenue instruments (taxes on income, consumption, and property/wealth) and discussing their trade-offs according to the criteria.

## Examples of Pedagogical Content

On the rationale that the coursework includes lecture, assignments, student discussions on policy topics, and a research report, some examples of each form of pedagogical content are provided in this section.

### Technical Skills Assignment

The most rapid area of evolution is in technical skills for constructing inferential statistics related to the tax policy criteria. These are often valuable skills for recent graduates to obtain to get their first position. Our approach has been to use assignments to (1) introduce a common technical task (e.g., construct an indicator, perform a forecast, etc.); (2) have the students do data manipulation according the necessary methodology for the task; and (3) communicate the results to a decision maker with an emphasis on both clear writing and excellent data visualization. The appendix provides a stylized example for measures of regional fiscal disparities, which students complete in R Markdown using a provided accompanying dataset.

### Lecture: Substitution Effects as Efficiency (Illustrative Numerical)

Economic efficiency is perhaps the most difficult of the policy criteria to grasp. Often confused for other concepts like "economic growth," economic efficiency (or welfare) results from policies that avoid distorting choices made by producers and consumers. Consider that if you tax only Coca-Cola, consumers will be incentivized to be made worse-off because of the distortion in choice. In such a case welfare can be increased by either relieving the tax, or by taxing more goods (like Pepsi). Counterintuitive results like this Pepsi vs. Coke example illustrates why the emphasis on substitution effects is perhaps one of the most difficult theoretical ideas to convey in public finance theory. Nevertheless, much of tax policy involves defining the base of taxable margins and understanding why it is important to "plug holes" in the tax code is an important element of tax policy analysis. Below is a numerical example used to illustrate the theory in class.

Let Table 3.1 represent how much better off a person is, measured in dollars of marginal benefits, as the increase their consumption across three goods: beer,

**TABLE 3.1** Marginal benefit/price ratio of consumer goods to hypothetical buyer

| Item | Beer | Pretzel | Nacho |
|------|------|---------|-------|
| 1st | 120 | 90 | 70 |
| 2nd | 100 | 75 | 60 |
| 3rd | 80 | 60 | 50 |
| 4th | 60 | 55 | 40 |
| 5th | 40 | 40 | 30 |

Note: All prices $1

pretzels, and nachos. Their patterns of consumption also exhibit diminishing marginal utility, because the incremental gains are increasing at a decreasing rate: the first beer betters the consumer off by $120, the second beer only by $100, and the third by $90. A preference profile that consumed two beers, one pretzel, and one nacho would experience ($120+$100+$90+$70=) $380 in benefits.

The next task is to assign prices to these three goods and give the consumer a budget constraint, then we can predict their path of consumption. The rule of consumption is that the household will buy the product with the highest marginal benefit to price ratio so long as it is affordable within the budget constraint. We can make this simple to start with by setting the price equal to $1 for each of the three goods in Table 3.1, so that the values in the above table are unchanged (i.e., 120/1=120; 90/1=90, etc.). When spending the first dollar, the first beer has the highest marginal benefit to price ratio (120>90>70), so the first dollar goes to the first beer. The second dollar represents a choice between the second beer (100), the first pretzel (90), or the first nacho (70), of which the second beer has the highest payoff. With the third dollar, the consumer will choose the first pretzel (90) over the third beer (80) or first pretzel (70). If we continue, the pattern of expenditures is the form provided in Table 3.2.

The total sum of gains in the above table yields $595, and with introspection you can see that there is no other combination of these three items for which a budget of $7 can generate a higher level of utility for the consumer. If the government were to levy a tax that took $1 from the budget, then the consumer would not be able to spend the seventh dollar and their total dollarized utility would fall from $595 to $535.

Suppose our strategy though is to levy a beer tax of $1 per unit and that this raises the price of beer to $2. It would be incorrect to assume that the pattern of consumption would remain unchanged; we must solve the new expenditure pattern out under the new relative prices. Now the marginal benefit ratios drop to half for beer, and the table is modified to what is shown in Table 3.3.

Table 3.3 shows now the first dollar is best spent on the pretzel, not beer (i.e. 90>70>60), the second dollar is spent on the second pretzel (i.e. 75>70>60), and

**TABLE 3.2** Buyer's utility maximizing choices from Table 3.1 under a $7 budget constraint

| Dollar Spent | Choice | Gain |
|---|---|---|
| 1st | Beer | $120 |
| 2nd | Beer | $100 |
| 3rd | Pretzel | $90 |
| 4th | Beer | $80 |
| 5th | Pretzel | $75 |
| 6th | Nacho | $70 |
| 7th | Any | $60 |

**TABLE 3.3** Marginal benefit/price ratio of consumer goods to hypothetical buyer

| Item | Beer | Pretzel | Nacho |
|---|---|---|---|
| 1st | 60 | 90 | 70 |
| 2nd | 50 | 75 | 60 |
| 3rd | 40 | 60 | 50 |
| 4th | 30 | 55 | 40 |
| 5th | 20 | 40 | 30 |

Note: Beer price = $1 + $1 tax, other prices = $1

the third is on the first nacho (i.e. 70>60~60). By the time the consumer gets to the fourth dollar, all three units will offer a marginal benefit to price ratio of 60, and the last $4 remaining in the budget is just enough to purchase all three after accounting for the $1 tax payment to the government when the one beer is purchased. To calculate the total gains, the marginal benefits in Table 3.1 are employed to calculate the new total welfare provided in Table 3.4.

The total gains in Table 3.4 add up to $475 to the household, $120 less than the pre-tax budget, and $1 to the government in tax revenue. The $1 in revenue collected is the same as if we had levied an income tax of $1, but the income tax would have had higher total gains ($535 instead of $475). These higher losses under the selective tax on beer relative to the income tax represent the "excess burden" stemming from the distortion in choices over the pattern of consumption.

We can replicate the income tax result, thereby improving on the selective beer tax result, by levying a consumption tax at a rate of 1/6. The table of marginal benefits is now divided by a price of ($1+1/6) in Table 3.5, but this will not affect the rank ordering of goods and leave the pattern of consumption undistorted from the original no-tax scenario. Consequently, the pattern of consumption will remain unchanged from the first example, except that the consumer will exhaust their budget on the sixth purchase instead of the seventh, identical to the consequence of the $1 income tax (see Table 3.6).

**TABLE 3.4** Buyer's utility maximizing choices from Table 3.3 under a $7 budget constraint

| Dollar Spent | Choice | Gain |
|---|---|---|
| 1st | Pretzel | 120 |
| 2nd | Pretzel | 100 |
| 3rd | Nacho | 90 |
| 4th to 7th | 1 of each | 240 |

**TABLE 3.5** Marginal benefit/price ratio of consumer goods to hypothetical buyer

| Item | Beer | Pretzel | Nacho |
|---|---|---|---|
| 1st | $120/(1+1/6)$ | $90/(1+1/6)$ | $70/(1+1/6)$ |
| 2nd | $100/(1+1/6)$ | $75/(1+1/6)$ | $60/(1+1/6)$ |
| 3rd | $80/(1+1/6)$ | $60/(1+1/6)$ | $50/(1+1/6)$ |
| 4th | $60/(1+1/6)$ | $55/(1+1/6)$ | $40/(1+1/6)$ |
| 5th | $40/(1+1/6)$ | $40/(1+1/6)$ | $30/(1+1/6)$ |

Note: All prices = $1 + $1/6 tax

**TABLE 3.6** Buyer's utility maximizing choices from Table 3.5 under a $7 budget constraint

| Total Spent | Choice | Gain |
|---|---|---|
| 1+1/6 | Beer | 120 |
| 2+2/6 | Beer | 100 |
| 3+3/6 | Pretzel | 90 |
| 4+4/6 | Beer | 80 |
| 5+5/6 | Pretzel | 75 |
| 7 | Nacho | 70 |

This "broad-base, low rate" approach yields total gains of $535 to the consumer and $1 of tax revenue, equivalent in tax revenue but better for the consumer than the selective tax on beer. These outcomes are summarized in Table 3.7. In economic parlance, the $1 tax on beer only contained "excess burden." That is, in altering the pattern of consumption through "substitution effects," the selective tax on beer contained ($535-$475=) $60 burden to the household *in excess* of what that would result from a broad tax on income or sales.

## Student-led Discussion of Policy Debates

One way of increasing student engagement with the material is by asking students to engage in a policy debate on tax issues. To accomplish this, students are provided

**TABLE 3.7** Comparison of efficiency outcomes for different policy choices

| Policy | Consumer Gains from Trade | Tax Revenues |
|---|---|---|
| No taxes | $595 | $0 |
| $1 income tax | $535 | $1 |
| $1 tax on beer only | $475 | $1 |
| $1/6 tax on any transaction | $535 | $1 |

with a prompt that includes several topics that are discussed in class, to which students must respond with a professionally prepared memo. The prompt and instructions are provided below.

Prompt: Policy advisers are often asked to prepare memos summarizing issues to get decision makers "up to speed" on a topic. Oftentimes, these topics are only vaguely or broadly defined. This is the case in each of the following topics:

• Sales taxation of e-commerce;
• State taxation of remote work;
• A wealth tax in the United States;
• Dark store property assessment; and,
• Criminal justice fees.

In advance of class devoted to each issue you will prepare a single-page memo addressing a policy maker on "what are the issues" on this subject. For each, I have provided a handful of relevant readings to get you started, which you should supplement with your own readings. Your memo is due at the start of class, and from there as a class you will begin a discussion on what you thought the key issues were, how they fit or conflicted with different goals, important insights from materials you read, and so on.

## Final Analytical Project Topics

A second assignment that works well is to require students to complete a final analytical project for the course. The analytical report attempts to simulate work that fiscal staff in a budget agency, revenue department, legislative service agency, or research organization would be assigned.

## Description for Students

You will undertake an investigation whose end product is a report and a presentation. Many of the topics I have designed because of immediate interest from stakeholders, and I would like your report to be directly influential.

## Guidelines for the Report

1.  Several of the topics will require that you propose options for dealing with a problem. Some topics may require analysis of tax laws, others may require some use of quantitative analysis. What you do will depend on your topic.
2.  The report should clearly explain the policy, the methods used to examine the policy, and the conclusions you have reached.
3.  You will research the topic using academic studies, government documents, reports of independent research organizations, and data relevant to the topic at hand. You may source your academic studies from the *National Tax Journal*, *International Tax and Public Finance*, *State Tax Notes*, *Tax Notes*, *Tax Notes International*, *Public Budgeting & Finance*, *Public Finance Review*, the *American Economic Journal: Economic Policy*, and the *Journal of Public Economics*, among others.
4.  You should support your claims by more than theoretical arguments. Many of these topics have been studied extensively so there are plenty of empirical results to draw from. Keep in mind that policy analysis in the real world requires a lot of assumptions; this analytical report is no different. However, you are expected to justify your assumptions.
5.  Ideally, you should go to the source for any data you use, rather than working with data that has already been cleaned and analyzed by other analysts. If the data originate with the Internal Revenue Service, then use data from the Internal Revenue Service source, not the product of some other researcher's manipulation of those data. Regardless, document clearly where your data comes from, and indicate if that data was cleaned by another researcher.
6.  Many helpful materials are available on the internet, but use extreme caution because such sources widely vary in quality. In particular, do not be misled by biased work prepared by narrow-interest NGOs. NGO is not the same thing as unbiased. Indeed, most NGOs are both biased and unaccountable. Having ".org" at the end of the web address is not a guarantee of either quality or of lack of bias. So be extremely careful as you read such reports.
7.  Most of the topics have the potential for extensive data analysis, particularly related to tax estimation and forecasting, which is why we cover that early in the course. Provide clear detail and documentation of what you do in this part of the analysis, and follow steps for reproducible work (as we will do on the early homework assignments).

## Deliverables

1.  **Report:** You will prepare a professional report on your investigation.
    a.  Audience: Your audience is a policymaker who is exceptionally smart but knows almost nothing about taxes.

     b.   Deliverables: Because the policymaker is very busy, s/he does not have the time to read an extensive report. Therefore, your report should include two parts:

         i.   An illustrative executive summary;

         ii.  Full length report.

     c.   Page limits: There is no page limit on the length of the report; the policymaker will have an aide dig through the report for clarifying information if required. The illustrative summary should be no more than ten pages, not including cover page.

2.   **Presentation**: You will brief the class on your work in the last two weeks of class. The presentation length is TBD (to be determined). The presentation will be in a form that would be appropriate for delivery to a legislative committee, an investigatory task force, or a budget agency.

## Grade/Rubric

Your report grade will be based on your executive summary and the extent to which your full report supports the executive summary. Things to consider:

1.   Addresses the major issues of the policy (e.g., goal fit; items in the policy criteria);
2.   How well does the executive summary address the prompt for the topic you selected?
3.   How well does the full report support the executive summary?
4.   How easy is it to find the supporting information in the full report?
5.   Quality of writing, presentation of graphical information (data visualization/tables/graphs, etc.), and formatting of references.

## Examples of Topics

Examples of topics for the report that are drawn from my previous courses include:

1.   TIF (tax incremental financing) in Sault St. Marie, Michigan (real-time client): The city manager is challenged by frequent turnover on the city council that repeatedly needs educated on the "lay of the land" in tax increment financing. The city councilors will typically have no previous exposure to the idea of TIF, what it is, how it works, the trade-offs, what exists in the city, and what options exist for them in pursuing development strategies. The audience for this document is the city council (current and future). Recommendations for improvement are welcome.
2.   Comparative analysis of TIF state policy in Michigan, Wisconsin, and Indiana (real-time client): State legislators in Michigan are interested in the effectiveness of TIFs in the state relative to their adjacent neighbors. In particular, there

is a general perception that Wisconsin TIFs "work better" than Michigan but it is anecdotal. Benchmark the TIF idea and provide a comparative analysis of the three states. Are there statutory differences? Do they have more process and overview? Access to capital projects? Are there different take-up rates of TIFs across the states, and if so, how do they differ? Audience is Michigan state legislator.

3.  Fiscal stress test: Pick a state with either no income or sales tax and conduct a budget stress test (aka fiscal stress test). Design a simple sales or income tax proposal for this state to adopt, and provide an analysis of how this adoption would affect the state's fiscal stability/sustainability.

4.  Wheel tax in Bloomington, Indiana: Indiana allows municipalities to adopt a wheel tax (IC 6-3.5-11). Write a report on the implications of Bloomington adopting such a tax, with the city council in mind as an audience. You'll have to educate the city councilors on the policy, its trade-offs, and so on. A most interesting and important component will be tax estimation.

5.  County local option income tax in Monroe County, Indiana: In the February 2020 "state of the city" address, the Mayor of Bloomington made the case that the County should pass an income tax, the proceeds for which are shared among certain taxing units (including Bloomington). Provide an analysis of this proposal with the intended audience being the citizens of Monroe County.

6.  Marijuana tax: Design an Indiana excise tax for legalized recreational marijuana. You must define the rate structure and base, the remittance policy (who remits the tax, to which agency, and how frequently), and a compliance (audit) mechanism. You will estimate the net revenue (revenue and administrative costs) that Indiana could collect from the tax and describe how the revenues are to be used. You will also discuss how the choices you have made impact the characteristics (efficiency, equity adequacy etc.) of the tax you have designed. You may inform your choices by reference to the taxes in states that have legalized recreational marijuana, although you may choose some other structure if you believe it to be more appropriate for Indiana.

7.  Road mileage tax: The road mileage tax is viewed as a promising revenue mechanism to fill the gap in states' highway funds. Design a road mileage tax for the state of Indiana. Your report should provide a detailed account of how the fee would be administered, including but not limited to: rate structure, tax base (e.g., all miles, in-state miles, in-state and out-of-state miles, etc.), mileage collection technology, remittance policy, compliance (audit mechanism), and revenue estimation. Be sure to justify your choices and explain how your fee stacks up against the standard criteria for evaluation of tax policies.

8.  E-commerce: The supreme court recently ruled (in *South Dakota V. Wayfair*) that South Dakota's decision to require out-of-state firms to collect sales taxes on transactions to South Dakota residents on the basis of physical presence is constitutional. This landmark ruling is expected to have significant impacts

on the taxation of e-commerce. How have states responded to this ruling? In particular, are states changing their sales tax laws to mimic South Dakota? What is the tax revenue impact of this ruling? How are states evolving on e-commerce taxation on the issue?

9. Pre-populated tax forms: The personal income tax is administered with blank tax forms at all levels of government in the US. Several countries administer personal income taxes with pre-populated tax forms. Your report should provide a detailed proposal for a pre-populated tax return system in the US. You may restrict your analysis to a single state or the federal government. Your proposal should be specific: coverage (all taxpayers or only a subset?); timing of forms and payments; role of employers vis-à-vis employees; responsibility for errors, among others. You should also discuss the impact of your proposal on the characteristics of the income tax.

10. Carbon tax on motor vehicles: Propose a carbon tax on motor vehicles for a state or country of your choosing. Your proposal must cover definition of tax base, tax rate, remittance policy, audit strategy, and penalty. Provide estimates of the tax policy for revenues and discuss the fairness and efficiency impacts of the policy.

11. Property tax exemptions: Indiana local governments differ considerably in the extent to which they host properties that are exempt from property taxation because they are owned by another government or by an exempt non-profit entity. Examine Indiana policy with regard to treatment of such property, identify the general magnitude of the problem (if you believe it to be a problem), and make any policy recommendation you believe necessary.

12. Dark store assessment: Some recent rulings have dictated "dark store assessment" of large retailers in Indiana for the real property tax. Examine the nature of the issue, how it impacts local governments and local economies, and what options are possible. Your analysis should include estimates of the revenue impacts. The Indiana Local Development Public Finance Model can be of some assistance here.

13. LSA report (three+ options): These are topics routinely undertaken by the Indiana Legislative Services Agency.[3] In each case, your target audience is the state legislature, and your report will cover proposal details and "lay of the land" information (i.e., you assume the state legislature is ignorant of the topic except for what you write in the report):

   a. A geographically targeted economic development area that captures incremental tax revenues (e.g., enterprise zones, professional sports and convention development areas, community revitalization districts, or certified technology parks). These are programs authorized by the state but administered by local governments. Many of these were published in 2016/2017 if you are interested in a model to look at and then specify your topic similarly.

    b.    Evaluate cigarette tax rate or alcoholic beverage tax rates (would require considering the effect of elasticity).

    c.    Look at local adoption of food and beverage taxes for cities or counties (of particular interest is revenue potential at different rates).

14.  Topic of your own choosing, subject to approval.

## Conclusions

Revenue policy provides many avenues for analysts to provide value-added information to decision makers. Like many subjects of public administration, it requires some training in hard skills that are often valuable to new entrants (e.g., data visualization) that are likely to atrophy quickly in market value and the wisdom that knowledge of theory can provide for the unforeseeable problems and challenges. This chapter largely emphasizes the latter and argues that practice in a seminar-style group discussion is likely to build this capability for the long term.

## Acknowledgments

We are deeply indebted to our late colleague John L. Mikesell. Professor Mikesell taught the school's Seminar in Revenue Theory for decades and generously shared a wealth of curricular materials and pedagogical wisdom. The authors also appreciate helpful comments and suggestions on this chapter from editors Meagan Jordan and Bruce McDonald.

## Notes

1  Ross (2018) surveys a wide range of tax policy criteria ranging from Adam Smith's *Wealth of Nations* to current textbooks and policy think tanks and notes the considerable similarity despite ranging differences in other perspectives.

2  Slemrod and Gillitzer (2014) provide a hierarchy of behavioral responses in a tax systems approach.

3  Examples are available at: http://iga.in.gov/legislative/2021/publications/tax_incentive_review/#document-cd74e97c

4  If there are considerable differences in prices from one region to another in the nation, it will be also necessary to adjust revenue capacity for those price differences. The idea is to identify the capacity to provide government services from revenue capacity and if service costs are distinctly different, the capacity measure must make an adjustment.

5  For an application of the total taxable resources measure, see Mikesell (2007). This source also identifies several weaknesses of the representative tax system.

6  An application of the RTS approach is available from Yilmaz et al. (2006).

7  The Canadian provincial equalization program is based on a constitutional requirement: "Parliament and the government of Canada are committed to the principle of making equalization payments to ensure that provincial governments have sufficient revenues to provide reasonably comparable levels of public services at reasonably comparable levels of taxation" (Subsection 36(2) of the Constitution Act, 1982).

## References

Martin, I. W., Mehrotra, A. K., & Prasad, M. (2009). *The new fiscal sociology.* Cambridge University Press.

Mikesell, J. L. (2007). Changing state fiscal capacity and tax effort in an era of developing government, 1981–2003. *Publius: The Journal of Federalism, 37*(4), 532–550.

Mikesell, J. L. (2011). *Fiscal administration: Analysis and applications for the public sector, 8th edition.* Wadsworth Cengage Learning.

Milbourn, G. C. (2002). *Management advisory report: Taxpayers continue to receive incorrect answers to some tax law questions* (Report 2002-40-086). Treasury Inspector General for Tax Administration.

Ross, J. M. (2018). Welfare effects of selective taxation: Economic efficiency as a normative principle. In A. J. Hoffer & T. Nesbit (Eds.), *For your own good: Taxes, paternalism, and fiscal discrimination in the twenty-first century* (pp. 41–58). The Mercatus Center.

Slemrod, J. B., & Gillitzer, C. (2014). Insights from a tax-systems perspective. *CESifo Economic Studies, 60*(1), 1–31.

Yilmaz, Y., Hoo, S., Nagowski, M., Rueben, K., & Tannenwald, R. (2006). Measuring fiscal disparities across the U.S. states: A representative revenue system/representative expenditure system approach, fiscal year 2002 (Working Paper 2006-06-02). *New England Public Policy Center.*

## Appendix: Assignment on Fiscal Disparity

## Measuring Fiscal Capacity and Fiscal Effort of Subnational Governments

Subnational governments have different capacities to finance government services from revenue sources assigned them because they have differing endowments of those sources. Central governments often use transfers to equalize fiscal capacity among their regional governments and regional governments similarly often use transfers to equalize capacity among their localities, that is, to reduce horizontal fiscal imbalance or fiscal disparity. In order to equalize, governments need a calculable and transparent quantitative measure of that capacity. What they require is a measure of the ability of government to obtain resources for public purposes. A uniform index must be used, but there is no unambiguous measure of capacity, in part because capacity depends on what taxes are available to the subject government (allowing local governments to levy a retail sales tax would add to capacity measured under some indices) and in part because actions taken by other governments often changes capacity of the subject government (an irrationally high tax rate levied by a neighboring government may well increase the size of the local economy and therefore its capacity under some indices). And there are always problems created by absence of appropriate data. Nevertheless, a number of alternate measures have been proposed and used by governments. What all attempt is to gauge the potential ability of the lower-tier government to raise revenue from its own sources so that a higher tier government might equalize capacity in an equitable and efficient fashion.[4]

Measured revenue capacity will be a compromise index. The measure should be reasonably transparent, should be reasonably simple, should not produce incentives for lower-tier governments to reduce their efforts to raise revenue or to encourage economic activity, should reflect actual fiscal systems, and should use data that are available and reasonably reliable. Data availability is often a major problem for local jurisdictions, although it can also force use of proxy indicators for states and regions as well. The measure will not be perfect, but it does need to be *operational, open, and non-distorting.*

## Measures of Fiscal Capacity

### Current or Lagged Revenue Collections

The amount of revenue collected affords a simple measure – what the government has been able to raise is an index of its capacity. Data are readily available and that is its almost exclusive advantage. Disadvantages are several: while collections are influenced by the economy of the region or locality, they are also influenced by compliance rates, enforcement efforts, and choices that the subject government may have made about tax rates or bases. Because collections equal the tax base multiplied by the tax rate, collections will not be a true measure of capacity alone. Furthermore, the measure potentially reduces the incentive for the subject government to raise revenue for itself – an increased capacity may cut the amount of the equalization transfer from the higher tier government. Some of the incentive problem can be reduced by using collections from some prior base year, possibly with adjustments made to those collections – but that reduces transparency in the process and adds to suspicions that data has been manipulated.

### Personal Income per Capita

Personal income per capita is widely used in equalization formulae because incomes of the population in a market economy provide a good index of the size of the economic base and, hence, how much the government might be able to raise from its revenue system. However, data on personal income are not quite so readily available as revenue collections, there are issues of data quality as well (activity outside the official economy does not get counted, for instance, but then it probably produces little revenue either), and some regional or local tax bases can be driven by personal income from outside their jurisdictions (taxes coming from tourism or from natural resources may, for instance, be driven by personal income measured outside). If data are available for the particular local jurisdiction in question, they likely will be available with a considerable lag. And personal income only crudely is linked to the revenue bases actually allowed regional or local governments, so such an index of capacity really has little to do with the fiscal system in place. Adding a new tax to local revenue portfolios, for instance, would cause no change in measured personal income per capita, even though it could dramatically alter absolute fiscal capacity and the relative capacity of localities within a region (some having much greater endowment of the new tax base than others).

## Gross Regional Product

Gross regional product is the total value of goods and services produced by a region's economic resources (land, labor, and capital) over a period of time and does reflect the economic base potentially taxable by the government. The measure is broader than personal income because it gauges income in the region without regard to the residence of the worker or producer; incomes earned by non-residents would be included and economic activity driven by non-resident spending in the region. However, this measure is also divorced from the actual revenue system – different components of gross regional product may be taxed quite differently by the system and the distribution of those components may differ radically across regions. Relatively high gross regional product may not necessarily translate into a similarly high capacity to apply tax. Furthermore, there may be tax system issues: business profits might be taxed at the home office instead of where income is earned. That would make gross regional product a misleading index of what the revenue system could yield, although still being a better index than personal income.

## Total Taxable Resources

Total Taxable Resources (TTR) adjusts gross regional product by adding income received by residents but produced out of the region and income produced in the region by non-residents and by subtracting indirect business taxes paid to the national government and national subsidies received in the region. The additions reflect payments that would realistically be part of the regional revenue base but are not in ordinary gross regional product while the subtractions reflect payments that would not realistically be in the regional revenue base but are measured in gross regional product. Although total taxable resources represent a methodological improvement over gross regional product, it does not represent the way in which tax systems actually reach economic activity. The US Department of Treasury annually estimates TTR for the states because the estimates are used in formulas that allocate Federal funds for the Community Mental Health Service and Substance Abuse Prevention and Treatment block grant programs to the states.[5] The measure is not generally available for local jurisdictions.

## Representative Tax System

The Representative Tax System (RTS) measures the amount of revenue that a region or locality could raise if it made average tax effort on its economic base.[6] The approach, pioneered by the US Advisory Commission on Intergovernmental

Relations, used by Canada in its provincial equalization transfer system,[7] and frequently applied in fiscal system analysis, proceeds by:

1.  Identifying collections from each revenue source available to the lower-tier governments;
2.  Estimating what the potential base is for each source in each region (this is an "ideal" measure of what the tax would be for each state, for instance, personal consumption expenditure for a retail sales tax or all cigarettes sold in the state, without regard for any exemptions, credits, etc., that might cause the actual base in the state to diverge from that ideal);
3.  Determining the representative rate is for each base by dividing the national total actual collections from the base by the national total ideal base (for instance, total general sales tax collections divided by total personal consumption expenditures);
4.  Estimating the revenue from each source that the lower-tier government could raise if it levied that representative tax rate (multiply the representative rate by the ideal base for each state);
5.  Aggregating the collections to obtain total revenue capacity for each state:
    a.  Dividing the total for each state by its population.
    b.  Aggregating total capacities for each state to obtain a national total.
    c.  Dividing the national total by national population.
6.  Divide state per capita capacity by national per capita capacity and multiply by 100. That gives the RTS index for each state.

The RTS capacity index provides an excellent indicator of the aggregate fiscal capacity because it uses the revenue system actually available to the lower-tier government, is based on actual fiscal choices made by lower-tier governments, works with available data, and, when used in a transfer formula, does not discourage governments from full use of revenue options available to them. The measure will be transparent if data are not confidential.

The same RTS data can be used to calculate a tax effort index. The index simply equals, for each state, total actual collections divided by total tax capacity multiplied by 100. Logically it measures the degree to which the state is using its tax resources more or less heavily than is typical for the nation as a whole.

The logic employed for calculating the RTS capacity measure is sometimes applied to the spending side of finance to compute a Representative Expenditure System (RES) measure. RTS and RES are then compared for each state to estimate the fiscal gap at capacity.

## Your Assignment

The learning management system file for the course contains a file "Data for RTS." All data in the file are actual. In that file, you will find state tax collections for several important taxes that states levy. For purposes of this exercise, assume that these are the only taxes they levy. The file also includes several other variables that you may use as measures of the ideal base for these taxes: personal consumption expenditure for the general sales tax, motor fuel gallonage for the motor fuel tax, personal income for the individual income tax, utility receipts in state GDP for the utility tax, cigarettes sold for the tobacco tax, and state GDP for the corporate income tax. (Only the last is a stretch – corporate profits are not available at the state level and GDP is not a horrible proxy.)

Do the following: Your response should be in the form of a memo addressed to the state budget director.

1. Prepare RTS fiscal capacity measures for each state. Which are the top five and bottom five states in measured fiscal capacity?
2. Prepare RTS tax effort measures for each state. Which are the top five and bottom five states in measured tax effort?
3. Compare results from the RTS fiscal capacity measure with what you would conclude from using either per capita income or per capita GDP as a capacity measure.
4. Does the evidence suggest that low fiscal capacity states exert greater effort to provide state government services?

## (Optional) Extend Your Skills with Maps

Maps are a popular and effective way of displaying data. An assignment like this is exactly the kind of setting where it might be valuable, where you are comparing something like capacity across states anyway.

# 4

# PUBLIC BUDGETING MECHANICS

*Katherine G. Willoughby and Colt Jensen*

This chapter discusses teaching students about public budgeting mechanics—budget cycles and timelines, budget formats and their purposes, and continuous improvement efforts of governments such as participatory budgeting and strategic planning—to advance budgeting processes and bolster budget outcomes. The focus is on how to use government budget documents and resources "in real time" to build student knowledge about these concepts and enhance their skills to develop and manage public budgets. Public budgeting, channeling Kingdon's (1984) book *Agendas, Alternatives, and Public Policies* regarding the public policy making process, brings together money, problems, politics, and priorities, the result is a budget that then (usually) serves as a foundation for future ones. In other words, the mechanics of budgeting are messy yet time constrained, with outcomes resulting from the decisions surrounding money, problems, politics, and priorities made in specific contexts and, often, given a dash of both good and bad luck.

The challenge in teaching students about public budgeting mechanics is that while there are some similar overarching characteristics of the various components, no two governments conduct such work in exactly the same way. For example, governments around the world exhibit a wide variety of fiscal years—many operate from July 1 to June 30, but others from January 1 to December 31, or October 1 to September 30, or April 1 to March 31. For example, the U.S. intergovernmental system includes an array of cycles: the current federal government budget year is from October 1 to September 30, a state government may have a cycle that runs from July 1 to June 30, and a local government may operate its fiscal year from January 1 to December 31. The U.S. federal government has an annual (one year) budget cycle which it rarely sticks to, with no requirement to balance, while almost half of state governments have biennial (two-year) budget cycles, and virtually all have some sort of requirement to pass a balanced budget.

DOI: 10.4324/9781003240440-4

Governments engage a cornucopia of budget formats. Many still use a strictly line-item, object of expenditure format, but plenty engage in some form of performance or program format, a target based or envelop format, or a hybrid that comingles two or more formats. Explaining the multiple budget cycles, fiscal years, and budget formats engaged by national and subnational governments around the world is challenging for these reasons, but knowledge of such variations is vital for any student seeking to go into practice, at whatever level of government and in whatever country. Throw into the mix the fact that many governments have trouble adhering to their own rules, policies, and protocols of timelines and formats, and many engage reforms halfheartedly or poorly, or drop them prematurely given new administrations or lagging championship, or before they have had time to produce results, and the real challenges of building student skill and knowledge of what to expect and how to operate in the public budgeting world is fully laid bare.

## Student Learning Objectives

The typical learning for an MPA core course in public budgeting include the following: Upon completion of the course, students will be able to

- Describe the environment of taxing and spending by governments worldwide—the legal framework in which these processes occur, as well as the economic, social, cultural, organizational, and technological factors that shape the decisions that determine public revenues and expenditures;
- Explain the public budgeting process—development, deliberation and passage, execution, and audit—and articulate how such process is impacted by various institutions, participants, and stakeholders, and in light of special circumstances, such as natural disasters or public safety crises;
- Apply budget and financial calculations, metrics, and analyses to evaluate government fiscal health and persuasively communicate information regarding budget and policy alternatives related to such governments; and,
- Identify ways of managing financial resources, solve budget problems, and make spending proposals to achieve organizational goals.

These objectives contribute to student advancement in all MPA program competencies espoused by the Network of Schools of Public Policy, Analysis, and Administration (NASPAA) in general, but specifically advance mastery of the second (to participate in the public policy process) and third (to analyze, synthesize, think critically, solve problems, and make decisions) competencies. In terms of student learning and skills regarding public budgeting mechanics of cycles, development of budget priorities, formats, and reforms specifically, the first two learning outcomes above are addressed predominantly using the exercises included in this chapter. Toward that end, the budget mechanics exercises included here seek to boost student knowledge and skill regarding the following:

- Discernment of various budget types used by governments to develop and manage budgets;
- Access of government budgets, determination of budget format(s), and understanding of the contents of budget documents;
- Understanding of the multiplicity of public budgeting cycles and timelines; and,
- Ability to distinguish and characterize different public budgeting reforms and, specifically, explain various components of modern performance budgeting.

Students should leave the course with a firm understanding of the current research about public budgeting, the wide variety of contexts within which governments must budget and operate, the multiplicity of budget mechanics that governments around the world engage, the difficult challenges that modern governments face in reaching financial sustainability, and the analytical approaches to evaluating public organizations and their fiscal health.

## Essential Knowledge About Public Budgeting Mechanics

An essential element of teaching budget mechanics is addressing government timelines for development, deliberation and appropriation, execution, and audit of the budget. Most students have little understanding of the origination of budget cycles—that governments typically established fiscal years to accommodate farming schedules and crop cycles. That is, legislative sessions were often held in winter months, with closure later in the spring, and the start of the fiscal year set to begin in a summer (harvesting) month. Governments can and do change budget cycles from their original fiscal years, for all sorts of reasons. For example, Papua, New Guinea changed its fiscal year to coincide with those of donors, given the weight and influence of donor funds on its economy. The U.S. Congress moved the start of the federal fiscal year forward from July 1 to October 1 in 1974 to provide more deliberative time regarding budget matters. The City of Atlanta changed its fiscal year from a January 1 to December 31 to July 1 to June 30, in part to better coordinate with the State of Georgia fiscal year.

Students should investigate budget cycles in governments all around the world and at every level. Begin by presenting a sample of budget cycles for students to compare across different governments. For instance, the example of budget cycles presented in Table 4.1 of the City of New York, the State of Georgia, and the U.S. federal government can be used to display cycle differences across governments. This comparison illustrates the relatively short cycle of a local government compared to a state or that of a national government. When considering

**TABLE 4.1** Budget timelines of United States governments

| Month | New York City | State of Georgia | U.S. Federal Government |
|---|---|---|---|
| **July** | New Fiscal Year begins. | New Fiscal Year begins. | |
| **August** | | Governor sets revenue estimate for next year's budget (FY+1). Governor's guidelines sent to agencies to develop next year's budget. | |
| **September** | Mayor releases Capital Commitment Plan (FY+1 and beyond). | State agencies submit their budget requests to the Office of Planning and Budget (OPB) given guidelines from the Governor. Requests include funding needs, such as salaries of employees, operational costs, technologies, and rent for office space. Agencies submit strategic plans alongside their budget request. Plans detail how the agencies will use their funds to improve services, increase employee retention, and enhance efficiency. | Fiscal Year ends. |
| **October** | Community Boards complete their Capital and Expense Budget (FY+1) consultations with City agencies. Community Boards submit their Capital and Expense Budget (FY+1) priorities to OMB. | OPB analyzes all agency budget requests to ensure that they further the state's policy goals in a cost-effective manner. OPB analysts meet with the Governor and his staff to brief him on the requests and offer recommendations based on their analyses. | New Fiscal Year begins. |

| | | | |
|---|---|---|---|
| **November December** | The Mayor releases a Financial Plan updating the Adopted (Current) Budget. | Governor formulates his own formal recommendations for the General Assembly, that are published in the Governor's Budget Report. | President submits budget for FY+1 to Congress the February prior. The Budget and Accounting Act of 1921 created a statutory role for the President to develop a consolidated federal budget proposal and submit it to Congress prior to the start of each fiscal year. Prior to this, agencies submitted their budget requests directly to Congress, and the President was left out of the budget process. The President's budget submission reflects the President's policy priorities and offers a set of recommendations regarding federal programs, projects, and activities funded through appropriations acts as well as any proposed changes to revenue and mandatory spending laws. |
| **January February** | The Mayor releases the Preliminary Budget for FY+1. The Mayor releases the Preliminary Ten-Year Capital Strategy if it is an odd calendar year. Community Boards receive responses to their budget priorities. | The General Assembly receives Governor's Budget Report within five days of convening in January. Legislators review the Governor's recommendations and develop appropriations bill that begins in the House and specifies how much money will be appropriated to each agency at a program-level. House passes bill and sends on to the Senate. Senate reviews the bill and adopts a substitute, which is then sent back to the House for acceptance or rejection. If two chambers do not agree on a version of the bill, a conference committee is convened, made up of members from both chambers. Conference committee compromises on appropriations, and the newest version of the bill is sent to both chambers for a vote. | Congressional Budget Office submits report on the economic and budget outlook to Budget Committees for FY+1. |

*(continued)*

**TABLE 4.1** Cont

| Month | New York City | State of Georgia | U.S. Federal Government |
|---|---|---|---|
| **March** | The Community Boards review the Preliminary Budget (FY+1) and submit a written response to the Mayor. Borough Boards submit their priorities to the Mayor and City Council. | | |
| **April** | The City Council submits its operating budget. The Borough Presidents issue recommendations for the Preliminary Budget (FY+1). The City Council holds hearings and proposes recommendations for the Preliminary Budget (FY+1). | Once the same version of the bill has passed both the House and Senate, it is sent to the Governor, who has 40 days to sign it before it automatically becomes law. The Governor maintains the constitutional right to strike out portions of the bill with his line-item veto. Once the bill is signed into law, Budget for FY+1, OPB compiles a document that summarizes all budgetary changes, known as the Budget in Brief that contains financial summaries and budget highlights. | Around April, prior to the President's submission of the budget for the FY+1, OMB coordinates its development by issuing various circulars, memoranda, and other guidance documents to the heads of executive agencies. OMB Circular No. A–11 is issued annually, an extensive document that provides agencies with an overview of applicable budgetary laws, policies for the preparation and submission of budgetary estimates, and information on financial management and budget data systems. Circular A–11 also provides agencies with directions for budget execution and guidance regarding agency interaction with Congress and the public. |

|  | | | |
|---|---|---|---|
| **May** | The Mayor submits the Executive Budget (FY+1) and the Message of the Mayor. The Mayor releases the Ten-Year Capital Strategy if it is an odd calendar year. Community Boards receive responses to their budget priorities. | OPB works to ensure that each agency's spending does not exceed the amount appropriated for each of its programs. OPB reviews and authorizes annual operating budgets (AOBs) as well as monthly allotments, and projects and analyzes agency expenditures. | After the President has submitted the budget for the FY+1 to Congress, Committees submit views and estimates to Budget Committees. The Senate Budget Committee reports concurrent resolution on the budget. Then, Congress completes action on concurrent resolution on the budget. After Congress completes action on concurrent resolution on the FY+1 budget, annual appropriations bills may be considered in the House. |
| **June** | The Executive Budget (FY+1) is adopted by the City Council, becoming the Adopted Budget. Fiscal Year ends. | Fiscal Year Ends. | Then, House Appropriations Committee reports last annual appropriation bill for FY+1. Congress completes action on reconciliation legislation for FY+1 budget. House completes action on annual appropriations bills for FY+1. |

Sources: Mayor's Office of Management and Budget (2021), Governor's Office of Planning and Budget (2021), and Saturno (2020).

cycles, such timelines do not account for breakdowns of negotiations, political gridlock, or crises like natural disasters or international conflicts that can stall the process.

Further complicating understanding budget cycles is the fact that all phases of the budget process are occurring throughout each cycle. While the U.S. Congress deliberates about the new fiscal year budget, it may also be addressing supplemental appropriations, such as those necessary for a natural disaster or international conflict. Federal agencies are executing budgets while they are developing their requests for the new fiscal year budget, and an audit may be in process for the previous fiscal year budget as the new fiscal year budget gets underway. Budgetary activities from planning to execution related to the funding for a new fiscal year may stretch over an extended period of two calendar years (or longer). In the U.S., while local and state government budget processes, start (development) to finish (new fiscal year begins), generally fall within a six-month to 12-month period, respectively, the U.S. federal budget process is much longer (about 18+ months). And states that have biennial or two-year budget cycles are different from annual ones. Further complicating federal budgeting in the U.S. is the fact that many if not most of the 12 appropriations bills are rarely passed by the start of the fiscal year (October 1), with government often operating on continuing resolutions. Certainly, different fiscal years among levels of governments as well as the inability to stick to the budget timelines on the part of any government compromises budget planning by lower-level governments when programming is dependent upon intergovernmental grants, loans, and other funds. All of this adds complexity and messiness to budgeting that is confusing to students. Enlightenment about how budgeting works only comes by getting students into the weeds of budget cycles and then considering fiscal federalism—learning about the money trail up and down governmental levels.

To better understand budget timelines and cycles, you can use Table 4.1 to review those of different governments. Then, over the course of the next several weeks, students can be assigned in-class exercises that they complete, either in groups, with a partner, or individually, that expose them to government budget cycles, budgeting components, formats, and strategies. The exercise below regards budgeting by governments around the world. A three-hour class has three components. For the first hour, students are taken to the multiple websites and pointed to data about government development, governance structures, and government budgets and budgeting. Students are taken through the exercise using a sample government. After a short break, students are put into groups and assigned a specific government (include only those governments that have undergone an assessment by the Public Expenditure and Financial Accountability (PEFA) program since 2016 that applies the most recent assessment framework (accessible at: www.pefa.org)). Students work together for about 40 minutes to develop their government assessments. After a short break, class returns and students present by group. The strength of this exercise is the requirement that students parse through PEFA assessments that dig into the details of public budgeting and finance components. Also, the International Budget Partnership Open Budget Survey (accessible at: www.internationalbudget.org/) presents data on budget transparency and public accessibility to government finance documents and plans.

The first recommended exercise for understanding the budget process is provided in Table 4.2. Exercise 1 addresses the first two learning outcomes presented early. In researching governance structures and economic metrics, students are exposed to the legal frameworks and economic circumstances that governments operate in that contribute to determinations of public revenues and expenditures. Also, the exercise requires students to find out information regarding the effects of government budgeting decisions over time by referencing the most current World Governance Indices related to:

**TABLE 4.2** Exercise 1—governance, development, and budget mechanics

Directions:

Work in groups to complete an assessment of an assigned country/government. Collect appropriate metrics and other data to be able to answer the questions below.

Countries for Groups:

- Group 1: Botswana
- Group 2: Montenegro
- Group 3: Ukraine
- Group 4: El Salvador
- Group 5: Georgia.

Questions to Answer:

1. Would you classify this country as low-, medium-, or high-income? What is the state of development in this country? Justify your response.
2. What is the country's governance structure? Then, summarize perceptions of governance in this country using appropriate metrics.
3. How transparent is this government regarding its budget? Justify your assessment.
4. Check the government's most recent PEFA assessment. Explain components of the budgetary process that this government conducts well and those that are particularly challenging.

Access any of the organizations below to complete the exercise:

- Human Development Index
- World Factbook
- World Bank's World Development Indicators
- Worldwide Governance Indicators
- International Monetary Fund's Economic Outlook
- PEFA Assessments
- Open Budget Survey.

- Voice and Accountability
- Political Stability and Absence of Violence
- Governance Effectiveness
- Regulatory Quality
- Rule of Law
- Control of Corruption.

Students gain skills in distinguishing various budget documents and formats by accessing metrics on budget transparency provided by the International Budget Partnership that scores the multiple budgets and reports produced by governments on accessibility to the public, citizen engagement in budgeting, and budget oversight mechanisms. The PEFA assessments grade governments on seven pillars of public financial management that cover the following components:

- Budget reliability
- Transparency
- Management of assets and liabilities
- Policy-based fiscal strategy and budgeting
- Predictability and control in budget execution
- Accounting and reporting
- External scrutiny and audit.

Requiring students to identify PEFA grades for their assigned government that regard over 30 measures operationalizing the above components exposes them to the complexity of public budgeting and financial management systems, including budget timelines, cycles and format, budget development and strategy, and budget accountability through external scrutiny and audit.

Exercise 2, as provided in Table 4.3, engages students across several classes and requires each to individually take on budgeting in a single U.S. state government. Having worked through budgeting in different countries around the world in earlier classes, consideration of U.S. state governments provides a good avenue for comparison of like governments that exhibit a wide variety of budget cycles, types, and budget development strategies true laboratories!

Beginning with the items enclosed within the dotted box, students are guided on collecting the information necessary, using an unassigned state government as an example. These items regard the environment and budget mechanics of a state government. The following online resources can be accessed:

- State government portals
- State legislative budget and fiscal offices
- Gubernatorial/executive budget offices
- National Association of State Budget Officers (NASBO)
- National Conference of State Legislatures (NCSL).

**TABLE 4.3** Exercise 2—making calculations and comparisons

Directions:

Present information about your assigned state government's budget process, revenues, debt and long-term obligations, and expenditures.

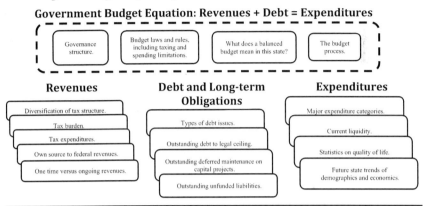

**Government Budget Equation: Revenues + Debt = Expenditures**

| Governance structure. | Budget laws and rules, including taxing and spending limitations. | What does a balanced budget mean in this state? | The budget process. |

| **Revenues** | **Debt and Long-term Obligations** | **Expenditures** |

Revenues:
- Diversification of tax structure.
- Tax burden.
- Tax expenditures.
- Own source to federal revenues.
- One time versus ongoing revenues.

Debt and Long-term Obligations:
- Types of debt issues.
- Outstanding debt to legal ceiling.
- Outstanding deferred maintenance on capital projects.
- Outstanding unfunded liabilities.

Expenditures:
- Major expenditure categories.
- Current liquidity.
- Statistics on quality of life.
- Future state trends of demographics and economics.

After taking students through a sample state government, they are afforded time in class to collect the information for their state and then to return to class with data about their state's fiscal year and budget cycle. Students must examine budget documents available from state budget offices in the executive and legislative branches, and comprehensive annual financial reports from the state auditor's office, as well as vital resources from the professional associations, NASBO and NCSL. The NASBO's periodic report, *Budgetary Processes in the States*, is particularly useful as it provides a comparative across the 50 states regarding budget timelines, cycles, formats, gubernatorial budget powers, budget balance requirements, tax and expenditure limitations, issuance of debt, and performance measurement application across the budget process. Once class resumes, students discuss their experiences collecting the information, challenges, and a brief description of their state's fiscal year and budget cycle. Subsequent classes then guide students through the sections below the dotted box, again using an unassigned state government as an example. Students create a folder with all collected information for their state that should include the variety of research reports and data from the many relevant foundations, research centers, and professional associations, as well as the that from state government portals, budget and fiscal offices, and so on, including budget documents, appropriation bills, comprehensive annual financial reports, performance reports, and the like. Students turn in a two-page summary of their state's budget process and fiscal circumstances at the conclusion of the exercise.

The purpose of this exercise is to introduce students to the wealth of public budgeting information readily available, exposure to relevant concepts surrounding public budgeting, real-world familiarity with budget mechanics, and the variability that exists even among like governments, rather than requiring a sophisticated analysis of government fiscal health. Further, students get hands-on experience learning about budget reforms, that are pervasive in the states and intertwined with cycles, timelines, and formats, and budget and policy strategic development. Calculations of fiscal ratios are introduced here, but that exercise is applied more rigorously in the research report that students complete with partners regarding a local government. Essentially, this exercise hits on all learning outcomes for the course and addresses skill building particularly well regarding budget mechanics. That is, students find and learn about government budget laws, cycles and timelines, budgetary processes, in addition to an introduction to multiple public budgeting concepts including revenue diversification and tax structure, public assets and liabilities, types of public debt, public expenditure categories, and budgeting results (quality of life and community metrics).

To help students gain an understanding of how the public may be brought into the budgeting dialogue as well as how governments develop budget strategies, the next exercise requires students to listen to a podcast by the IBM Center for the Business of Government[1] that reviews Willoughby, Dzigbede, and Gehl (2020). The report regards local government strategies to manage through natural weather-related disasters and teases out six important strategies that localities need to engage to bolster fiscal resiliency following a disastrous event. Details regarding the assignment are provided in Table 4.4 and the framework is presented in Figure 4.1.

Strategies calling on localities to generate vertical and horizontal networks and partnerships illustrate to students the importance of governments being all-inclusive in managing through both acute (such as disasters) and chronic (such as homelessness) problems. Further, the requirement of a whole of community approach that calls on everyone (business, nonprofit, community, individual and government) within a jurisdiction to participate in local planning and setting strategies shows students how the public can be involved in budgeting by and for their own government(s). The purpose of this exercise is to boost student knowledge about how governments develop budget priorities and plan for managing budgets when disaster strikes. Importantly, the exercise emphasizes how current circumstances—the modern disaster-prone environment—have exacerbated the long-standing public budgeting problem posed by Key (1940), "[o]n what basis shall it be decided to allocate x dollars to activity A instead of activity B?" (p. 1138).

In addition to frequent in-class exercises, generally completed in the relevant class session, students complete a semester-long research report with a partner. An overview of this report is provided in Table 4.5. The research report necessitates immersion into the budget and finance workings of a U.S. local government (population size 35,000–65,000). Report requirements are presented below and further engage students in learning about budget cycles, timelines and formats, development of budget agendas and strategies, and public participation opportunities.

**TABLE 4.4** Exercise 3—local strategies to boost resiliency following disaster

Directions:

You are assigned a partner and a city government that has experienced weather-related disaster within the last few years. To prepare for our next class, listen to the podcast below that discusses a framework of how localities adapt enterprise strategies to advance fiscal resiliency in times of disaster.

Also, before the next class, touch base with your group and assess and collect data for your assigned city government. Then, in our next class, we will begin with a discussion of the IBM report finding that are explained in the podcast. You will then work with your group for about 30 minutes to develop a summary assessment of their city that presents the following information to everyone:

- The city's engagement of any of the six strategies discussed in the podcast.
- A summary and justification of the assessment of the city's fiscal resiliency along the following fiscal resiliency grip.

| Not Resilient at All | Barely Resilient | Somewhat Resilient | Mostly Resilient | Completely Resilient |
|---|---|---|---|---|

Podcast:

IBM Center for the Business of Government: Katherine Willoughby, Komla Dzigbede, and Sarah Beth Gehl.

www.blochhousemedia.com/ibm/katherine_willoughby_abc.mp3

Cities for Groups:

- Group 1: Deerfield Beach, Florida
- Group 2: Tybee, Georgia
- Group 3: Sioux Falls, South Dakota
- Group 4: Cameron, Louisiana
- Group 5: Malden, Washington.

Especially helpful here is the requirement that students gain an understanding of the rhythm of budgeting by accessing government council meeting minutes over the course of six months to a year. Usually, class sessions in the latter half of the semester use questions from this assignment as in-class exercises. Students work with their partners for some period of these classes to complete relevant questions regarding their chosen city. Then, by the end of the term, students have completed much of the work for the report, providing them needed time for polishing their final product before submitting it.

Along with a variety of budget cycles and timelines, governments employ multiple types of budgets. Operating budgets account for day-to-day recurring costs of conducting government business. Generally, operating budgets are supported predominantly with tax receipts—those raised by the government through a determined tax structure. On the other hand, capital budgets support infrastructure like roads, bridges, government administration buildings, water

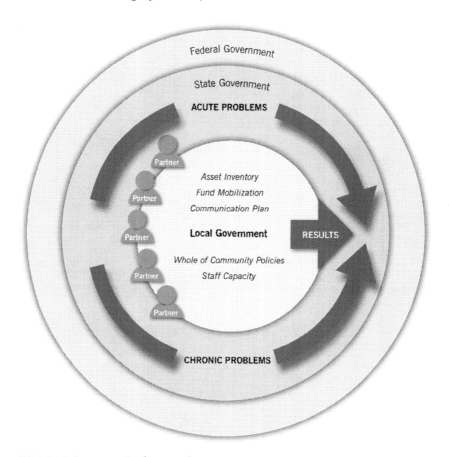

**FIGURE 4.1** An enterprise framework

Source: Willoughby et al. (2020, p. 33)

utilities, and recreational facilities. Unlike spending for operations that impact the current public, that for capital provides benefits to current and future generations. Therefore, governments are likely to borrow money to pay for infrastructure, allowing for long-term pay down of the debt over the life of the capital project. Also, governments often separate their operating and capital budgets, given the different funding streams that support each. Capital financing by governments may include cash (pay as you go), debt issuance, intergovernmental grants and/or loans, or by accessing a reserve or sinking fund (or some combination of these methods). Debt financing requires an assessment of the time value of money, to account for debt servicing (payback) over time.

Luckily, many, if not most, governments around the world provide relatively easy access to their budgets. Exposing students to these documents is as easy as assigning them a government to investigate and setting them loose to explore, as

**TABLE 4.5** Exercise 4—research report: budgeting in a pandemic

Directions:

Answer the questions below for the city of your choice from the U.S. Bureau of Census'
*American Cities 2020* excel spreadsheet posted to the course's learning management
system. You must choose a city with a population between 35,000 and 65,000 and one
that that is a state other than Georgia. Develop your findings into a research report
that explains the current and future budget and fiscal situation of the city as well as
any advancements and challenges as the pandemic continues. Documents and sources
to consider include the government's homepage, municipal code, and budgets by
fiscal year, budget highlights, comprehensive annual financial reports, council agendas,
meetings, meeting minutes, and mayoral addresses and local news stories. Present at least
one table and one chart or figure embedded in your report that displays relevant data to
justify your responses. You must develop original tables, charts, and/or figures—do not
cut and paste from documents that you can access for this report. A table might present
budget trend data for the city or a breakdown of revenues and expenditures for the
most recent fiscal year (or both!). Charts might include those indicating tax diversity or
fiscal status by year.

Make sure to address each question below, though, in any order that you consider
provides for the greatest flow and logic. City all sources accordingly.

1. Briefly describe the socio-economic, demographic, and geographic characteristics of
   the city. What is the governance structure of the city? Explain the budget cycle and
   format(s) used by the city.
2. What are the budget priorities of the current elected officials in this government? Do
   the priorities of t he executive and legislative branches of the city conflict? Justify your
   response.
3. Does this government have a diversified tax base? Justify your response.
4. What are predominant revenue sources for the city? Explain major expenditure
   categories. Describe city budget trends of the last five or six years.
5. What does the most recent auditor's option in the city's most recent Comprehensive
   Annual Financial Report tell you about financial reporting in the city?
6. Is the city in a better fiscal position this year compared to last year? Defend your
   response with appropriate metrics and data.
7. Does the city engage the public in budget-making? If so, how? Determine if the city
   shares information (and how) with the public about the results of spending public
   funds for community benefit. Does the city indicate engaging other budget reforms?
   Describe any reforms and results that you find.
8. Explain whether the city's mission and vision are reflected in its most recent
   budget.
9. Explain how COVID-19 does or does not impact the sustainability of the city's
   budget, if sustainability is defined as in the long-term, growth of spending does not
   exceed growth of revenues. Justify your response.
10. Explain and justify if budgeting in the city can be described by any public budgeting
    theories you have been introduced to in this course.

The report should be from 10–12 pages, double spaced and 10–12-point font, with
additional pages for charts, tables, graphs, title page, and references. Cite appropriately.

the several exercises and the research report assignment above so indicate. Still, it is worthwhile to use class time to introduce students to the wealth of budget types by accessing governments online, such as the State of Virginia's Department of Planning and Budget website, as shown in Figure 4.2.

Accessing Virginia's budget documents is especially appealing as it provides those that span the budget cycle—development, legislative appropriation (see "Other Budget Links" tab), and execution. The website also provides information about the capital budget, variances, transfers, and adjustments to the current budget, as well as access to a data portal that drills down into agency expenditures (see Other Budget Links tab). Just pulling up this website in class allows for rich discussion and exposure of public budgeting mechanics that include budget types, formats, cycles, accounting, and results. For example, a lecture might begin regarding the importance of budget transparency in supporting accountability to the public regarding budgeting decisions. Then, exposing government budgets online can engage students in a discussion of how governments might be scored regarding budget transparency and if the various budgets presented score well or not on any transparency metric considered. Students can be queried as to why they find some government budgets more or less transparent than others, for example.

Exposing students to the wide variety of budget formats is easy given continually advancing information technology and good governance transparency efforts worldwide. Of budget formats, the most elementary type is the line-item or object of expenditure, that affords legislative bodies the greatest control over executive spending. Notice the 2021 budget adopted by the City of Charlotte, North Carolina (see Figure 4.3). This budget lists expenditures simply by object of expenditure. Still, like many government budgets, Charlotte applies several formats, including details about budget adjustments, as well as performance data and determined changes to employee numbers (see Figure 4.4).

The State of Wyoming budget appropriation bill for Fiscal 2020–2022 is broken down by programs, not objects. Program budgets include information about revenues and expenditures for the major activities of an agency, allowing easy comparisons of resources available to the various programs. Figure 4.5 provides Wyoming's budget appropriation for Fiscal 2020–2022 for the Livestock Board. Notice the breakdown of funding for the various programs, number of full- and part-time employees authorized, and narrative to further explain funding authority.

Continually exposing students to government budget displays and pointing out formats advances their knowledge of the messiness of public budgeting. That is, it is the rare government that does not engage more than one and often several types of formats (as noted above, the City of Charlotte provides a line-item budget with performance data). Viewing government budgets in class can prompt robust conversation about the purposes of various formats, implementation benefits, and challenges of these formats, and the power-sharing results (or not) between branches of government given the use of specific formats. The repetition necessary

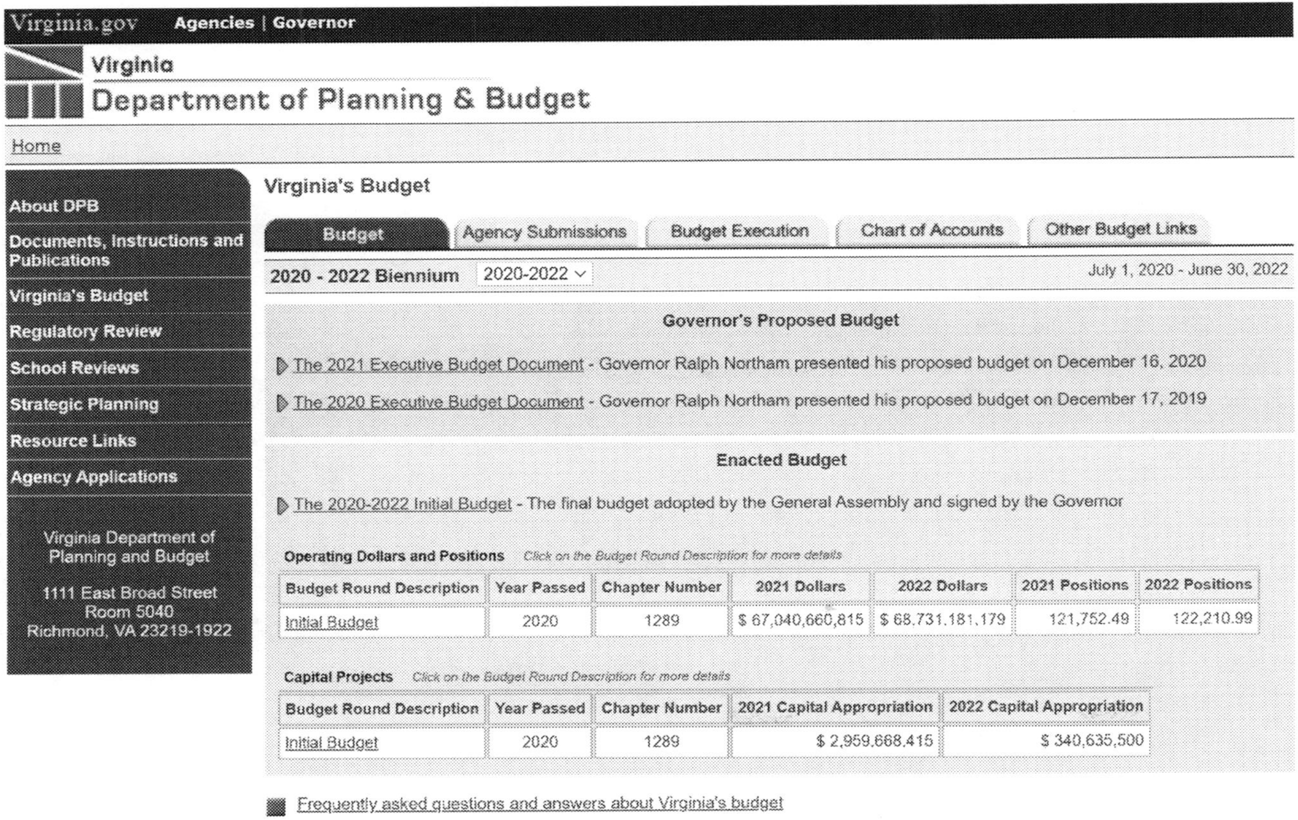

**FIGURE 4.2** State of Virginia budget documents

Source: Virginia Department of Planning and Budget (2021)

**Community Relations**

## Mission Statement

To empower, collaborate, engage, and promote opportunities to create positive outcomes.

## Department Overview

- Serve as the human relations agency for the City of Charlotte and Mecklenburg County
- Work to prevent discrimination and ensure fair practices and access for all
- Facilitate dialogue, mediation, and training to increase understanding and improve community harmony
- Provide training on the Americans with Disabilities Act (ADA) to help promote accessibility across the city

## Organizational Chart

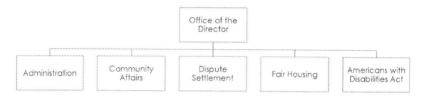

## Budget Overview

|  | FY 2018 Actual | FY 2019 Actual | FY 2020 Budget | FY 2021 Adopted | Percent Change FY 2020 FY 2021 |
|---|---|---|---|---|---|
| **Expenditures** |  |  |  |  |  |
| Personnel Services | $962,276 | $1,469,118 | $1,607,971 | $1,634,641 | 1.7 % |
| Operating Expenses | $97,006 | $162,208 | $86,263 | $72,413 | -16.1 % |
| Departmental Charges | - | -$256,172 | -$179,710 | -$179,710 | 0.0 % |
| **Total Expenditures** | **$1,059,282** | **$1,375,154** | **$1,514,524** | **$1,527,344** | **0.8 %** |

**FIGURE 4.3** City of Charlotte, budget for community relations, FY 2021

Source: City of Charlotte, NC (2021, p. 66)

to effect knowledge building of budgeting mechanics requires students to constantly examine public budgets, decipher and compare them, and talk about them. Essentially, part of every class can include a review of any one aspect of budgeting mechanics considered here.

## Teaching Philosophy and Knowledge-building Techniques

Typically (pre-pandemic), this course is offered in the classroom with all material accessible online through the university's learning management system (LMS). Students are expected to visit the course's LMS page frequently to stay up to date with announcements and emails related to 15-week semester progression. Further, all readings, videos, in-class exercises, assignments, and so on are posted to

**Community Relations**

## Performance Measure Highlights

| Objective | Measure | FY 2019 Actual | FY 2020 Target | FY 2021 Target |
|---|---|---|---|---|
| **Strategic Priority Area: Neighborhood Development (Safe, Healthy, and Inclusive Communities)** | | | | |
| Improve human relations work process for International Community | Number of collaborations and partnerships with the international community | 42 | 40 | 45 |
| Improve service delivery to Community Relations members, volunteers, customers, and partners | Average rating on Community Relations survey of members, volunteers, customers, and partners regarding service delivery on a 5.0 scale | 4.3 | 4.0 | 4.3 |
| Investigate housing discrimination | Number of housing discrimination cases investigated | 21 | 30 | 30 |
| Prevent housing discrimination | Number of fair housing conciliation attempts | 82 | 50 | 90 |
| Reduce interpersonal and community conflicts | Percent of cases referred to Community Relations that are successfully resolved | 87% | 85% | 87% |

## Full-Time Equivalent (FTE) Position Summary

| Position Title | FY 2020 FTE | Change in FTE | FY 2021 FTE |
|---|---|---|---|
| Administrative Officer I | 1.00 | - | 1.00 |
| Community Affairs Manager | 1.00 | -1.00 | - |
| Community Programs Coordinator | 1.00 | 1.00 | 2.00 |
| Community Relations Administrator | 1.00 | - | 1.00 |
| Community Relations Manager | 1.00 | - | 1.00 |
| Community Relations Specialist | 5.00 | - | 5.00 |
| Deputy Community Relations Director | 1.00 | - | 1.00 |
| Director of Community Relations | 1.00 | - | 1.00 |
| **Department Total FTE** | **12.00** | **-** | **12.00** |

**FIGURE 4.4** City of Charlotte, budget for community relations with performance measures and FTE count, FY 2021

Source: City of Charlotte, NC (2021, p. 68)

the course on this platform in content modules that represent each class session. Using the Willoughby (2021) e-book developed using Tophat.com, generally, students are assigned one chapter to read each week (excluding exam weeks and those that concern special topics, such as "Budgeting for Disasters"). Questions are embedded in most chapters that students must complete before class and then student responses are reviewed in the relevant class session. Most chapter questions require students to develop a written response based on the chapter topic. Table 4.6 presents an outline of the e-book and sample questions posed by each chapter.

2020                          STATE OF WYOMING                        20LSO-0442

|  | GENERAL | FEDERAL | OTHER | TOTAL |
|---|---|---|---|---|
| APPROPRIATION | FUND | FUNDS | FUNDS | APPROPRIATION |
| FOR | $ | $ | $    . | $ |

1  Section 051. LIVESTOCK BOARD

2

3  PROGRAM

| | | | | |
|---|---|---|---|---|
| 4  Administration | 1,598,989 | 21,186 | 329,185 SR | 1,949,360 |
| 5  Animal Health [1.] | 1,228,849 | | 245,866 SR | 1,474,715 |
| 6  Brucellosis [2.] | 983,052 | 416,216 | | 1,399,268 |
| 7  Estrays | 43,050 | | | 43,050 |
| 8  Brand Inspection | 1,851,039 | | 10,362,037 SR | 12,213,076 |
| 9  Predator Control Fees | | | 2,105,212 SR | 2,105,212 |
| 10  TOTALS | 5,704,979 | 437,402 | 13,042,300 | 19,184,681 |

11

12  AUTHORIZED EMPLOYEES

13  Full Time          17

14  Part Time           0

15  TOTAL             17

16

17  1.  Of this general fund appropriation, one hundred thousand dollars

18  ($100,000.00) and of this other funds appropriation, fifty thousand dollars

19  ($50,000.00)SR shall be deposited into the livestock law enforcement account

20  created under W.S. 11-18-120(a).

21

22  2.  It is the intent of the legislature that of this general fund

23  appropriation, one hundred thousand dollars ($100,000.00) not be included in

24  the livestock board's standard budget for the immediately succeeding fiscal

25  biennium.

**FIGURE 4.5**  State of Wyoming budget appropriation bill, FY 2021–2022

Source: H.B. 0001 (2020, p. 33)

As noted earlier, a three-hour class session is usually broken into three components that include: (1) lecture/discussion of chapter and questions (50–60 minutes), a break (10 minutes), (2) an in-class exercise conducted by students individually, with a partner, or in groups (30–40 minutes), a break (10 minutes), and (3) return to class for presentation and discussion of exercise results (45–60 minutes). Students are responsible for writing up their responses to in-class

**TABLE 4.6** Outline of public budgeting: theories and practice

| Chapter | Chapter Question |
|---|---|
| Introduction: Public Budgeting and Finance: Messy and Mesmerizing | Go to the City of Atlanta's Open Checkbook website: **https:// checkbook.atlantaga.gov/#!/year/All%20Years/** and drill down into the data for a department of your choice. What are you able to learn about revenues and spending in the department? What questions do you have after examining the cash flow of this department? |
| 1) The Psychology and Ethics of Public Budgeting and Finance | Of the edicts below, pick one that you consider as most important and realistically possible to apply to public finance officers. Then, pick one edict that you consider as difficult, if not impossible, to apply to these budgeters. Justify your choices in a sentence or two. In one or two concluding sentences, indicate how public budgeters can be taught to engage a democratic ethos when conducting their work.<br>An ethics code should:<br>• Avoid legalistic language and be easily digestible by the public.<br>• Be readily available to the public.<br>• Include comprehensive conflict of interest provisions which prohibits certain relationships while mandating disclosure.<br>• Cover corruption, abuse, fraud, bribery, other violations of the law, and non-criminal conduct which violates the code's conflict of interest provisions.<br>• Include an affirmative obligation to report suspected violations which affirmative obligation has its own enforcement mechanism.<br>• Have an independent enforcement mechanism for any violation.<br>• Contain adequate whistleblower protections for those who report violations.<br>• Cover the inducement of violations by private citizens. |
| 2) National Budgeting | Having read this chapter about national budgeting, can you list three things that you consider vital for a government to do to advance its budget process and outcomes? Explain in several sentences why you consider each vital to better budgeting. |
| 3) Budgeting in the American States | Pick a state government with performance budgeting law from the table presented in this chapter. Search for the law and determine if it has been amended or repealed. Describe your findings in a paragraph. |
| 4) Budgeting at the Local Level | Given what you have read about in this chapter, consider the experience of a small Tennessee town and its debt investment and management experience. The video, *Small Town, Big Debt*, is provided below. Be prepared to discuss reasons you think something like this happens in an industrialized country such as the United States. |

*(continued)*

**TABLE 4.6** Cont.

| Chapter | Chapter Question |
| --- | --- |
| 5) Executive versus Legislative Budgeting and the Role of the Courts | Consider the state government that you examined earlier in the semester for an in-class exercise regarding budget process, revenues, debt, and expenditures. Justify your assessment of the state's budget process as more empowering to the legislative or executive branch or balanced between the two. |
| 6) Funding Public Budgets | Explain in a paragraph the implications for a government with a constitutional provision that the tax system represents the principle of ability to pay. |
| 7) Public Budgeting Formats and Reforms | Discuss in two paragraphs the potential advantages and disadvantages of various budget formats for different audiences (legislators, chief executives, agency managers, and citizens). For example, compare a line-item with a performance format in terms of contributing to public understanding about government taxing, spending, programming, and service delivery. |
| 8) Public Budgeting Results | Research an example of human rights budgeting in a government that has not been mentioned in this chapter. How, if at all, has human rights budgeting, as practiced by this government, impacted quality of life of its public? |

Source: Willoughby (2021).

exercises that are posted to the content for that class session on the LMS. All synchronous online class sessions are recorded on Zoom and posted to the appropriate content module after the session concludes.

Thus, the course requires substantial reading and preparation, some individual and group work, completion of chapter questions, conduct of various exercises in class sessions, a research report, and one or, if selected, two written essay exams. The exams are budget cases that require students to make calculations and conduct analyses along with written assessments. Exams are administered through the course electronic platform and students access and return all exams, in-class exercises, other assignments, and term projects to this site. The course has evolved from including few exercises and multiple exams to including numerous in-class exercises (conducted individually, with a partner, or in groups), one research report (conducted with a partner), and one mid-term exam, with a final exam provided as optional to students. Several sample exams can be found in the appendix to this chapter that have been engaged with various timetables. That is, the Exam A is expected to be completed in one evening, Exam B completed within about 30 hours (overnight), and Exam C in one week. The various timetables expose students to different amounts of information and deadlines for conducting analyses and crafting clear, logical written responses that incorporate their calculations.

Expressed in this chapter is a teaching philosophy that embraces an active learning approach by applying multiple types of knowledge-building activities. As noted above, readings include one text online, but also published research papers and reports and other scholarship, as well as government budget and finance documents. Students conduct exercises that require them to search out data about governments "in real time," to interpret such data, draw conclusions, and communicate findings in unambiguous and compelling ways. Exams are an extension of the work on exercises, testing student ability to understand the budgeting context presented, analyze and interpret data, and present an assessment and/or decisions in direct, sensible, and efficient ways.

## Conclusion

In this chapter, an active pedagogical approach to the teaching of public budgeting mechanics is presented along with supporting exercises and assignments. This approach is designed to help students improve their understanding of the diversity of public budgeting cycles, timelines, and budget formats while recognizing important overarching themes of process regarding strategic development of budget priorities and while remaining accountable to the public. Outlining these themes as clearly defined learning objectives that are integrated with the NASPAA competencies can act as a valuable guide for students as well as instructors.

Since many students typically enter public budgeting courses with very limited understanding of the mechanics of public budgeting, having students frequently review, interpret, and make calculations based on actual government budgeting documents can help ensure that they are on track to achieve the learning objectives posed here. In addition to the development of technical budgeting skills, increased student understanding of the roles of budgetary actors, citizen participants, and the politics of the process are essential as each directly contributes to budgeting outcomes. These roles can be better understood by directing students to readings, exercises, assignments, and exams that engage them in analyzing and discussing budgetary context and in finding solutions to ubiquitous public budgeting problems.

Public budgeting, both for practitioners and as an academic discipline, continues to evolve. This makes it useful to annually revisit learning objectives, instructional documents, and readings to verify that they will adequately prepare students for their next professional or academic experience. The Association for Budgeting and Financial Management (ABFM) maintains a database of syllabi that are used to teach public budgeting courses at universities and colleges across the nation. The NASPAA website also tags scholarly articles related to the instruction of public budgeting from the *Journal of Public Affairs Education* or *Teaching Public Administration*. These two resources and journals can serve as a useful starting point for creating or revising public budgeting course materials.

## Note

1 The IBM Center for The Business of Government offers the *Business of Government Hour*, Interviews with Leaders free to listen and/or download and accessible at: www.businessofgovernment.org/interviews/4061.

## References

City of Charlotte, NC. (2021). Adopted FY 2021 budget: FY 2021–2025 capital investment plan. Retrieved from https://charlottenc.gov/budget/FY2021/adobted/FY2021_ Adopted_Budget_Book-Final_Draft.pdf

Governor's Office of Planning and Budget. (2021). The budget process. Retrieved from https://opb.georgia.gov/budget-information/budget-process

H.B. 0001, 2020 Biennium, 2020 Budget Sess. (Wy. 2020).

Key, V. O. (1940). The lack of a budgetary theory. *American Political Science Review*, *34*(6), 1137–1144.

Kingdon, J. (1984). *Agendas, alternatives, and public policies*. Little, Brown.

Mayor's Office of Management and Budget. (2021). New York City budget cycle. Retrieved from www1.nyc.gov/site/omb/about/new-york-city-budget-cycle.page

Saturno, J. V. (2020). *Introduction to the federal budget process*. Congressional Research Service.

Virginia Department of Planning and Budget. (2021). Virginia's budget. Retrieved from https://dpb.virginia.gov/budget/budget.cfm

Willoughby, K. (2021). *Public budgeting: Theories and practices*. Tophat.com.

Willoughby, K., Dzigbede, K., & Gehl, S. B. (2020). How localities continually adapt enterprise strategies to manage natural disasters. *IBM Center for the Business of Government*. Retrieved from http://businessofgovernment.org/report/how-localities-continually-adapt-enterprise-strategies-manage-natural-disasters

# 5

# CAPITAL BUDGETING AND DEBT FINANCING

*W. Bartley Hildreth*

While the operating budget requires the raising of revenue in one year to cover the costs of personnel and related service expenditures in that same year, the capital budget has a different focus. Capital budgeting, as practiced by state and local governments, focuses on the construction or purchase of high cost, almost irreversible, capital assets. A common source of the money to buy or build things comes from borrowed funds with repayment spread over the life of the capital asset from future revenues generated by that asset's use or from some other dedicated source.

This chapter seeks to advance the instruction of capital budgeting and debt management employed by American state and local governments, although the basic information applies in other settings. Relevant learning objectives and competencies are identified and then used to structure applications to teaching with multiple examples offered to assist the instructional process.

## Educational Objectives and Competencies

Both capital budgeting and debt management are examined by the following objectives and competencies (abbreviated as REMIT – respect environment, methods interpreted transparently):

- *Respect* the rules completely;
- Assess the *environment* thoroughly;
- Apply basic *methods* skillfully;
- *Interpret* results fairly; and
- Communicate *transparently*.

DOI: 10.4324/9781003240440-5

Each of these principles, in effect, are briefly described before using this framework to provide application that help operationalize each point.

## Respect the Rules Completely

Law defines public administration so that is the first order of attention, but other policies specified by management are just as compelling in a practical sense. All of these rules of the game are prescriptions, framed in shall/shall-not verbiage. Examples include: "A citizen panel shall review the capital improvement program ahead of the city council vote on the capital budget"; and "Debt shall not be used to cover operating deficits." Such rules specify the stakeholders involved in the process, as well as the constraints or procedures to follow. Capital budgeting and debt management operates within these prescribed rules.

## Assess the Environment Thoroughly

Management does not work in a vacuum; forces outside the organization can drive change. Political realities, social pressures, intergovernmental challenges, climate events, physical limitations, economic trends, market forces, and a host of other environmental factors impinge on carefully crafted budgets. Assessing such threats and opportunities, and making the necessary changes, puts constant pressure on management and its capital plans.

## Apply Basic Methods Skillfully

Financial choices rest on applying analytical methods skillfully. Some choices can rest on structured decision-making using nonquantitative methods, while others are best handled using financial calculations, such as those based on time value of money principles. Reasonable capital decisions rest on accurate calculations and structured decision-making.

## Interpret Results Fairly

Data-in produces data-out, but it is the application and interpretation of that data that matters. Just as fraught with meaning as a "balanced" budget (it depends on answers to "when" and "what"), so too is the basis for deciding. For example, where to locate a new regional park versus siting a new landfill, which side of the road to take more public easement, whether to lease or own a new facility, and how to structure a new debt issue. Moreover, "who benefits" and "who pays"? Disclosing assumptions and choices (even those options that were discarded, and why) is critical in promoting fairness.

## Communicate Transparently

All stakeholders in a capital investment decision expect access to full and timely information ahead of the deliberation and adoption process that leads to any official vote. Transparency requires attention to both the process and the results (Hildreth, 2005). Clarifying the implications for the current and future budgets, and tax levels, is expected. Timely and complete disclosures are needed by the lenders (investors) to gauge the value of their investments.

## Educational Applications

Capital budgeting and debt management are rich subjects with numerous books and materials to use in the classroom. The most recent comprehensive book on capital budgeting and debt management is by Marlowe, Rivenbark, and Vogt (2009), entitled *Capital Budgeting and Finance: A Guide for Local Governments*. This book is an excellent foundation for a course devoted exclusively to capital budgeting and financing. There are many books on municipal securities, the form of debt issued by state and local governments, but most are written for investors rather than issuers of the debt instruments. Appealing to both audiences, the standard is *The Fundamentals of Municipal Bonds* by the Securities Industry and Financial Markets Association (2011). For state and local government debt issuers, the most recent comprehensive book is by Johnson, Luby, and Moldogaziev (2014), entitled *State and Local Financial Instructions: Policy Changes and Management*. The Government Finance Officers Association (GFOA) provides numerous booklets on both capital budgeting and debt management. For example, Casey and Mucha's (2007) book, *Capital Project Planning and Evaluation: Expanding the Role of the Finance Officer*, not only has chapters on the essential components of capital projects (such as cost estimation and budgeting) but separate chapters on project-specific considerations (e.g., roads, water and wastewater systems, and convention centers and meeting facilities). There are numerous other books, book chapters, cases,[1] and articles that elaborate and expand on the topics. My publications on these topics further inform this chapter.[2]

There is no one-best-way to teach content. Recognizing that limitation, this section offers guidance and exercises based mostly on my experience. Included are a few examples shared from the work of others or that seem like reasonable ways to advance a particular topic. I use the aforementioned REMIT framework of objectives and competencies to structure the approaches to teaching.

## Respect the Rules Completely

Governments must adhere to fiscal policies, defined most clearly as prescriptions embedded in constitutions, statutes, ordinances, and law. Additionally, governing officials may establish management policies and procedures to further structure financial practices. Such policies may also flow from professional best practices (see National Advisory Council on State and Local Budgeting (1998) and Kavanagh and Williams (2004)).[3] Fiscal policies range from general principles to local practice. To ensure clarity, most fiscal policies are stated as a prescription (i.e., shall, must, or will-do). An exercise can reinforce the "rule of law" principle.

*Exercise 1.* After the class has completed its study of the content on capital budgeting and debt management, students must formulate a "should" or "should not" sentence for each item in Table 5.1. This exercise forces the use and application of course content into a set of fiscal policy guidelines.

*Exercise 2.* For an asynchronous course, the fiscal policy statement exercise can serve as a weekly method of keeping students glued to the material. I have students identify five sentence-length fiscal policy statements based on the weekly set of course material (book chapter, journal articles, videos, etc.). As the student

**TABLE 5.1** Establishing capital budgeting and debt management policies

Debt should not be entered into lightly, but rather as a result of careful capital planning. Part of the preparation is thinking through the goals of capital budgeting and debt management, and developing appropriate guidelines. Formulate a "should" or "should not" statement for each. For example, a policy statement that defines a capital project could be framed this way: A capital project is defined as a non-recurring capital asset expenditure that has an expected useful life of more than 10 years and an estimated total cost of $50,000 or more.

- *Citizen participation.* Address participation by citizens in the capital planning and debt planning processes.
- *Collaboration.* Since capital projects often impact adjacent jurisdictions, address the value of coordinating and partnering with other organizations.
- *Define a capital project.* Specify the dollar size and life span of the project that makes it a capital project instead of an operating budget item.
- *Project life.* Tie debt to economic life of a project.
- *Legal limits.* Isolate any legal restrictions.
- *Funding of ongoing operations compared to capital projects.* Link operating revenue to ongoing operations.
- *Importance of maintaining existing capital assets.* Recognize that maintaining existing assets may be more cost effective than the acquisition or construction of new facilities.
- *Time period covered in capital improvements planning.* Identify the number of years into the future for which capital projects will be specified.
- *Priority criteria for ranking proposed capital projects.* Specify the rational used to evaluate capital projects.
- *Funding method.* Extent of search for alternative sources of funding instead of local tax dollars.
- *Public-private partnerships.* State the policy on the use of public-private partnership to achieve capital projects.
- *Least costly alternative.* Emphasis placed on determining the least costly method and type of financing.
- *Purpose of debt.* State the need for a debt financing option.

**TABLE 5.1** Cont.

- *Use of short-term debt.* Specify conditions for use of debt of one year or less.
- *Use of variable-rate debt.* Address conditions when, and if, it is appropriate to use variable interest-rate obligations.
- *General obligation security.* Clarify when the full faith and credit can be extended.
- *Revenue security.* Identify when pledges of dedicated revenues can be made.
- *Interest rates.* Specify any limits on the use of variable rates instead of fixed rates.
- *Lease arrangements.* Clarify conditions for use of lease-purchase and other lease arrangements, including appropriation debt.
- *Conduit bonds.* Provide criteria for serving as conduit issuer.
- *Taxable bonds.* Identify any limits on the use of taxable debt.
- *Debt service constraints.* State the policy on structure options, such as level of debt service or level of principal.
- *Maturity.* State payout period in average length of maturity.
- *Redemption features.* Clarify the use of "call" option or early redemption features.
- *Credit enhancement.* Establish criteria for use of bond insurance.
- *Liquidity providers.* Establish criteria for use of letter of credit and other liquidity providers.
- *Bank loans.* Clarify conditions for use of a direct bank loan instead of a debt issue.
- *Derivatives.* Specify conditions for use of derivative products.
- *Credit objective.* Plan for maintaining or improving the independent credit rating.
- *Debt capacity.* Set the terms for internal debate on what is affordable.
- *Debt coordination.* Clarify any work with overlapping and underlying debt issuers to coordinate debt plans to temper joint debt appetite.
- *Competitive sales.* Specify any preference for competitive sale.
- *Negotiated sales.* Specify conditions under which negotiated sales can occur.
- *Benchmark pricing.* Establish criteria or methods for determining comparable indicators of market prices.
- *Winning price.* Evaluate and select winning bid based on "net interest cost" or "true interest cost."
- *Use of Municipal Advisor.* Specify conditions when independent financial advisors will be used to help with debt issuance.
- *Selection of outside professionals.* Provide criteria and method for selection of bond counsel, financial advisor, underwriter, trustee, and other professionals hired to assist in the transaction.
- *Refunding criteria.* Clarify criteria to be used in evaluating a proposal to re-issue debt.
- *Primary market disclosure.* Recognize the obligations under applicable securities laws, bond undertaking agreements, and market expectations.
- *Secondary market disclosure.* State the legal necessity of making event notices and the obligation to make continuing disclosure.
- *Investor relations.* Identify the contact person for investors.
- *Arbitrage compliance.* State the necessity to meet tax law regarding arbitrage rules.
- *Investment of proceeds.* Translate tax laws into spend-down policy.
- *Responsibility.* Assign responsibility for all elements of debt and capital budget policy.
- *Adoption of policy.* Announce obligation to get legislative approval of these policies.
- *Monitoring and revising policy.* Provide for ongoing review and revision, as necessary, of debt policy.

reads each chapter, they should try to identify the important concepts that could be stated as a generic fiscal policy statement or sets of principles for the material covered in that chapter. Hint: Almost every paragraph or subheading in a textbook introduces a new concept and the material is full of normative statements because laws are structured that way (e.g., the city will adopt a balanced budget; or a budget for the upcoming year should be adopted before the fiscal year begins). These generic descriptive statements should reflect *the big issues covering the full scope of that week's material* and not merely summary statements from the covered material. Thus, the five statements should not cluster around one part of the chapter topic, but reflect the entire content of that particular module segment (readings and videos). A minimum goal of the exercise is to gain comfort that the student has read and viewed all the material. Students should consider the substantive pros and cons (advantages and disadvantages) of each statement before submitting the list for grading with notice that they could be called upon to explain their entries. In essence, the five fiscal policy statements provide the big take-away principles for that week's scope of coverage. I remind students that governments do not do things, people do. Thus, students should not frame a statement with something similar to: "Governments should construct a capital budget that ..." Instead, frame the statement more directly: "The capital budget should ..."

Each week, the students submit their work to an assignment folder on the learning management system. I use this grading rubric: Good work – five clear, generic statements that adequately reflect the scope of material for this week (4 points); Weak – one or more statements are weak or inarticulate, statements cluster instead of spread across the full scope of the week's materials (3 points); Unsatisfactory – does not address requirements, attempts are largely inaccurate or incomplete, missed pro/con when asked, not read or view the assigned material (1 point); Missing (0 points). Over a 15-week class, the total of all possible points (15*4=60) is converted to base 100, hopefully with most students scoring 100. Given the machine capability to track time on task, it is easy to tell if a student skipped viewing an assigned video. My goal is for each student to score all points (Good Work) so if one or more statements in a week are unclear or not fitting the material, I offer a "revise and resubmit"-type response (with my reasons) and give them 48 hours from my posting to resubmit. I may offer several opportunities, but at a point a grade will be assigned. All of the submissions together represent the student's own set of Recommended Fiscal Policy Guidelines for the course, and collectively counts a certain percentage (30 percent) of the course grade.

*Exercise 3.* For an on-campus class, I use most of the same rules as in Exercise 2, but I have divided each class week among the students (several to each weekly book chapter, for example). They must formulate a sentence-length fiscal policy statement for each of the five most important concepts covered that week that they are able to give the pro/con for each, if asked. Examples include: a capital projects plan will be developed and updated annually; and a capital project is defined as a non-recurring capital asset expenditure that has an expected useful life of more than x years and an estimated total cost of $x or more. They post that list to an open discussion board by book chapter. Students must review all postings (by the others) each week. By the end of the course, all students have access to a collection of weekly fiscal policy statements covering the entire course. For a final assignment, each student then compiles into a logical manner what they want to submit as their set of Recommended Fiscal Policy Guidelines that covers the entire course and major concepts therein. This set can be used to compare to the actual practices found in a local community that they pick to study. I assigned 25 percent of the course grade for this assignment.

### Assess the Environment Thoroughly

For capital budgeting, the built environment looms large in consideration of what other physical facilities might be needed going forward. Specifying these needs can emerge from observing the deteriorating condition of roads and bridges, finding the remaining life of expensive equipment such as the high volume air conditioners on buildings, assessing the demand for regional parks to accommodate an expanding population, recognizing the obligation to preserve public health through the provision of clean water and sewer services, identifying any deficiencies in meeting new building codes for old public buildings, responding to the opportunity to spur economic development by providing infrastructure around a new industrial site, and answering the call to deal with other pressing needs.

By design, a capital budget helps implement a comprehensive plan covering public needs over a long horizon (such as 20 to 30 years) in managing growth and development patterns. Demographic changes can highlight, for example, the need for more recreation sites for a younger population, highways to handle vehicle congestion for the working population, extending utility service to serve growth in the surrounding area, and zoning constraints on businesses locating in residential neighborhoods.

*Exercise 4.* The built environment we enjoy is dependent upon public capital assets, ranging from the visible roads and streetlights to the underground infrastructure such as the water and sewer pipes. As busy people, we are so accustomed to those public capital assets that we give little thought to their condition. Students could be required to report on their observations of potential capital project needs during a tour (walk or drive) around the city. An assessment tool could be as simple as having the student judge the physical and working condition of a list of common capital assets based on their own (limited) knowledge. The purpose is not to catch all the flaws or problems with mechanical or physical elements, but to get students to focus on these public capital assets apart from the surrounding area. Giving them a week or more to see (or, better yet, visit where possible) a fire station, airport, water or sewer plant, recreation facility, bridge, street condition, road congestion points, sidewalks, bike path, street lights, storm drains, and other

**TABLE 5.2** Sample capital facilities inventory

| Facility | Year Built or Acquired | Latest Major Improvement | Condition | Extent of Use | Target Date for Rebuilding or Expansion |
|---|---|---|---|---|---|
| Town Hall | 1972 | – | Fair | Heavy | 2024 |
| Fire Station | 1974 | – | Fair | Moderate | 2026 |
| Northside Park | 1985 | – | Good | Heavy | 2031 |
| South Street | 1965 | 2015 | Fair | Heavy | 2024 |
| Landfill | 1997 | – | Good | Heavy | 2028 |

public facilities. Interviewing users and studying population trends can add to the assignment. Overall, the task is to improve the student's observation (and listening) skills about the physical plant of a community. This exercise provides direct experience in the first step of capital improvement planning which is the development of an inventory of existing physical facilities by the age, last major improvement, physical condition, extent of use, and a target date for replacement or expansion of each facility, as shown in Table 5.2.

*Exercise 5.* An exercise designed to engage students in the implications of a proposed major capital project is to have them list the three most important issues that would have to be decided before the new project could be accomplished. I used this question: Assume the State of Georgia announced plans to construct a new Northern Arc outer-perimeter Interstate Highway Loop that would connect I-75 to I-85 at least 20 miles north of the current circular loop around the city (I-285). Besides the costs (and who pays?), I look for recognition that siting the project (including "taking" private land and its implications) looms large in such an undertaking.

*Exercise 6.* Due to the long lifespan and high cost of capital assets, capital budgeting decisions engender community interest and debate. Most local governments recognize the imperative of giving citizens a meaningful input by requiring community meetings or even a special citizen panel or committee to play significant roles in the development of capital improvement plans. Students could be tasked with identifying for a nearby city what, if any, differences in citizen participation activity occur between local consideration of the annual operating budget and the multiyear capital improvements plan.

Capital assets serve to meet the social and economic needs of a community. Assessing social-economic trends requires more attention than covered here.[4] An instructional activity for those programs (universities) that provide student access to a Bloomberg Terminal is detailed.

*Exercise 7.* After students have received an assigned state government (although it could be a local governmental entity), they are to use the available Bloomberg Terminal to assess the financial and social-economic conditions affecting that jurisdiction, as detailed in Table 5.3. This exercise was offered for voluntary, extra credit. While the immediate instructional goal is to assess the student's ability to conduct a reasonable analysis, another goal is to introduce students to the value-added of the Bloomberg Terminal that is the standard used by sophisticated market experts.

**TABLE 5.3** Bloomberg assignment

The Bloomberg Terminal:

Bloomberg is a computer system for professionals in business (primarily finance) and other industries to access, monitor, and analyze real-time financial market data and place trades on its electronic trading platform. The system also provides up-to-date news, price quotes, and messaging across its network.

The Bloomberg Terminal allows students to: monitor real-time financial market changes and their effects; track financial market news; compare stocks and company information; access industry overviews; track foreign exchange, gold and oil trade information; and much more!

For students the advantages of having access to Bloomberg are significant. Today's business and finance graduates must be both intellectually and technically savvy to succeed beyond the classroom. Complex concepts are best grasped through practical examples and immersion. The Bloomberg Terminal allows students to learn how to analyze financial markets, assess economic scenarios and interpret the key news developments that impact the global economy. Students can watch the interaction of world events and market behaviors in real time and acquire marketable skills that improve the odds of landing the job you want.

Assignment:

Write a five-page report for your assigned state about different financial and non-financial trends that could have implications for the finances/budget of your state government. To complete this assignment, you will use the Bloomberg Terminal that is located [give the location]. You have the flexibility to choose the trends that you think are important for your state government. However, it should pertain to the major themes covered in this course. Please ensure that each set of data you include is accompanied by an explanation of the implications it could have for your state government. For example: An increasing population above the age of 60 could mean an increasing share of state budgets to expenditures on Medicaid and retirement benefits. Some other components you could look at are:

1) Labor Market Indicators such as Population over the age of 60, Unemployment, Percentage of People for each level of education.
2) Economic Activity Indicators such as the cost of Medicare per enrollee, percentage of households receiving food stamps.
3) Government Sector Indicators: Trends of state tax collections from taxes such as corporate income tax, individual income tax, vehicle tax.
4) Personal Sector Indicators: Trends of median incomes per household, income and benefits.

(*continued*)

**TABLE 5.3** Cont.

---

5) National Accounts: Per Capita GDP, Per Capita Income.
6) Municipal Bonds: These are debt obligations issued by state and local governments and agencies to borrow funds in order to finance new infrastructure projects or refinance outstanding bonds. These bonds are issued in the capital markets. This process typically involves municipal securities dealers or banks acting as underwriter between the issuer and investors. The underwriter agrees to purchase all the bonds from an issuer and then resells those bonds to investors. Typical investors include individuals, banks, insurance companies, trusts, mutual funds, hedge funds, and corporations, among others. Some aspects this report could contain are the descriptions of the municipal bonds issued by the issuer of your choice, history of the bonds issued, the range of coupon rates that the issuers typically face and the kind of investors who invest in the official bond.
7) Latest news developments that impact the economy.
8) You could also use the Bloomberg Market Concepts system [not described here] to supplement your discussion about your assigned state.

Through this assignment you must showcase the knowledge you have received from this course. Therefore, please ensure that you interpret the indicators that you mention in your report and assess what implications it could have for the finances of your respective state government. This assignment should be five pages, double-spaced, with regular margins and font. Also ensure that the data you include in the form of graphs or tables is formatted well so that it is easy for the reader to understand the content.

[For a debt management course, the Bloomberg Terminal offers a wide range of additional opportunities for advanced work and inquiry.]

---

Debt issuance requires a team of specialists, including but not limited to bond counsel, municipal advisors (the regulatory term for "financial advisors"), credit rating agencies, and, of course, the initial purchaser to the securities, the underwriter (or investment banking firm(s)) as well as the ultimate purchaser, the investors.

*Exercise 8.* Network analysis offers a way to identify and analyze all the relationships involved in a debt issuance transaction. Students could explore a particular debt sale through the conduct of interviews and the review of documents (capital budgets, timeline, bond disclosure documents, official voting records, engagement letters, closing memorandums, credit rating presentations, etc.). The goal is to plot all the parties and their relationships, especially noting any repeat relationships on prior bond transactions. Students could write a paper on the debt issuance process. In a different approach, I had a student (in an independent study) develop a case based on a compiled set of all the material from the start to the finish of one bond transaction and then used that product in other classes to show the details involved in the debt issuance process.

Public-private partnerships are an interesting way to fund needed capital projects (including, but not limited to, arenas, stadiums, toll roads, parking decks, technology, and government buildings).

*Exercise 9.* Public-private partnerships are bespoke arrangements, meaning that each one is unique in many ways. Focusing on a project finance case study is a way to ground students in the intricate arrangements required to pull off one of these partnerships. The published cases offered by many outlets provide the detail to explore project financing.[5] You can temper enthusiasm with the topic of mega-projects and cost overruns.[6]

## Apply Basic Methods Skillfully

There is a robust repertoire of analytical methods to deploy in capital budgeting and debt management. Each proposed capital project has its own characteristics of costs, benefits, operational implications, and unique challenges. New capital projects can impact the operating budget by requiring staffing to operate, ongoing maintenance, and the payback of any borrowed money to initiate the project in the first place.

*Exercise 10.* After identifying a specific capital project need that they have observed, studied documents found online or that were obtained from the city, and perhaps even interviewed relevant local officials (such as the public works manager or city council member for that district) to fully understand the options to fix or replace, students should fill-out a form, such as the capital request form in Table 5.4. In reviewing the submissions, check on the accuracy of the information and its eligibility as determined by the definition of a capital project contained in the fiscal policy statement (see the above section "Respect the Rules Completely").

In capital budgeting, after compiling all the capital request forms, the next task is to prioritize the laundry list of proposed projects. While it might sound best to select the highest benefits to cost ratio projects, that is unlikely in government since there are some projects that loom larger as a need or demand than sheer monetary value can justify. Array all the proposed projects into a sequence with the highest priority projects at the top and so on down the list. Then projects to be accomplished in the first year must be grouped together, separated from projects for the second year, and so on, for the five or six years covered by the Capital Improvements Program.

*Exercise 11.* Each proposed project must be examined compared to the others. By subjecting each project to a set of criteria, the relative priority of one over the next can be clarified. An open discussion is used to develop the priority criteria with the evolving discussion visually displayed in front of the class. One set of criteria is shown in Table 5.5.

The core financial calculation in capital budgeting and debt management is the time value of money because cash flow timing has economic consequences.

**TABLE 5.4** Capital improvement project detail sheet

City of _____
1) Description and Location:
2) Justification:
3) Current Status (check which applies):
   a. New proposal
   b. Design stage
   c. Land acquisition
   d. Site improvement
   e. Actual construction

4) Estimated costs:
   a. Engineering: $ ____
   b. Architect: $ ____
   c. Land & right-of-way: $ ____
   d. Site improvement: $ ____
   e. Construction: $ ____
   f. Furniture and equipment: $ ____
   g. Other: $ ____
   h. Contingencies: $ ____
   i. Total project costs (sum of 'a' to 'h'): $ ____
   j. Less trade, if any: $ ____
   k. Net project costs ('i' less 'j'): $ ____

5) Project expenditures by year:
   a. First year: $ ____
   b. Second year: $ ____
   c. Third year: $ ____
   d. Beyond third year: $ ____

6) Suggestive source of financing:
7) Effect on annual operating cost after completion:
   a. Change in personnel force (yes/no): _____
      i. How many (+ or -): _____
   b. Salary and wage costs per year: $___
   c  Other annual recurring costs: $___

A dollar today is worth more than a dollar that will be received at some future date (money now versus money later). This is different than a change in purchasing power, termed inflation. Rather the time value of money recognizes the alternative use of money, termed opportunity value. Interest is the return received for investing that money; compound interest is the interest that an investment earns on the interest previously earned. Albert Einstein said it best: "The most powerful force in the universe is compound interest."

*Exercise 12.* A simple way to help students understand the time value of money is to use a basic example. As shown in Table 5.6, assume $100 today can be invested at 10 percent compound interest for two years. How much is that investment

**TABLE 5.5** Ranking method

---

1) Highest priority projects are those required to:
   a. Complete or make fully usable an existing major capital facility;
   b. Complete already programmed improvements;
   c. Remedy a condition endangering the public health, safety, or welfare;
   d. Provide facilities necessary for a critically needed community program; and,
   e. Achieve a minimal level of community services.
2) Lower priority projects are those appropriate to:
   a. Conserve and improve existing facilities;
   b. Achieve a standard level of community services;
   c. Allow a growing, progressive area to stay in competition with other areas; and,
   d. Channel growth in a manner economical to providing community services.
3) Lowest Priority Projects are those designed to:
   a. Raise community facilities and services to an optimum level;
   b. Provide for the convenience and comfort of the public; and
   c. Improve the social, cultural, economic, and aesthetic value of the community.

---

worth at the end of the second year? The answer is $121: the original investment of $100; $10 in interest earned that first year; another $10 in interest earnings in the second year; and $1 of interest earned on the first year's $10 of interest. Derivations of the basic formula allow for solving for any of the unknown four factors: the present value; the future value; the interest rate; or the number of compounding periods. Classroom examples and quizzes applying different time value of money formulas reinforce learning.[7]

*Exercise 13.* A more difficult time value of money topic is how to handle annuities, or a level series of payments or receipts made at regular intervals for a determined period of time. Figure 5.1 provides slides for covering this topic. Classroom examples and quizzes applying different time value of money formulas reinforce learning.

*Exercise 14.* Spreadsheet software packages offer formulas that facilitate use of time value of money calculations for different applications. Two formulas that add value are shown in Table 5.7. Classroom examples and quizzes applying these formulas reinforce learning.

*Exercise 15.* An application that relies upon the use of time value of money principles is Life Cycle Cost Analysis [LCCA]. LCCA is a process of evaluating the total cost of a facility or project over its useful life. By comparing the life cycle costs of varying options (from leasing to owning), LCCA can advance consideration of the most cost-effective solution. The State of Washington provides a spreadsheet model and examples of its application which can be employed by students to evaluate local projects or to replicate the recent examples on the state's website (see Office of Financial Management, 2019).

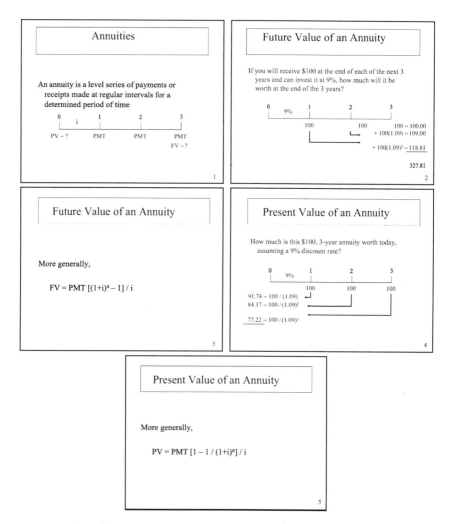

**FIGURE 5.1** Annuities

The capital budget is only as good as the plan for financing the proposed projects. Financing plans rest on expected levels of future recurring own-source revenues and expenditures, savings (fund balances), reasonably expected external funds (intergovernmental aid), and amounts available by borrowing against future revenues (debt). If capital plans cover a five- to seven-year period, then financial projections should cover the same span, even if in broad terms. The usual start is to focus on the General Fund to show the annual difference, if any, between operating revenues and operating expenditures. If projected revenues exceed forecasted expenditures over this multiyear period, the gap offers the opportunity to schedule a pay-as-you-go capital program.

**TABLE 5.6** Time value of money calculations

Example:

You have the opportunity to invest $100 (Principal or Present Value; P or PV) earning interest (I) at a rate (r) of 10% per year. What will the investment be worth after 1 year? After 2 years?

| Yr 0 | 10% | Yr 1 | 10% | | Yr 2 |
|------|-----|------|-----|---|------|
| $100 | | $110 | | | $121 |

| | After 1 Year | | | After 2 Years | |
|---|---|---|---|---|---|
| P = | | = $100 | P = | | = $100 |
| I = | 100 x 0.10 | = $10 | I = | 100 x 0.10 | = $10 |
| | | $110 | I = | 100 x 0.10 | = $10 |
| | | | I = | 10 x 0.10 | = $1 |
| | | | | | $121 |

Determine Future Value:

$$FV = PV (1 + r)t$$

| | | |
|---|---|---|
| FV = | 100 (1 + .10)1 | = $110 |
| FV = | 100 (1 + .10)2 | = $121 |

Determine Present Value:

$$PV = FV / (1 + r)t$$

| | | |
|---|---|---|
| PV = | 110/(1 + .10)1 | = $100 |
| PV = | 121/(1 + .10)2 | = $100 |

Determine Rate:

$$PV = FV / (1 + r)t$$

$$t = \frac{\log(\frac{110}{100})}{\log(1+.10)} = 1$$

$$FV / PV = (1 + r)t$$

$$t = \frac{\log(\frac{121}{100})}{\log(1+.10)} = 2$$

$$\log (FV / PV) = t [\log (1 + r)]$$

$$t = \frac{\log(\frac{FV}{PV})}{\log(1+r)}$$

*Exercise 16.* Students could be tasked with developing a financial plan based on certain assumptions, based for example on a local capital improvement plan. Table 5.8 shows what to include in a financial plan. It provides a sequence to isolate the gap that capital financing or other new sources of funds might help resolve.

*Exercise 17.* Students could be tasked with searching for intergovernmental aid opportunities for a particular type of project, such as renewing certain infrastructure projects in a distressed area of town. Students can use the grants.gov website in their search. The results can be reported back to the class or written as a memo about grant opportunities to the city mayor.

**TABLE 5.7** Using excel functions

---

1) Excel payment function ['PMT']: = PMT (rate, n period, PV, FV)

   Example: Monthly payment on $34,500 car, for 4 years @ 2.9% per year [need to convert rate and time to monthly]
   =PMT (.029/**12**, 4★**12**, 34500,0)
   = (762.11) per month

   Example: Village is considering a new library that costs $10 million, with 30-year maturity and average bond rate will be 5%, based on a level of debt service. What is a quick estimate of annual debt service?
   =PMT (5%,30 years, $10 million)
   = $650,514

2) Excel payment function ['PMT']: = PMT (rate, n period, PV, FV)

   Example: What would be the bond issue size if we only had the rate (5%), number of periods (30) and the yearly debt service we could pay ($650,514)?
   =PV (.05, 30,650514)
   =?

---

*Exercise 18.* New development can impose costs as well as benefits on a community. Fiscal impact analysis offers a tool for estimating that impact.[8] The local newspaper or TV station often feature stories on the development of new subdivisions, office buildings, or shopping plazas as well as major industrial development projects. The class could be tasked with developing a case study of one or more of these significant private investment efforts and the implications for the public at large. Table 5.9 offers a set of calculations that can be introduced for use by students exploring the impact of a proposed new development in a community. A class exercised using this set of calculations is provided in Table 5.10.

In considering the issuance of debt, several methods can aid student learning.

*Exercise 19.* An exercise is useful to clarify the difference between a bond coupon and yield. The coupon rate is the interest rate expressed as a percentage of the principal amount set at the time of debt issuance. For example, a $1,000 bond with a coupon rate of 3 percent would pay the investor $30 per year. In contrast, the current yield is the ratio of annual amount of interest on a security to the purchase (market) price, stated as a percentage. At original issuance (reoffering) the coupon and current yield are the same, 3 percent. In subsequent trading, however, if that same bond was purchased at a premium of $1,200, it would have a current yield of 2.50 percent, but if it was purchased for $800, the current yield would be 3.75 percent. Table 5.11 shows this relationship. It helps students to have assignments or quizzes to reinforce the difference between fixed coupon rate and the (market) current yield.

*Exercise 20.* Calculating standard debt ratios, especially when compared to industry mediums for similar governments, offers valuable insights on the viability of incurring more debt. Table 5.12 offers a model multiyear debt plan based on

**TABLE 5.8** Model financial plan

*Current Year*

| Line | | Characteristics | FY | FY+1 | FY+2 | FY+3 | FY+4 | FY+5 |
|------|---|-----------------|-----|------|------|------|------|------|
| 1. | | Revenues | | | | | | |
| 2. | – | Expenditures | | | | | | |
| 3. | – | Capital outlays | | | | | | |
| 4. | – | Debt service | | | | | | |
| 5. | = | Gross funds flow | | | | | | |
| 6. | – | Capital Improvement Plan | | | | | | |
| 7. | + | Project revenues | | | | | | |
| 8. | = | Net funds flow | | | | | | |

A separate financial plan is needed for each accounting fund, using the following basic definitions:

1) Revenues should be those of a recurring nature. A separate line could show the start-of-year fund balance. If one-time general revenues are expected, then create a new line that could be labeled "special revenues." This additional line might include future revenues generated from the eventual use of new capital projects.
2) Expenditures should be those of a recurring nature. If one-time outlays are expected, create a new line. This "special expenditure" row could include future expenditures required to operate, maintain, and repair new capital projects.
3) Capital outlays are fixed assets that do not meet the dollar size or other conditions necessary for a capital improvement, and therefore are handled out of general operations. They are listed in this separate line to highlight their nature and importance relative to the Capital Improvements Program.
4) Debt service on outstanding long-term debt. Any debt issued for new capital improvement projects would have its debt service appear here as perhaps a separate line.
5) The result of subtracting expenditures, capital outlays, and debt service from revenues. If there is a required fund balance policy, then an amount equal to that set aside could be entered as a new line before deriving the amount listed as gross funds flow.
6) This line shows the yearly appropriations contained in the multiyear capital improvements plan.
7) This should include any revenues directly associated with the proposed capital improvements, such as a construction grant, new debt proceeds (with subsequent debt service showing up in row 4), or other revenues contingent on adoption of the capital improvement plan. Subsequent revenues that may be generated by a finished capital project (such as fees generated by use of the new facility) may show up as a special revenue line, and associated expenditures may be listed in a special expenditure line.
8) The net figure reveals the gap, if any, remaining after taking into account all operating and capital plans. Each year's net funds flow (end-of-year fund balance) becomes available for the subsequent year's use.

debt levels, key statistical indicators, and standard debt ratios. Students are assigned a local government to analyze its debt ratios in order to assess the impact of its debt plan. This table displays, by year, the amount of debt outstanding at the start of the year, and the changes in that level that result from retiring old debt and issuing (and repaying) new debt. The table captures the effect that new debt issued in one year becomes "new debt retired" in subsequent years. Additional data are required on actual and projected levels of population, property values, personal

**TABLE 5.9** Fiscal impact analysis – projecting revenue from new development

---

Earned Income Tax:

Assumption: Family spends 20 percent of its monthly income on housing. Thus, to obtain annual income:
housing costs (per month) × 5 × 12
    or
monthly housing cost × 60

Example: Locality faces development of 1,000 single-family houses and 500 garden apartments. The local income tax rate is 0.5 percent.

Residential (1,000 single-family houses)
Average monthly housing costs × 60 = Average annual income
(taxes, debt service, insurance)
Example: $500 × 60 = $30,000

Residential (500 apartments)
Average monthly rent × 60 = Average annual income
Example: $250 × 60 = $15,000

Residential (Combined)
Annual income x income tax rate x number of units = Total Rev.

|  |  |  |  |  |
|---|---|---|---|---|
| $30,000 | 0.005 | 1,000 | = | $150,000★ |
| $15,000 | 0.005 | 500 | = | 37,500★ |
|  |  |  |  | $187,500 |

★Assumes 100 percent occupancy

Fines, Forfeitures, and Penalties:

Example: Residential (1,000 single-family homes)

| Total Annual Revenues Collected from Fines and Forfeitures | ÷ | Current Estimate Population | = | Per Capita Revenue from Fines & Forfeitures |
|---|---|---|---|---|
| $64,000 | ÷ | 16,000 | = | $4.00 |
| Per Capita Revenue from Fines & Forfeitures | × | Anticipated Development Population | = | Total Revenue from Fines and Forfeitures Due to Growth |
| $4.00 | × | 4,300 | = | $17,200 |

Water and Sewerage:

| Daily Water Consumption by Type of Facility (gallons/day) | × | Number of Days | × | Number of Dwelling Units | = | Total Annual Water Consumption for Domestic Purpose (gallons) |
|---|---|---|---|---|---|---|
| 250 (single family) | × | 365 | × | 1,000 | = | 91,250,000 |
| 200 (apartments) | × | 365 | × | 500 | = | 36,500,000 |
| Total Annual Water Consumption | × | Water Rates | + | Sewer Rate | = | Total Revenue from Water and Sewerage Charges Due to Growth |

**TABLE 5.9** Cont.

| 91,250,000 | × | $1.50/ 1,000 Gal. | + | 50/1000 Gal. | = | $182,500 |
|---|---|---|---|---|---|---|
| 36,500,000 | × | $1.50/ 1,000 Gal. | + | 50/1,000 Gal. | = | $73,000 |

Property Tax:

Residential Units for Sale (1,000 single-family homes),
Given Assessed Value and Local Tax Rate

| Entity: Assessed Value | × | Local Tax Rate | × | No. of units | = | Total Revenues |
|---|---|---|---|---|---|---|
| Municipality: $40,000 | × | $0. /$100 | × | 1,000 | = | $376,000 |
| School District: 40,000 | × | $2.81/$100 | × | 1,000 | = | $1,124,000 |

Source: Burchell and Listokin (1980)

**TABLE 5.10** Fiscal impact analysis exercise

Exercise:

Make a revenue estimate of new development in the city.

Earned Income Tax:

☐ Family spends 20% of its monthly income on housing.
☐ Estimate of family housing costs for single-family house (taxes, debt service and insurance) is $500.
☐ Average monthly garden home rent is $250.
☐ Locality faces development of 1,000 single-family houses and 500 garden apartments.
☐ The local income tax is 0.5 percent.
☐ Assume 100 percent occupancy once constructed.
☐ What is the estimated revenue for the local government?

Fines, Forfeitures, and Penalties (FFP):

☐ New residential subdivision of 1,000 single-family homes
☐ Each home is estimated to have an average of 4.3 residents
☐ Total revenue now from FFP is $64,000 per year
☐ Current estimated population is 16,000
☐ What is the estimated revenue for the local government?

income, revenues, and debt service. Debt ratios result from dividing debt figures by relevant statistics. This debt plan highlights the effect of planned debt on key debt ratios. Rapid increases in debt ratios raise a red flag in credit evaluations that requires explanation. Naturally, future year estimates are sensitive to some error.

*Exercise 21.* The existing debt attached to enterprise operations, such as water and sewer utilities, carry coverage ratios. These ratios can be used to determine

**TABLE 5.11** Relationship of fixed coupon and current year

*A $1,000 Bond (Par) Purchase by Investor, for one year*

| Purchase Price (A) | Fixed at Deb Issuance | | Current Yield (D=C/A) | |
| | Coupon (B) | Interest (C) | | |
| --- | --- | --- | --- | --- |
| $1,000 | 3.00% | $30 | 3.00% | Par Bond |
| $800 | 3.00% | $30 | 3.75% | Discount Bond |
| $1,200 | 3.00% | $30 | 2.50% | Premium Bond |

Note: C = A⋆B and it fixes interest amount on the security regardless of subsequent purchase price
Price is the amount of proceeds the debt issuer receives as well as the amount of capital committed by the investor until repayment by the issuer

Coupon sets the annual amount of interest the debt issuer has to pay to the investor

Interest is the amount that is paid by the debt issuer and received by investor on that amount of principal

Current yield is the value of the investment to the investor given the purchase price, but it does not change the issuer's debt service amounts due the investor

the additional debt that can be serviced based on future revenue estimates without diluting existing bondholder claims. Table 5.13 shows how to determine if there is any additional debt capacity given the coverage ratio that must be honored, and, if so, how much new debt can be supported. Although this is a simple example, it drives home the impact of the coverage ratio limitations in planning new debt for an enterprise operation.

*Exercise 22.* Sizing a bond issue. An excellent instructional video by Peter Orr shows how to size a level-debt structure (for a $400 million bond issue): https://youtu.be/bZgqfjFXO18. I have used this video in settings where students have already identified a project and its costs, so the task is to structure a level-debt structure, as in Table 5.14. You do need an interest rate scale which can be obtained by using the fixed interest (coupon) rate scale from a recent bond issue. You can search for a recent bond issuance for a particular local community on the Municipal Securities Rulemaking Board's website at: https://emma.MSRB.org.

*Exercise 23.* Debt issuers sell their bonds through either a competitive auction or through negotiation with underwriters. In either case, the underwriters agree to purchase all the bonds with an expectation of reselling (reoffering) the securities to ultimate investors. The debt issuer must determine the basis for computing the bids. The traditional method, now seldom used, is termed Net Interest Cost (NIC) while the preferred method is True Interest Cost (TIC) which takes into account the time value of money. Table 5.15 shows the basic calculations. These examples use an annual interest payment while most municipal bonds are sold with the annual amount paid semi-annually. Classroom exercises and quizzes applying NIC and TIC formulas reinforce learning.

**TABLE 5.12** Model debt plan

| Line | Characteristics | Past Year FY-1 | Current Year FY | FY+1 | FY+2 | FY+3 | FY+4 | FY+5 |
|---|---|---|---|---|---|---|---|---|
| | **Debt Levels** [a][b] | $ | $ | $ | $ | $ | $ | $ |
| 1 | Debt outstanding at start of fiscal year | 71 | 74 | 74 | 76 | 75 | 76 | 78 |
| 2 | Minus old debt retired | 10 | 10 | 9 | 8 | 7 | 7 | 8 |
| 3 | Minus new debt retired | 0 | 0 | 3 | 5 | 7 | 8 | 9 |
| 4 | Plus new debt to be issued | 13 | 10 | 14 | 12 | 15 | 17 | 18 |
| 5 | Debt outstanding at end of year | 74 | 74 | 76 | 75 | 76 | 78 | 79 |
| 6 | Estimated overlapping debt | | | | | | | |
| | **Statistics** | | | | | | | |
| 7 | Population | | | | | | | |
| 8 | Personal income | | | | | | | |
| 9 | Full value of property | | | | | | | |
| 10 | Revenues [c] | | | | | | | |
| 11 | Debt service | | | | | | | |
| | **Debt Ratios** | | | | | | | |
| 12 | Debt per capita (line 5/ line 7) | | | | | | | |
| 13 | Debt to income (line 5/ line 8) | | | | | | | |
| 14 | Debt to full value (line 5/ line 9) | | | | | | | |
| 15 | Debt service to revenue (line 11/line 10) | | | | | | | |
| 16[d] | Debt plus overlapping debt to full value (lines 5 and 6 summed, then divided by line 9) | | | | | | | |

a. If debt levels are expressed in thousands or millions of dollars, be sure to convert statistics and debt ratios accordingly.
b. Debt could be gross direct debt but is usually direct net debt. Principal amount only.
c. Revenues usually defined as locally generated, non-enterprise operating revenue.
d. Additional lines of characteristics can be added to see, for example, the effect on tax rates.

*Exercise 24.* To an investor, the value of a bond is the present value of the cash flow of all future payments to be received on that bond (i.e., the periodic interest received and the return of the principal at maturity). The discount rate used to calculate that present value is the yield on the bond. Table 5.16 shows the formula so classroom exercises and quizzes can reinforce learning.

*Exercise 25.* Bond prices are sensitive to changes in interest rates. Investors are concerned about the possibilities of bond prices going down as interest

**TABLE 5.13** Revenue coverage capacity example

| Year | Debt Service | Required Coverage @1.3X | Estimated Revenue | 'Actual' Coverage | Excess of Over Required | Excess of Coverage (@1.3x) to Leverage | Additional Debt Capacity* Maximum Leverage of Excess @ 1.3X |
|------|---------|---------|---------|---------|---------|---------|---------|
| | | | | | | | Revenue Coverage Capacity Example Based on a 1.3 times Coverage Ratio |
| | (1) | (2) = (1)*1.3 | (3) | (4)= (3)/(1) | (5)= (3)-(2) | (6)= (5)/1.3 | 30 yr @ 7% |
| 2022 | $638,600 | $830,180 | $1,240,603 | 1.94 | $410,423 | $315,710 | $3,917,658 |
| 2023 | $635,645 | $826,339 | $1,332,320 | 2.10 | $505,982 | $389,217 | $4,829,804 |
| 2024 | $633,645 | $823,739 | $1,444,658 | 2.28 | $620,920 | $477,630 | $5,926,935 |
| 2025 | $635,650 | $826,345 | $1,481,443 | 2.33 | $655,098 | $503,922 | $6,253,183 |
| 2026 | $636,405 | $827,327 | $1,632,585 | 2.57 | $805,259 | $619,430 | $7,686,528 |

*Row formula: –PV(.07,30, column 6)

Note: Year, Debt Service, the 1.3x Coverage Ratio, and Revenue are hypotheticals, the remaining items are calculated

**TABLE 5.14** Debt project assignment

You are to propose to bond finance a project. Determine the purpose and monetary amount of the capital project (e.g., build a new public building, large park, or new road). Estimate the timing and cost of land acquisition and the design and build process. Prepare a level of debt service schedule. Prepare and defend your results.

---

Notes to the Instructor: There are other elements that can be added to the assignment depending upon the focus of the class.

Add these requirements for the class members: Address the specific debt policies that will guide your proposed financing plan. Clarify you plans for picking and working with all the major participants in the debt issuance process (such as the municipal advisor, bond counsel, underwriters, rating firms, paying agent/trustee). What are your specific plans for attracting investors? Prepare your presentation as if giving to the credit rating firms.

Invite an expert panel of two to four local finance officers, elected officials, and/or bond market experts to sit as a review board with feedback on how to improve the work.

**TABLE 5.15** Basis for determining cost of capital

Net Interest Cost:

A method to determine the average annual interest expense for a bond issue. The total
dollar amount of interest over the life of the bonds is adjusted by the amount of the
premium or discount bid, and then reduced to an average annual rate. This exhibit
shows interest paid annually, not semi-annually.

| Annual Maturity Dates | Principal | Coupon | Interest | Total Interest: Coupon Payments Per Maturity | Bond Year Dollars |
|---|---|---|---|---|---|
| A | B | C | D=B*C | E=A*D | F=A*B |
| 1 | $10,000,000 | 2.00% | $200,000 | $200,000 | $10,000,000 |
| 2 | $20,000,000 | 2.25% | $450,000 | $900,000 | $40,000,000 |
| 3 | $20,000,000 | 2.50% | $500,000 | $1,500,000 | $60,000,000 |
| 4 | $20,000,000 | 2.75% | $550,000 | $2,200,000 | $80,000,000 |
| 5 | $30,000,000 | 3.00% | $900,000 | $4,500,000 | $150,000,000 |
| | $100,000,000 | | $2,600,000 | $9,300,000 | $340,000,000 |
| | NIC = Total Interest/Bond Year = Sum E/Sum F = | | | | 2.74% |

True Interest Cost:

To discount all future cash flows so that the sum of their present value equals the bond
proceeds. This exhibit shows interest paid annually, not semi-annually.

| Annual Maturity Dates | Principal | Coupon | Interest | Interest Paid Per Year | Cash Flow: Annual Debt Service |
|---|---|---|---|---|---|
| A | B | C | D=B*C | E | F=B+E |
| | | | | | -**$100,000,000** |
| 1 | $10,000,000 | 2.00% | $200,000 | **$2,600,000** | $12,600,000 |
| 2 | $20,000,000 | 2.25% | $450,000 | $2,400,000 | $22,400,000 |
| 3 | $20,000,000 | 2.50% | $500,000 | $1,950,000 | $21,950,000 |
| 4 | $20,000,000 | 2.75% | $550,000 | $1,450,000 | $21,450,000 |
| 5 | $30,000,000 | 3.00% | $900,000 | $900,000 | $30,900,000 |
| | $100,000,000 | | **$2,600,000** | $9,300,000 | $109,300,000 |

To do Internal Rate of Return (IRR) in spreadsheets, must put initial
investment as negative

TIC = Internal Rate of Return [IRR (cash flow range, rate estimate)]=    2.73%

**TABLE 5.16** Valuing a bond with annual coupon

$$Bond\,Value = C\left[\frac{1 - \dfrac{1}{(1+r)^t}}{r}\right] + \frac{F}{(1+r)^t}$$

Consider a bond with a coupon rate of 10% and annual coupons. [C is the coupon amount paid each period.] The par or face [F] value is $1,000 and the bond has 5 years to maturity. The yield to maturity [r] is 11%. What is the value of the bond?

Using the formula:
- B = PV of annuity + PV of lump sum
- B = 100[1 − 1/(1.11)$^5$] / .11 + 1,000 / (1.11)$^5$
- B = 369.59 + 593.45 = 963.04

        [thus, it is a DISCOUNT BOND, with Price at 96.304 per 100 par]

rates rise. While introductory business finance textbooks cover the material as would textbooks on investments, there are other sources (see Johnson, Luby, and Moldogziev, 2014). Classroom exercises and quizzes on these topics reinforce learning.

State and local governments typically issue serial bonds, meaning that a portion of the outstanding bonds mature at regular intervals until all the bonds have matured. Given the life span of the funded capital project, it is not uncommon to find 30-year maturities. In contrast, a term bond is where all the outstanding bonds have a common maturity date which could be several decades out. Regardless, these long-term obligations may have been issued with interest rates higher than current rates or the bond covenants contained restrictions that now appear onerous. Issuing new bonds to replace existing bonds is a traditional approach but there are now federal tax law restrictions on advance refunding. Therefore, restructuring existing debt obligations calls for careful analysis, both financial and legal.

*Exercise 26.* Debt restructuring requires an analysis and comparison of different financing structures. Table 5.17 provides an assignment based on City of Chicago transactions but it could be revised for a debt issuer closer to you. The assignment requires technical skills.

Securities are sold initially into the primary market and the subsequent buying and selling of those bonds occurs in the secondary market. Publicly available trade data became available in the early 2000s by the Municipal Securities Rulemaking Board (emma.msrb.org). Analyzing trade data can reveal information of value to debt issuers and analysts. For example, how does the market react to an event (e.g., negative news) concerning a debt issuer?

*Exercise 27.* Secondary trading activity can inform an issuer on market reactions (measure by bond prices) to an event. Table 5.18 provides an exercise that calls for a pricing analysis and discussion surrounding Puerto Rico bonds.

**TABLE 5.17** Financial structure and debt service analysis

You are the Managing Director of the Public Finance Division of SPEA & Associates, a municipal financial advisory firm specializing in debt financing strategies. Recently, a potential client sent your firm a request for qualifications (RFQ) for financial advisory services to help them restructure their debt portfolio.

To demonstrate your firm's expertise and analytical capabilities, a section of the RFQ requires you to analyze a debt refinancing/restructuring transaction of the City of Chicago, and offer a candid evaluation of their debt financing strategy. The primary source of information for your analysis is the July 15, 2015, Series A & B bond issue [https://emma.msrb.org]. You are encouraged to use other sources of information as well (e.g., Comprehensive Annual Financial Reports, newspaper articles, etc.).

Your analysis must contain a general and technical analysis of the debt restructuring/refunding.

General Analysis – To analyze the debt refunding/restructuring transaction, use the fundamental principles, specific polices and best practices found in Johnson, Luby & Moldogaziev (2014) and Luby (2014) as the analytical framework. Often in refinancing/restructuring debt transactions there are several tradeoffs in terms of benefits versus costs, risks versus rewards, intergenerational equity, etc. Your report should demonstrate and analyze such trade-offs.

1. Analyze the City's 2015 Series A & B debt issue, including the overall financing decision, uses of proceeds and the city's decision to use tax-exempt and taxable bonds.

Technical Analysis – Prior to the bond issue the City publically floated the idea of issuing zerials (zero coupon serial bonds), and there were concerns raised over issuing taxable GO bonds. The bond issued is a combination of tax-exempt and taxable bonds, but has no serial bonds. The city is currently examining the same two ideas, but under the new federal tax code that decreased the highest federal marginal tax rate by 9%.

2. Compare the 2015 financing structure used with a new financing structure where: A) expected tax-exempt and taxable yields are subject to the current federal marginal tax rate structure; and B) an alternative zerial issue, with zerial yields adjusted on the tax-exempt bonds +110 basis points, and the taxable bonds +125 basis points.

Compare the financing structures in terms of debt service, TIC, gross (net) proceeds, and any other measure you think important.

Write a memo that analyzes and compares the different financing structures, covering both general and technical analysis. The memo must not exceed 6 pages. Use double-spacing, 12pt. font and 1" margins. In addition to the 6-page text, include a section that illustrates the main points of the memo with graphs and/or tables, and another section with a technical appendix of your calculations. The memo should demonstrate your general knowledge of debt financing in the municipal market, and your specific understanding and technical ability to implement a complex refunding and/or restructuring financing for a less than prime-rated municipal issuer in the future.

Note: Assignment provided by Craig Johnson, Indiana University

**TABLE 5.18** Secondary market pricing

The assignment is for a two-part discussion forum.

Discussion Forum 1: Secondary Market Bond Pricing Analysis

For Discussion Forum 1 analyze the pricing of 3 bonds with the following CUSIP numbers: 74514LE86, 74526QZB1, and 74529JLM5.

[The first six digits of the CUSIP# identifies the issuer (74514L); the next two digits identifies the issue (E8); and the last digit is a check number (as in enabling checking for errors) (6).]

Use the CUSIP# to search for the bonds in EMMA. EMMA has secondary market trading data in the tab "Trading Activity" and in the "Continuing Disclosure" section in the tab "Disclosure." Along with other information, the official statement contains information on "Security" and "Disclosure" which should be helpful. Use other sources as needed.

Your assignment is to analyze the secondary market trading activity of the 3 bonds. Use price data. You can create graphs in EMMA which can help you visualize the data and tables that help you understand trading days. In EMMA you can create graphs and tables showing trades in either prices or yields. I suggest you use prices first to understand a time series and then tables with prices and yields to understand particular trades. Do not copy and paste graphs or tables from EMMA into discussion forum posts. It's fine to create and post your own brief table or graph if it helps readers understand the main point you're making in the text.

In your analysis compare and contrast bond prices (yields) for the 3 bonds from: a) the date of issuance to the present, and b) from the date that the last bond was issued to the present (thereby using the same time period for all 3 bonds).

Also, compare and contrast bond price (yield) trends for the 3 bonds, particularly the highs (peaks) and lows (troughs) of the 3 bonds.

1. What is the substantive reason behind a bond hitting a particular inflection point? Compare and contrast several specific inflection points for all three bonds, and more general aspects of bond price (yield) changes. Analyze bond prices (yields) based upon the nature of the repayment security pledge and the market's understanding of ability and willingness to pay at the time of issue, and bond price changes that likely result from new information to the market and/or "events" worthy of continuing disclosure in EMMA. Limit your discussion to a technical analysis of the data.

Discussion Forum 2: The Impact of Financial Policy and Management Decisions

Do not post on Discussion Forum 2 before you have made at least two posts on Discussion Forum 1.

1. Discuss the decision to issue the 3 bond issues (from Discussion Forum 1). What was the impact on Puerto Rico and the municipal securities market? What was the impact of issuing the bonds and the subsequent secondary market bond price changes on specific stakeholder groups, including issuers, taxpayers, ratepayers, intermediaries, and investors (primary market buyers, and secondary market traders (sellers and buyers))?

2. What went wrong and how should it be fixed?

3. Do recent bond sales and other restructuring actions help solve the problems? If so, how? If not, why not?

4. What are your suggestions for government officials going forward?

Note: Assignment provided by Craig Johnson, Indiana University

## Interpret Results Fairly

Capital projects are expensive and almost irreversible. Location decisions affect the surrounding community as well as the delivery of related services, and even ongoing budget costs. For example, building a new fire station can impact service equity. Spreading the cost over a reasonable period of time of facility use (termed pay-as-you-use) meets the intergenerational equity principle (those who benefit pays), while saving money over years to build a facility that only benefits those after it is open fails that same principle.

*Exercise 28.* An instructional approach is to distribute and discuss a newspaper article on environmental justice.[9] Alternatively, a case study, such as the water crisis in Flint, Michigan offers a startling case to elicit discussion about the interaction of service delivery decisions (to change water intake) on the (old) built infrastructure, and, now, the cost of remediation.

An increasing concern is the distributional aspects of capital investments, measured by spending by district (such as city council districts). Directing attention to Austin, Texas and Portland, Oregon where there are robust discussions on distributional equity of public services could enliven classroom discussion.

*Exercise 29.* An advanced exercise would have students use GIS software to (roughly) plot a nearby city's distribution of proposed capital projects by district. Distributional analysis generates lively classroom discussion.

Finance officials violate equity concerns when they hide money in obscure accounting funds, or even in fund balances that are not publicly highlighted, only to pull the money out at the last minute to "solve" a crisis faced by elected officials. A related equity question can arise in the transfer of money from a cash-rich accounting fund (such as a profitable enterprise utility) to a cash-poor fund (such as the General Fund). The equity issue arises when the payers of enterprise operations (especially business and industry which pay for heavier use of the water and sewer system) end up subsidizing the General Fund which may disproportionately benefit homeowners who do not want to pay higher property taxes to pay for all the services wanted out of the General Fund.

*Exercise 30.* An instructional approach is to distribute information about the use of transfers and its impact on taxation and user charges compared to foregone investment in the utility physical plant.[10] A related discussion concerns the appropriateness of fund balances – what is too much and why.

## Communicate Transparently

Information is power, so there is a compelling need to solicit information from all affected by decisions early and throughout the capital budgeting and debt management processes, and to use that information in formulating public decisions. Capital assets have enormous impact on the community so siting issues have to have community support. These choices affect tax rates (Hildreth & Miller, 2003), utility charges, budget levels (to cover debt service) and service delivery, and political careers.

The capital budget represents the current buy-or-build projects in a rolling multiyear improvement plan. Communicating this information in a timely and comprehensive manner calls for well-designed budget documents.

*Exercise 31.* An instructional method is to have class members assess the communication value of a capital budget from a state or local government. Fundamentally, the capital budget document should provide the jurisdiction's fiscal policies as covered in Table 5.1. Explaining these items should infuse and structure the entire capital budget document. A good start is to assign Mack (2019). Debt affordability studies offer a way to assess the impact of existing and proposed debt in a community or state. Almost every state produces such a document, although it might go by a different name. Usable information includes studies by the Pew Charitable Trusts (2018) and Weiner (2013).

*Exercise 32.* Class members are assigned different states with the task of finding and reviewing that state's debt affordability study and assessing the methodology of how that state assesses its "affordability" and what trends over time emerge from studying the most recent five years of those reports. Comparing results across states can be revealing. Of course, the sources cited in the prior footnote offer a comparative framework.

Capital market disclosure practices have financial and legal implications. The willingness of investors to buy particular state or local bonds rests on investor assessment of risk and return. Information is king. Therefore, the official disclosure documents prepared by government officials provide the coveted details that allow investors to make financial investment decisions. Given the centrality of these disclosure documents to market makers, securities regulators expect that debt issuers will make accurate and timely disclosure of material information. Failure to do so opens those officials and the governmental entity itself to legal sanction, often in the form of fraud-on-the-market allegations.[11]

*Exercise 33.* The formal debt disclosure document is termed the "Official Statement" (OS) upon the issuance of debt by American state and local governments (or, in other markets, termed the prospectus or offering circular). Management prepares this legal document for distribution to potential investors. Students of state and local debt management have to become familiar with this core financial document. Table 5.19 offers a basic checklist for students to look for certain aspects usually contained in the cover sheet of the OS.[12]

*Exercise 34.* Exploring the OS in more detail can be useful. Students can prepare a risk assessment of a revenue bond transaction. This assignment requires a careful reading of the complete OS with special attention to the security and sources of payments for the bonds, including the pledged assets, the flow of funds which refers to the order and timing in which pledged revenues may be used (often called the "waterfall" of money into successive separate accounting funds), priority of liens, rate covenants, additional bonds coverage, required reserve accounts, and the use

**TABLE 5.19** Quick reading of the official market disclosure document

Use the cover of the "Official Statement" to find the following information (although some of the items may not be relevant to your document).
Issuer's name:
General Obligation Bond or Revenue Bond?
Refunding Bonds?
Amount borrowed:
Purpose (Use) of Bond proceeds: Moody's Bond Rating:
Maturity (from when to when):
Interest payment dates (semi-annual?): Registered?
Book-entry?
Denomination?
Financial guaranty insurance used:
Letter of credit used:
Underwriter(s):
Bond Counsel:
Disclosure Counsel:
Underwriters' Counsel:
Dated date (see bottom left):

**TABLE 5.20** Case analysis of a revenue bond financing

Write a brief memo that describes and analyzes a major revenue bond financing sold in your assigned state. You can choose a revenue bond financing from any level of government in your state, as long as it does not involve a school district or a pooled financing like a revolving fund.

In your memo provide a description of the financing transaction, including background information; analyze the cash flow structure, diversity and strength of revenue and repayment sources; the most important legal structures; and finally analyze the overall risks and benefits of the financing. You must use the official marketing documents, and other sources, to write the report (maximum 3 pgs. (12 pt. font, double-spaced, 1" margins)).

Note: Assignment provided by Craig Johnson, Indiana University

of surplus revenues. Recent financial results and feasibility studies incorporated into the OS offer insights and plans. Litigation, environmental, and financial risks require attention also. Tables 5.20 and 5.21 offer two assignments, one for a case analysis of a revenue bond financing and the second, a more detailed assignment, that requires more attention to the bond covenants and project financing.

Investors generally require an independent assessment of the risk of a potential investment, usually by a regulated credit rating organization.[13] These organizations assess the ability and willingness of the borrowing entity to repay the money on time and in full.

**TABLE 5.21** Enterprise revenue bond analysis: bond covenants and project financing

You are an Associate in the Public Finance Division of SPEA & Associates, an investment banking firm specializing in the analysis of enterprise revenue bonds and project financing deals. Recently, a potential client sent your firm a request for proposals for financial advisory work on their new capital improvement campaign. [Instructor: If needed, you can conduct a Google search for an RFP for financial advisory services for revenue bond.] Your managing director has assigned you the task of drafting an important segment of the response.

To demonstrate your firm's expertise and analytical capabilities, you've been asked to analyze the risks and benefits of a sophisticated enterprise revenue bond issue, focusing on the use of bond covenants to manage project financing risks.

Your report (maximum 6 pages, double-spaced, 12 pt. font, 1 inch margins) must analyze the major risks associated with the enterprise revenue project financing, focusing on the ability of the bond covenants to balance the risks and rewards of the financing structure and contractual obligations to different stakeholder groups.

In the report include an analysis of the major bond covenants (rate, flow of funds, additional bonds, etc.) that are designed to mitigate specific project financing risks. The risks involved in a potential project financing may include, but are not necessarily limited to the following areas: Regulatory and Legal, Technological, Construction, Supply, Demand and Sales Revenue, Production Processes, Operations and Management, Debt Service Repayment.

Your memo must include the following:

1. A detailed exposition of the specific risks associated with the project and their magnitude;
2. An analysis of the legal arrangements and financing techniques incorporated into the financing structure to mitigate or eliminate certain risk factors; and
3. Where appropriate, a thorough discussion of specific legal arrangements and financial techniques that *should have* been used to reduce risks to particular stakeholder groups.

Your proposal will be evaluated largely on your ability to clearly and succinctly demonstrate an understanding of the appropriate use of bond covenants in a project financing; the potential client is especially looking for indications that you will be able to creativity structure future project financing deals.

Note: Assignment provided by Craig Johnson, Indiana University

*Exercise 35.* Students can use the rating criteria from one of the credit rating organizations to develop a rating for a particular bond transaction. Table 5.22 details an assignment for a credit quality analysis of a general obligation bond issued by a state government. This exercise may best fit a group project with sufficient time to explore the jurisdiction borrowing the money, its purpose, and other details.

Capital budgeting and debt management involve the allocation and financing of a capital project. Managing the construction or acquisition process requires project management skills not covered here, but are no less important. When the

**TABLE 5.22** State GO credit quality analysis

As a member of a major rating agency, provide a credit quality analysis of an assigned state General Obligation debt issue as of the date of issue. [Find the documents at: https: emma.msrb.org] You must evaluate the debt issue's overall credit quality and determine if the state is an excellent, good, fair or poor credit. Also, evaluate recent trends in credit quality and categorize them as improving, stable, or deteriorating.

Use the official statement (prospectus) of the bond issue as the primary, but not sole, source of information. [The instructor should provide links to rating criteria publications that are available from the major credit rating firms.]

You are required to analyze the state's:

1. Socio-demographic and economic condition;
2. Budgetary and financial condition;
3. Cash and debt financial management; and
4. Administrative capacity and political leadership.

The entire report must be no more than 18 double-spaced pages, not including mandatory exhibits, cover page, and a one-page executive summary (single-spaced) and reference section (if needed). The body of the report must be double-spaced, use 12 pt. font and 1" margins. If necessary, use footnotes to amplify the discussion in the text (do not use endnotes).

The written report is due in one month. Oral presentations and Q&A will take place in class. Your oral presentation must be no longer than 5 minutes.

The written report is worth 70% and the oral presentation is worth 30% of the GO Credit Analysis score.

Note: Assignment provided by Craig Johnson, Indiana University

financing is through the issuance of tax-exempt securities, there are detailed tax law procedures that must be followed, else the securities could be ruled taxable to the considered consternation (and legal challenge) by investors losing the tax-exemption. One of the constraints on spending tax-exempt bond proceeds is that the funds have to be expended within certain deadlines (such as 10 percent within one year, 30 percent within two years, etc.).[14] These spend-out requirements prevent the debt issuer from borrowing tax-exempt funds and then investing those proceeds in higher-yielding instruments, thus obtaining arbitrage earnings.

## Concluding Class Activities

Instructors differ on course design, especially on the use of midterms and final examinations. Although I do not use midterms for graduate classes, I have redesigned courses for online only instruction. The following methods show the different designs for in-class and asynchronous online classes.

In a regular in-class course, I use a two-part final exam (and no midterm exam). The first part of the final exam is a two-week take-home set of discussion questions with options. I only ask for a formal comprehensive outline instead of a written essay. When they turn in their answers, the students have to sign a statement confirming that they have not communicated with anyone about the take-home segment. The second part of the final exam is an in-class, open-book set of calculation questions, with more points available than needed to score the maximum. The overall exam grade is a weighted total (with the student picking the weight of 40, 50 or 60 percent for the in-class segment) of the in-class and take-home segments.

In an online (asynchronous) class, I have a weekly set of open-book quizzes scored mechanically. I do it weekly to capture the freshness of the material before moving to the next week. The weekly questions are a mix of multiple choice and fill-in-the-blank answers to calculation problems, with hints about formatting (e.g., the required number of digits, $ and % signs, etc.) since it is scored mechanically. I give a two-day window to take the quiz but a limit of two hours with three attempts allowed and the highest score automatically used for the gradebook. I allow the missed questions to show after each attempt.

## Conclusion

This chapter provides an instructional framework for coverage of capital budgeting and debt management. Course objectives and competencies are organized by REMIT: *Respect* the rules completely; assess the *environment* thoroughly; apply basic *methods* skillfully; *interpret* results fairly; and, communicate *transparently*. The chapter offers a set of exercises to give emphasis to these principals of good management of capital budgeting and financing.

## Notes

1 Two examples of relevant cases come from the GFOA (1993). These are Straussman's case, "The Stafford County Jail: A Case of Judicial Intervention in Public Management," and Vogt's case, "Capital Budgeting in City of Parkrose."
2 Cited at https://BartHildreth.com.
3 GFOA provides further information on best practices at: www.gfoa.org/best-practices.
4 An excellent source on economic analysis is Galambos and Schreiber (1978). For an example of doing social-economic analysis for transportation projects, see Forkenbrock and Weisbrod (2001).
5 Several relevant cases are found in the collections offered by the Kennedy School, Harvard Business Publishing, the Humphrey School, and the Evans School. Although it is not focused on public finance, I have used Lyonnet du Moutier's (2010) case study on project finance and agency theory.
6 See, for example, Siemiatycki (2005).
7 Instead of providing a test bank of questions for this exercise and the two that follow, I refer you to a business finance textbook with multiple time value of money examples.
8 A good source is Kotval and Mullin (2006).

9 One source, for example, is the Environmental Equity program at UCLA: https://innovation.luskin.ucla.edu/environmental-equity/. Another source is from the Environmental Protection Agency: www.epa.gov/environmentaljustice.

10 I have used the case of water fund transfers in Cobb County, Georgia: www.cobbcounty.org/node/622.

11 The Office of Municipal Securities in the Securities and Exchange Commission provides this helpful source: www.sec.gov/municipal/oms-enforcement-actions.html.

12 Search for a community or state government official statement: https://Emma.msrb.org.

13 In the U.S., the Securities and Exchange Commission regulates "nationally recognized statistical rating organizations" or NRSROs, such as Moody's Investors Service, Inc., S&P Global Ratings, and Fitch Ratings, Inc., as listed at: www.sec.gov/ocr/ocr-current-nrsros.html

14 Check the Internal Revenue Code for the current rules.

## References

Burchell, R. W., & Listokin, D. (1980). *The fiscal impact guidebook: A practitioner's guide*. U.S. Government Printing Office.

Casey, J. P., & Mucha, M. J. (2007). *Capital project planning and evaluation: Expanding the role of the finance officer*. Government Finance Officers Association.

Forkenbrock, D. J., & Weisbrod, G. E. (2001). *Guidebook for assessing the social and economic effects of transportation projects*. National Academy Press.

Galambos, E., & Schreiber, A. (1978). *Making sense out of dollars: Economic analysis for local governments*. National League of Cities.

Government Finance Officers Association. (1993). *Practical exercises in local government finance: Concepts and practices*. Government Finance Officers Association.

Hildreth, W. B. (2005). Tax transparency. In J. J. Cordes, R. Ebel, & J. Gravelle (Eds.), *Encyclopedia of taxation and tax policy* (2nd ed., pp. 429–430). Urban Institute Press.

Hildreth, W. B., & Miller, G. J. (2003). Can the Riverside community afford a massive debt-financed capital improvements program? In A. Khan & W. B. Hildreth (Eds.), *Case studies in public budgeting and financial management* (pp. 273–283). Marcel Dekker.

Johnson, C. J., Luby, M. J., & Moldogaziey, T. T. (2014). *State and local financial instructions: Policy changes and management*. Edward Elgar.

Kavanagh, S., & Williams, W. A. (2004). *Financial policies: Design and implementation*. Government Finance Officers Association.

Kotval, Z., & Mullin, J. (2006). *Fiscal impact analysis: Methods, cases, and intellectual debate*. Lincoln Institute of Land Policy.

Luby, M. (2014). Not all refinancings are created equal: A framework for assessing state and local government debt refinancing measures. *State and Local Government Review*, *46*(1), 52–62.

Lyonnet du Moutier, M. J. (2010). Financing the Eiffel Tower: Project finance and agency theory. *Journal of Applied Finance*, *20*(1), 127–141.

Mack, M. (2019). A guide to online financial transparency. *Government Finance Review*, *35*(6), 8–13.

Marlowe, J., Rivenbark, W. C., & Vogt, A. J. (2009). *Capital budgeting and finance: A guide for local governments*. International City/County Management Association.

National Advisory Council on State and Local Budgeting. (1998). *Recommended budget practices: A framework for improving state and local government budgeting*. Government Finance Officers Association.

Office of Financial Management. (2019). Facility life cycle cost model. *State of Washington.* Retrieved from https://ofm.wa.gov/facilities/facility-life-cycle-cost-model

Pew Charitable Trusts. (2018). *Strategies for managing state debt: Affordability studies can help states decide how much to borrow.* Pew Charitable Trusts.

Securities Industry and Financial Markets Association. (2011). *The fundamentals of municipal bonds.* Securities Industry and Financial Markets Association.

Siemiatycki, M. (2005). *Cost overruns on infrastructure projects: Patterns, causes, and cures.* Institute on Municipal Finance and Governance, University of Toronto.

Wiener, J. (2013). *A Guide to state debt affordability studies: Common elements and best practices.* Federal Reserve Bank of Boston.

# 6

# FINANCIAL MANAGEMENT

*Craig L. Johnson and Yulianti Abbas*

Governmental accounting and financial reporting are essential elements in understanding and managing government finances. Government finances are accounted for and reported via a system of controls, rules and requirements. Financial information flows through the accounting system and is used internally by financial managers and reported to external stakeholders such as taxpayers and ratepayers, creditors, investors, and financial intermediaries.

Governmental accounting and reporting education in a financial management course or program is not intended to train future bookkeepers or accountants. But it must provide students with the ability to effectively communicate with bookkeepers and accountants, other budgeting and finance professionals, as well as other administrators, policymakers, and stakeholders.

Students should learn basic financial management concepts, theories, and practices; how information flows throughout the accounting and reporting system; how to read and interpret financial reports; and how to communicate to external stakeholders on the financial condition of the government. Governmental accounting and reporting from a public financial management perspective educates future professionals in the public, not-for-profit, and business sectors about the financial activities of governments and other public benefit organizations like utilities and health care organizations. But it is less focused on the inputs of the accounting process and more focused on understanding the outputs of the process and the usefulness of the information generated for public sector officials and other external stakeholders.

Throughout the course, we recommend that instructors use financial documents prepared by financial management professionals. For a financial management

DOI: 10.4324/9781003240440-6

course that emphasizes accounting and financial reporting, the Comprehensive Annual Financial Report is a great learning vehicle and should be fully utilized.

The Comprehensive Annual Financial Report contains the basic financial statements, the notes to the financial statements, the Management Discussion and Analysis (MD&A), and the Required Statistical Information (RSI). All sections of the Comprehensive Annual Financial Report can make an important contribution to the financial management learning experience. Of course, it is essential for students to learn how to read and interpret the information in the basic financial statements, but the notes to the financial statements are essential to fully understand what is being conveyed in the financial statements. The MD&A provides background on the important financial activities of the government over the year, and a narrative window into what to look for in the financial statements. The MD&A should be required reading, prior to reading the financial statements.[1] The RSI, though typically not audited, provides time-series data on a multitude of financial, social, demographic and economic variables for financial analysis and can be used to conduct project-based financial analysis.

## Learning Objectives of Financial Management

A financial management course should incorporate theories relevant to financial management from public administration, budgeting and finance, and public policy, but it should be a hands-on course focused on the practice of managing government finances. The subject lends itself to project-based, real-world instruction and learning. The following are the learning objectives for a course in financial management that focuses on governmental accounting and financial reporting:

1. What are the basic principles of governmental accounting and financial reporting?
2. Who is the Governmental Accounting Standards Board (GASB) and what are Generally Accepted Accounting Principles (GAAP)?
3. How does information flow through the accounting system and accounting cycle?
4. What is the basic accounting equation and the governmental accounting equation?
5. What are the basic financial statements?
6. What is a Comprehensive Annual Financial Report, what information is in the report, and how is such information used?
7. How information in financial reports is used to create financial ratios?
8. How are cash and investments accounted for and reported in the Comprehensive Annual Financial Report?
9. What are the risks associated with short-term investments?

## What's in This Chapter?

This chapter covers financial management from the perspective of issues related to governmental accounting and reporting. It focuses on providing instructors with the knowledge, instructional guidance and teaching approach that they can use to teach their students to use the information provided in financial reports to make financial management decisions. The chapter provides an overview of several financial management concepts coupled with instructional guidance, practical examples, and exercises in the appendix.

The chapter continues with a review of the basic principles of governmental accounting and financial reporting. Then we discuss the role of GAAP and GASB. Next, we cover the accounting cycle, the basic accounting equation, and the governmental accounting equation. Then the chapter turns to financial reports and the Comprehensive Annual Financial Report. We review the financial reporting model, the basic financial statements, and the notes to the basic financial statements. We then cover the fund financial statements and the government-wide financial statements. The chapter also describes the information in the MD&A and RSI sections of the Comprehensive Annual Financial Report, and some basic information needed to start the process of conducting governmental financial condition analysis.

## The Basic Principles of Governmental Accounting and Financial Reporting

According to GASB Statement No. 1, "financial reporting plays a major role in fulfilling government's duty to be publicly accountable in democratic society" (GASB, 1987). Financial reporting is essential because it enables users to evaluate the financial performance of government officials and thereby hold government officials accountable.

One way of approaching teaching the basics of governmental accounting and reporting in a financial management course is to use a conceptual framework to establish basic principles. These basic principles are the thread that ties together data and managerial activities throughout the accounting and reporting process. In order for stakeholders to trust the information produced, the principles by which it's produced should be clearly conveyed and diligently implemented. These principles should be highlighted throughout the course whenever possible so that students understand how they are implemented in practice throughout the process.

There are three underlying principles that government financial managers should use when handling accounting data and generating financial reports: transparency, accountability, and control. The transparency principle is based on the idea that the finances of government should be open and easy to understand, not secretive or obscure. The underlying financial flows and financial condition of government should be easy to determine. The accounting books should present an honest picture of the government.

Two other important principles are accountability and control. The public and other stakeholders should be able to use the accounting system and financial reports to hold government officials accountable for their actions. Government officials do not own their organizations. They are stewards and hold a public trust. The accounting system should provide the necessary information to enable the public to evaluate the quality of their stewardship and hold government officials accountable.

Using the accounting system to hold officials accountable is very much related to using the accounting system to control the behavior of officials. Internal controls are an explicit component of financial management. Internal controls are used throughout the accounting system to limit, prescribe, and dictate actions to reduce fraud and corruption by government officials. On the front end, the internal control system is designed to catch fraud and inappropriate actions before they occur. On the back end, the audit process assesses the appropriateness of the actions taken and is documented in the independent audit report. A basic, ongoing systematic check on fraud and corruption in government involves the managing of finances through the internal control accounting system.

There are several operational principles used to make sure the information produced is of value to decision-makers. Accounting data must be complete and comprehensive, accurate, and consistent. Data should be complete and comprehensive in the sense that it should cover all relevant transactions, activities, and organizations associated with the government that need to be included to understand the governments financial condition.

In addition, the information provided must be accurate, meaning it reflects what has actually occurred. The principle of consistency refers to information being produced the same way each time. Each data element or piece of information should be accounted for in the same way. Accounting systems use particular measurement focus and basis of accounting (MFBA) standards to implement the principle of consistency.

There are three different basis of accounting (cash, modified accrual, full accrual) and two different measurement foci (current financial resources and economic resources). It is essential that a government's accounting system use the same MFBA for all accounting transactions. While different fund types may use different MFBA, the same fund type should use the same basis of accounting and measurement focus. Otherwise, the information in the financial statements is not comparable.

It is also important that the same MFBA is used for the same financial statements across all governments for comparability purposes. Governmental funds use current financial resources and modified accrual. Government-wide and proprietary and fiduciary fund statements use economic resources and full accrual (often referred to as simply accrual).

Governmental fund figures are reconciled to the economic resources and full accrual basis for presentation in the government-wide financial statements. One area commonly required to be reconciled is noncurrent assets and liabilities, which are not reported in governmental funds but are reported in the government-wide statements. Such reporting of noncurrent, longer-term assets and liabilities is an important advantage of using the government-wide statements to understand the government's longer-term, as opposed to short-term, financial condition. Going through the reconciliation statements helps students understand the impact of the different MFBA standards across financial statements. The reconciliation statements of the budgetary basis fund balances, as well as governmental funds, are important.

Financial reports should also be complete and comprehensive, accurate and consistent, and they must also be understandable, comparable, reliable and timely. They must be understandable in the sense that an average person should be able to read and understand the information in the report. The MD&A section should be written for the non-accountant stakeholder to understand. In terms of comparability, a financial report of a particular state government, for example, should be comparable to all state governments. Financial information should be accounted for and reported using the same MFBA, making their results comparable.

Reliability is related to accuracy, but reliability specifically covers the trustworthiness of the financial statements. Users of financial statements must trust the information presented. Finally, to be of value to decision-makers, financial reports must be made available in a timely manner. The value of financial information diminishes over time, and financial information may be of no value to decision-makers if it is not available when a decision has to be made.

It is important to note that while the above conceptual framework and basic principles may seem generic, they are used every day in making decisions about the data input into the accounting process, how that data is processed, and the outputs that are produced. In order for students to understand why certain rules and requirements exist, it is important to highlight how, when, and why principles are implemented.

## The Role of GAAP and GASB in the Accounting Process

The abovementioned principles can only be implemented across the government sector if there is an organization that is responsible for creating and overseeing standards. The GASB is an independent organization responsible for establishing the accounting and reporting standards for state and local governments. These standards provide a system of principles and practices that are implemented throughout the accounting systems of most governmental entities. GASB standards cover all subnational governments in the United States which includes general governments (towns, cities, counties, states), and special purpose governments (i.e., special taxing districts, school and utility districts, public authorities, etc.).

GASB is responsible for establishing the basic set of accounting and reporting guidelines which are referred to as GAAP. GAAP contains accounting and reporting principles and practices that have been determined to be appropriate standards for all governmental entities to use when accounting for and reporting financial information in the public sector. GAAP provides both general philosophical principles and very detailed practical guidance.

It is important to convey to students that what constitutes GAAP is under constant review by GASB and changes to GAAP regularly occur in the form of new concepts and statements, but only after substantial deliberation and consultation throughout the practitioner, user, and academic communities. The last major overhaul of the reporting model was GASB Statement No. 34 which was published in June 1999, but the official process to overhaul the reporting model began in 1985 (Smith, 2009). Lesser changes to GAAP do not regularly take 14 years, but the process of changing standards is formal, deliberate, and involves substantial consultation with public input. Students can benefit by tracing the path a new idea takes to becoming official GASB guidance in the form of a new, official GASB statement. It lets them see into the black box of the world of creating accounting rules that are intended to improve financial management practice. In addition, these new rues often generate new scholarly empirical research which can be used in the course to develop the student's ability to read, understand, and potentially contribute to the professional financial management literature and practice. But the process to professional understanding and practice begins with understanding the process. The next section covers the basics of the accounting cycle.

## The Accounting Cycle

The accounting cycle defines the repeated steps taken to transform decisions into financial statements. Decisions are reflected in the transactions made by the entity. The cycle starts from identifying and classifying transactions in a systematic way. In identifying transactions, two attributes are considered: (1) whether the transactions have financial impact, and (2) whether the transactions can be measured reliably. Only transactions that have financial impact and can be measured reliably are recorded. Transactions are classified and recorded under the appropriate accounts, for example a cash receipt transaction will be recorded under the cash account and revenue account, respectively.[2]

A journal entry is used to record transactions. The journal entry is then posted to a ledger. A ledger shows the balance of each individual account and posting is intended to update the balance. The balance from the ledger is used to create a trial balance. The trial balance shows all of the entity's individual accounts. In accrual-based accounting, adjustments are sometimes needed to correct account balances. The financial statements are prepared from the trial balance. At the end of the accounting cycle, the entity will record a closing journal entry to close all temporary accounts (e.g., revenues, expenses).

The time to record a transaction varies based on the accounting basis. Cash basis accounting records only cash transactions. If a transaction does not involve a cash receipt or payment, the transaction will not be recorded. Accrual basis accounting records transactions when they occur. Revenues are recorded when earned. For example, if an entity makes a sale, the revenues will be recorded under the accrual basis regardless of the cash receipts. Similarly, expenses are recorded when incurred. For example, an entity has to record expenses for services it used regardless of whether it has made the cash payment. The modified accrual basis is commonly used by government entities in preparing the governmental fund report. The modified accrual basis uses the current financial resources focus, which means no noncurrent assets or long-term debt is recorded. Under this basis, revenues are recorded when available and measurable while expenditures are recorded when the related liability is recognized. This is typically when a good or service has been purchased and when payment is due.

## The Basic Accounting Equation

An entity records and classifies transactions under the appropriate accounts. These accounts are created based on an accounting equation. The basic accounting equation is as follows:

Assets = Liabilities + Owner's Equity

A transaction is recorded in an entity's accounts by keeping the right side and the left side of equation balanced. For example, if an entity issued a notes payable, the transaction will be recorded as an increase in assets (for the proceeds received from the notes payable issuance) and an increase in liabilities (for the notes payable).

An asset generally shows the resources owned by the entity. An asset is expected to bring a future benefit for the entity. A liability shows a claim on the entity's resources. Owner's equity represents the residual claim on the entity resources. A liability represents an outsider's claim; equity represents an insider's (owner's) claim. Owner's equity is usually divided into paid-in capital and retained earnings:

Assets = Liabilities + Paid-in Capital + Retained Earnings

Paid-in capital represents an owner's investment while retained earnings are the amount earned and kept for future use. The two major items affecting retained earnings are revenues and expenses. Revenues represent inflows of resources and expenses represent outflows of resources. Revenue increases retained earnings while an expense reduces retained earnings.

In accordance with the accounting equation, an entity can create a set of accounts that best represent their financial condition. For example, assets are commonly classified into current assets and noncurrent assets. Current assets represent benefits that are expected to be received within one operating cycle. Current assets can further be classified into more detail, such as cash and cash equivalent, short-term investment, prepaid expenses, and so on. Similarly, liabilities are commonly classified as short-term liabilities and long-term liabilities. The short-term liabilities are those payable within the business' operating cycle.

## The Basic Governmental Accounting Equation

The basic governmental accounting equation comprises the elements of net position and is the following:

$$\text{Net Position} = \text{Assets} + \text{Deferred Outflows of Resources} - \text{Liabilities} - \text{Deferred Inflows of Resources}$$

It is based on GASB Concepts Statement 4 (GASB, 2007). As in the basic accounting equation described in the prior section, it includes assets and liabilities. Assets are resources that the government owns. Liabilities are the amount of resources that the government owes. Net assets can be derived by simply subtracting total liabilities from total assets, but that figure does not include deferred inflows of resources and deferred outflows of resources. Therefore, the net asset figure is not the same as net position, which does include deferred resources. The inclusion of deferrals makes the current governmental accounting equation different than the previous one described in Statement No. 34 in 1999, which was based on net assets and did not explicitly include deferrals.

Deferrals are not assets or liabilities, nor revenues or expenses, since they are not related to the current year. Deferrals represent an inflow or outflow of resources related to future years. With a deferral the event has already occurred, however, the recognition of the event is deferred to future periods. The recognition is deferred until the future when the inflows and outflows are related (GASB, 2013).

Prior to the inclusion of deferrals into the accounting equation, deferrals were not separated out from current year revenues and expenses. So they were included fully as assets and liabilities in the current year. As a consequence, some government financial condition results, as presented in the financial statements, were misleading. Moreover, it provided inappropriate incentives for government officials to undertake certain financial arrangements if they could record all future revenue upfront.

The governmental accounting equation is focused on the government's financial position, called net position. Unlike business accounting which uses owner's equity, governmental accounting is focused on interperiod equity. Interperiod equity is determined by the government's net position. Net position is the difference between assets and deferred outflows, and liabilities and deferred inflows. If total revenues exceed expenses, then the change in net position is positive and the government runs a surplus and interperiod equity increases. On the other hand, if expenses exceed revenues, then the government runs a deficit (negative change in net position) and must use previously accumulated surplus resources or push obligations into the future, decreasing interperiod equity.

The change in net position can be thought of as the "bottom line" from government operations. A positive change in net position indicates that the government is financially better off from current year operations, and a negative change in net position indicates that the government is now worse off from current year operations.

Deferrals are important to explicitly include in the accounting equation in order for the interperiod equity figure to be accurate. Of course, only cash flows that took place during the year should be included, but in addition, only those cash flows that are related to the current fiscal year should be included. So revenues and expenses transactions that occur in the fiscal year, but that are related to a future year, should be recognized as deferred revenues and deferred expenses, rather than revenues and expenses.

## Financial Reporting and the Basic Financial Statements

Financial reporting is central to the financial management function and is a way for government officials to convey to stakeholders that they are good financial stewards and meeting their transparency, accountability, and control goals. Financial reporting is central to the enterprise of governing in a modern, open, and free society and provides a record to evaluate the quality of governance. As Johnson (2009, p. 390) puts it:

> Financial reporting is one of government's most important responsibilities. Governments have an ethical obligation to produce financial reports that stakeholders – taxpayers, citizens, creditors, vendors, among others – can read and understand and provide the most accurate, transparent, comprehensive, and complete picture of their government. Financial reports must enhance, not hinder, the stakeholders' ability to understand, monitor, and evaluate how government finances are being managed. An outcome of the many managerial, accounting, and auditing activities undertaken by government and outside firms should be annually audited financial statements that inform stakeholders.

Subnational government officials produce financial reports for the public based on GASB Statement No. 34, which created a new and fundamentally different financial reporting model when it was published in 1999 (GASB, 1999). When the new financial reporting model was created, it was intended to help users better understand the financial activities of government, and those same intentions are still important today. Specifically, users of financial reports should be able to:

> Assess the finances of government in its entirety;
> Determine whether the government's overall financial position improved or deteriorated;
> Evaluate whether the government's current-year revenues were sufficient to pay for current-year services; and
> Make better comparisons between governments.
>
> *Johnson, 2009, p. 391*

It is important to appreciate that the financial reporting model is not in tablets etched in stone or a holy scripture. While most aspects of the initial GASB 34 reporting model remain intact to this day, there have been several important changes over the years and it is currently being formally reexamined by GASB for potential improvements. GASB published a draft document of potential improvements in June 2020 for public review and comments (GASB, 2020). If the draft is finalized in its current form, it would make several changes to some of the fund statements and required supplementary information, but no major changes to the basic government-wide financial statements. At the end of this process, it is likely that changes to the reporting model will be made, but only after a thorough public discussion of the costs and benefits of doing so. A parallel discussion in the classroom can be had to discuss important contemporary topics which has the additional value of socializing future financial managers into the profession.

## Government-wide Financial Statements

A comprehensive and comparative perspective on the financial condition of state and local governments begins with the government-wide financial statements. The government-wide financial statements are the first set of basic of financial statements in the Comprehensive Financial Annual Report because they present the governmental entity as a comprehensive unit. A thorough and practical understanding of government-wide financial statements is an important element of a public financial management education. It can distinguish students coming out of public management (affairs/policy) programs from their business school counterparts. If the public financial management graduate can demonstrate his or her practical ability to use government-wide financial statements in decision-making, it can provide them with a comparative advantage on the job market.

The government-wide financial statements are third-party, audited financial statements. Therefore, the information provided by government-wide statements has been validated by certified accounting professionals using widely accepted national accounting and reporting standards and authoritative rules. This is not the case with information from several non-audited or self-reported sources, such as the U.S. Census Bureau or the Fiscal Survey of the States.

In order to assess the quality of the financial reports, one should read the independent auditor's report. For a government with a good financial management and accounting system, you expect to see a "clean" or unmodified audit report. Meaning that in the opinion of the auditor, the financial statements are created according to GAAP, and that in all material respects the financial statements present a fair representation of the government's financial condition. Good financial management practice dictates that government officials strive for a "clean" audit opinion. Also, debt sold in financial markets by issuers with a clean opinion is likely to receive a discount compared to modified audit opinions.

Perhaps the most important improvement to financial reporting from the implementation of government-wide financial statements has been the ability to now view a government as a whole governmental entity rather than a series of funds, and to be able to compare such governments to each other. The two basic financial statements, the Statement of Net Position and the Statement of Activities, present information about the government as a whole, which is referred to as the primary government. The Statement of Activities is similar to a corporate income statement, and the Statement of Net Position is similar to a corporate balance sheet. Both financial statements provide a broad overview of the government's finances. The statements provide both short-term and long-term information on the government's financial condition which enables stakeholders to access the financial condition of the government at the end of the fiscal year.

Government-wide financial statements consolidate and reconcile the information from several different fund statements into two basic financial statements. Looking across the different governmental funds and other fund types, it was, and still can be, difficult to evaluate the government as a whole because of the sheer number of funds and all the different basis of accounting and measurement foci across fund types. The government-wide statements consolidate the different funds and reconcile the different MFBAs across fund types to produce two statements using only the accrual basis of accounting and economic resources measurement focus. This has improved the user's ability to understand the longer-term financial condition of government.

The government-wide financial statements present separate columns for governmental activities and business-type activities. The two are distinguished largely on how their operations are financed. Business-type activities are intended to be self-sustaining operations financed though prices charged in exchange for goods and services. An example is a state lottery. Prices are charged for chances to win a prize. Revenue for business-type activities typically comes from user charges, fees, and licenses, but not typically general revenues. Governmental activities are primarily financed with general tax dollars and intergovernmental aid that supports traditional public services like education, health and human services, environmental protection, the legal system, and so on. The sum of governmental and business-type activities equals the primary government. The primary government-total is shown in a separate column and represents the governmental entity as a whole.

Component units are also accounted for on the government-wide financial statements. Component units are tax exempt entities that raise or hold economic resources for the direct benefit of the government, but that are legally separate and distinct from the government (GASB, 2002). The state university system, for example, is a component unit in several states. Component unit information is presented separately from primary government information. Component units are not reported as a part of the total primary government, but the financial condition of a component unit is important to understand, especially if it runs a structural deficit and is being subsidized by primary government general revenues. Including component units in the financial statements and discretely presenting their information separate from governmental and business-type activities increases the comprehensiveness of the financial report.

### Statement of Net Position

The Statement of Net Position is the government's balance sheet. It presents all of the government's financial and capital resources in a format where assets plus deferred outflows of resources, minus liabilities minus deferred inflows of resources equals net position. Moving some of the terms around, it can be viewed as assets plus deferred outflows equal liabilities plus deferred inflows, plus net position. Either way, the focus is on net position and whether the financial position of the government is either stable, improving, or deteriorating.

Figure 6.1 shows the Statement of Net Position for the State of California ending the 2019 fiscal year. Assets are presented first in the Statement of Net Position. Assets are listed in their order of liquidity. California presents current assets and noncurrent assets separately, as recommended by GASB. The separation enables the user to easily and consistently determine the amount of short-term and long-term assets for further analysis. Notice that capital assets are listed toward the bottom of noncurrent assets, and are itemized by land and different types of physical improvements: highway infrastructure, buildings, construction, and so on.

Moving from left to right under primary government, there is a column for government activities, business-type activities, and a total column. The total column is simply the addition of governmental and business-type activities, but conceptually is important because it represents the total primary government. Notice that the components units are presented in a separate column at the end, and though important to understand in terms of their potential draw on government resources, they are not a part of the total primary government.

Deferred outflows of resources are displayed after total assets at the bottom of Figure 6.1. After all the assets are summed, deferred outflows are added to obtain the line: total assets and deferred outflows of resources. Notice that for the primary government, deferred outflows make up 8.4 percent of total assets and deferred outflows. The figure also displays the Statement of Net Position's liabilities and deferred inflows of resources. Liabilities are also broken down into current and noncurrent, and are listed in order of maturity. Following the total liabilities line is deferred inflows of resources and then total liabilities and deferred inflows of resources. Notice that the amount of deferred inflows of resources adds $22 billion to the $362 billion in total liabilities.

| | Primary Government | | | Component |
| | Governmental Activities | Business-type Activities | Total | Units |
|---|---|---|---|---|
| **ASSETS** | | | | |
| Current assets: | | | | |
| Cash and pooled investments | $ 60,263,614 | $ 7,383,985 | $ 67,647,599 | $ 2,814,435 |
| Amount on deposit with U.S. Treasury | ~~~ | 3,717,242 | 3,717,242 | ~~~ |
| Investments | 607,430 | 2,994,955 | 3,602,385 | 8,166,937 |
| Restricted assets: | | | | |
| Cash and pooled investments | 581,464 | 999,183 | 1,580,647 | 288,562 |
| Investments | ..... | ..... | ..... | 40,342 |
| Due from other governments | ~~~ | 292,355 | 292,355 | ~~~ |
| Net investment in direct financing leases | 12,105 | 11,868 | 23,973 | |
| Receivables (net) | 17,797,081 | 2,157,008 | 19,954,089 | 6,309,315 |
| Internal balances | (191,044) | 191,044 | ..... | ~~~ |
| Due from primary government | ~~~ | ~~~ | ..... | 222,053 |
| Due from other governments | 31,068,148 | 444,522 | 31,512,670 | 155,027 |
| Prepaid items | 216,791 | 69,471 | 286,262 | 4,529 |
| Inventories | 69,969 | 15,263 | 85,232 | 266,839 |
| Recoverable power costs (net) | ~~~ | 88,000 | 88,000 | |
| Other current assets | 38,203 | 3,697 | 41,900 | 448,632 |
| Total current assets | 110,463,761 | 18,368,593 | 128,832,354 | 18,716,671 |
| Noncurrent assets: | | | | |
| Restricted assets: | | | | |
| Cash and pooled investments | 143,195 | 745,756 | 888,951 | 55,798 |
| Investments | ..... | 352,860 | 352,860 | 70,584 |
| Loans receivable | ~~~ | 1,954,696 | 1,954,696 | |
| Investments | ~~~ | 2,070,884 | 2,070,884 | 35,891,433 |
| Net investment in direct financing leases | 253,833 | 208,216 | 462,049 | ~~~ |
| Receivables (net) | 6,777,439 | 472,679 | 7,250,118 | 2,901,483 |
| Loans receivable | 3,373,943 | 5,304,523 | 8,678,466 | 3,126,293 |
| Recoverable power costs (net) | ~~~ | 837,000 | 837,000 | |
| Long-term prepaid charges | 1,158 | 1,467,006 | 1,468,164 | 134 |
| Capital assets: | | | | |
| Land | 20,473,440 | 306,207 | 20,779,647 | 1,442,899 |
| State highway infrastructure | 78,418,144 | ~~~ | 78,418,144 | ~~~ |
| Collections – nondepreciable | 22,682 | 27,473 | 50,155 | 554,898 |
| Buildings and other depreciable property | 32,753,402 | 15,807,714 | 48,561,116 | 56,078,435 |
| Intangible assets – amortizable | 2,630,788 | 433,466 | 3,064,254 | 1,784,908 |
| Less: accumulated depreciation/amortization | (16,142,867) | (6,573,874) | (22,716,741) | (28,699,015) |
| Construction/development in progress | 16,149,346 | 3,257,564 | 19,406,910 | 4,360,384 |
| Intangible assets – nonamortizable | 592,549 | 118,807 | 711,356 | 10,344 |
| Other noncurrent assets | ~~~ | 29,820 | 29,820 | 455,058 |
| Total noncurrent assets | 145,447,052 | 26,820,797 | 172,267,849 | 78,033,636 |
| **Total assets** | 255,910,813 | 45,189,390 | 301,100,283 | 96,750,307 |
| **DEFERRED OUTFLOWS OF RESOURCES** | 24,864,723 | 3,000,868 | 27,865,591 | 10,834,877 |
| **Total assets and deferred outflows of resources** | $ 280,775,536 | $ 48,190,258 | $ 328,965,794 | $ 107,585,184 |

(continued)

**FIGURE 6.1** Statement of Net Position, State of California, June 30, 2019

Note: Amounts in thousands

Source: Office of the State Controller (2019)

| | Primary Government | | | |
|---|---|---|---|---|
| | Governmental Activities | Business-type Activities | Total | Component Units |
| **LIABILITIES** | | | | |
| Current liabilities: | | | | |
| Accounts payable | $ 35,908,393 | $ 571,116 | $ 36,479,509 | $ 4,220,427 |
| Due to component units | 222,053 | | 222,053 | — |
| Due to other governments | 10,817,194 | 326,574 | 11,143,768 | — |
| Revenues received in advance | 2,050,018 | 372,260 | 2,422,278 | 1,613,694 |
| Tax overpayments | 5,930,342 | — | 5,930,342 | — |
| Deposits | 460,966 | — | 460,966 | 1,146,004 |
| Contracts and notes payable | 4,581 | — | 4,581 | 11,281 |
| Unclaimed property liability | 1,047,738 | — | 1,047,738 | — |
| Interest payable | 1,119,817 | 62,135 | 1,181,952 | 24,424 |
| Securities lending obligations | — | — | — | 991,052 |
| Benefits payable | — | 527,078 | 527,078 | — |
| Current portion of long-term obligations | 6,240,109 | 2,581,483 | 8,821,592 | 4,277,889 |
| Other current liabilities | 651,056 | 575,381 | 1,226,437 | 2,169,340 |
| Total current liabilities | 64,452,267 | 5,016,027 | 69,468,294 | 14,454,111 |
| Noncurrent liabilities: | | | | |
| Loans payable | 199,063 | — | 199,063 | 17,370 |
| Lottery prizes and annuities | — | 682,929 | 682,929 | — |
| Compensated absences payable | 3,666,981 | 206,770 | 3,873,751 | 364,726 |
| Workers' compensation benefits payable | 3,958,475 | 5,131 | 3,963,606 | 488,169 |
| Commercial paper and other borrowings | 1,032,760 | 778,497 | 1,811,257 | 1,854 |
| Capital lease obligations | 363,129 | 295,214 | 658,343 | 372,104 |
| General obligation bonds payable | 74,762,282 | 807,597 | 75,569,879 | — |
| Revenue bonds payable | 14,912,983 | 13,275,970 | 28,188,953 | 22,973,611 |
| Mandated cost claims payable | 1,815,450 | | 1,815,450 | — |
| Net other postemployment benefits liability | 69,441,716 | 14,765,563 | 84,207,279 | 20,355,755 |
| Net pension liability | 81,299,874 | 8,730,246 | 90,030,120 | 18,439,837 |
| Revenues received in advance | — | 8,048 | 8,048 | 12,215 |
| Other noncurrent liabilities | 2,128,019 | 268,122 | 2,396,141 | 2,976,451 |
| Total noncurrent liabilities | 253,580,732 | 39,824,087 | 293,404,819 | 66,002,092 |
| **Total liabilities** | 318,032,999 | 44,840,114 | 362,873,113 | 80,456,203 |
| **DEFERRED INFLOWS OF RESOURCES** | 17,468,047 | 4,587,487 | 22,055,534 | 7,179,642 |
| **Total liabilities and deferred inflows of resources** | $ 335,501,046 | $ 49,427,601 | $ 384,928,647 | $ 87,635,845 |

| | Primary Government | | | |
|---|---|---|---|---|
| | Governmental Activities | Business-type Activities | Total | Component Units |
| **NET POSITION** | | | | |
| Net investment in capital assets | $ 112,279,950 | $ 2,534,257 | $ 114,814,207 | $ 14,902,116 |
| Restricted: | | | | |
| Nonexpendable – endowments | — | 1,693 | 1,693 | 7,471,853 |
| Expendable: | | | | |
| Endowments and gifts | — | — | — | 12,974,311 |
| General government | 4,176,720 | 192,993 | 4,369,713 | — |
| Education | 848,496 | 144,161 | 992,657 | 1,441,553 |
| Health and human services | 3,424,992 | 2,047,041 | 5,472,033 | — |
| Natural resources and environmental protection | 5,234,161 | 2,729,142 | 7,963,303 | — |
| Business, consumer services, and housing | 4,218,802 | 22,414 | 4,241,216 | — |
| Transportation | 9,033,482 | 6,293 | 9,039,775 | — |
| Corrections and rehabilitation | 76,730 | 4,941 | 81,671 | — |
| Unemployment programs | — | 7,798,582 | 7,798,582 | — |
| Indenture | — | — | — | 629,421 |
| Statute | — | — | — | 2,067,910 |
| Budget stabilization | 14,358,422 | — | 14,358,422 | — |
| Other purposes | — | — | — | 17,875 |
| Total expendable | 41,371,805 | 12,945,567 | 54,317,372 | 17,131,070 |
| Unrestricted | (208,377,265) | (16,718,860) | (225,096,125) | (19,555,700) |
| **Total net position (deficit)** | (54,725,510) | (1,237,343) | (55,962,853) | 19,949,339 |
| **Total liabilities, deferred inflows of resources, and net position** | $ 280,775,536 | $ 48,190,258 | $ 328,965,794 | $ 107,585,184 |

FIGURE 6.1 Continued

Figure 6.1 brings the two sides of the governmental accounting equation together to display net position. It shows several components of net position: net investment in capital assets; restricted (non-expendable and expendable); and unrestricted. Net investment in capital assets represents capital assets minus depreciation and any debt used to acquire the capital assets, as well as any related deferred inflows and outflows of resources. Restricted net position consists of assets that have restrictions associated with their use minus liabilities and deferred inflows of resources associated with their use. Unrestricted net position is a residual figure. It is the figure after net investments in capital assets and restricted net position are subtracted from net position.

The unrestricted net position of -$225 billion is a residual figure and is calculated as follows:

(total assets and deferred outflows of resources – total liabilities and deferred inflows of resources) – (net position, net investment in capital assets + net position, restricted) = unrestricted net assets

$$(\$328.9\text{-}\$384.9) - (\$114.8\text{+}\$54.3) = \$\text{-}225$$

The net position of the State of California is -$55.9 billion in 2019, which is a cause for concern. But it is less than the -$70 billion in 2018. The change in net position year-over-year shows an improvement, but also indicates a long way to go for the state to reach solvency.

## Statement of Activities

The Statement of Activities presents information on the flow of resources over the fiscal year. It is similar to a corporate income statement, but it is not an income statement. General government units are not financed by providing goods and services and earning income, they are financed with mandatory taxes and other revenues which are not earned, they are levied and received.

Figure 6.2 shows the Statement of Activities for the State of California for the fiscal year ended June 30, 2019. On the left-hand side, it lists the functions and programs the primary government provides for governmental activities and then business-type activities. Below the primary government, the component units are shown. Notice that the University of California is classified as a component unit whereas the California State University is a part of the primary government. This indicates that the University of California system has substantial, independent budget authority, and the California State University system does not.

The second column contains expenses, and the next three columns are program revenues: charges for service, operating grants and contributions, and capital grants and contributions. Governmental activities are not expected to be self-sustaining, so most of their expenses are not covered through charges. In contrast, business-type activities are expected to be self-sustaining and the reader can see that most business-type programs charge for services at a level that is expected to cover expenses. But some may fall short.

The next section of the statement covers Net (Expense) Revenues and Changes in Net Position. The top of this section shows whether or not the function or program ran a surplus or deficit for the year. Notice that most lines in the governmental activities section are in deficit in the total column, whereas most lines

| | | Program Revenues | | |
| | | | Operating | Capital |
| | | Charges | Grants and | Grants and |
| FUNCTIONS/PROGRAMS | Expenses | for Services | Contributions | Contributions |
| **Primary government** | | | | |
| Governmental activities: | | | | |
| General government.............. | $   17,900,629 | $    5,755,165 | $    1,438,133 | $        ....... |
| Education ............................. | 75,643,779 | 78,445 | 7,597,743 | ....... |
| Health and human services........ | 144,936,676 | 13,874,296 | 82,667,677 | ....... |
| Natural resources and environmental protection........................... | 9,774,290 | 6,644,917 | 290,509 | ....... |
| Business, consumer services, and housing............. | 2,133,480 | 1,206,126 | 157,518 | ....... |
| Transportation............................ | 17,022,071 | 7,093,122 | 2,274,694 | 1,561,483 |
| Corrections and rehabilitation............. | 15,153,502 | 10,993 | 75,588 | ....... |
| Interest on long-term debt.............. | 3,995,597 | ....... | ....... | ....... |
| Total governmental activities............. | 286,560,024 | 34,663,064 | 94,501,862 | 1,561,483 |
| Business-type activities: | | | | |
| Electric Power........................ | 913,000 | 913,000 | ....... | ....... |
| Water Resources ......................... | 1,199,823 | 1,172,134 | ....... | ....... |
| State Lottery............................. | 7,435,755 | 7,473,452 | ....... | ....... |
| Unemployment Programs ................. | 13,229,332 | 14,039,030 | ....... | ....... |
| California State University .............. | 9,779,084 | 3,529,083 | 2,044,729 | ....... |
| State Water Pollution Control Revolving............... | 49,860 | 95,703 | 12,504 | ....... |
| Safe Drinking Water State Revolving............... | 19,371 | 25,762 | 68,129 | ....... |
| Housing Loan............................. | 54,402 | 60,002 | ....... | ....... |
| Other enterprise programs ............ | 109,113 | 105,687 | ....... | ....... |
| Total business-type activities ........... | 32,789,740 | 27,414,853 | 2,125,362 | ....... |
| **Total primary government**............. | $   319,349,764 | $    62,077,917 | $    96,627,224 | $    1,561,483 |
| **Component Units** | | | | |
| University of California......... | 40,906,746 | 25,681,303 | 10,437,522 | 59,966 |
| California Housing Finance Agency ............... | 180,958 | 48,052 | 100,000 | ....... |
| Nonmajor component units ............... | 2,222,698 | 1,062,891 | 723,827 | 32,279 |
| Total component units............. | $    43,310,402 | $    26,792,246 | $    11,261,349 | $    92,245 |

General revenues:
  Personal income taxes......................................
  Sales and use taxes ........................................
  Corporation taxes ..........................................
  Motor vehicle excise tax ...................................
  Insurance taxes.............................................
  Managed care organization enrollment tax ...................
  Other taxes................................................
  Investment and interest income.............................
  Escheat ...................................................
  Other......................................................
Transfers .....................................................
  Total general revenues and transfers.......................
    Change in net position ................................
Net position (deficit) – beginning, restated...................
Net position (deficit) – ending................................

(continued)

**FIGURE 6.2**  Statement of Activities, State of California, June 30, 2019

Note: Amounts in thousands

Source: Office of the State Controller (2019)

| Net (Expenses) Revenues and Changes in Net Position | | | |
|---|---|---|---|
| Primary Government | | | |
| Governmental Activities | Business-type Activities | Total | Component Units |
| $  (10,707,331) | | $  (10,707,331) | |
| (67,967,591) | | (67,967,591) | |
| (48,394,703) | | (48,394,703) | |
| (2,838,864) | | (2,838,864) | |
| (769,836) | | (769,836) | |
| (6,092,772) | | (6,092,772) | |
| (15,066,921) | | (15,066,921) | |
| (3,995,597) | | (3,995,597) | |
| (155,833,615) | | (155,833,615) | |
| | $  —— | —— | |
| | (27,689) | (27,689) | |
| | 37,697 | 37,697 | |
| | 809,698 | 809,698 | |
| | (4,205,272) | (4,205,272) | |
| | 58,347 | 58,347 | |
| | 74,520 | 74,520 | |
| | 5,600 | 5,600 | |
| | (2,426) | (2,426) | |
| | (3,249,525) | (3,249,525) | |
| $  (155,833,615) | $  (3,249,525) | $  (159,083,140) | |
| | | | $  (4,727,955) |
| | | | (32,906) |
| | | | (403,701) |
| | | | $  (5,164,562) |
| $  100,657,551 | $  —— | $  100,657,551 | $  —— |
| 41,006,121 | —— | 41,006,121 | —— |
| 14,625,724 | —— | 14,625,724 | —— |
| 7,632,365 | —— | 7,632,365 | —— |
| 2,734,068 | —— | 2,734,068 | —— |
| 2,562,919 | —— | 2,562,919 | —— |
| 3,790,987 | —— | 3,790,987 | —— |
| 706,637 | —— | 706,637 | 2,787,634 |
| 447,401 | —— | 447,401 | —— |
| | —— | | 2,738,007 |
| (3,930,906) | 3,930,906 | | —— |
| 170,232,867 | 3,930,906 | 174,163,773 | 5,525,641 |
| 14,399,252 | 681,381 | 15,080,633 | 361,079 |
| (69,124,762) | (1,918,724) | (71,043,486) | 19,588,260 |
| $  (54,725,510) | $  (1,237,343) | $  (55,962,853) | $  19,949,339 |

**FIGURE 6.2** Continued

in the business-type activities section are in surplus. The major exception being the California State University line, which shows a deficit of $4.2 billion. Even though the system received over $2 billion in operating grants and contributions, and charges for services amounted to over $3.5 billion, the system still ran a substantial operating deficit.[3]

Most governmental activities get most of their money to operate from general revenues, which is listed in the bottom section of the Statement of Activities. Revenues are shown in order of the size of their contribution. It shows that the personal income tax makes up most of the state's general revenues, followed by sales and use taxes, and corporate taxes.

After general revenues there is a line for transfers which shows that $3.9 billion was transferred from governmental activities to business-type activities. The notes to the financial statements on page 168 indicate that the $3.9 billion amount was a transfer from the general fund to the California State University system enterprise fund, which is a direct subsidy from state general revenues (State of California, 2019).

Finally, at the bottom of the statement is net position information. It shows the changes in net position; net position (deficit) – beginning, restated;[4] and net position (deficit) - ending. The change in net position is the "bottom line" of annual financial performance. It is $15 billion and shows that, overall, the state had a good financial year. The $15 billion change in net position resulted in a substantial reduction in the overall net position deficit, from -$71 billion to -$55.9 billion. While the state still has a substantial cumulative deficit, fiscal year 2019 was a good year financially for the state.

## Fund Financial Statements

An understanding of fund financial statements is important for students learning public financial management. In contrast to the government-wide financial statements that show the government as one entity, the fund financial statements present funds as separate entities with their own resources and liabilities. It is common for governmental entities to have legal and contractual restrictions on their revenues and expenditures. Revenues and related expenditures with different legal or contractual restrictions are recorded in a separate fund. Fund accounting thus controls the use of financial resources to comply with the imposed restrictions.

While governments may have several types of funds, GASB 34 requires only the general fund and the major funds to be reported under separate columns in the fund financial statements. All nonmajor funds are shown in aggregate only.[5] A government entity can choose to report a fund as a major fund if it believes that the fund is particularly important to financial statement users. The fund financial statement thus presents in detail funds that are material in size and/or play an important role in the operation of government.

Fund financial statements can be very complex; therefore, it is important to teach students on the information that is most useful in understanding a particular fund financial statement. Fund balance has been considered to be the most universally and widely used piece of governmental financial information (GASB, 2010). The two major areas of information related to the fund balance in the fund financial statements are: (1) the fund balance from the balance sheet; and (2) the changes in fund balance from the Statement of Revenues, Expenditures, and Changes in Fund Balances. The fund balance shows the amount of current financial resources available in a particular fund at the balance sheet date, while the changes in fund balance shows the results of the fund's activities over one operating cycle.

In understanding fund information, it is also important to understand the nature of the fund in the operations of government. Students should be able to identify the three types of funds based on the services and activities provided by government: the governmental fund, the proprietary fund, and the fiduciary fund. Understanding the information provided in the three types of fund financial statements is necessary to develop a detailed picture of the financial condition of government.

## The Governmental Fund

The governmental fund shows the major government operations. It is important to note that the activities accounted for in the governmental fund are similar to the governmental activities in the government-wide financial statements. The main difference is the governmental fund focuses only on current financial resources. The accounting basis used is the modified accrual basis. Revenues are recorded when they are measurable and available to pay a current period obligation. Expenditures are recorded when they are incurred and will be paid from current financial resources. The governmental fund thus shows how government manages its short-term financial resources to comply with legal and contractual requirements. Using the information in the governmental fund statement, students will be able to measure the short-term financial performance of a government entity.

Students also need to understand that there are several types of governmental funds. Financial statement users commonly place the most emphasis on the General Fund. The General Fund is the primary governmental fund that accounts for resources received and used for general government services. Other types of governmental funds include the special revenue funds that account for specific revenue sources; the debt service funds account for resources that are intended to pay debt principal and interest; the capital projects funds account for resources intended for capital outlays; and, the permanent funds account for resources of which only their earnings can be used to support government programs.

In analyzing the balance sheet of the governmental funds statement, it is important to mention to students that fund balance is not shown only as one aggregate total number, but also in detail form. The classification shows fund balance based on the relative strength of the constraints that control how specific amounts of funds can be spent. This detailed presentation of the fund balance enables financial statement users to assess a fund's liquidity and the government's financial flexibility. In brief, GASB 54 classifies fund balance into:

a.  Nonspendable fund balance accounts for resources that are not in a spendable form (e.g., inventories);
b.  Restricted fund balance accounts for resources that are restricted by constitution, external resource providers, or through enabling legislation;
c.  Committed fund balance accounts for resources that do not meet the restricted criteria but their use is determined by formal action of the government's highest level decision-making authority;
d.  Assigned fund balance accounts for resources that do not meet the restricted nor the committed criteria but have a specific purpose; and,
e.  Unassigned fund balance accounts for the resources that do not meet the other criteria. Unassigned fund balance will only show up in the General Fund as other funds account for resources for specified purposes.

Another important piece of information in the governmental fund's financial statement is the stabilization fund.[6] GASB 54 requires a government entity to report the stabilization fund in the fund balance. This information is important as it informs financial statement users of the government's financial health and the resources available to cover fiscal shocks. For example, a decrease in the stabilization fund might indicate that the government is experiencing a condition that limits its ability to perform normal operations and may be less prepared to overcome fiscal shocks. According to GASB 34, the stabilization fund can be shown on the fund balance in the balance sheet or in the notes to the financial statement. The stabilization fund can be reported as a restricted or committed fund, depending on the existence of legal or constitutional constraints on the fund.

Instructors can use information from the governmental funds statements to teach financial management. Figure 6.3 shows the Balance Sheet-Governmental Funds for the State of California in 2019. Instructors can point out that, in addition to the General Fund, the major funds reported are Federal, Transportation, Environmental and Natural Resources, and Health Care Related Program. Other funds are aggregated under Nonmajor Governmental Funds. Note that the State of California does not report a debt service fund or the capital project fund as a major fund in its governmental fund statement.

The next analysis involves interpreting the numbers in the governmental fund statement. The far-right column of the figure reports the total governmental fund's assets as $130 billion and total liabilities and deferred inflows of resources for governmental fund as $75 billion. The total fund balance for the governmental fund is $55 billion ($130 billion–$75 billion). The first fund column of the figure shows the balance sheet for the General Fund. The General Fund's total assets are $49 billion, and the total liabilities and deferred inflows of resources is $31 billion. The fund balance is thus $49 billion minus $31 billion, or $18 billion. This number generally shows that the current financial resources available for the primary government function on the balance sheet date is roughly $18 billion.

The fund balance information in the General Fund shows that out of the $18.56 billion fund balance, $1.18 billion is a nonspendable fund, $14.8 billion is restricted, and $1.78 billion is committed. There is no assigned fund balance for the general fund and the amount of fund balance that is not nonspendable, restricted, committed, or assigned (or unassigned) is $765 million. It is important to note that the fund balance is further explained in the notes to the financial statement.

In the notes to the financial statement, the government explains the restrictions imposed on the fund balance. The State of California's 2019 Comprehensive Annual Financial Report disclosed that the nonspendable fund balance consists of long-term interfund receivables, loans receivable, and legal or contractual requirements. The restricted fund balance is restricted by external constraints such as debt covenants and contractual obligations, constitutional provisions and statutes. Second, a fund balance schedule is presented in the notes to financial

| | General | Federal |
|---|---|---|
| **ASSETS** | | |
| Cash and pooled investments | $ 25,686,637 | $ 359,294 |
| Investments | | |
| Receivables (net) | 17,440,580 | 5,544 |
| Due from other funds | 3,126,488 | |
| Due from other governments | 2,267,323 | 27,057,959 |
| Interfund receivables | 1,173,670 | |
| Loans receivable | 31,811 | 221,900 |
| Other assets | 1,727 | |
| Total assets | $ 49,728,236 | $ 27,644,697 |
| | | |
| **LIABILITIES** | | |
| Accounts payable | $ 2,404,879 | $ 898,149 |
| Due to other funds | 6,120,501 | 23,189,228 |
| Due to component units | 163,305 | |
| Due to other governments | 3,621,013 | 3,205,467 |
| Interfund payables | 4,814,193 | |
| Revenues received in advance | 533,902 | 96,907 |
| Tax overpayments | 5,930,342 | |
| Deposits | 2,990 | |
| Unclaimed property liability | 1,047,738 | |
| Other liabilities | 435,278 | 29,808 |
| Total liabilities | 25,074,141 | 27,419,559 |
| **DEFERRED INFLOWS OF RESOURCES** | 6,086,213 | 1,950 |
| Total liabilities and deferred inflows of resources | 31,160,354 | 27,421,509 |
| **FUND BALANCES** | | |
| Nonspendable | 1,180,575 | |
| Restricted | 14,834,597 | 223,188 |
| Committed | 1,787,142 | |
| Assigned | | |
| Unassigned | 765,568 | |
| Total fund balances | 18,567,882 | 223,188 |
| Total liabilities, deferred inflows of resources, and fund balances | $ 49,728,236 | $ 27,644,697 |

(continued)

**FIGURE 6.3** Balance Sheet – Governmental Funds, State of California, June 30, 2019

Note: Amounts in thousands

Source: Office of the State Controller (2019)

| Transportation | Environmental and Natural Resources | Health Care Related Programs | Nonmajor Governmental | Total |
|---|---|---|---|---|
| $ 8,068,483 | $ 11,399,975 | $ 1,738,155 | $ 11,328,615 | $ 58,581,159 |
| — | — | — | 607,430 | 607,430 |
| 1,288,924 | 490,891 | 3,838,924 | 1,366,550 | 24,431,413 |
| 1,675,616 | 400,000 | 60,706 | 1,097,733 | 6,360,543 |
| 8,059 | 11,685 | 1,604,741 | 104,374 | 31,054,141 |
| 1,242,708 | 1,974,641 | 277,938 | 1,056,542 | 5,725,499 |
| — | 308,691 | 39,329 | 2,768,442 | 3,370,173 |
| 23,758 | — | — | 12,718 | 38,203 |
| $ 12,307,548 | $ 14,585,883 | $ 7,559,793 | $ 18,342,404 | $ 130,168,561 |
| | | | | |
| $ 711,564 | $ 351,419 | $ 68,269 | $ 645,335 | $ 5,079,615 |
| 417,608 | 71,953 | 6,151,536 | 577,654 | 36,528,480 |
| 5,958 | 2,500 | — | 50,290 | 222,053 |
| 724,131 | 73,072 | 8,154 | 3,868,192 | 11,500,029 |
| 510,143 | 178,569 | — | 70,929 | 5,573,834 |
| 17,072 | 236,950 | 3,586 | 153,411 | 1,041,828 |
| — | — | — | — | 5,930,342 |
| 2,865 | 791 | — | 453,038 | 459,684 |
| — | — | — | — | 1,047,738 |
| 495,300 | 7,790 | — | 170,381 | 1,138,557 |
| 2,884,641 | 923,044 | 6,231,545 | 5,989,230 | 68,522,160 |
| 123,413 | 39,176 | 192,466 | 279,207 | 6,722,425 |
| 3,008,054 | 962,220 | 6,424,011 | 6,268,437 | 75,244,585 |
| | | | | |
| — | — | — | 12,760 | 1,193,335 |
| 9,249,016 | 5,144,478 | 1,055,843 | 10,656,584 | 41,163,706 |
| 50,478 | 8,479,185 | 79,939 | 1,385,376 | 11,782,120 |
| — | — | — | 19,247 | 19,247 |
| — | — | — | — | 765,568 |
| 9,299,494 | 13,623,663 | 1,135,782 | 12,073,967 | 54,923,976 |
| $ 12,307,548 | $ 14,585,883 | $ 7,559,793 | $ 18,342,404 | $ 130,168,561 |

**FIGURE 6.3** Continued

statement. The schedule details the components of each type of fund balance. As shown in Figure 6.4, the restricted fund balance in the General Fund is divided based on government functions. The budget stabilization fund constitutes the largest part of the restricted fund. Out of the $18.56 billion fund balance, $14.35 billion is the budget stabilization fund.

The second fund report that is important in analyzing governmental financial condition is the Statement of Revenue, Expenditures, and Changes in Fund Balances – Governmental Funds. Figure 6.5 shows the total governmental funds revenue is $300.10 billion and the total governmental funds expenditure is $296.61 billion, resulting in $3.49 billion excess of revenues over expenditures. For the General Fund only, the total revenue is $140.50 billion, and the total expenditure is $129.11 billion. The excess of revenues over expenditures in the General Fund

| | General Fund | Federal Fund | Transportation Fund | Environmental and Natural Resources Fund | Health Care Related Programs Fund | Nonmajor Governmental Funds |
|---|---|---|---|---|---|---|
| **Nonspendable** | | | | | | |
| Long-term interfund receivables ... | $ 1,173,670 | $ — | $ — | $ — | $ — | $ — |
| Long-term loans receivable.......... | 6,905 | — | — | — | — | — |
| Other.............................. | — | — | — | — | — | 12,760 |
| Total nonspendable............... | 1,180,575 | — | — | — | — | 12,760 |
| **Restricted** | | | | | | |
| General government ..................... | 14,846 | — | — | 1,922 | 1 | 3,951,852 |
| Education............................... | 178,111 | 404 | 1,384 | — | 95,455 | 573,142 |
| Health and human services.......... | 200,399 | 257 | — | 89,148 | 960,387 | 2,174,801 |
| Natural resources and environmental protection........... | 4,367 | 1,574 | — | 5,029,044 | — | 199,176 |
| Business, consumer services, and housing........................ | 2,377 | 220,953 | 221,241 | 24,364 | — | 3,749,867 |
| Transportation........................ | — | — | 9,026,391 | — | — | 7,091 |
| Corrections and rehabilitation ...... | 76,075 | — | — | — | — | 655 |
| Budget stabilization................... | 14,358,422 | — | — | — | — | — |
| Total restricted..................... | 14,834,597 | 223,188 | 9,249,016 | 5,144,478 | 1,055,843 | 10,656,584 |
| **Committed** | | | | | | |
| General government .................... | 769,283 | — | — | 17,387 | — | 351,846 |
| Education.............................. | 101,502 | — | — | — | — | 61,863 |
| Health and human services........... | 904,437 | — | 431 | — | 79,939 | 250,716 |
| Natural resources and environmental protection........... | 4,604 | — | 3 | 8,389,105 | — | 579,486 |
| Business, consumer services, and housing......................... | — | — | — | 72,693 | — | 135,970 |
| Transportation........................ | — | — | 50,044 | — | — | 5,164 |
| Corrections and rehabilitation ...... | 7,316 | — | — | — | — | 331 |
| Total committed | 1,787,142 | — | 50,478 | 8,479,185 | 79,939 | 1,385,376 |
| **Assigned – general government**..... | — | — | — | — | — | 19,247 |
| **Unassigned** ........................... | 765,568 | — | — | — | — | — |
| **Total fund balances**................... | $ 18,567,882 | $ 223,188 | $ 9,299,494 | $ 13,623,663 | $ 1,135,782 | $ 12,073,967 |

**FIGURE 6.4** Schedule of Fund Balances by Function, State of California, June 30, 2019

Note: Amounts in thousands
Source: Office of the State Controller (2019)

is thus $11.39 billion. After accounting for the other financing sources and uses, the net change in the General Fund balance is $6.3 billion.

The excess of revenues over expenditures indicates a surplus or that the government is able to raise current revenues more than their current expenditures. The net change in fund balance adjusts the surplus/deficit with other sources/ disbursements other than the fund's main activities. Additionally, from the figure, the financial statement user can see that most of the General Fund revenue is generated from taxes. The amount of personal income taxes is $95 billion, which contributes 68 percent of the total general fund revenues. The other two taxes, sales and uses, and corporation taxes, contribute approximately 28 percent of the total general fund revenues.

## The Proprietary Fund

The second type of fund statement is the proprietary funds statement. Students need to be able to differentiate a proprietary fund from a governmental fund. There are two categories of proprietary funds: internal service and enterprise. They are

| | General | Federal |
|---|---|---|
| **REVENUES** | | |
| Personal income taxes............ | $   95,026,913 | $   ~~ |
| Sales and use taxes................. | 25,701,417 | ~~ |
| Corporation taxes.................. | 14,038,348 | ~~ |
| Motor vehicle excise taxes....... | 95,590 | ~~ |
| Insurance taxes..................... | 2,734,068 | ~~ |
| Managed care organization enrollment tax....... | ~~ | ~~ |
| Other taxes.......................... | 588,040 | ~~ |
| Intergovernmental.................. | ~~ | 96,078,529 |
| Licenses and permits............... | 8,119 | ~~ |
| Charges for services................ | 380,347 | ~~ |
| Fees................................... | 17,205 | ~~ |
| Penalties............................. | 270,302 | 133 |
| Investment and interest............ | 687,833 | ~~ |
| Escheat.............................. | 447,399 | ~~ |
| Other................................ | 508,046 | ~~ |
| Total revenues................... | 140,503,627 | 96,078,662 |
| **EXPENDITURES** | | |
| Current: | | |
| General government.............. | 5,895,961 | 1,446,287 |
| Education .......................... | 66,686,716 | 7,614,054 |
| Health and human services ...... | 35,158,002 | 82,189,959 |
| Natural resources and environmental protection ...... | 3,155,461 | 274,514 |
| Business, consumer services, and housing...... | 535,863 | 146,909 |
| Transportation.................... | 13,878 | 3,824,786 |
| Corrections and rehabilitation.... | 12,293,950 | 75,626 |
| Capital outlay..................... | 50,506 | ~~ |
| Debt service: | | |
| Bond and commercial paper retirement...... | 2,579,311 | 10,320 |
| Interest and fiscal charges......... | 2,743,505 | 1,070 |
| Total expenditures.............. | 129,113,153 | 95,583,525 |
| Excess (deficiency) of revenues over (under) expenditures...... | 11,390,474 | 495,137 |
| **OTHER FINANCING SOURCES (USES)** | | |
| General obligation bonds and commercial paper issued ...... | ~~ | ~~ |
| Refunding debt issued............. | ~~ | ~~ |
| Premium on bonds issued......... | 117,747 | ~~ |
| Remarketing bonds issued........ | ~~ | ~~ |
| Payment to remarket long-term debt...... | ~~ | ~~ |
| Capital leases...................... | 50,506 | ~~ |
| Transfers in........................ | 697,211 | ~~ |
| Transfers out....................... | (5,871,863) | (500,603) |
| Total other financing sources (uses) ...... | (5,006,399) | (500,603) |
| Net change in fund balances...... | 6,384,075 | (5,466) |
| **Fund balances – beginning**........ | 12,183,807 * | 228,654 |
| **Fund balances – ending** ........... | $   18,567,882 | $   223,188 |

\* Restated

(continued)

**FIGURE 6.5** Statement of Revenues, Expenditures, and Changes in Fund Balances – Governmental Funds, State of California, June 30, 2019

Note: Amounts in thousands
Source: Office of the State Controller (2019)

distinguished based on the restrictions on financial resources. The internal service fund is used to record activities related to providing goods or services to other funds, to other departments of the primary government, or to other governments. The enterprise fund is used to record activities related to providing goods and services to external parties for which a fee is charged.

The proprietary fund statement reports enterprise funds as business-type activities and internal service funds. The activities in enterprise funds are the business-type activities reported in the government-wide financial statements. The proprietary fund statement separates the activities based on the government's

| Transportation | Environmental and Natural Resources | Health Care Related Programs | Nonmajor Governmental | Total |
|---|---|---|---|---|
| $ ...... | $ ...... | $ ...... | $ 1,774,163 | $ 96,801,076 |
| 925,818 | ...... | ...... | 14,458,391 | 41,085,626 |
| ...... | ...... | ...... | ...... | 14,038,348 |
| 7,323,574 | 87,354 | ...... | 125,847 | 7,632,365 |
| ...... | ...... | ...... | ...... | 2,734,068 |
| ...... | ...... | 2,562,919 | ...... | 2,562,919 |
| ...... | 190,204 | ...... | 2,910,287 | 3,688,531 |
| ...... | ...... | 2,973,863 | 815,358 | 99,867,750 |
| 5,180,473 | 424,396 | ...... | 3,573,957 | 9,186,945 |
| 165,125 | 131,117 | 4 | 279,439 | 956,032 |
| 1,580,243 | 2,650,726 | 5,337,523 | 3,555,725 | 13,141,422 |
| 12,957 | 117,217 | 5,803 | 639,864 | 1,046,276 |
| 165,973 | 244,146 | 39,762 | 183,429 | 1,321,143 |
| ...... | ...... | ...... | 1,357 | 448,756 |
| 111,112 | 3,462,333 | 398,464 | 1,114,632 | 5,594,587 |
| 15,465,275 | 7,307,493 | 11,318,338 | 29,432,449 | 300,105,844 |
| | | | | |
| 449,290 | 173,136 | 2,809 | 11,295,663 | 19,263,146 |
| 8,260 | 2,010 | 207,495 | 552,653 | 75,871,188 |
| 2,318 | 57,095 | 11,354,509 | 15,781,706 | 144,543,589 |
| 194,498 | 5,193,577 | 186 | 251,541 | 9,069,777 |
| 96,344 | 154,306 | ...... | 1,079,987 | 2,813,409 |
| 13,635,140 | 409,565 | ...... | 9,969 | 17,893,338 |
| ...... | ...... | ...... | 1,686,190 | 14,055,766 |
| ...... | 165,089 | ...... | 71,892 | 287,487 |
| 1,421,031 | 1,904,861 | 97,490 | 4,431,812 | 10,444,825 |
| 47,235 | 21,009 | 424 | 1,158,110 | 3,971,353 |
| 15,854,116 | 8,080,648 | 11,662,913 | 36,319,523 | 296,613,878 |
| (388,841) | (773,155) | (344,575) | (6,887,074) | 3,491,966 |
| | | | | |
| 859,810 | 1,332,100 | 285,595 | 1,149,260 | 3,626,765 |
| 1,102,285 | 1,190,065 | ...... | 2,980,175 | 5,272,525 |
| 210,245 | 259,163 | 615 | 415,567 | 1,003,337 |
| 100,000 | ...... | ...... | 311,340 | 411,340 |
| (100,000) | ...... | ...... | (311,340) | (411,340) |
| ...... | ...... | ...... | ...... | 50,506 |
| 1,419 | 165,245 | 175,284 | 3,375,091 | 4,414,250 |
| (1,636,020) | (64,629) | ...... | (224,980) | (8,298,095) |
| 537,739 | 2,881,944 | 461,494 | 7,695,113 | 6,869,288 |
| 148,898 | 2,108,789 | 116,919 | 808,039 | 9,561,254 |
| 9,150,596 * | 11,514,874 | 1,018,863 * | 11,265,928 * | 45,362,722 |
| $ 9,299,494 | $ 13,623,663 | $ 1,135,782 | $ 12,073,967 | $ 54,923,976 |

**FIGURE 6.5** Continued

major business activities. An understanding of the proprietary fund statement is needed to assess the self-sustainability of the business activities run by a government. Business activities should be self-sustaining enterprises in the sense that they should not rely on money from government general revenues to operate.

To analyze the proprietary fund statements, students need to understand the three types of financial statements required for the proprietary funds and the accounting basis used to record transactions. Accrual basis accounting is used to record transactions in propriety funds. The three financial statements are the Statement of Net Position, the Statement of Revenues, Expenses, and Changes in Fund Net Position, and the Statement of Cash Flows. Similar to the balance sheet for the governmental funds, the Statement of Net Position shows the assets, liabilities, and fund balance for each major fund. The Statement of Revenues, Expenses, and Changes in Fund Net Position shows the surplus or deficit and changes in fund balance. The Statement of Cash Flows shows cash inflows and outflows for a particular fund. This statement is not required for the governmental fund. For the proprietary fund, the Statement of Cash Flows provides important information about the liquidity of a government's business activities. A lack of liquidity reduces operational flexibility and limits a government's ability to respond to changes in the environment.

The statement of cash flows explains the cash inflows and outflows under three types of activities: operating, investing, and financing. The operating cash flows are considered the most important type of cash flows. A negative operating cash flow balance means that business activity is not generating enough operating cash to cover operating expenditures.

In teaching the proprietary fund statement, instructors can start by pointing out the major funds reported in the proprietary fund statement and their differences with the funds reported in the governmental funds. Using a specific fund, instructors can ask students to calculate net assets from the statement of net position and changes in net assets from the statement of revenues, expenses, and changes in fund net position. It is important to note that a surplus may be recorded for one business activity, while a deficit is experienced by another. The statement of cash flows shows a unique picture of government financial condition. Instructors might want to point out that the cash surplus/deficit in the Statement of Cash Flows differs from the surplus/deficit reported in the Statement of Revenues, Expenses, and Changes in Net Position.

## The Fiduciary Funds

The fiduciary fund financial report records resources held by a governmental entity in a trustee or agent capacity for others. Fiduciary funds generally include pension, other employee benefit programs, trust funds, investment trust funds, private-purpose trust funds, and agency funds. The government-wide financial statements exclude fiduciary activities since the government cannot use the resources of fiduciary activities to support its programs (GASB, 1999).

Fiduciary funds use the accrual basis accounting and measure the flow of economic resources including short-term and long-term resources. Two major financial reports for the fiduciary funds are the Statement of Fiduciary Net Position that shows the fund balance and the Statement of Changes in Fiduciary Net Position that shows the changes in fund balance. Fiduciary funds statements are important for public accountability and to assess the government's ability to manage funds it does not own, but that it holds in trust. One of the most important trust funds is the pension fund. This fund records resources that are required to be held in trust for the members and beneficiaries of the government's pension plans.

In teaching about the use of fiduciary funds, instructors can start by asking students to identify the type of funds reported in the fiduciary funds statement. Instructors can point out the information in the Pension and Other Employee Benefit (OPEB) Trust fund and ask students to determine whether the fund is in surplus or deficit. By examining the Statement of Changes in Fiduciary Net Position, students can also determine the sources of financing for a particular fiduciary fund and the total amount paid and payable to participants for the current period.

## Reconciliation Between Government-wide Financial Statements and Fund Financial Statements

Understanding the relationship between government-wide financial statements and the fund financial statements can help students learning financial management understand the role of each financial statement in assessing government operations and financial condition. As mentioned in the previous section, the government-wide financial statements do not record fiduciary activities. Therefore, information about the role of government as the trustee of fiduciary funds, and an understanding of the ability of the government to manage fiduciary funds, can only be assessed using the fiduciary funds financial statements. As for the business-type activities, financial statement users can get the information from the business-type activities in the government-wide financial statement as well as the proprietary fund statements. Since both statements use the accrual basis of accounting, no reconciliation is needed.

There is, however, a significant difference in the recording of governmental activities. Governmental fund financial statements use the modified accrual basis focusing only on current financial resources. In contrast, the government-wide financial statement uses the full accrual basis. The governmental fund balances thus will be different than the net assets or net position of governmental activities in the government-wide statements. Similarly, the net change in fund balances in governmental funds will be different than the change in net position of governmental activities in the government-wide financial statements. To help financial users understand why different numbers are presented, GASB 34 requires government entities to reconcile the differences between fund financial statements and the government-wide financial statements. The reconciliation should be presented in a table among the financial statements. The most common reconciliations involve:

- Reconciling governmental fund balances and the net assets of governmental activities, including:
    - Fixed assets: The governmental fund statement measures and records only current financial resources; and,
    - Long-term liabilities: The governmental fund statement only accounts for liabilities that are due and payable in the current period.

- Reconciling the net change in fund balances in governmental funds and the change in net position of governmental activities, including:
  - Depreciation expense: The governmental fund statement does not record long-term assets, so no depreciation expenses are recorded;
  - Deferred revenue: The governmental fund statement only accounts for revenues that were available to pay current period expenditures; and
  - Accrued expenses: The governmental fund statement only accounts for expenditures that require the use of current financial resources not accrued expenses.

## Required Supplementary Information

RSI is information that is essential to understanding government financial condition. Without the RSI, the financial statements might not provide sufficient contextual information and time-series data to broadly inform decision-making. Therefore, understanding government financial statements and financial condition requires students to be informed about the RSI, its components, and its uses.

According to GASB 34, the RSI that should be presented in the government financial report includes:

a.  The MD&A section;
b.  The budgetary comparison schedules;
c.  Infrastructure asset disclosure for governments that use the modified approach for reporting infrastructure assets; and,
d.  Other supplementary information as required by other standards.

### Management Discussion and Analysis

In the MD&A section government administrators commonly share their opinion and analysis regarding entity performance over the year. A brief overview of the financial condition, such as comparisons of the current year to the prior year, and an explanation of whether financial condition has improved or deteriorated compared to prior years are commonly found in the MD&A. The MD&A also provides an analysis of the causes of significant changes in financial performance. Other financial information commonly found in the MD&A includes the analysis of budget variance and an overview of capital assets and long-term debt. The MD&A also provides a discussion of conditions that are expected to affect future government financial position.

### The Budgetary Comparison Schedules

Budget information is very important for users of government financial information. To complement the financial statement information, budgetary comparison schedules should be provided in the RSI. According to GASB 34, the schedule should be prepared for the general fund and for each major special revenue fund that has a legally adopted annual budget. The budgetary comparison schedules should present: (a) the original budget, (b) the final appropriated budgets, and (c) the actual inflows, outflows, and balances. The budgetary comparison schedule enables financial statement users to measure the variance between the appropriated budget and initial budget, as well as the variance between appropriated budget and final budget amounts. Since the budget is recorded using the budgetary basis of accounting, a schedule showing a reconciliation of the budget to meet GAAP requirements is also provided.

### Infrastructure Asset Disclosure for Governments that Use the Modified Approach for Reporting Infrastructure Assets

A government entity can choose to report its infrastructure assets using the modified approach which does not require the government to report depreciation expense but capitalizes all costs that add to the capacity and efficiency of the infrastructure assets. All costs related to maintenance and preservation are expensed. GASB 34 requires information regarding these infrastructure assets to be presented in the RSI. The information includes the description of the infrastructure assets, a detailed condition assessment, and the budgeted and actual preservation costs for the infrastructure assets.

### Other Required Supplementary Information

The RSI should also include the Schedule of Changes in Net Pension Liability and Related Ratios, Schedule of Changes in Net OPEB Liability and Related Ratios, Schedule of State Pension Contributions, and Schedule of OPEB Contributions. These schedules are typically provided for the last five years to help financial statement users assess the adequacy of pension and OPEB financing. A low funding ratio might indicate future financial problems related to paying pension and OPEB obligations.

Government entities are also required to provide additional information in the Statistical Section of the Comprehensive Annual Financial Report. This section is very important because it provides data on government finances and related areas for the most recent ten years thereby showing the trend in many important financial measures. GASB 34 defines five categories of information that should be presented in the Statistical Section, which are:

- Financial
- Revenue capacity
- Debt capacity
- Demographic and economic
- Operating.

Students learning government financial statement analysis should be aware of the existence of the statistical section. The information in the statistical section can help students understand the historical financial performance of the government entity and compare the past performance to the current condition as presented in the government financial reports.

## Extensions and Concluding Remarks

After students understand the structure, components, and information contained in the government financial reports, they can analyze the information using financial analysis techniques. Financial report analysis uses the numbers extracted from the government-wide and fund financial statements to measure the financial condition of the government. Financial analysis also uses the notes to the financial statements and information in the RSI. The RSI complements the financial statements by providing management's discussion and analysis of the financial condition, budget-related information, and a variety of historical financial information.

The notes to the financial statements contain valuable information providing a detailed description of the account balances and transactions reported in the financial statements. They also contain several tables and schedules providing a more detailed look at specific aspects of the financial statements. For example, they provide detailed information describing the governments' cash and investments, and categorize and explain the risks associated with short-term investments. The Comprehensive Annual Financial Report commonly contains a discussion of the governments cash management and investment strategy, the types of securities the government is authorized to invest in, and several schedules describing the value of investments, along with investment risks, such as interest rate risk, credit risk, and foreign currency risk. In all, stakeholders can use this information to determine the appropriateness of the government's investments and assess whether or not the government is following the wise old investment strategy of PLR: first get your principal back; second maintain liquidity; then, and only then, go after return.

Students can use the data in the financial reports to conduct several types of financial analysis. They can conduct year-over-year analysis and disaggregate the analysis over governmental activities, business-type activities and component units, as well as different types of funds. They can use the historical data in the financial statements and statistical section to conduct time-series or panel data analysis. Also, groups of students can use the data to work on a level of government (cities, counties, states, etc.) to create benchmarks. For example, a student can analyze a city relative to benchmarks created by the class from a sample of similar cities. This can deepen their understanding of the city they're responsible for analyzing, and also deepen their overall understanding of the entire sector.

However, students should understand that financial reports have limitations. First, financial reports measure past events, which might not always reflect the current situation. Second, some financial information might have been measured using estimates or judgments under certain rules or conventions that have evolved over time. Also, financial reports do not measure nonfinancial data. In the government environment, nonfinancial data such as the political environment, socio-demographic, and economic conditions might have a significant influence on government financial condition. Therefore, to make informed decisions, financial statement users need to combine the information from the financial reports with other relevant information to deliver the kind of analysis that decision-makers need to make good decisions.

This chapter's goal was to present the importance of governmental accounting and financial reporting as a part of understanding and teaching public financial management. Though it was necessary to describe basic accounting terms and concepts, our focus was on understanding how accounting and financial reporting is used by financial managers to inform stakeholders about the financial performance of government.

Financial management is an integral part of the financial integrity and transparency system of government. Stakeholders want to know whether or not the government's resources are being raised and spent in the amounts and for the purposes intended. The information in the financial statements is used to strengthen financial accountability. Creditors require information about whether governments are likely to be able to pay their future bills in full and on time. Financial managers use the financial information provided in financial reports to convince creditors that they are a good credit risk. Without such an assurance, investors are less likely to provide state and local governments with the money they need, and at the cost they can prudently afford, to provide essential services to the public, like schools, roads, and bridges. Good financial management and accurate, comparable, complete, comprehensive, consistent, reliable, timely, and understandable financial information is necessary to maintain the flow of funds to governments from investors and maintain the trust of all stakeholders.

## Notes

1 We also suggest that instructors encourage students to read financial information from newspapers and periodicals along with the MD&A to get another perspective on the financial issues covered in the MD&A.

2 A chart of accounts shows the list of accounts used by an entity to categorize its financial resources, obligations, or inflow/outflow of resources. The purpose of this categorization is to provide more detailed information regarding an entity's financial condition.

3 Please note that the components units' column shows that the University of California system ran an even larger deficit of $4.7 billion.

4 It is not uncommon for a government to restate (revise) its beginning net position from the net position-ending of the previous year.

5 The definition of a major fund based on GASB statement 34 is as follows: (a) for each individual governmental or enterprise fund, the total assets, liabilities, revenues, or expenditures/expenses are at least 10 percent of the corresponding total (assets, liabilities, and so forth) for all funds of that category (governmental or enterprise); (b) for each individual governmental or enterprise fund, the total assets, liabilities, revenues, or expenditures/expenses are at least 5 percent of the corresponding total for all governmental and enterprise funds combined.

6 Designated money used for stabilization purposes is sometimes referred to as a stabilization account.

## References

Bogui, F. B. (2009). *Handbook of governmental accounting*. CRC Press.

Governmental Accounting Standards Board. (1987). *Summary of concepts statement no. 1. Objectives of financial reporting*. Governmental Accounting Standards Board.

Governmental Accounting Standards Board. (1999). *Statement no. 34 of the Governmental Accounting Standards Board, basic financial statements – and management's discussion and analysis – for state and local governments*. Governmental Accounting Standards Board.

Governmental Accounting Standards Board. (2002). *Summary of statement no. 39. Determining whether certain organizations are components units – an amendment of GASB statement no. 14*. Governmental Accounting Standards Board.

Governmental Accounting Standards Board. (2007). *Concepts statement 4. Elements of financial statements*. Governmental Accounting Standards Board.

Governmental Accounting Standards Board. (2010). *Statement no. 60. Accounting and financial reporting service concession arrangements*. Governmental Accounting Standards Board.

Governmental Accounting Standards Board. (2011). *Statement no. 63. Financial reporting of deferred outflows of resources, deferred inflows of resources, and net position*. June 2011. Governmental Accounting Standards Board.

Governmental Accounting Standards Board. (2013). *A plain-English guide to deferrals*. Governmental Accounting Standards Board.

Governmental Accounting Standards Board. (2020). *Financial reporting model improvements. Exposure draft. Proposed statement of the Governmental Accounting Standards Board*. Governmental Accounting Standards Board.

Johnson, C. L. (2009). Government-wide financial benchmarks for state governments. In F. B. Bogui (Ed.), *Handbook of governmental accounting* (pp. 389–408). CRC Press.

Johnson, C. L., Kioko, S. N., & Hildreth, W. B. (2012). Government-wide financial statements and credit risk. *Public Budgeting & Finance, 32*(1), 80–104.

Mead, D. M. (2018). *An analyst's guide to government financial statements*. Governmental Accounting Standards Board.

Office of the State Controller. (2019). *State of California comprehensive annual financial report. For the fiscal year ended June 30, 2019*. Office of the State Controller.

Smith, G. R. (2009). The growth of GAAP. In F. B. Bogui (Ed.), *Handbook of governmental accounting* (pp. 1–70). CRC Press.

## Appendix: Exercises

### Instructor's Note

The exercises in the appendix are written for instructors to use with city government financial statements and reports and other sources of city-level information. Please note that mid-size and larger cities are more likely to have a Comprehensive Annual Financial Report that is complete and that students can access as a pdf with a simple download. Other levels of government may also be used. Any entity that implements GASB accounting and financial reporting standards can be used in the assignments and exercises. Therefore, instructors can use different levels of governments: school districts, cities, counties, and states, for example. Instructors can also use different types of public benefit organizations: utilities, health care organizations, higher education institutions, and so on. Unless otherwise indicated, we suggest students use the financial statements and reports of the city of their choice for the following exercises.

## Exercise 1: Budgetary Versus GAAP Basis of Accounting

1. What is the difference in financial condition between the budgetary basis and GAAP basis of accounting shown on the Reconciliation of Budgetary Basis Fund Balances of the General Fund and Major Special Revenue Funds to GAAP Basis Fund Balances?
2. What is the difference in fund balances across the different funds (i.e., general fund, different special revenue funds, etc.)?

## Exercise 2: Duration of Assets and Liabilities

GASB recommends, but does not require, that all governments display short-term and long-term assets and liabilities in the financial statements. Check and see if your city makes the separation. If not, can you distinguish between your city's short-term and long-term assets and liabilities?

## Exercise 3: Deferred Resources

What deferred outflows of resources and deferred inflows of resources are recorded by your city? Describe each deferral and explain why each is recorded as a deferral. Also, what is their impact on net position?

## Exercise 4: Component Units

Are the component unit's reported on the financial statements essential for understanding the financial activities of the city? Would not including the component units of the city be misleading? Why?

## Exercise 5: Major Funds Definition

1. Identify and list funds reported in the separate columns of the governmental funds statement.
2. Choose another city and repeat question (1). Compare and contrast the type of funds reported in the governmental funds statements of the two cities.

## Exercise 6: Types of Fund Financial Statements

What funds are reported in the governmental fund, the proprietary fund, and the fiduciary fund statements? Describe which activities are included in each fund statement and explain why they are included.

## Exercise 7: Governmental Fund

Using General Fund information determine the:

1. Total fund balance;
2. Percent of total fund balance that is not nonspendable, restricted, committed, and assigned;
3. Main sources of revenues in the Statement of Revenues, Expenditures, and Changes in Fund Balances; and
4. Net change in fund balance.

## Exercise 8: Proprietary Fund

Use Figures 6.A1, 6.A2, and 6.A3, which show the financial report for the proprietary funds of the State of California in 2019, to determine the:

1. Net assets of each fund reported in the statement of net position.
2. Surplus/deficit of each fund reported in the Statement of Revenues, Expenses, and Changes in Fund Net Position; which fund experienced the largest deficit in 2019?
3. Total cash increase/decrease for each fund reported in the Statement of Cash Flows.
4. Compare your answers in (2) and (3). Do you see any differences? Explain.

   Answer questions 1–4 for the city of your choice.

## Exercise 9: Fiduciary Fund

Figures 6.A4 and 6.A5 show the Statement of Fiduciary Net Position of the State of California in 2019. For the Pension and Other Employee Benefit Trust Funds, determine the:

1. Total assets and deferred outflows and the total liabilities and deferred inflows;
2. Net position balance and whether there is any restriction on the fund balance;
3. Net change in position (fund balance);
4. Sources of addition to the pension and other employee benefit trust fund in 2019;
5. Kind of deductions to the pension and other employee benefit trust fund in 2019.

   Answer questions 1–5 for the city of your choice.

## Exercise 10: Reconciliation

Using the Reconciliation of the Governmental Fund Balance Sheet to the Statement of Net Position, describe the items that account for the differences between the governmental activities reported in the Statement of Net Position and the Governmental Funds Balance Sheet? How do those differences affect your understanding of the financial condition of the government?

Using the Reconciliation of the Statement of Revenues, Expenditures, and Changes in Fund Balances of Governmental Funds to the Statement of Activities, describe the items that account for the differences between the governmental activities reported in the Statement of Activities and the Statement of Revenues,

| | Electric Power | Water Resources |
|---|---|---|
| **ASSETS** | | |
| Current assets: | | |
| Cash and pooled investments | $ ---- | $ 708,971 |
| Amount on deposit with U.S. Treasury | ---- | ---- |
| Investments | ---- | ---- |
| Restricted assets: | | |
| Cash and pooled investments | 688,000 | ---- |
| Due from other governments | ---- | ---- |
| Net investment in direct financing leases | ---- | ---- |
| Receivables (net) | 2,259 | 155,303 |
| Due from other funds | 7,720 | 1,582 |
| Due from other governments | ---- | 207,380 |
| Prepaid items | ---- | ---- |
| Inventories | ---- | 4,893 |
| Recoverable power costs (net) | 88,000 | ---- |
| Other current assets | ---- | ---- |
| Total current assets | 785,979 | 1,078,129 |
| Noncurrent assets: | | |
| Restricted assets: | | |
| Cash and pooled investments | 582,000 | 163,653 |
| Investments | 302,000 | 50,860 |
| Loans receivable | ---- | ---- |
| Investments | ---- | ---- |
| Net investment in direct financing leases | ---- | ---- |
| Receivables (net) | ---- | ---- |
| Interfund receivables | ---- | 96,048 |
| Loans receivable | ---- | 10,105 |
| Recoverable power costs (net) | 837,000 | ---- |
| Long-term prepaid charges | ---- | 1,466,584 |
| Capital assets: | | |
| Land | ---- | 188,965 |
| Collections – nondepreciable | ---- | ---- |
| Buildings and other depreciable property | ---- | 5,378,648 |
| Intangible assets – amortizable | ---- | 39,626 |
| Less: accumulated depreciation/amortization | ---- | (2,276,510) |
| Construction/development in progress | ---- | 2,078,333 |
| Intangible assets – nonamortizable | ---- | 111,900 |
| Other noncurrent assets | ---- | ---- |
| Total noncurrent assets | 1,721,000 | 7,308,212 |
| **Total assets** | 2,506,979 | 8,386,341 |
| **DEFERRED OUTFLOWS OF RESOURCES** | 70,000 | 296,613 |
| Total assets and deferred outflows of resources | $ 2,576,979 | $ 8,682,954 |

(continued)

**FIGURE 6.A1** Statement of Net Position – Proprietary Funds, State of California, June 30, 2019

Note: Amounts in thousands
Source: Office of the State Controller (2019)

| Business-type Activities – Enterprise Funds | | | | | Governmental Activities |
| State Lottery | Unemployment Programs | California State University | Nonmajor Enterprise | Total | Internal Service Funds |
|---|---|---|---|---|---|
| $ 829,472 | $ 3,637,655 | $ 848,213 | $ 1,359,674 | $ 7,383,985 | $ 1,682,455 |
| ..... | 3,717,242 | ..... | ..... | 3,717,242 | ..... |
| 60,150 | ..... | 2,934,805 | ..... | 2,994,955 | ..... |
|  |  |  |  |  |  |
| ..... | ..... | ..... | 311,183 | 999,183 | 581,464 |
| ..... | ..... | ..... | 292,355 | 292,355 | ..... |
| ..... | ..... | 11,868 | ..... | 11,868 | 486,012 |
| 569,546 | 1,187,994 | 197,183 | 44,723 | 2,157,008 | 88,093 |
| 4,333 | 22,209 | 11,177 | 32,258 | 79,279 | 608,191 |
| ..... | 40,477 | ..... | 196,665 | 444,522 | 14,007 |
| ..... | ..... | 69,442 | 29 | 69,471 | 216,791 |
| 7,130 | ..... | ..... | 3,240 | 15,263 | 69,969 |
| ..... | ..... | ..... | ..... | 88,000 | ..... |
| 3,697 | ..... | ..... | ..... | 3,697 | ..... |
| 1,474,328 | 8,605,577 | 4,072,688 | 2,240,127 | 18,396,828 | 3,746,982 |
|  |  |  |  |  |  |
| ..... | ..... | 103 | ..... | 745,256 | 143,195 |
| ..... | ..... | ..... | ..... | 352,860 | ..... |
| ..... | ..... | ..... | 1,954,696 | 1,954,696 | ..... |
| 771,874 | ..... | 1,279,428 | 19,582 | 2,070,884 | ..... |
| ..... | ..... | 208,216 | ..... | 208,216 | 7,829,752 |
| ..... | 80,281 | 392,398 | ..... | 472,679 | ..... |
| ..... | 839,806 | ..... | 12,439 | 948,293 | 38,536 |
| ..... | 35,591 | 59,491 | 5,199,336 | 5,304,523 | 3,770 |
| ..... | ..... | ..... | ..... | 837,000 | ..... |
| 422 | ..... | ..... | ..... | 1,467,006 | 590 |
|  |  |  |  |  |  |
| 18,798 | ..... | 97,172 | 1,272 | 306,207 | 2,080 |
| ..... | ..... | 27,473 | ..... | 27,473 | ..... |
| 321,168 | 28,556 | 10,053,368 | 25,974 | 13,807,714 | 674,915 |
| ..... | 244,118 | 147,961 | 1,761 | 433,466 | 75,724 |
| (130,994) | (70,834) | (4,075,988) | (19,548) | (6,573,874) | (532,598) |
| ..... | ..... | 1,179,125 | 106 | 3,257,564 | 1,282,497 |
| ..... | ..... | 6,907 | ..... | 118,807 | ..... |
| ..... | ..... | 26,666 | 3,154 | 29,820 | ..... |
| 981,268 | 1,157,518 | 9,402,320 | 7,198,772 | 27,769,090 | 9,518,461 |
| 2,455,596 | 9,763,095 | 13,475,008 | 9,438,899 | 46,025,918 | 13,265,443 |
| 73,060 | 89,316 | 2,456,788 | 15,091 | 3,000,868 | 514,390 |
| $ 2,528,656 | $ 9,852,411 | $ 15,931,796 | $ 9,453,990 | $ 49,026,786 | $ 13,779,833 |

(continued)

FIGURE 6.A1 Continued

Expenditures, and Changes in Fund Balances of Governmental Funds? How do those differences affect your understanding of the financial condition of the government?

## Exercise 11: MD&A

1. The MD&A section should be written so that the average citizen and stake-holder can understand the basic financial activities of the government over the fiscal year and the basic financial outcomes. There is some controversy as to whether or not it achieves this goal. What are the characteristics of your city's MD&A section that makes it accessible to the average citizen? What more could government officials do to make it more accessible and more useful to the average citizen?

| LIABILITIES | Electric Power | Water Resources |
|---|---|---|
| Current liabilities: | | |
| Accounts payable | $ 1,741 | $ 172,753 |
| Due to other funds | 238 | 52,356 |
| Due to other governments | — | 289,335 |
| Revenues received in advance | — | — |
| Deposits | — | — |
| Contracts and notes payable | — | — |
| Interest payable | 17,000 | 13,794 |
| Benefits payable | — | — |
| Current portion of long-term obligations | 832,000 | 191,376 |
| Other current liabilities | — | — |
| Total current liabilities | 850,979 | 719,614 |
| Noncurrent liabilities: | | |
| Interfund payables | 607 | 57,470 |
| Lottery prizes and annuities | — | — |
| Compensated absences payable | — | 25,703 |
| Workers' compensation benefits payable | — | — |
| Commercial paper and other borrowings | — | 689,984 |
| Capital lease obligations | — | — |
| General obligation bonds payable | — | 10,685 |
| Revenue bonds payable | 1,711,000 | 3,075,542 |
| Net other postemployment benefits liability | 5,393 | 771,286 |
| Net pension liability | 4,000 | 527,333 |
| Revenues received in advance | — | — |
| Other noncurrent liabilities | — | 149,976 |
| Total noncurrent liabilities | 1,721,000 | 5,307,979 |
| Total liabilities | 2,571,979 | 6,027,593 |
| DEFERRED INFLOWS OF RESOURCES | 5,000 | 1,489,012 |
| Total liabilities and deferred inflows of resources | 2,576,979 | 7,516,605 |
| NET POSITION | | |
| Net investment in capital assets | — | 783,286 |
| Restricted: | | |
| Nonexpendable – endowments | — | — |
| Expendable: | | |
| Construction | — | — |
| Debt service | — | 383,063 |
| Security for revenue bonds | — | — |
| Lottery | — | — |
| Unemployment programs | — | — |
| Other purposes | — | — |
| Total expendable | — | 383,063 |
| Unrestricted | — | — |
| Total net position (deficit) | — | 1,166,349 |
| Total liabilities, deferred inflows of resources, and net position | $ 2,576,979 | $ 8,682,954 |

(continued)

**FIGURE 6.A1** Continued

2. Using the MD&A section of the Comprehensive Annual Financial Report, identify the information in the report that demonstrates the government's ability to effectively implement the three underlying principles of handling accounting data and generating financial reports, described in Section 6.4 of the text: transparency, accountability and control.

## Exercise 12: Budgetary Comparison Schedules

1. Using the Budgetary Comparison Schedule, what is the difference in the original (proposed) budget, the final (adopted) budget, and the actual amounts. Why do these differences occur? How much are they determined by changes in policy, administrative actions, or external factors like changes in the economy?

2. There are typically several line items that have substantial positive and negative variances, what are the causes of those variances?

| Business-type Activities – Enterprise Funds | | | | | Governmental Activities |
| State Lottery | Unemployment Programs | California State University | Nonmajor Enterprise | Total | Internal Service Funds |
|---|---|---|---|---|---|
| $ 56,297 | $ 40,702 | $ 291,670 | $ 7,917 | $ 571,080 | $ 409,604 |
| 441,283 | 71,513 | 21,866 | 22,834 | 610,090 | 328,653 |
|  | 36,637 |  | 602 | 326,574 | 58,053 |
| 2,383 | 48,636 | 321,194 | 47 | 372,260 | 1,008,190 |
|  |  |  |  |  | 1,282 |
|  |  |  |  |  | 23,441 |
|  |  |  | 31,341 | 62,135 | 96,538 |
|  | 527,078 |  |  | 527,078 |  |
| 1,072,103 |  | 331,874 | 154,130 | 2,581,483 | 599,348 |
| 268 | 44,963 | 530,145 | 5 | 575,381 | 17,933 |
| 1,572,334 | 769,529 | 1,496,749 | 216,876 | 5,626,081 | 2,543,042 |
| 12,979 |  | 133,419 | 21,999 | 226,474 | 1,111,083 |
| 682,929 |  |  |  | 682,929 |  |
|  | 59,019 | 112,521 | 9,527 | 206,770 | 144,835 |
| 3,013 |  |  | 2,118 | 5,131 | 46,324 |
|  |  | 88,513 |  | 778,497 |  |
|  |  | 295,214 |  | 295,214 |  |
|  |  |  | 796,912 | 807,597 |  |
|  |  | 6,682,306 | 1,807,122 | 13,275,970 | 8,424,622 |
| 231,853 | 599,198 | 13,128,996 | 28,837 | 14,765,563 | 2,028,065 |
| 126,042 | 300,413 | 7,733,251 | 39,207 | 8,730,246 | 1,206,073 |
|  |  | 8,048 |  | 8,048 |  |
|  |  | 97,466 | 20,680 | 268,122 | 29,629 |
| 1,056,816 | 958,630 | 28,279,734 | 2,726,402 | 40,050,561 | 12,990,631 |
| 2,629,150 | 1,728,159 | 29,776,483 | 2,943,278 | 45,676,642 | 15,533,673 |
| 51,222 | 123,830 | 2,888,140 | 30,283 | 4,587,487 | 433,379 |
| 2,680,372 | 1,851,989 | 32,664,623 | 2,973,561 | 50,264,129 | 15,967,052 |
| 208,972 | 201,840 | 1,336,605 | 3,554 | 2,534,257 | 534,879 |
|  |  | 1,693 |  | 1,693 |  |
|  |  | 43,570 |  | 43,570 | 208,099 |
|  |  | 38,975 | 258,323 | 680,361 |  |
|  |  |  | 2,087,404 | 2,087,404 |  |
| 93,646 |  |  |  | 93,646 |  |
|  | 7,798,582 |  |  | 7,798,582 |  |
|  |  | 61,616 | 2,180,388 | 2,242,004 |  |
| 93,646 | 7,798,582 | 144,161 | 4,526,115 | 12,945,567 | 208,099 |
| (454,334) |  | (18,215,286) | 1,950,760 | (16,718,860) | (2,930,197) |
| (151,716) | 8,000,422 | (16,732,827) | 6,480,429 | (1,237,343) | (2,187,219) |
| $ 2,528,656 | $ 9,852,411 | $ 15,931,796 | $ 9,453,990 | $ 49,026,786 | $ 13,779,833 |

FIGURE 6.A1 Continued

| | Electric Power | Water Resources |
|---|---|---|
| **OPERATING REVENUES** | | |
| Unemployment and disability insurance | $    — | $    — |
| Lottery ticket sales | — | — |
| Power sales | (5,000) | 96,308 |
| Student tuition and fees | — | — |
| Services and sales | — | 1,053,344 |
| Investment and interest | — | — |
| Rent | — | — |
| Grants and contracts | — | — |
| Other | — | — |
| Total operating revenues | (5,000) | 1,149,652 |
| **OPERATING EXPENSES** | | |
| Lottery prizes | — | — |
| Power purchases (net of recoverable power costs) | (16,000) | 290,908 |
| Personal services | — | 392,703 |
| Supplies | — | — |
| Services and charges | 11,000 | 100,562 |
| Depreciation | — | 94,191 |
| Scholarships and fellowships | — | — |
| Distributions to beneficiaries | — | — |
| Interest expense | — | — |
| Amortization of long-term prepaid charges | — | — |
| Other | — | — |
| Total operating expenses | (5,000) | 878,364 |
| Operating income (loss) | — | 271,288 |
| **NONOPERATING REVENUES (EXPENSES)** | | |
| Donations and grants | — | — |
| Private gifts | — | — |
| Investment and interest income | 918,000 | 22,482 |
| Interest expense and fiscal charges | (918,000) | (116,481) |
| Lottery payments for education | — | — |
| Other | — | (204,978) |
| Total nonoperating revenues (expenses) | — | (298,977) |
| Income (loss) before capital contributions and transfers | — | (27,689) |
| Transfers in | — | — |
| Transfers out | — | — |
| Change in net position | — | (27,689) |
| Total net position (deficit) – beginning | — | 1,194,038 * |
| Total net position (deficit) – ending | $    — | $ 1,166,349 |

* Restated

(continued)

**FIGURE 6.A2** Statement of Revenues, Expenditures, and Changes in Fund Balances – Proprietary Funds, State of California, June 30, 2019

Note: Amounts in thousands
Source: Office of the State Controller (2019)

| Business-type Activities – Enterprise Funds | | | | | Governmental Activities |
|---|---|---|---|---|---|
| State Lottery | Unemployment Programs | California State University | Nonmajor Enterprise | Total | Internal Service Funds |
| $ — | $ 13,969,174 | $ — | $ — | $ 13,969,174 | $ — |
| 7,388,050 | — | — | — | 7,388,050 | — |
| — | — | — | — | 91,308 | — |
| — | — | 2,198,195 | — | 2,198,195 | — |
| — | — | 607,889 | 111,648 | 1,772,881 | 3,575,293 |
| — | — | — | 145,792 | 145,792 | 24,348 |
| — | — | — | — | — | 417,092 |
| — | — | 79,131 | — | 79,131 | — |
| — | — | 254,378 | 3,129 | 257,507 | — |
| 7,388,050 | 13,969,174 | 3,139,593 | 260,569 | 25,902,038 | 4,016,733 |
| | | | | | |
| 4,715,593 | — | — | — | 4,715,593 | — |
| — | — | — | — | 274,908 | — |
| 99,664 | 372,865 | 6,634,906 | 59,128 | 7,559,266 | 1,129,432 |
| 14,080 | — | 1,589,485 | 44,152 | 1,647,717 | 30,633 |
| 730,177 | 51,665 | — | 48,395 | 941,799 | 2,391,932 |
| 18,815 | 17,263 | 379,786 | 1,087 | 511,142 | 65,006 |
| — | — | 915,286 | — | 915,286 | — |
| — | 12,786,647 | — | — | 12,786,647 | — |
| — | — | — | 34,135 | 34,135 | 364,505 |
| — | — | — | — | — | 129 |
| — | — | — | 7,239 | 7,239 | — |
| 5,578,329 | 13,228,440 | 9,519,463 | 194,136 | 29,393,732 | 3,981,637 |
| 1,809,721 | 740,734 | (6,379,870) | 66,433 | (3,491,694) | 35,096 |
| | | | | | |
| — | — | 2,044,729 | 80,633 | 2,125,362 | — |
| — | — | 55,003 | — | 55,003 | — |
| 85,380 | 69,856 | 204,813 | 27,326 | 1,327,857 | 5,263 |
| (32,202) | (892) | (259,621) | (38,610) | (1,365,806) | (2,331) |
| (1,825,224) | — | — | — | (1,825,224) | — |
| 22 | — | 129,674 | 259 | (75,023) | (112,651) |
| (1,772,024) | 68,964 | 2,174,598 | 69,608 | 242,169 | (109,719) |
| 37,697 | 809,698 | (4,205,272) | 136,041 | (3,249,525) | (74,623) |
| — | — | 3,934,300 | 1,750 | 2,936,050 | 2,220 |
| — | — | — | (5,144) | (5,144) | (49,281) |
| 37,697 | 809,698 | (270,972) | 132,647 | 681,381 | (121,684) |
| (189,413) | 7,190,724 | (16,461,855) | 6,347,782 * | (1,918,724) | (2,065,535)* |
| $ (151,716) | $ 8,000,422 | $ (16,732,827) | $ 6,480,429 | $ (1,237,343) | $ (2,187,219) |

FIGURE 6.A2 Continued

| | Electric Power | Water Resources |
|---|---|---|
| **CASH FLOWS FROM OPERATING ACTIVITIES** | | |
| Receipts from customers/employers | $ (5,000) | $ 1,092,325 |
| Receipts from interfund services provided | ...... | ...... |
| Payments to suppliers | (9,000) | (478,709) |
| Payments to employees | (1,000) | (392,703) |
| Payments for interfund services used | ...... | ...... |
| Payments for Lottery prizes | ...... | ...... |
| Claims paid to other than employees | ...... | ...... |
| Other receipts (payments) | 10,000 | 129,892 |
| Net cash provided by (used in) operating activities | (5,000) | 350,805 |
| **CASH FLOWS FROM NONCAPITAL FINANCING ACTIVITIES** | | |
| Changes in notes receivable and capital leases receivable | ...... | ...... |
| Changes in interfund receivables | ...... | ...... |
| Changes in interfund payables and loans payable | ...... | ...... |
| Receipt of bond charges | 883,000 | ...... |
| Proceeds from general obligation bonds | ...... | ...... |
| Retirement of general obligation bonds | ...... | ...... |
| Proceeds from revenue bonds | ...... | ...... |
| Retirement of revenue bonds | (753,000) | ...... |
| Interest received | ...... | ...... |
| Interest paid | (139,000) | ...... |
| Transfers in | ...... | ...... |
| Transfers out | ...... | ...... |
| Grants received | ...... | ...... |
| Lottery payments for education | ...... | ...... |
| Net cash provided by (used in) noncapital financing activities | (9,000) | ...... |
| **CASH FLOWS FROM CAPITAL AND RELATED FINANCING ACTIVITIES** | | |
| Acquisition of capital assets | ...... | (649,078) |
| Proceeds from sale of capital assets | ...... | ...... |
| Proceeds from notes payable and commercial paper | ...... | 585,075 |
| Principal paid on notes payable and commercial paper | ...... | (475,763) |
| Proceeds from capital leases | ...... | ...... |
| Payment on capital leases | ...... | ...... |
| Retirement of general obligation bonds | ...... | (25,975) |
| Proceeds from revenue bonds | ...... | 405,805 |
| Retirement of revenue bonds | ...... | (129,400) |
| Interest paid | ...... | (89,223) |
| Grants received | ...... | ...... |
| Net cash provided by (used in) capital and related financing activities | ...... | (378,559) |
| **CASH FLOWS FROM INVESTING ACTIVITIES** | | |
| Purchase of investments | ...... | (252,772) |
| Proceeds from maturity and sale of investments | ...... | 252,618 |
| Change in loans receivable | ...... | 819 |
| Earnings on investments | 44,000 | 21,034 |
| Net cash provided by (used in) investing activities | 44,000 | 21,699 |
| Net increase (decrease) in cash and pooled investments | 30,000 | (6,055) |
| Cash and pooled investments – beginning | 1,240,000 | 878,679 |
| Cash and pooled investments – ending | $ 1,270,000 | $ 872,624 |

* Restated

(continued)

**FIGURE 6.A3**  Statement of Cash Flows – Proprietary Funds, State of California, June 30, 2019

Note: Amounts in thousands
Source: Office of the State Controller (2019)

| | Business-type Activities – Enterprise Funds | | | | | Governmental Activities |
| --- | --- | --- | --- | --- | --- | --- |
| | State Lottery | Unemployment Programs | California State University | Nonmajor Enterprise | Total | Internal Service Funds |
| $ 7,390,296 $ | 13,983,271 $ | 2,787,552 $ | 353,686 $ | 25,602,130 $ | 14,045 |
| — | — | 3,678 | 3,678 | 4,629,351 |
| (257,962) | (19,091) | (1,607,046) | (92,368) | (2,464,176) | (1,935,490) |
| (83,759) | (213,600) | (5,397,993) | (32,109) | (6,121,164) | (985,521) |
| (7,582) | (12,997) | — | (2,846) | (23,425) | (15,704) |
| (4,893,812) | — | — | — | (4,893,812) | — |
| (505,915) | (12,768,292) | — | — | (13,274,207) | (540,761) |
| 565,907 | (54,215) | (637,510) | (748,344) | (734,270) | (417,008) |
| 2,207,173 | 915,076 | (4,854,997) | (518,303) | (1,905,246) | 748,912 |
| — | — | (18,012) | — | (18,012) | 328,554 |
| — | 96,232 | — | 2,409 | 98,641 | — |
| — | — | (123,050) | 6,937 | (116,113) | 174,928 |
| — | — | — | — | 883,000 | — |
| — | — | — | 277,960 | 277,960 | — |
| — | — | — | (14,830) | (14,830) | — |
| — | — | 89,815 | 100,806 | 190,621 | — |
| — | — | (29,069) | (65,280) | (847,349) | — |
| — | — | 23,293 | — | 23,293 | — |
| — | — | (29,814) | (64,229) | (233,043) | (1,421) |
| — | — | 3,607,887 | 1,750 | 3,609,637 | 2,220 |
| — | — | — | (5,144) | (5,144) | (49,281) |
| — | — | 2,171,199 | 69,403 | 2,240,602 | — |
| (1,815,267) | — | — | — | (1,815,267) | — |
| (1,815,267) | 96,232 | 5,692,249 | 309,782 | 4,273,996 | 455,000 |
| (30,508) | — | (945,843) | (6,864) | (1,632,293) | (760,913) |
| 24 | 23 | 13,050 | 83 | 13,180 | 3,322 |
| — | — | — | — | 585,075 | — |
| — | — | — | — | (475,763) | — |
| — | — | 9,087 | — | 9,087 | — |
| — | — | (569,274) | — | (569,274) | — |
| — | — | — | — | (25,975) | — |
| — | — | 762,076 | — | 1,167,881 | 139,506 |
| — | — | (1,654) | — | (131,054) | (518,640) |
| — | (892) | — | — | (90,115) | (575) |
| — | — | 54,020 | — | 54,020 | — |
| (30,484) | (869) | (678,538) | (6,781) | (1,095,231) | (1,137,300) |
| (39,821) | — | (10,573,282) | (16,265) | (10,882,140) | — |
| 52,207 | (746,869) | 10,327,619 | 14,898 | 9,900,473 | — |
| — | — | — | — | 819 | — |
| 26,968 | 69,856 | 120,927 | 26,628 | 309,413 | 5,299 |
| 39,354 | (677,013) | (124,736) | 25,261 | (671,435) | 5,299 |
| 400,776 | 333,426 | 33,978 | (190,041) | 602,084 | 71,911 |
| 428,696 | 3,304,229 | 814,338 | 1,860,898 * | 8,526,840 | 2,335,203 |
| $ 829,473 $ | 3,637,655 $ | 848,316 $ | 1,670,857 $ | 9,128,924 $ | 2,407,114 |

(continued)

**FIGURE 6.A3**  Continued

| | Electric Power | Water Resources |
|---|---|---|
| **RECONCILIATION OF OPERATING INCOME (LOSS) TO NET CASH PROVIDED BY (USED IN) OPERATING ACTIVITIES** | | |
| Operating income (loss) | $ —— | $ 271,288 |
| Adjustments to reconcile operating income (loss) to net cash provided by (used in) operating activities: | | |
| Depreciation | —— | 94,191 |
| Provisions and allowances | —— | —— |
| Amortization of premiums and discounts | —— | —— |
| Amortization of long-term prepaid charges and credits | —— | 18,369 |
| Other | —— | 129,892 |
| Change in account balances: | | |
| Receivables | 10,000 | (45,123) |
| Due from other funds | —— | —— |
| Due from other governments | —— | (166,769) |
| Prepaid items | —— | —— |
| Inventories | —— | 545 |
| Net investment in direct financing leases | —— | —— |
| Recoverable power costs (net) | (16,000) | —— |
| Other current assets | —— | —— |
| Other noncurrent assets | —— | —— |
| Loans receivable | —— | —— |
| Deferred outflow of resources | 1,000 | —— |
| Accounts payable | —— | (100,231) |
| Due to other funds | —— | (2,238) |
| Due to component units | —— | —— |
| Due to other governments | —— | 78,235 |
| Deposits | —— | —— |
| Contracts and notes payable | —— | —— |
| Interest payable | —— | —— |
| Revenues received in advance | —— | —— |
| Other current liabilities | —— | —— |
| Benefits payable | —— | —— |
| Lottery prizes and annuities | —— | —— |
| Compensated absences payable | —— | —— |
| Other noncurrent liabilities | —— | 72,646 |
| Deferred inflow of resources | —— | —— |
| Total adjustments | (5,000) | 79,517 |
| **Net cash provided by (used in) operating activities** | $ (5,000) | $ 350,805 |
| **Noncash investing, capital, and financing activities:** | | |
| State's contribution for pension benefits and OPEB | $ —— | $ —— |
| Long-term debt retirement from bond issuance | —— | 109,080 |
| Amortization/defeasance of bond premium and discount | 53,000 | 27,287 |
| Amortization of deferred loss on refundings | 27,000 | 10,362 |
| Unclaimed lottery prizes directly allocated to another entity | —— | —— |
| Interest accreted on annuitized prizes | —— | —— |
| Unrealized gain on investments | —— | —— |
| Interest accreted on zero coupon bonds | —— | —— |
| Contributed capital assets | —— | —— |
| Change in accrued capital asset purchases | —— | —— |
| Other assets paid through long-term debt | —— | —— |
| Other miscellaneous noncash transactions | —— | —— |

(continued)

**FIGURE 6.A3** Continued

| | Business-type Activities – Enterprise Funds | | | | | Governmental Activities |
|---|---|---|---|---|---|---|
| | State Lottery | Unemployment Programs | California State University | Nonmajor Enterprise | Total | Internal Service Funds |
| $ | 1,809,721 | $ 740,734 | $ (6,379,870) | $ 66,433 | $ (3,491,698) | $ 35,096 |
| | 18,815 | 17,263 | 379,786 | 1,087 | 511,142 | 65,006 |
| | 4,027 | | | (111) | 3,916 | |
| | | | | (458) | (458) | (91,239) |
| | | | | | 18,369 | 129 |
| | 26 | | (22,618) | (14,495) | 92,805 | 13,817 |
| | (24,002) | 2,566 | (26,927) | 656 | (82,830) | 10,299 |
| | (63) | (8,098) | (17,947) | (4,725) | (30,833) | (72,426) |
| | | (3,654) | | (1,088) | (371,511) | 3,070 |
| | 923 | | (9,564) | 62 | (8,579) | 16,976 |
| | 162 | | | 69 | 776 | 2,520 |
| | | | | | | 512,666 |
| | | | | | (16,000) | |
| | 3,552 | | | | 3,552 | |
| | | | | 977 | 977 | |
| | | | | (582,675) | (582,675) | |
| | | 44,021 | 1,615,763 | 30,034 | 1,690,818 | 190,708 |
| | (10,751) | 32,573 | 14,366 | 3,127 | (68,916) | (118,104) |
| | (9,834) | (45,632) | | 12,211 | (45,493) | 172,232 |
| | | | | | | 98 |
| | | 2,023 | | 5 | 88,263 | (22) |
| | | | (4) | | (4) | (673) |
| | | | | | | 866 |
| | | | | 1,038 | 1,038 | (4,640) |
| | 206 | 11,531 | (7,253) | (14) | 4,470 | 49,270 |
| | 784 | (11,851) | (1,223) | 471 | (11,819) | 830 |
| | | 18,356 | 26,225 | 6,322 | 58,703 | 18 |
| | 387,513 | | | | 387,513 | |
| | | 3,842 | 13,936 | 551 | 18,329 | 4,611 |
| | 26,094 | 38,191 | (1,822,821) | (16,235) | (1,792,125) | (246,003) |
| | | 73,211 | 1,383,154 | (21,345) | 1,435,020 | 195,807 |
| | 397,452 | 174,342 | 1,524,873 | (584,736) | 1,586,448 | 713,816 |
| $ | 2,207,173 | $ 915,876 | $ (4,854,997) | $ (518,303) | $ (1,905,246) | $ 748,912 |

(concluded)

| $ | | $ | $ 326,113 | $ | $ 326,113 | $ |
| | | | | | 109,080 | |
| | | | 32,159 | | 112,446 | |
| | | | 6,147 | | 43,449 | |
| | 45,423 | | | | 45,423 | |
| | 32,202 | | | | 32,202 | |
| | 39,164 | | | | 39,164 | |
| | 18,277 | | | | 18,277 | |
| | | | 7,825 | | 7,825 | |
| | | | 9,835 | | 9,835 | |
| | | | 89,670 | | 89,670 | |
| | | | 24,599 | 2,255 | 26,854 | 109,984 |

**FIGURE 6.A3** Continued

| | Private Purpose Trust | Pension and Other Employee Benefit Trust | Investment Trust Local Agency Investment | Agency |
|---|---|---|---|---|
| **ASSETS** | | | | |
| Cash and pooled investments | $ 113,197 | $ 3,264,944 | $ 24,735,365 | $ 4,284,516 |
| Investments, at fair value: | | | | |
| Short-term | .... | 15,857,095 | .... | .... |
| Equity securities | 4,700,510 | 317,399,932 | .... | .... |
| Debt securities | 2,931,223 | 161,788,992 | .... | .... |
| Real estate | 289,136 | 73,473,072 | .... | .... |
| Securities lending collateral | .... | 27,129,823 | .... | .... |
| Other | 1,443,868 | 73,492,132 | .... | .... |
| Total investments | 9,364,737 | 669,141,046 | .... | .... |
| Receivables (net) | 29,131 | 9,160,099 | .... | 4,584,617 |
| Due from other funds | 38 | 3,096,812 | .... | 27,322,360 |
| Due from other governments | .... | .... | .... | 140,365 |
| Interfund receivable | .... | .... | .... | 199,063 |
| Loans receivable | .... | 2,783,321 | .... | 15,145 |
| Other assets | 245,011 | 739,389 | .... | 805,929 |
| Total assets | 9,752,114 | 688,185,611 | 24,735,365 | $ 37,351,995 |
| **DEFERRED OUTFLOWS OF RESOURCES** | .... | 179,825 | .... | |
| Total assets and deferred outflows of resources | 9,752,114 | 688,365,436 | 24,735,365 | |
| **LIABILITIES** | | | | |
| Accounts payable | 47,643 | 5,426,723 | .... | $ 21,235,401 |
| Due to other governments | .... | 11 | 150,513 | 13,184,549 |
| Tax overpayments | .... | .... | .... | 7,613 |
| Benefits payable | .... | 3,632,592 | .... | .... |
| Revenues received in advance | .... | .... | .... | 679 |
| Deposits | 245,011 | .... | .... | 2,109,815 |
| Securities lending obligations | .... | 27,111,004 | .... | .... |
| Loans payable | .... | 2,787,398 | .... | .... |
| Other liabilities | 8,396 | 8,176,839 | .... | 813,938 |
| Total liabilities | 301,050 | 47,134,567 | 150,513 | $ 37,351,995 |
| **DEFERRED INFLOWS OF RESOURCES** | .... | 138,056 | .... | |
| Total liabilities and deferred inflows of resources | 301,050 | 47,272,623 | 150,513 | |
| **NET POSITION** | | | | |
| Restricted for pension and other postemployment benefits | .... | 623,237,339 | .... | |
| Held in trust for: | | | | |
| Deferred compensation participants | .... | 17,840,285 | .... | |
| Pool participants | .... | .... | 24,584,852 | |
| Individuals, organizations, or other governments | 9,451,064 | 15,189 | .... | |
| Total net position | $ 9,451,064 | $ 641,092,813 | $ 24,584,852 | |

**FIGURE 6.A4** Statement of Fiduciary Net Position, State of California, June 30, 2019

Note: Amounts in thousands
Source: Office of the State Controller (2019)

| | Private Purpose Trust | Pension and Other Employee Benefit Trust | Investment Trust Local Agency Investment |
|---|---|---|---|
| **ADDITIONS** | | | |
| Contributions: | | | |
| Employer | $ ----- | $ 25,574,412 | $ ----- |
| Plan member | ----- | 9,384,427 | ----- |
| Non-employer | ----- | 5,334,860 | ----- |
| Total contributions | ----- | 40,293,699 | ----- |
| Investment income: | | | |
| Net appreciation (depreciation) in fair value of investments | 102,226 | 29,921,335 | ..... |
| Interest, dividends, and other investment income | 441,212 | 11,757,940 | 526,689 |
| Less: investment expense | (3,900) | (2,072,615) | ----- |
| Net investment income | 539,538 | 39,606,660 | 526,689 |
| Receipts from depositors | 5,148,758 | ----- | 27,306,652 |
| Other | ----- | 169,317 | ----- |
| **Total additions** | **5,688,296** | **80,069,676** | **27,833,341** |
| **DEDUCTIONS** | | | |
| Distributions paid and payable to participants | ----- | 42,794,148 | 524,819 |
| Refunds of contributions | ----- | 386,557 | ----- |
| Administrative expense | 373 | 549,617 | 1,870 |
| Interest expense | 143 | 105,309 | ----- |
| Payments to and for depositors | 4,913,953 | 610,086 | 25,270,760 |
| **Total deductions** | **4,914,469** | **44,445,717** | **25,797,449** |
| Change in net position | 773,827 | 35,623,959 | 2,035,892 |
| Net position – beginning | 8,677,237 | 605,468,854 | 22,548,968 |
| Net position – ending | $ 9,451,064 | $ 641,092,813 | $ 24,584,852 |

**FIGURE 6.A5** Statement of Changes in Fiduciary Net Position, State of California, June 30, 2019

Note: Amounts in thousands
Source: Office of the State Controller (2019)

# 7

# AUDITING AND INTERNAL CONTROLS

*Carl J. Gabrini*

Auditing and internal controls is not glamorous topic. It is a topic, however, that is important for MPA students to learn as many government or not-for-profit managers will be affected by an audit or by the internal controls in some way while they perform their duties. Both topics also have the potential to affect the reputations and fortunes of organizations and their people. This chapter focuses on teaching students about the role of auditing and internal controls in public organizations along with any associated limitations. It also addresses the importance of linking them to a broader discussion of ethical behavior.

In reading this chapter it might be helpful to place it into context with other chapters in this book. Auditing and internal controls are associated with budgeting, financial accounting and reporting, and the financial statements contained in an organization's annual reports (Comprehensive Annual Financial Report or CAFR in government). These are topics covered in Chapters 4, 6, 8, and 9. Internal controls are the policies, procedures, and practices management designs and implements to ensure that everyone focuses on achieving the operational and strategic goals of the organization. Auditing, on the other hand, offers assurance to interested parties that outputs and outcomes align with pre-established criteria, which can include the goals of the organization. Internal controls affect all aspects of an organization including the reports they produce, and auditors offer assurance to stakeholders as to the quality of those reports.

Government and not-for-profit entities issue reports covering a wide variety of subjects, including operations, legal and regulatory compliance, and financial condition and performance. All these reports are prepared using data and information obtained from systems governed by management's system of internal controls. External consumers often require that entities offer assurance to the accuracy, completeness, and timeliness of the reports. Entities engage external experts,

DOI: 10.4324/9781003240440-7

often professional accounting firms, who conduct audits, examinations, reviews, and other types of assurance services on those reports. The assurance or opinion offered often extends to the systems and internal controls affecting the information contained in the reports. Stakeholders use the reports to make important decisions potentially affecting financial and political support of the entities.

Audits and internal controls are relevant to students of public administration because of the close association between the services provided by government and not-for-profit entities, the reports they issue, and the external stakeholder groups that consume the reports. Students need to understand the nature and role of audits and internal controls; specifically, how to interact with auditors, and why following policies and procedures is important to mission success. Students should be able to explain the relationship between effective internal control and audits and the ethical climate inside organizations. Finally, students should be able to explain the link between effective systems of internal control and positive audit outcomes with an organization's reputation and stakeholder support.

The next section of this chapter will introduce suggestions about the core competencies and learning objectives that should be the focus when teaching about audit and internal controls. The second section offers pedagogical approaches to teaching about audit and internal controls, including suggested available resources, topics to cover, and teaching strategies and methods. The third section will focus on suggested approaches to assess students' comprehension of the material such as suggested assignments and projects. The last section will include a summary and concluding comments on teaching strategies for audit and internal controls.

## Learning Objectives and Core Competencies

Covering auditing and internal controls in a limited amount of time is a challenge. To overcome the challenge, it is important to focus on the most important learning objectives that can be taught and learned within the available time. My suggestions in this section are based on the assumption that most courses in public financial management will include one week or one three-hour course period devoted to accounting, financial reporting, auditing, and internal controls. Given that time constraint, and my experience both as an auditor and instructor, I suggest the lesson or unit focus on the annual independent financial audit. This can be accomplished by focusing on three core competencies: (1) Explaining an audit, (2) Describing the audit process, and (3) Summarizing the possible audit outcomes. The discussion of internal controls should be integrated into the larger discussion of financial audits. Specifically, internal controls addressed with financial audits center on those associated with producing the financial statements. Focusing on the independent financial audit and the three competencies will allow you to efficiently organize and effectively present the topic to your students. Framing the discussion of audit and internal controls using these three core competencies

**TABLE 7.1** Suggested learning outcomes

Students should be able to:

1 Explain the nature and purpose of a financial audit
2 Compare a financial audit with other types of audits
3 Describe the steps in the audit process
4 Discuss the professional standards followed by auditors
5 Explain the contents of an audit report including the types of opinions
6 Discuss Single Audits required at the Federal and state level

should also make it easier for your students to appreciate the topics importance and master the material.

Table 7.1 illustrates a set of sample learning objectives associated with the three core competencies from the previous paragraph. The nature and role of internal controls can be integrated into these learning objectives with the focus being on those controls related to financial accounting and reporting. Coverage of internal controls would include discussing key controls such as segregation of duties. This is one of the most important internal control strategies for all organizations. Separation of duties helps prevent fraud and guard against errors by having different individuals authorize transactions, process transactions, and manage custody of the assets. Consider the purchasing and disbursements cycle (Wallace, 1991). Typically, one individual will generate a requisition for inventory, another will review and approve it, another will place the purchase order, another will receive the inventory, another will approve the receipt, another will process payment, and finally another will authorize the disbursement. Even in this process usually a separate individual approves vendors. The main goal is to operate an effective and efficient process but with sufficient safeguards to protect the organization from one individual being able to conceal fraud or errors. All major processes within the government or not-for-profit should be designed to incorporate sufficient separation and oversight to ensure the integrity of the operations and the veracity of reports on the process.

## Pedagogical Strategies

This section focuses on how to approach teaching students about government and not-for-profit auditing. Recall that earlier I suggested focusing on three core competencies: explaining an audit, describing the process, and summarizing the possible outcomes. In this section I will break this down by offering you some resources for learning to build more effective lesson plans and for possible reading materials for your students. I will then discuss the topics that, based on my experience, are most important for students to learn about. I will close out this section of the chapter with suggestions of teaching strategies I have used and found successful.

## Information Sources

There are many sources of information on audits of government and not-for-profits that can be used in developing lesson plans and assigned to students as reading material. Most of these resources are free to faculty and students, making them an attractive option to supplement textbook reading. In the tables below I list many of the sources I have used over the years. The lists are not exhaustive but do provide a rich assortment of government and private sources of information. I point out those resources that may require a subscription to access their materials.

The following tables present links to websites that contain information that will be useful in teaching about public sector auditing. The tables include names and addresses for sites containing information about Federal Single Audits, Generally Accepted Government Auditing Standards (GAGAS), standards governing audits of private companies listed on the major stock exchanges, and the accounting standards that govern how information is recorded by public and private organizations. Some of the websites are for various professional representing members employed in internal audit functions or those serving in state audit functions.

Table 7.2 contains a partial list of websites focusing on guidance from federal level organizations that may apply to all levels of government, private organizations, and not-for-profits. The GAO website contains links to audits and audit resources relevant to discussions of auditing of federal level agencies. Additionally, the site is home of the GAGAS, also known as the *Yellow Book*. GAGAS applies to most audits of federal, state, and local government. The standards contain guidance about auditor behavior and actions, planning and conducting an audit, and reporting on

**TABLE 7.2** Federal websites

| | |
|---|---|
| Government Accountability Office (GAO) | www.gao.gov |
| Generally Accepted Government Auditing Standards (GAGAS) | www.gao.gov/yellowbook/overview |
| Office of Management and Budget (OMB) | www.whitehouse.gov/omb |
| OMB Circulars | www.whitehouse.gov/omb/information-for-agencies/circulars |
| Single Audit Act | No single site exists. Check individual agency or state auditor sites. |
| Federal Accounting Standards Advisory Board | www.fasab.gov |
| Securities and Exchange Commission (SEC) | www.sec.gov |
| Public Company Accounting Oversight Board (PCAOB) | www.pcaobus.org |
| Generally Accepted Auditing Standards (GAAS) | www.aicpa.org/research/standards/auditattest.html |

**TABLE 7.3** State, local, and professional websites

| | |
|---|---|
| National Association of State Auditors, Comptrollers and Treasurers (NASACT) | www.nasact.org/state_auditor_welcom |
| Government Finance Officers Association (GFOA) | www.gfoa.org |
| Association of Inspectors General | https://inspectorsgeneral.org |
| Association of Local Government Auditors | www.algaonline.org |
| Financial Accounting Standards Board | www.fasb.org |
| Government Accounting Standards Board | www.gasb.org |

**TABLE 7.4** Example websites, Florida

| | |
|---|---|
| Joint Legislative Audit Committee | www.leg.state.fl.us/committees/jlac/ |
| Florida Auditor General | www.flauditor.gov |
| Florida Statutes Annual Financial Audit Reports | www.flsenate.gov/Laws/Statutes/2019/218.39 |
| Office of the Chief Inspector General | www.flgov.com/inspector_general |
| City of Tallahassee Financial Transparency | www.talgov.com/transparency/transparency.aspx |
| Palm Beach County Office of Inspector General | www.pbcgov.com/OIG/ |

the audit results. The other sites listed contain information related to administering and accounting for government grants and contracts (OMB) as well as more general accounting and auditing information that applies to private and not-for-profit organizations (SEC, PCAOB, GAAS).

Table 7.3 contains sites with information more relevant to state and local governments as well as not-for-profits. The Government Finance Officers Association (GFOA) website is home to information on the Excellence in Financial Reporting certificate program. The GFOA produces a set of detailed standards that state and local governments may elect to follow in preparing their annual report. If they meet all the criteria, they can earn a certificate to display in their annual report stating they have done so. The certification is important to stakeholders trying to assess the quality of the financial reporting of these entities. The Financial Accounting Standards Board (FASB) and Governmental Accounting Standards Board (GASB) websites are links to the major accounting standard setting bodies for private companies, state and local governments, and not-for-profits. The remaining sites in the table are for professional groups associated with government accounting and auditing.

Table 7.4 presents examples of sites where instructors and students may find information on auditing in the State of Florida. Each state has its own laws controlling the financial reporting and auditing of local governments. Instructors supplying a table similar to the example above would help students learn about the states where they live and work. The example for Florida has information on internal and external audits of state, county, municipal, and special purpose entities. It would be fairly straightforward to use the Florida table as a template for any state's audit information. As for not-for-profit organizations, I often refer to the National Council of Nonprofits for current materials and information on auditing not-for-profits (see National Council of Nonprofits, 2021a).

## Defining the Types of Characteristics of Audits

Based on my experience teaching auditing, I suggest the outline in Table 7.5 for how you might consider organizing the presentation of materials to the students. The first topic involves defining an audit and explaining how an audit fits in the broader classification of services provided by professional accountants and auditors. There are two basic classes of services, assurance services and non-assurance services (American Institute of Certified Public Accountants [AICPA], 2015). Assurance services are those that result in the auditor issuing an opinion or conclusion. Non-assurance services do not result in the issuance of an opinion by the auditor. Auditing is considered an assurance service because it results in the auditor reaching an opinion or conclusion on some subject matter such as the financial statements. Further, auditing is an attestation service within the class of assurance services. Attestation services are a subset of assurance services that require the provider to be independent of the subject matter. Other attestation services include examinations, reviews, and agree–upon–procedures. What they all have in common is that something is examined or reviewed against established criteria and an opinion is offered on the results. Examples of non-assurance services includes tax services and most management consulting engagements.

The first topic involves defining an audit and explaining how an audit fits in the broader classification of services provided by professional accountants and auditors. There are two basic classes of services, assurance services and

**TABLE 7.5** Topics in governmental and not-for-profit auditing

- What is an audit?
  - Name the distinct types of audits
  - Who performs audits?
- Why are audits important?
- How are audits performed?
- What are auditors' responsibilities versus management's responsibilities?
- How are audit outcomes communicated?
- What are the possible outcomes?
- How are audits and internal controls related?

non-assurance services (AICPA, 2015). Assurance services are those that result in the auditor issuing an opinion or conclusion. Non-assurance services do not result in the issuance of an opinion by the auditor. Auditing is considered an assurance service because it results in the auditor reaching an opinion or conclusion on some subject matter such as the financial statements. Further, auditing is an attestation service within the class of assurance services. Attestation services are a subset of assurance services that require the provider to be independent of the subject matter. Other attestation services include examinations, reviews, and agree-upon-procedures. What they all have in common is that something is examined or reviewed against established criteria and an opinion is offered on the results. Examples of non-assurance services include tax services and most management consulting engagements.

Audits can be divided into external audits, internal audits, and regulatory audits. My focus here is on external audits, which includes the financial audit. Internal audit is a management oversight tool that operates as part of the entity's system of internal control and risk management. Regulatory audits include audits by government agencies such as the Internal Revenue Service, state departments of revenue, departments of environmental protection, and departments of labor. External audits of state agencies, counties, and local governments are performed by either private, independent certified public accounting firms or by state-level audit agencies such as state auditor general offices. The key criterion for external auditors is that they be independent of the organization they are auditing. Some states contract some or all of their audit activity to private CPA firms as part of a trend to privatize government services.

Audits are important to both government and not-for-profit organizations, and for similar reasons. The GFOA (2021) best practice on audit procurement starts out "properly performed audits play a vital role in the public sector by helping to preserve the integrity of public finance functions, and by maintaining citizens' confidence in their elected leaders." The Government Accountability Office's (GAO, 2018) *Government Auditing Standards* states in the introduction that "audits provide essential accountability and transparency over government programs." According to the National Council of Nonprofits (2021b), independent audits serve to ensure confidence of stakeholders essential to the financial viability of not-for-profits and may aid in preserving their tax-exempt status. Independent financial audits are not required for public entities and not-for-profits. It is important to understand state law affecting the requirement. Generally, the larger the organization, the more likely it is that the organization is required to have an independent financial audit completed on an annual basis.

## The Audit Process

Audit performance is organized and systematic. The audit standards applicable to public entity audits requires that they be planned, supervised, performed, and completed following rigorous principles and rules. Regardless of who performs the independent financial audit, an engagement letter is prepared and signed by both parties. The letter details the audit to be performed and the responsibilities of the auditors and agency or not-for-profit. Public entities and government not-for-profits follow GAGAS while private not-for-profit audits follow GAAS. The standards can be thought of as nested as a Russian doll. GAAS applies to all audits while GAGAS applies to audits of public entities, and Single Audit Act rules apply to those public and not-for-profit entities that meet the expenditure threshold (currently $750,000). The standards get more extensive as one moves from GAAS to GAGAS to Single Audit.

The basic steps in the audit process begin with planning. Planning involves writing an audit plan and performing preliminary procedures to develop or update an understanding of the organization. This is followed by performing procedures to evaluate control risk and help determine the nature, extent, and timing of the specific audit tests. Once the audit program is finalized, audit testing is conducted, and results are reviewed by audit team leaders. As levels of review are completed, the results are evaluated and any findings are drafted. Typically, some form of debriefing is conducted with the entity audited to go over the results of the audit and provide the entity an opportunity to respond to any findings. The last phase is finalizing and releasing the audit report.

The performance of the audit requires cooperation between the audit team and the staff of the entity audited. Members of the public or not-for-profit must prepare as much for the audit as the auditors. Staff must be briefed on the nature and timing of the audit. Documents and data required by the auditors must be gathered and turned over by the staff. Typically, a detailed inventory is maintained of all requests and all items turned over. While audits are independent, a good working relationship must exist between the auditors and auditee to ensure a successfully completed audit. Problems in the conduct of the audit could affect the outcome of the audit.

The annual financial statements contained in the annual reports and the related notes are a product of the accounting system of the entity. That system is guarded by a system of internal controls related to financial accounting and reporting (ICFR). Therefore, auditors must consider ICFR in the conduct of their audit. The auditors will examine the organization's internal controls related to financial reporting. The controls are the responsibility of management. Information on internal controls can be found on the web under Committee of Sponsoring Organizations of the Treadway Commission (COSO). The site contains both free and subscription-based information about internal controls (COSO, 2021). An alternative site for information on risk management and internal controls is the International Organization for Standardization (ISO, 2021). They maintain standard ISO 31000 (Risk Management) and standard ISO 27001 (Information Security Management). These standards provide additional information about managing risk in organizations. The nature, timing, and extent of various audit testing will depend on the auditor's assessment of those internal controls. Management of government and not-for-profit entities must pay careful attention to the system of internal controls. Since they are management's responsibility, management must understand all activities and processes under their direction and control in order to ensure there are adequate controls focused on achieving the organization's strategic and operating goals. These goals usually include complying with applicable laws and regulations, safeguarding financial and nonfinancial assets, and reliable and accurate reporting of the organization's financial performance and condition.

The reporting phase of the audit is one that is of great concern to leadership of any government or not-for-profit entity. It is at this stage of the audit where the auditors reveal what they found and concluded regarding the financial statements and notes. It is also at this stage where management learns whether there were any findings related to Federal or state funds spent, or whether any findings or comments resulted from the auditor's consideration of the organization's internal controls. How these communications are handled is just as important as the conduct of the audit itself. I personally participated in meetings that went very badly because of how messages were delivered by the auditors and received by management. It is important to remain professional at all times. The goal of any audit should be to arrive at a professional opinion about the subject matter audited, offering constructive criticism and appropriate advice for curing any findings.

Chapter 9 of the GAO's *Government Auditing Standards* specifies the contents of an audit report. Reports are to include the objectives, scope, and methodology of the audit, the audit results, a summary of the views of responsible officials, and the nature of any confidential or sensitive information omitted (GAO, 2018, pp. 195–196). Audit findings are included in the audit results section of the audit report. They typically include four elements. First is the condition that was found during the conduct of the audit. The second element is the criteria or standards used to measure performance or activity. The third element is the cause. Often this is the auditor's professional opinion based on the information obtained during the audit. The fourth element is the effect of the condition. It is important to understand the significance of the effect of the condition on what is being audited. This is often stated as being the difference between the expected result and the observed result.

The auditor's opinion on the financial statements and related notes can be classified as unmodified, modified, disclaimed, or adverse. Unmodified refers to a clean opinion without any explanatory language or qualifications. A modified opinion may include explanatory language or a qualification of the opinion on certain portions of the financial statements or notes. A disclaimer of opinion indicates the audit was not completed due to a scope limitation. That means the auditor was unable to gain access to information they needed to complete the audit. An adverse opinion means that the auditors concluded the financial statements and notes were not fairly stated. Audit reports of governments and some not-for-profits will include a report on internal control as well as a report on the Single Audit Act. These can include findings and questioned costs. Findings classified as material and significant. Other items of note are often communicated in a management letter from the auditors. As an additional resource, the AICPA publishes audit guides that serves as a resource for planning and conducting an audit of government and not-for-profit organizations. The guides also make a useful resource for additional reading for the course or for students who want additional information.

## Teaching Strategies

To this point in the section, I have introduced sources of information about auditing and the important topics that should be considered in planning a class session on this topic. The last topic I want to share is teaching strategies I have used in my classes that I have found worked well based on feedback from students. Auditing can be dry and technical so finding methods to encourage students to engage in the topic is important. I prefer to employ interactive lesson plans that rely partly on the students' advance preparation and group work in class, ending with a class discussion and my summarizing the main lessons learned.

When I teach auditing, I prefer to use the flipped class methodology. It is more effective if students have completed some preliminary work prior to covering the material in class. The work assigned may range from reading a chapter from their course textbook to reading a sample of audit reports. I usually assign them to read the annual report and the related audit report of a city close by to enhance students' connection with the material. Once the material is covered in class, I ask the students to complete an assignment to assess their comprehension of the reading material. In the next section on student assessment, I describe several examples of assignments that could be used, but by no means should this limit one's imagination with creating new innovative assignments. I prefer students complete the assignments individually, but they can be easily given as group assignments as well. During the class meetings, rather than lecture, I prefer to use simulations or cases taken from the textbook. I divide the class session into two halves. In the first half students break into groups and collaborate on possible solutions. In the second half we come back together and discuss their solutions, and I facilitate to help them connect the simulation or case to the material they read. The use of more interactive and collaborative teaching and learning strategies offers students an opportunity to experience how auditors often work together as a team and not just individually, alone in a cubicle.

During the class meeting time I also like to include ethics and standards of conduct in the discussion. The GAO's (2018) *Government Auditing Standards* includes a discussion of standards of conduct for auditors, but there are also standards of conduct and ethical statements published by many of the professional organizations serving those that work in government and not-for-profit organizations. My experience in auditing and accounting has exposed me to many situations that presented ethical challenges. I share my own experiences, those that I witnessed as an auditor, and others that I learned about from colleagues. The main point I try to get across to the students in class is that challenges are real and are more likely to occur than most realize. I suggest using the American Society for Public Administration's (2021) *Code of Ethics* as a framework for an ethics discussion, but it is also useful to use any state or local government laws or ordinances instituting a code of ethics or conduct for public officials and employees.[1] An example I use in my courses is the Georgia Municipal Association's (2021) Cities of Ethics program.

Several ideas I have found useful in teaching include the use of one-minute papers. I offer a brief situation and ask students to write for one minute a response to that situation. It may be related to their role during an audit, some internal control issue, or an ethical situation. After the minute is up I would either have them discuss their responses in small groups or with the entire class. I also use video clips that I find either on government web sites or through YouTube that we watch and discuss. An example is a video clip on YouTube from the City of Greenville, South Carolina, announcing the results of their financial audit (City of Greenville, SC, 2009). I have made extensive use of guest speakers when available. When planned ahead, the guest speaker can be a fun and interesting way to engage students with auditing. There are more ways to spice up a class than I can cover here. We are only limited by our imaginations and institutional policies.

## Student Assessment

In this section I offer five assignment suggestions you may consider using in your courses to help students learn more about auditing and internal controls (additional suggestions can be obtained from Copley [2018] and Reck, Lowensohn, and Neely [2019]). The assignments described below focus on selecting an auditor, adopting an audit committee, reading an audit report, and evaluating internal controls. These assignment suggestions offer students an opportunity to examine topics they may experience if employed in local government. You may modify the assignments to apply to a state agency or not-for-profit setting as well.

### Assignment: Auditor Selection and Independence

The first assignment suggestion involves selecting an auditor and evaluating threats to the auditor's independence. Instructors should consider using the state where they are teaching and the residence of the students taking the course when selecting a setting for the scenario. The learning goals of the assignment include finding the state law affecting local government audit requirements and contracting for professional services. Students will learn what to include in a request for proposal (RFP) for audit services and what factors they should choose to evaluate the proposals they receive. Finally, students will learn to evaluate the independence of auditors and threats to their independence.

The scenario being as follows: students put themselves into the role of finance director for a city or county within their state. They are new to the role and receive notification that their current auditor will no longer be able to serve as their independent auditor for the coming year. Instructors should ask students to complete the following tasks:

1. Explain the state law governing financial reporting and auditing of local governments;
2. Summarize the state law affecting contracting for professional services;
3. Write a list of items to include in a request for proposal for annual financial audit services; and,
4. List factors they would consider when evaluating and selecting the winning proposal.

The next part of the assignment will focus the student's attention on auditor independence. As noted in the earlier section on pedagogical strategies, auditors must be independent of the entities they audit. It is equally important for those in management to understand the independence requirement and be prepared to evaluate potential threats to their independence. A key resource to aid students with this assignment include the GAO's (2018) webpage that covers GAGAS. Students should refer to it before beginning to write their responses. Instructors should ask students to complete the following tasks:

1. Define auditor independence;
2. Explain the importance of auditor independence; and
3. Explain at least three things that might threaten auditor independence.

If the assignment is completed before the class discussion it can be used as a framework to guide the class discussion for that day and supplemented with other information important to students that will likely be in a position to experience being on the receiving end of an audit. This assignment can easily be modified to focus on a not-for-profit setting. Not-for-profit audits are conducted under standards issued by the AICPA and are available on their website.

## Assignment: Citizen Engagement

A second assignment that might be useful involves citizen engagement, oversight, and internal controls. Students are to assume the role of the city or county director of finance. They recently read an article in *Governing* magazine that mentioned local government audit committees. Their city or county has never had an audit committee. The assignment requires the student to research the idea of forming an audit committee and to find helpful resources to refer to in creating one. The following is a list of sample tasks you might include in the assignment:

1.  List and describe resources you would use to help you design and implement an effective audit committee;
2.  Write a list of items you would include in the audit committee's charter;
3.  Discuss options for composing membership on the audit committee. Consider looking at other local government audit committees for examples;
4.  Explain the relationship that would develop between the director of finance, the audit committee, the independent auditor, and the legislative branch; and
5.  Write a memo to the city council or county commission proposing the formation of an audit committee. Make sure to address the benefits of an audit committee, its role, and composition in city or county governance.

The audit committee assignment can easily be modified to a not-for-profit situation by changing the wording to refer to a real or fictitious not-for-profit organization and refer to a board instead of the city council or commission.

## Assignment: Research Papers/Essay Questions

A third assignment suggestion can focus student's attention on auditing standards, types of audits, and audit outcomes. Instructors may change the assignment based on their interests or course learning outcomes. I offer the following topics for possible research papers or essay assignments:

1.  Compare and contrast GAGAS with Generally Accepted Auditing Standards (GAAS).
    a.  How do these audit standards impact audits of state and local government?
2.  Discuss the nature and scope of audits performed under the Single Audit Act of 1984.
    a.  When must a government or not-for-profit have a Single Audit performed?
    b.  What programs are subject to be included in a Single Audit?
3.  Explain the relationship between assurance, audit, and attestation?
    a.  What are the standards that apply to each of the above for government?
    b.  What are the standards that apply to each of the above for not-for-profits?
4.  Discuss the differences between the financial statement audit, performance audit, and compliance audit.

## Assignment: Reviewing an Audit Report

My fourth assignment suggestion requires students to read and understand the contents of an audit report. Audit reports may be selected from state and local government annual reports or from a not-for-profit entity. I offer two options for the assignment, but others may be created depending on your requirements or interests.

1.  The instructor can use the text of an actual audit report, fictionalize the names of the auditor and the government or not-for-profit organization, and intentionally embed errors into the audit report letter. The instructor would ask students to compare the audit report provided with the right audit standards and find any mistakes and explain how to correct them.
2.  The instructor can assign or allow students to choose a CAFR for a state, county, or city, or choose a not-for-profit entity, find the auditor's report and answer the following questions:
    a.  Who performed the audit?
    b.  What did they audit?
    c.  What standards did the auditors follow?
    d.  What type of opinion did the auditor issue?
    e.  Explain what, if any, differences exist in the audit report you read, and an unmodified opinion letter as illustrated in the auditing standards?
    f.  According to the auditor's report what are the auditor's responsibilities?
    i.  What are management's responsibilities?

## Assignment: Reviewing an Audit Report

The last suggestion focuses students on the topic of internal controls. In my courses I most often provide students with a written procedure narrative or a flow chart of a process. For example, I might give them a purchase-card process narrative or flow chart. Any business process performed within state or local government may be used in this assignment. I selected purchase-card transactions because it is fairly straightforward and easy to explain. More complex processes might distract from the lesson, which is to recognize internal controls or their absence.

Instructors interested in this assessment first must decide if the setting will be state or local government. Once the setting is decided the actual policy related to purchase-cards should be obtained either through a search of state statutes and policies or by request of the local government. After drafting the narrative or flowchart, the instructor should change the narrative or flowchart to create internal control weaknesses for the students to locate when they attempt the assignment. I think choosing a smaller local government as the setting is best because they often receive findings related to inadequate separation of duties due to smaller staffs and limited budgets.

The students are asked to read the narrative and find the internal controls present and where they are weak or missing. A more advanced variation of the assignment would include asking students to suggest ways to correct weaknesses and address missing controls. This assignment can be used as a framework to hold a discussion of internal controls and their importance in organizations.

## Conclusion

Auditing is important to ensuring accountability, transparency, and stewardship in government and not-for-profit organizations. This is not a new or novel observation. Over 25 years ago in an article published in the *Maine Townsmen* noted that independent audit is integral to a sound financial management program (Reny, 1984). This is true particularly in times when organizations experience fiscally challenging times. A well-designed and conducted independent audit can help leaders identify weaknesses in internal controls, operations, and financial management and point toward strategies for addressing them. The advantages of an independent audit are most realized when those in charge of governance are knowledgeable of them and embrace their relevance and importance.

This chapter has introduced methods for teaching auditing, internal controls for financial reporting, and related ethics issues. The topic can appear dry and technical if viewed through the lens of a traditional lecture; however, applying more innovative teaching techniques and engaging students early with the material using examples may help them find it relevant and increase interest and attention. To cover the material given the time usually made available, I suggested focusing on three core competencies that address what is an audit, how are audits performed, and what are the possible outcomes. These core competencies can be expanded using the information sources and outline provided earlier based on the amount of time allocated to the topic during the semester. Additionally, I included five versatile suggestions to use as assignments. They can be used to prepare students for the class meeting or as an assessment of what they learned after the class session.

The primary focus of this chapter has been on independent financial audits of government and not-for-profits. However, the materials and methods presented in this chapter may be applied to internal audits as well as external audits, and to the distinct types of audits, attestation, or assurance services. The GAO's *Government Auditing Standards* contain information that is relevant to performance audits (also referred to as operational audits) as well as compliance audits. Information about internal audit can be obtained through the Institute of Internal Auditors (2021) and the Association of Local Government Auditors (2021). My goal in writing this chapter was to encourage instructors to include auditing in their financial management courses and to offer some suggestions on how that might best be accomplished.

## Note

1 For guidance of using the American Society for Public Administration's *Code of Ethics* in the MPA classroom, see El Baradei (2020) and King, Agyapong, and Roberts (2019).

## References

American Institute of Certified Public Accountants. (2015). *CPA services*. Retrieved from www.aicpa.org/Advocacy/State/DownloadableDocuments/Attest-Services-Chart-Color-Nonfillable.pdf

American Society for Public Administration. (2021). *Code of ethics*. Retrieved from www.aspanet.org/ASPA/Code-of-Ethics/Code-of-Ethics.aspx

Association of Local Government Auditors. (2021). *Association of local government auditors*. Retrieved from https://algaonline.org

City of Greenville, SC. (2009). Financial audit confirms city's sound financial condition. *YouTube*. Retrieved from https://youtu.be/_JMiL_WtS3U

Committee of Sponsoring Organizations of the Treadway Commission. (2021). Welcome to COSO. Retrieved from www.coso.org

Copley, P. A. (2018). *Essentials of accounting for governmental and not-for-profit organizations*. McGraw-Hill.

El Baradei, L. (2020). Ethics education in public affairs programs: What do faculty around the globe have to say? *Journal of Public Affairs Education*. https://doi.org/10.1080/15236803.2020.1818023

Government Accountability Office. (2018). Government auditing standards 2018 revision. Retrieved from www.gao.gov/products/gao-18-568g

Government Finance Officers Association. (2021). Best practice: Audit procurement. Retrieved from www.gfoa.org/materials/audit-procurement

Georgia Municipal Association. (2021). Cities of ethics. Retrieved from www.gacities.com/About/Awards-and-Certifications/Cities-of-Ethics.aspx

Institute of Internal Auditors. (2021). *Institute of internal auditors home page*. Retrieved from https://na.theiia.org/Pages/IIAHome.aspx

International Organization for Standardization. (2021). Standards. Retrieved from www.iso.org/popular-standards.html

King, S. M., Agyapong, E., & Roberts, G. (2019). ASPA code of ethics as a framework for teaching ethics in public affairs and administration: A conceptual content analysis of MPA ethics course syllabi. *Journal of Public Affairs Education*. https://doi.org/10.1080/15236803.2019.1640560

National Council of Nonprofits. (2021a). Nonprofit audit guide. Retrieved from https://councilofnonprofits.org/nonprofit-audit-guide

National Council of Nonprofits. (2021b). What is an independent audit? Retrieved from www.councilofnonprofits.org/nonprofit-audit-guide/what-is-independent-audit

Reck, J., Lowensohn, S., & Neely, D. (2019). *Accounting for governmental & nonprofit entities*. McGraw-Hill.

Reny, R. (1984). *Municipal audit: Integral to sound financial management*. Maine Municipal Association.

Wallace, W. (1991). *Handbook of internal auditing controls*. Prentice Hall.

# 8

# FINANCIAL CONDITION ANALYSIS

*Craig S. Maher*

Within the first year in faculty position in an MPA program, I received a telephone call from a local city administrator asking me if a student or students in my class could be assigned a project where they produced a financial condition analysis for his community (I still have that report, nearly 20 years later, and still share it with students in my public financial management course). A few years later, I asked one of my MPA students, who was a deputy city comptroller, to give a presentation on financial reporting with a focus on the implications of the upcoming Governmental Accounting Standards Board (GASB) 34 changes to Comprehensive Annual Financial Reports. These two stories have stayed with me during my career for a couple of reasons, the first is that financial condition analysis is salient to students and practitioners. It can be a highly effective tool for distilling a great amount of financial information into a tangible tool for guiding policy. As an instructor, financial condition analyses are effective in demonstrating the interconnectedness of financial, demographic, and economic data. Second, many students in most MPA programs bring a great deal of experience to the classroom (granted few will be comptrollers), and harnessing that experience is what makes teaching these students so enjoyable. In the case of financial condition analysis, students may not initially understand how the fiscal data are collected and analyzed, but many are better at explaining the context behind the numbers because they typically choose to examine organizations where they are employed.

Over the years, it has also become apparent that technical writing is a skill that needs development for many MPA students. As a previous MPA program chair and board member for local government/finance associations, I frequently ask stakeholders what the top needs are from employers of our graduates. Regardless of the venue, written and oral communication skills top the list of needs. One of

DOI: 10.4324/9781003240440-8

the challenges with writing skills is training students for the breadth of writing styles necessary to be successful in the program and in the profession.

Requiring students to write financial condition analyses where the audience is public officials or government staff is far more valuable to the students' career development than treating the assignments like typical research projects. This means training students to produce shorter and more concise assignments, such as memos, rather than longer research papers. An added benefit of financial condition analyses is that the course design and expectations can be linked directly to program competencies. For instance, the financial reporting learning outcomes as they relate to our program core competencies focus on analytical skills, written and verbal communication skills and policy analysis. An example of how the course assignments are linked to program competencies is provided below:

Program Competency: To Lead and Manage in Public Governance

Understand the core management systems that impact the functioning of public and non-profit organizations, including financial management.

Course assignment: Prepare a 3–4-page report (single-spaced) describing the economic, political, and fiscal environment for the entity you have decided to examine. Included in the paper should be an analysis of the city's revenue structure based on the previous weeks' readings and discussions: what are positives and negatives? This is an excellent opportunity to effectively use tables and/or graphs.

To be consistent with the upcoming assignments, base your analysis of any economic or fiscal trends on the past 5 years. Questions to consider:

1. What are the city's economic and socioeconomic characteristics?
   a. Population (current and patterns)
   b. Economic base (major employers/industries)
   c. Recent unemployment rates
   d. Tax base
2. What are the entity's major revenue sources (major types of own-source; intergovernmental)?
3. What is the entity's government structure? What are the existing restrictions on taxes/assessment/expenditures (TELs) and are there any exemptions and/or methods to override the limitations? Does the entity have a home-rule charter that affords them additional powers, for instance the ability to ignore TELs?

As described in greater detail by Maher, Ebdon and Bartle (2020), course assignments that utilize financial condition analysis enhance students' understanding of financial management, designing, and executing research, thinking critically (especially when confronted with making sense of the ratios and offering policy recommendations), and communicating. It is very important to encourage students to write, think and present financial condition analyses where the intended audience is policymakers. This helps prepare students for their careers by forcing them to write and present information more clearly, concisely and, in many cases, more forcefully.

## Financial Condition and Financial Condition Analysis

Financial condition can be as straightforward as tracking the inflows and outflows of financial resources where a financially "healthy" entity would reflect revenues exceeding expenditures. Other definitions include not only the ability to meet these short-term, budgetary needs, but also long-term liabilities and service-level needs (Nollengerber, 2003). According to McDonald and Maher (2019, p. 271), financial condition has four elements[1]:

> the capacity of a municipality to meet its immediate or short-term financial obligations, (b) the capacity of a municipality to meet its financial obligations over a budgeted fiscal year, (c) the capacity of a municipality to meet its long-term financial obligations, and (d) the capacity of a municipality to finance the base level programs and services as required by law. This multi-dimensional approach allows for a balancing of where the municipality is in terms of meeting the future needs of the organization with the needs and demands of its residents.

How one empirically assesses financial condition has been a work in progress for 40-plus years. In general terms, the most frequently used tools for financial condition analysis fall along the lines of some form of trend analysis, benchmarking to peers or some combination of the two. For instance, The International City/ County Management Association's (ICMA) Financial Trend Monitoring System (FTMS) offers 27 indicators that are tracked over a ten-year period (see Nollenberger, 2003). The trajectory of each indicator is then assessed relative to some identified benchmark. For instance, one of ICMA's indicators is intergovernmental revenue and the measure is calculated as a ratio of general revenues as a percentage of total general revenues. According to ICMA, a "warning trend" is when the municipality's intergovernmental revenues ratio increases over time since it is revenue over which the community has no control. There are thus two defining attributes of this analysis, a trend analysis for a set of metrics selected by the municipality and assessment of each metric independently, meaning that the ratios are not aggregated into some cumulative score, or assessment.

Alternatively, the Government Finance Officers Association's (GFAO) publications by Brown's (1993) "10-Point Test" and Maher and Nollenberger's (2009) "Revisiting Ken Brown's 10-Point" are based on benchmarking to similar-sized communities. Brown (1993) identifies ten financial ratios that are designed to reflect revenues, expenditures, debt, and operating position. Brown's four-step process for financial condition analysis consists of: (1) calculating the ten ratios from municipal annual financial reports; (2) comparing each ratio to other similar-sized municipalities; (3) generating a score for each ratio based on quartile rankings and then summing the ten scores for each ratio; and (4) assessing a summary score based on Brown's scoring scheme.

There has been much written about these financial condition techniques. The consensus seems to be that ICMA's list of ratios is too extensive, time-consuming and cumbersome. Conversely, Brown's (1993) ratios are too heavily focused on the general fund, ignore enterprise funds, and the creation of a summative score that aggregates important dimensions of financial health is less meaningful. Maher, Ebdon and Bartle (2020) offer techniques for conducting financial condition analyses that attempt to capture the straightforward nature of Brown's approach, but also includes government-wide data (therefore enterprise funds) and a five-year trend analysis. The same approach will be discussed later in this chapter.

## Comprehensive Annual Financial Report

Before students can conduct financial condition analyses, a basic understanding of financial reporting is required. The primary resource for financial condition analysis is the audited annual financial report, or AFR. In many states, there is a requirement that AFRs be completed by an independent auditor. The detail of these reports can vary but the most complete and generally consistent is the Comprehensive Annual Financial Report. Comprehensive Annual Financial Report requirements are established by the GASB. GASB's vision and mission statements emphasize the importance of AFRs for the purpose of guiding policy.

Figure 8.1 illustrates the core components of a Comprehensive Annual Financial Report. These include the Management Discussion & Analysis (MD&A) section, two distinct sets of financial statements, notes to the financial statements and supplemental required information. The MD&A is meant to serve as an overview of a community's financial position that can be understood by stakeholders (elected officials, citizens, bond rating agencies) and is required to contain certain elements, including:

- Discussion of the Basic Financial Statement
- Condensed Comparative Data
- Overall Analysis
- Fund Analysis
- Budget Variances in the General Fund
- Capital Asset & Long-term Debt Activity
- Infrastructure
- Other Potentially Significant Matters

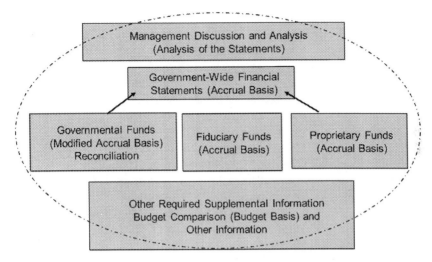

**FIGURE 8.1** Structure of Comprehensive Annual Financial Reports

Source: Finkler (2005)

The MD&A is written by the community's finance team, not the auditor. The various analyses in the MD&A can help the reader, including students, understand the financial position of the community from the perspective of the finance team.

The funds statements are where most of the data necessary to calculate financial condition ratios are available. There are two sets of financial statements, government-wide and fund-based statements. Government-wide statements were created for the purpose of providing an overall perspective for the entity that combines governmental and business-type activities, as well as long-term assets and liabilities. These statements are followed by fund statements, governmental and business-type (proprietary). The last section reconciles differences between the government-wide and funds statements.

The funds statements are followed by rather extensive Notes to Financial Statements and Major Required Supplementary Information. The Notes to Financial Statements includes pension and other post-employment benefits (OPEBs) data, policies for things such as asset capitalization and applying restricted and unrestricted resources, beginning and ending balances of long-term liabilities, investment policies, and so on. The Major Required Supplementary Information includes a budgetary comparison – including the original budget, final amended budget, and actual revenues, expenditures, and fund balances. It should also include infrastructure condition and maintenance data for governments using the Modified Approach for Infrastructure Assets. Finally, and quite valuable to students conducting financial condition analysis, the section includes debt, economic, and demographic data.

Several more recent (within past 10–15 years), modifications to Comprehensive Annual Financial Reports include GASB 44 and 54. Prior to 2010, fund balances were reported in the general fund as reserved and unreserved. Since 2010, fund balances have been reported on a five-category scale: non-spendable; restricted; committed; assigned; and unassigned. In essence the categories refer to their relative availability. For purposes of recording accessible reserves, assigned and unassigned balances are reported (Maher, 2013). GASB 44 refers to information required in the statistical section; more specifically, financial trends information, revenue capacity information, debt capacity information, demographic and economic information, and operating information. The statistical section should include ten-year trends in three types of operating information - government employment levels, operating statistics, and capital asset information. A government's statistical section should now also include trend information on governmental fund balances and principal employers. Finally, the statistical section will include ten-year trend information about net assets and changes in net assets. The debt information presented in the statistical section will also be more comprehensive due to the inclusion of information from the government-wide financial statements and notes.

## Financial Condition Analysis

Earlier, the case was made that financial condition analyses are valuable for assessing program competencies. It is also the case that these analyses are valuable tools for communities as they face fiscal and economic challenges/uncertainty. The fiscal challenges facing communities due to COVID-19 and the lingering effects of the Great Recession (2007–2009) have highlighted the value in conducting financial condition analyses. According to Berne and Schramm (1986), financial condition means "being able to meet their financial obligations as they come due, in both the short run and the long run" (p. 67). How does one know when a community is doing well or needs to take corrective action? How does one assess financial condition? According to Hendrick (2011), the following conditions need consideration when evaluating financial condition:

- *Adaptation and Fit*: Several approaches to assessing financial condition are based on the premise that a government in good financial condition has adapted and continuously adapts fiscal structure (tax levy, fund balance, debt level) to the environment and other circumstances (residential or commercial, growth, aging infrastructure, wealth of revenue source).
- *Relative*: Fit is assessed with ratios: revenue/spending; revenue/combined size of tax bases (revenue burden); fund balance/spending; GO debt/equalized assessed valuation.
- *Varying definitions*: For instance, a municipality that generates over 60 percent of their revenue from sales taxes (including state sales taxes) will have to adapt differently (have different strategies and solutions) and have a different

standard for financial condition than one that gets over 60 percent of its revenue from property taxes.

- The sales tax dependent government may have to maintain a higher fund balance, especially if they are small. A property tax dependent municipality may have to maintain steadier levels of capital investment than a municipality that depends on sales tax (where get large infuses of revenue during good times). Bigger and wealthier municipalities (surplus resources) may not need higher fund balance.

A government is in good financial condition if it has adapted its fiscal structure to its environment, the fiscal structure "fits" or is "balanced" with the environment. The financial condition must be assessed *relative* to features of the jurisdiction and government. What defines good financial condition will vary for different governments depending on their circumstances. Finally, not all strategies, solutions, and practices are correct for all circumstances. This is what makes these analyses so challenging and why understanding context is so important.

These attributes are generally consistent with the dimensions of financial condition as reported by ICMA Financial Condition Monitoring System (Nollenberger, 2003). Given the nature of ICMA, an organization that supports professional managers in city and county government, the dimensions are a bit more precise. According to Nollenberger (2003), positive financial condition means that a community has:

1. The ability to generate enough cash over 30 days to pay bills – *cash solvency*;
2. The ability to generate enough revenue over its normal budgetary period to meet expenditures and not incur deficits – *budgetary solvency*;
3. The ability to pay all the costs of doing business, including expenditures that normally appear in each annual budget, as well as those that will appear only in the years in which they must be paid – *long-run solvency*; and,
4. Ability to provide services at the level and quality that are required for the health, safety and welfare of the community and that its citizens desire – *service-level solvency*.

## Tools for Financial Condition Assessment: Part 1 – Using Governmental Fund Statement

There currently exists a dizzying array of financial condition assessment tools. I will focus on two for the sake of expediency. The first is a very common tool – "The 10-Point Test of Financial Condition: Toward an Easy-to-Use Assessment Tool for Smaller Cities" by Brown (1993). Supported by the GFOA as a leading measurement of fiscal health, Brown's 10-Point Test measures four aspects of a jurisdiction's financial condition: revenues, expenditures, operating position, and debt structure (see Figure 8.2).

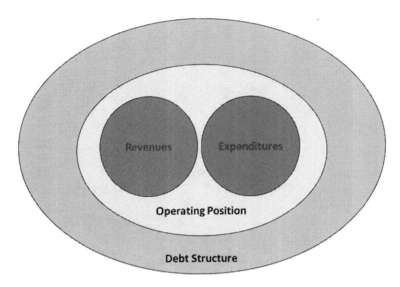

**FIGURE 8.2** Brown's dimensions of fiscal condition

The data are available in Audited Annual Financial Reports and Comprehensive Annual Financial Reports. It is important to note that Brown's tool was published by the GFOA prior to GASB 34 and thus focuses exclusively on governmental funds. The process requires calculating ten ratios using data from the Comprehensive Annual Financial Report, compare each ratio to others for similar-sized governments, assigning a score (-1,0,1,2) based on the quartile in which the ratio is located, summing the scores for all ratios and assess a summary grade. For this exercise, I will focus on Detroit, Michigan. Table 8.1 provides the calculation of each of the ten ratios based on Detroit's 2017 Comprehensive Annual Financial Report. Figures 8.A1 and 8.A2 show where each of the values are found and Figure 8.A3 provides a six-year trend (2008–2012, 2017) of each of Brown's ten ratios.

According to Brown (1993), the next steps are, for each ratio, compare the value to the same ratio for similar-sized municipalities. Score each ratio from -1 to 2 and then sum all ten scores to get an overall score and compare it to other municipalities. Cities with cumulative scores of 10 or more are "among the best"; scores of 5-9 are "better than most"; scores of 1-4 are "about average"; scores of 0 to -4 are "worse than most" and; scores below -4 are "among the worst" (p. 24). Using current fiscal data and applying it to Brown's scheme is challenging given the differences in timeframes. The more than 30-year difference, at a minimum, requires adjusting the per capita ratios for inflation. Figuring out the appropriate inflation index is, itself, a challenging endeavor. There is also growing evidence that combining ratios that capture different facets of fiscal condition into one summative score is ineffective (McDonald & Maher, 2019). Furthermore,

**TABLE 8.1** Brown's 10-Point Test for Detroit, MI, FY 2017

| Ratio | Measurement | Explanation |
|---|---|---|
| Total governmental revenues divided by population | $1,344,474,794 / 672,795 = $1,983 | The expectation is that relatively higher per capita revenues offer less revenue growth opportunities. |
| General fund revenues from own sources divided by general fund revenues | ($988,938,222 − $162,389 − $197,831,755 − $799,306) / $988,938,222 = 0.80 | The expectation is that the closer to 1.0 the better since local officials prefer control over revenues and they have no control over intergovernmental aid. |
| General fund sources from other sources as a percentage of general fund revenues | $0 / $988,938,222 = 0.00 | Transfers of revenues from other sources such as enterprise funds are generally frowned upon. |
| Operating expenditures divided by total expenditures | ($1,222,441,522−$71,074,891) /$1,222,441,522=0.94 | A higher ratio (near 1.0) is an indication that funds are not being sufficiently expended for capital improvements. |
| Total revenues divided by total expenditures | $1,334,474,793 / $1,222,441,522 = 1.09 | A ratio of 1.0 or higher means that governmental revenues are equal to or greater than governmental revenues. |
| Unreserved general fund revenues divided by general fund revenues | ($168,966,674 + $62,280,192 + $60,253,830 + $50,000,000 + $90,148,163 + $47,895,504) / $988,938,222 = 0.48 | There is a great deal of uncertainty of what an adequate ratio should be, but for the purpose of this exercise, the larger the ratio the better. |
| General fund cash and investments divided by general fund liabilities | $517,113,529 / $239,373,792 = 2.16 | Municipalities tend to have conservative cash management policies, so it is not uncommon to see ratios of 2.0 or higher. For the exercise, the higher the ratio the better. |
| General fund liabilities divided general fund revenues | $239,373,792 / $988,938,222 = 0.24 | According to Brown, this ratio is "self-explanatory." For this exercise, a lower ratio is a positive sign. |

(continued)

**TABLE 8.1** Cont.

| Ratio | Measurement | Explanation |
|---|---|---|
| General obligation debt divided by population | $1,850,000,000 / 672,795 = $2,749.72 | Higher per capita general obligation debt relative to similar-sized municipalities is perceived as negative sign. |
| Debt service as a percentage of total revenues | ($77,078,797 + $97,109,299 + $4,163,414) / $1,334,474,794 = 0.13 | Like general obligation debt, higher debt service relative to similar-sized municipalities is perceived as fiscally "unhealthy." |

These figures are from Detroit, Michigan's (2017) Comprehensive Annual Financial Report. See Figures 8.A1 and 8.A2 for more detail.

there is also the problem that different cities operate under different fiscal rules, making comparisons difficult. This latter point is one of the reasons Hendrick (2011) asserts that context matters. For instance, if a city has a revenue cap (e.g., Colorado's TABOR, see Decker, 2021; Maher, Park, & Harrold, 2016) and lower per capita revenues ratio it does not mean that the city has greater opportunity for revenue growth. Understanding the fiscal and political environment in which the cities operate is critical for interpreting and explaining these financial ratios.

My approach in the classroom to these challenges is to: (1) require an analysis of the political, structural, economic, and demographic environment for the community of study; (2) prohibit students from calculating a summative index, rather students are challenged to describe the ratios from Brown's broader framework of revenue and expenditure structures, operating position and debt structure; (3) make each student's fiscal ratio data available to the class so that a "mini" comparison group of city fiscal data can be generated for class use; and (4) require the students to focus less on comparisons across communities and, instead, shift their attention to trends over time (usually require a 5-year trend analysis). Figure 8.A3 provides a six-year analysis of each of the ten ratios for years 2008–2012 and 2017. The point for this period is to demonstrate Detroit's fiscal condition heading into its 2013 bankruptcy filing and comparing how the city has fared in more recent years.

Students are asked to write an assessment of these data by focusing on the most recent year and describing the city's financial strengths and weaknesses relative to the years 2008–2012. In the case of Detroit, the city struggled with its operating position heading into bankruptcy and in 2017, was in much stronger position. Note, for instance, ratio 5; Detroit struggled with general fund revenues falling below expenditures in fiscal years 2008–2009 and 2011–2012, but in 2017, the ratio is much stronger. Even more dramatic is the reversal in unreserved fund balances. The city had negative unreserved fund balances from 2008–2012, but in 2017, Detroit's unreserved general fund balance is nearly half of general fund revenues. The same applies to general fund cash and investments as a percentage of general fund liabilities – substantial improvement in 2017 compared to years 2008–2012. The two areas of modest concern are: declining per capita governmental revenues (ratio 1) and growing per capital general obligation debt (ratio 9).

## Tools for Financial Condition Assessment: Part 2 – Using Government-wide Statements

Another criticism of Brown's 10-Point Test is that it focuses exclusively on the general fund (Maher & Nollenberger, 2009). Several worthwhile studies offer ratios based on government-wide financial statements that include both governmental and business-type activities. For this exercise, the focus is on Maher (2013), "Calculating Ratios Using Maher's Measuring Financial Condition: An Essential Element of Management During Periods of Fiscal Distress." Similar to Brown, the ratios focus on financial position (revenues, expenditures and reserves), financial performance (change in assets), general support rate (own-source revenues relative to expenditures), liquidity (cash and investments), and solvency (long-term debt).

The example of calculations, which are provided in Table 8.2, will be of combined governmental and business-type activities. It is advised that these funds also be assessed separately. Like the Brown (1993) calculations, Figure 8.A6 provides a six-year trend analysis of these ratios for years 2008–2012 and 2017. Students and instructors learn that the calculations are the easy part – just a matter of plugging numbers into a spreadsheet – and that interpretation is the challenge. The tendency for students is to simply describe the trends for each ratio, one by one. This is insufficient on a couple of levels: (1) the student does not appreciate the interconnectedness of the ratios, making it more difficult to make policy recommendations, and (2) as a policy document that is supposed to be written for policy makers (see Maher, Ebdon, & Bartle, 2020), a simple description of trends will lose your audience. As I state in my course syllabus, "[t]he emphasis of the writing needs to be on explaining the context behind selected ratios." Students who simply describe trends without investigating the patterns in the trends will not get high scores.

For the Detroit, MI example, I added both per capita revenues and expenditures to the same graph. The reason is that, perhaps more important than the trend, or how 2017 compares to the pre-bankruptcy years, visualizing revenues to expenditures is important to assessing an entity's financial condition. In all years, Detroit's expenditures exceeded revenues. Given this revenue to expenditure imbalance, and since local and state governments cannot run budget deficits, one's attention should then shift to liquidity measures. There are two key ratios of liquidity: cash, investments, and receivables relative to current liabilities, and

**TABLE 8.2** Maher's measuring financial condition for Detroit, MI, FY 2017

| Ratio | Measurement | Explanation |
| --- | --- | --- |
| Per capita revenues | ($611,237,538 + $239,604,308 + $7,971,197 + $1,055,568,796) / 672,795 = $2,845.42 | Trending patterns particularly in conjunction with per capita expenditures should be examined. |
| Per capita expenditures | $1,967,189,817 / 672,795 = $2,923.91 | Trending patterns, particularly in conjunction with per capita revenues should be examined. |
| Intergovernmental aid divided by total revenues | ($239,607,308 + $7,971,197 + $197,831,755) / $1,914,384,812 = 0.23 | Greater reliance on intergovernmental aid weakens the community's financial position. |
| Assigned and unassigned general fund balance divided by general fund expenditures | ($168,966,674 + $62,280,192 + $60,253,830 + $50,000,000 + $90,148,163 + $47,895,504) / $880,310,267 = 0.545 | The larger the fund balance, the stronger the community's financial position. |
| Unrestricted net position divided by expenses | $-1,184,661,604 / $1,967,189,817 = -0.60 | The larger the ratio, the stronger the financial position. |
| Change in net position divided by total assets | $-210,759,525 / $5,614,992,060 = -0.038 | Measures the extent to which, each year, assets grew or declined. |
| Cash, investments, and receivables divided by current liabilities | ($805,943,974 + $286,519,250 + $34,016,952 + $412,699,290) / ($5,086,456,143-$2,835,114,438-$139,064,635) = 0.73 | Local governments tend to have conservative cash management strategies. It is not surprising to see values of 2.0 or higher. |
| General obligation debt divided by equalized valuation★ | $1,850,000,000 / $6,700,000,000 = 0.28 | Trends in the ratio should be examined over time, perhaps also in conjunction with total assets. It is also important to examine the ratio relative to existing state and/or locally imposed debt limits. |
| Long-term liabilities divided by assets | $2,835,114,438 / $5,614,992,060 = 0.50 | This is a broader measure of debt and includes post-employment benefits. |

See Figures 8.A4 and 8.A5 for more detail.

★ These data are found in the notes section of the Comprehensive Annual Financial Report.

general fund balance relative to general fund expenditures. Here the results are mixed: it is not uncommon to find cash, investments, and receivables as a percentage of current liabilities in excess of 200 percent, since cities tend to have conservative cash management strategies (Chaney, 2005). In the case of Detroit, this ratio was 74 percent in 2017, lower than any year from 2009–2012. Conversely, the city had a much stronger general fund balance in 2017 (54 percent of general fund expenditures) compared to years 2008–2012 when the city ran negative balances.

Another sign that Detroit has not fully recovered from bankruptcy is continued negative ratios for change net position (change in net position as a percent of total assets) and unrestricted net assets (unrestricted net assets as a percentage of government-wide expenditures). The latter "focuses on the net assets accumulated and available for the provision of future government services" (Chaney, Mead, & Schermann, 2002, p. 28). The former ratio "asks if a community experienced an addition to or subtraction from its total assets within a given year" (Maher, 2013, p. 24).

The ratios also reveal mixed signals for long-term liabilities. General obligation debt relative to property valuation is higher in 2017 compared to years 2008–2012. On the other hand, using a broader measure of long-term liabilities relative to assets, Detroit is in a stronger position in 2017 compared to those prior years. Both ratios could be construed as a positive sign for Detroit in that overall liabilities are lower, at least with respect to assets, and general obligation debt, the least costly form of borrowing, is growing which is a signal that borrowers are more willing to buy general obligation bonds following Detroit's default on its GO bond payments in 2013.

## Summary

Financial condition analysis is an important tool for faculty and students in MPA programs. It offers practical skills that include technical writing, financial report analysis, and a better understanding of budgeting and financial management in the public sector. The assignment(s) also enable students to focus on a community of their choosing, which gives students greater buy-in to the experience (see Maher, Ebdon, & Bartle, 2020). Several questions that are useful for class discussions are provided in Table 8.3.

With the advent of GASB 34 and the subsequent development of professional and academic literature, students and faculty have an array of financial condition analysis tools at their disposal. For this chapter, I offer two of those ratio analyses; one focuses on governmental funds and the other focuses of governmental-wide statements. The two analyses provide some consistency (Detroit's general fund reserves balances stronger) and more nuanced results. These are functions of fund-type differences – general fund vs. government-wide that includes business-type activities – and less straightforward interpretations of data. For instance, a negative

**TABLE 8.3** Discussion questions

| | |
|---|---|
| Question 1: | Complete the financial condition analysis for Detroit using government-wide financial statement by calculating the ratios for governmental funds and business-type funds. Discuss differences in the ratios across the funds. |
| Question 2: | What are the most important economic and demographic data to include in a financial condition analysis and how should those data be incorporated into the analysis. |
| Question 3: | Using the Detroit data, write a two-page memo describing Detroit's financial condition in 2017. |
| Question 4: | Conduct a financial condition analysis for a city of your choice. Compare that city's fiscal health to Detroit. |
| Question 5: | Class assignment – using Brown's financial condition ratios, generate a comparison group of ratios and quartiles from the cities selected by each student and then replicate Brown's analysis for each city. Discuss the strengths and weaknesses of such an approach. |

unrestricted net position could simple be a function of government policies (see Maher, 2013).

These projects also highlight the fact that calculating the ratios is the easy part, the more challenging and important part of these assignments is understanding the meaning of the ratios. This can be a challenge for both students and instructors. Part of the challenge is the lack of benchmarks or best-practices (however, see Kavanaugh, 2012) and the other is importance of context. The latter point means that students need to read and understand the Management and Discussion Analyses in the Comprehensive Annual Financial Reports and they should be required to study the community's economic and demographic data trends (see Maher, Ebdon, & Bartle, 2020). Furthermore, requiring students to understand the interconnectedness of some of the ratios is a valuable exercise otherwise the analysis will lack depth of understanding of a community's financial condition.

For students who are using government-wide financial statements, they should be encouraged to calculate three ratios for each measure – governmental-type activities, business-type activities, and total primary government. Patterns in these trends could be quite different and the implications could have different policy consequences. This also offers an opportunity for class discussion about the differences between governmental and business-type activities.

I also hope that the examples made clear the value of conducting trend analyses. While there is value in comparisons to peer entities, identifying those peers and conducting the data collection is challenging/time-consuming. To address some of challenges associated with data collection, instructors are encouraged to require students share their data. As a policy document, however, it can be challenging to convince policymakers that the communities selected for comparison are appropriate. For this reason and from an analytical perspective, students should be required to conduct a trend analysis for each ratio, typically five years, because it is in those trends one can get a real appreciation of the financial position of a community.

Lastly, this piece assumes that Comprehensive Annual Financial Reports are available for communities. This is not necessarily the case, especially for smaller communities. While less common and more questionable, analyses using budget data are possible. In this case, ensuring the comparability of data is paramount. This requires greater emphasis on trend analysis and if comparisons are conducted, assurances that the data classifications and timing are consistent. See Maher, Oh, and Liao (2020) for an example of fiscal condition analysis using budget data for Nebraska counties.

## Note

1 For a longer discussion on fiscal health and the measurement approaches utilized, see McDonald (2017, 2018, 2019).

## References

Berne, R., & Schramm, R. (1986). *The financial analysis of governments*. Prentice-Hall.

Brown, K. W. (1993). The 10-point test of financial condition: Toward an easy-to-use assessment tool for small cities. *Government Finance Review, 9*(6), 21–26.

Chaney, B. (2005). Analyzing the financial condition of the City of Corona, CA: Using a case to teach the GASB 34 government-wide financial statements. *Journal of Public Budgeting, Accounting and Financial Management, 17*(2), 180–201.

Chaney, B., Mead, D., & Schermann, K. R. (2002). The new governmental financial reporting model: What it means for analyzing government financial condition. *Journal of Government Financial Management, 51*(1), 26–31.

City of Detroit. (2017). *Comprehensive annual financial report for the fiscal year ended June 30, 2017*. City of Detroit, MI.

Decker, J. W. (2021). An (in)effective TEL: Why county governments don't utilize their maximum allotted property tax rate. *Public Administration*. https://doi.org/10.1111/padm.12756

Finkler, S. A. (2005). *Financial management for public, health, and not-for-profit organizations*. Pearson.

Hendrick, R. (2011). *Managing the fiscal metropolis: The financial policies, practices, and health of suburban municipalities*. Georgetown University Press.

Kavanaugh, S. (2012). *Financial policies*. Great Plains Government Finance Officers Association.

Maher, C. S. (2013). Measuring financial condition: An essential element of management during periods of fiscal stress. *Journal of Government Financial Management, 62*(1), 20–25.

Maher, C. S., Ebdon, C., & Bartle, J. R. (2020). Financial condition analysis: A key tool in the MPA curriculum. *Journal of Public Affairs Education, 26*(1), 4–10.

Maher, C. S., & Nollenberger, K. (2009). Revisiting Kenneth Brown's 10-point test. *Government Finance Review, 25*(5), 61–66.

Maher, C. S., Oh, J. W., & Liao, W. J. (2020). Assessing fiscal distress in small county governments. *Journal of Public Budgeting, Accounting and Financial Management, 32*(4), 691–711.

Maher, C. S., Park, S., & Harrold, J. (2016). The effects of tax and expenditure limitations on municipal pension and OPEB funding during the Great Recession. *Public Finance and Management, 16*(2), 121–146.

McDonald, B. D. (2017). Measuring the fiscal health of municipalities (Working Paper No. WP17BM1). Lincoln Institute of Land Policy.

McDonald, B. D. (2018). Local governance and the issue of fiscal health. *State and Local Government Review, 50*(1), 46–55.

McDonald, B. D. (2019). The challenges and implications of fiscal health. *South Carolina Journal of International Law and Business, 15*(20), 78–99.

McDonald, B. D., & Maher, C. S. (2019). Do we really need another municipal fiscal health analysis? Assessing the effectiveness of fiscal health systems. *Public Finance and Management, 19*(4), 268–291.

Nollenberger, K. (2003). *Evaluating financial condition: A handbook for local government.* International City/County Managers Association.

# Appendix

## City of Detroit, Michigan

Balance Sheet
Governmental Funds

**June 30, 2017**

| | General Fund | Other Governmental Funds | Totals |
|---|---|---|---|
| **Assets** | | | |
| Cash and cash equivalents Brown Ratio #7 | $  517,113,529 | $  201,223,022 | $  718,336,551 |
| Investments | - | 10,360,636 | 10,360,636 |
| Accounts and contracts receivable: | | | |
| Estimated withheld income taxes receivable | 23,468,899 | 54,555 | 23,523,454 |
| Utility users' taxes receivable | 3,906,981 | - | 3,906,981 |
| Income tax assessments | 74,268,869 | - | 74,268,869 |
| Special assessments | 24,669,919 | 541,890 | 25,211,809 |
| DIA and foundation receivable | 186,046,059 | | 186,046,059 |
| Property tax receivable | 80,277,933 | 10,036,778 | 90,314,711 |
| Loans receivable | - | 100,841,010 | 100,841,010 |
| Trade receivables | 197,922,006 | 36,699,041 | 234,621,047 |
| Total accounts and contracts receivable | 590,560,666 | 148,173,274 | 738,733,940 |
| Allowance for uncollectible accounts | (276,958,316) | (140,104,494) | (417,062,810) |
| Total accounts and contracts receivable  Net | 313,602,350 | 8,068,780 | 321,671,130 |
| Due from other funds | 59,386,882 | 53,598,816 | 112,985,698 |
| Due from fiduciary funds | 2,381,066 | | 2,381,066 |
| Due from component units | - | - | |
| Due from other governmental agencies | 44,548,590 | 41,825,906 | 86,374,496 |
| Advances to component units | 10,000,000 | - | 10,000,000 |
| Prepaid expenditures | 1,072,987 | 51,696 | 1,124,683 |
| Restricted cash | 130,527,277 | 45,333,691 | 175,860,968 |
| Other restricted assets | 9,227,868 | - | 9,227,868 |
| Other assets | 5,107,950 | - | 5,107,950 |
| Total assets | $  1,092,968,499 | $  360,462,547 | $  1,463,431,046 |
| **Liabilities** | | | |
| Accounts and contracts payable | $   38,745,405 | $   38,706,173 | $   77,451,578 |
| Accrued liabilities | 434,195 | 1,799,040 | 2,233,235 |
| Accrued salaries and wages | 21,713,994 | 1,145,919 | 22,859,913 |
| Due to other funds | 96,303,233 | 39,779,736 | 136,082,969 |
| Due to fiduciary funds | 3,745,203 | | 3,745,203 |
| Due to other governmental agencies | 18,436,914 | 23,960,957 | 42,397,871 |
| Due to component units | 2,673,088 | - | 2,673,088 |
| Income tax refunds payable | 15,440,330 | | 15,440,330 |
| Deposits from vendors and customers | 6,766,607 | 2,151,180 | 8,917,787 |
| Unearned revenue | - | 3,196,357 | 3,196,357 |
| Other liabilities | 31,432,918 | 7,467,781 | 38,900,699 |
| Accrued interest payable | 3,681,905 | - | 3,681,905 |
| Total liabilities | 239,373,792 | 118,207,143 | 357,580,935 |
| **Deferred Inflows of Resources** Brown Ratio #7, #8 | 260,802,179 | 7,639,208 | 268,441,387 |
| **Fund Balances** | | | |
| Nonspendable | | | |
| Prepaid expenditures and advances | 11,072,987 | 51,696 | 11,124,683 |
| Permanent fund principal  Nonexpendable | | 1,005,096 | 1,005,096 |
| Restricted for: | | | |
| Highway and street improvements | - | 54,444,951 | 54,444,951 |
| Police | - | 10,735,208 | 10,735,208 |
| Endowments and trusts  Expendable | - | 687,258 | 687,258 |
| Local business growth | - | 478,084 | 478,084 |
| Rubbish collection and disposal | - | 52,174,570 | 52,174,570 |
| Construction code | - | 18,509,391 | 18,509,391 |
| Grants | - | 14,772,891 | 14,772,891 |
| Capital acquisitions | - | 13,714,763 | 13,714,763 |
| QOL program | 54,675,178 | | 54,675,178 |
| Debt service | 27,500,000 | 31,905,618 | 59,405,618 |
| Committed for risk management operations | 20,000,000 | - | 20,000,000 |
| Assigned for: | | | |
| Budget reserve | 62,280,192 | - | 62,280,192 |
| Subsequent appropriations | 60,253,830 | | 60,253,830 |
| Capital acquisitions Brown Ratio #6; Maher Ratio #4 | | 37,810,881 | 37,810,881 |
| Blight and capital | 50,000,000 | - | 50,000,000 |
| Pension | 90,148,163 | - | 90,148,163 |
| Risk management operations | 47,895,504 | | 47,895,504 |
| Unassigned (deficit) | 188,066,674 | (1,674,211) | 167,292,463 |
| Total fund balances | 592,792,528 | 234,616,196 | 827,408,724 |
| Total liabilities, deferred inflows of resources, and fund balances | $  1,092,968,499 | $  360,462,547 | $  1,463,431,046 |

**FIGURE 8.A1**  Sources of Brown's 10-Point Test: Balance Sheet

Source: City of Detroit (2017)

## City of Detroit, Michigan

Statement of Revenue, Expenditures, and Changes in Fund Balances
Governmental Funds

**Year Ended June 30, 2017**

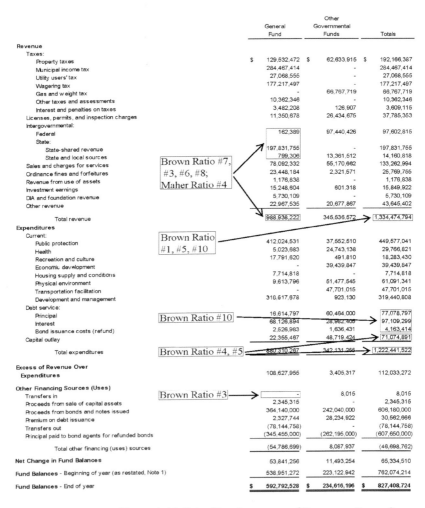

| | General Fund | Other Governmental Funds | Totals |
|---|---|---|---|
| **Revenue** | | | |
| Taxes: | | | |
| Property taxes | $ 129,532,472 | $ 62,633,915 | $ 192,166,387 |
| Municipal income tax | 284,467,414 | - | 284,467,414 |
| Utility users' tax | 27,068,555 | - | 27,068,555 |
| Wagering tax | 177,217,497 | - | 177,217,497 |
| Gas and weight tax | - | 66,767,719 | 66,767,719 |
| Other taxes and assessments | 10,362,346 | - | 10,362,346 |
| Interest and penalties on taxes | 3,482,208 | 126,907 | 3,609,115 |
| Licenses, permits, and inspection charges | 11,350,678 | 26,434,675 | 37,785,353 |
| Intergovernmental: | | | |
| Federal | 162,389 | 97,440,426 | 97,602,815 |
| State: | | | |
| State-shared revenue | 197,831,755 | - | 197,831,755 |
| State and local sources | 799,306 | 13,361,512 | 14,160,818 |
| Sales and charges for services | 78,092,332 | 55,170,662 | 133,262,994 |
| Ordinance fines and forfeitures | 23,448,184 | 2,321,571 | 25,769,755 |
| Revenue from use of assets | 1,176,838 | - | 1,176,838 |
| Investment earnings | 15,248,604 | 601,318 | 15,849,922 |
| DIA and foundation revenue | 5,730,109 | - | 5,730,109 |
| Other revenue | 22,967,535 | 20,677,867 | 43,645,402 |
| Total revenue | 988,938,222 | 345,536,572 | 1,334,474,794 |
| **Expenditures** | | | |
| Current: | | | |
| Public protection | 412,024,531 | 37,552,510 | 449,577,041 |
| Health | 5,023,683 | 24,743,138 | 29,766,821 |
| Recreation and culture | 17,791,620 | 491,810 | 18,283,430 |
| Economic development | - | 39,439,847 | 39,439,847 |
| Housing supply and conditions | 7,714,818 | - | 7,714,818 |
| Physical environment | 9,613,796 | 51,477,545 | 61,091,341 |
| Transportation facilitation | - | 47,701,015 | 47,701,015 |
| Development and management | 318,617,678 | 923,130 | 319,440,808 |
| Debt service: | | | |
| Principal | 16,614,797 | 60,464,000 | 77,078,797 |
| Interest | 68,126,894 | 28,982,405 | 97,109,299 |
| Bond issuance costs (refund) | 2,526,983 | 1,636,431 | 4,163,414 |
| Capital outlay | 22,355,467 | 48,719,424 | 71,074,891 |
| Total expenditures | 880,310,267 | 342,131,255 | 1,222,441,522 |
| **Excess of Revenue Over Expenditures** | 108,627,955 | 3,405,317 | 112,033,272 |
| **Other Financing Sources (Uses)** | | | |
| Transfers in | - | 8,015 | 8,015 |
| Proceeds from sale of capital assets | 2,345,315 | - | 2,345,315 |
| Proceeds from bonds and notes issued | 364,140,000 | 242,040,000 | 606,180,000 |
| Premium on debt issuance | 2,327,744 | 28,234,922 | 30,562,666 |
| Transfers out | (78,144,758) | - | (78,144,758) |
| Principal paid to bond agents for refunded bonds | (345,455,000) | (262,195,000) | (607,650,000) |
| Total other financing (uses) sources | (54,786,699) | 8,087,937 | (46,698,762) |
| **Net Change in Fund Balances** | 53,841,256 | 11,493,254 | 65,334,510 |
| Fund Balances - Beginning of year (as restated, Note 1) | 538,951,272 | 223,122,942 | 762,074,214 |
| **Fund Balances - End of year** | $ 592,792,528 | $ 234,616,196 | $ 827,408,724 |

Annotations on the statement: "Brown Ratio #7, #3, #6, #8; Maher Ratio #4" (pointing to revenue section); "Brown Ratio #1, #5, #10" (pointing to expenditures); "Brown Ratio #10" (pointing to debt service); "Brown Ratio #4, #5" (pointing to total expenditures); "Brown Ratio #3" (pointing to Transfers in).

**FIGURE 8.A2** Sources of Brown's 10-Point Test: Statement of Revenues, Expenditures, and Changes in Fund Balances

Source: City of Detroit (2017)

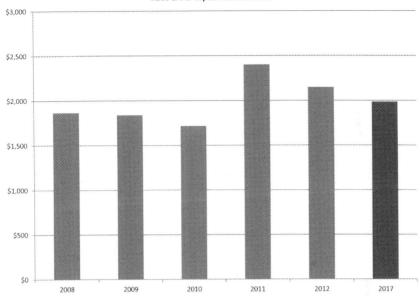

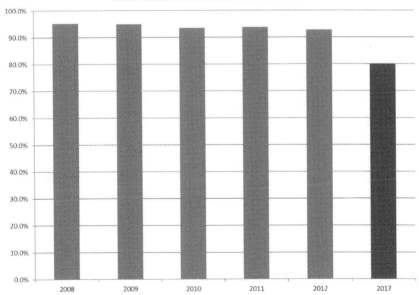

**FIGURE 8.A3** Brown's 10-Point Test: Detroit, MI

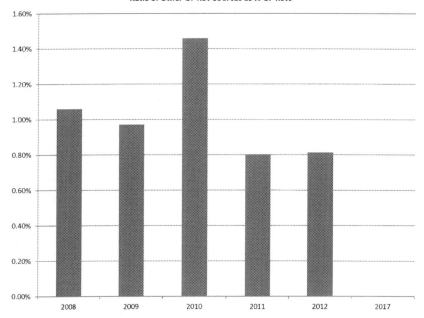

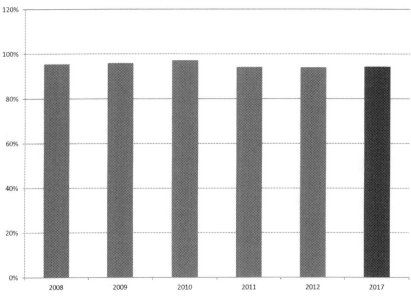

**FIGURE 8.A3** Continued

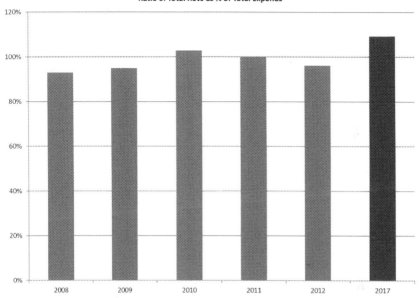

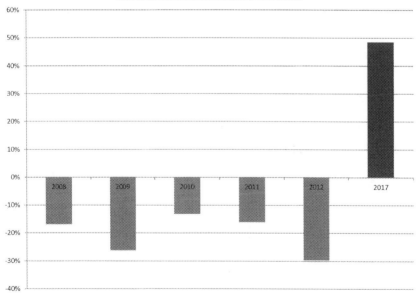

**FIGURE 8.A3** Continued

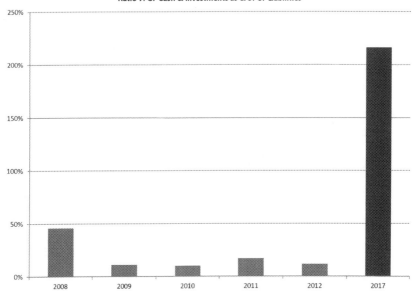

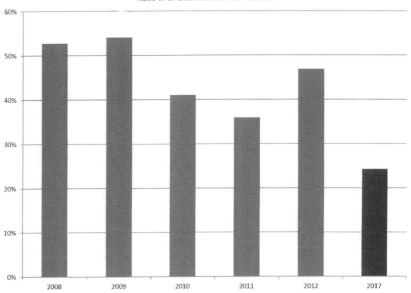

**FIGURE 8.A3** Continued

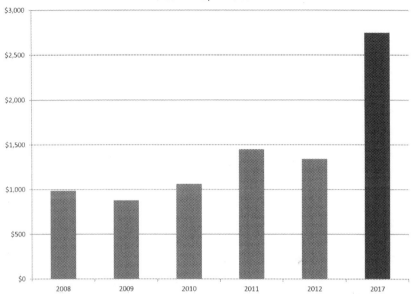

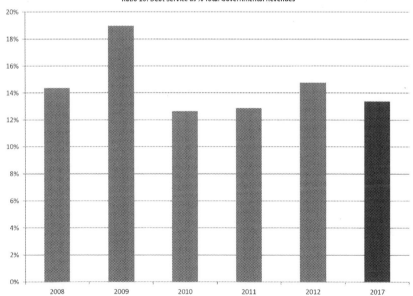

**FIGURE 8.A3** Continued

## City of Detroit, Michigan

Statement of Net Position

June 30, 2017

| | Primary Government | | | Component Units |
|---|---|---|---|---|
| | Governmental Activities | Business-type Activities | Totals | |
| **Assets** | | | | |
| Cash and cash equivalents | $  718,336,551 | $  87,607,423 | $  805,943,974 | $  92,931,494 |
| Restricted cash and cash equivalents | 175,860,968 | 110,658,282 | 286,519,250 | 26,881,577 |
| Investments | 10,360,636 | 23,656,316 | 34,016,952 | 117,758,182 |
| Accounts and contracts receivable - Net | 321,671,130 | 91,028,160 | 412,699,290 | 180,325,197 |
| Internal balances | (23,097,271) | 23,097,271 | - | - |
| Due from primary government | - | - | - | 6,852,928 |
| Due from fiduciary funds | 2,381,066 | 1,723,348 | 4,104,414 | - |
| Inventory | - | 8,853,331 | 8,853,331 | 3,439,538 |
| Due from other governmental agencies | 86,374,496 | 35,007,783 | 121,382,279 | 7,235,694 |
| Prepaid expenses | 1,124,683 | 788,855 | 1,913,538 | 2,683,985 |
| Advance to component unit | 10,000,000 | - | 10,000,000 | - |
| Loans, notes, and pledges receivable | - | - | - | 14,194,413 |
| Receivable from Great Lakes Water Authority | - | 1,062,342,235 | 1,062,342,235 | - |
| Other assets | 5,107,950 | - | 5,107,950 | 43,594,037 |
| Other restricted assets | 9,227,868 | - | 9,227,868 | 19,233,431 |
| Capital assets: | | | | |
| Nondepreciable | 426,408,914 | 236,707,539 | 663,116,453 | 894,756,898 |
| Depreciable - Net | 1,015,728,289 | 1,174,036,237 | 2,189,764,526 | 325,053,657 |
| Total capital assets - Net | 1,442,137,203 | 1,410,743,776 | 2,852,880,979 | 1,219,810,555 |
| Total assets | 2,753,485,280 | 2,855,508,780 | 5,614,992,060 | 1,734,941,031 |
| **Deferred Outflows of Resources** | 255,008,457 | 35,266,116 | 290,274,573 | 27,751,319 |
| **Liabilities** | | | | |
| Accounts and contracts payable | 77,451,578 | 17,935,486 | 95,387,064 | 31,736,215 |
| Accrued liabilities | 2,233,235 | - | 2,233,235 | - |
| Accrued salaries and wages | 22,859,913 | 886,719 | 23,746,632 | 797,350 |
| Accrued interest payable | 16,309,738 | 10,217,806 | 26,527,544 | 27,899,996 |
| Due to other governmental agencies | 44,845,322 | 119,997,934 | 164,843,256 | 8,532,861 |
| Due to primary government | - | - | - | - |
| Due to fiduciary funds | 3,745,203 | 8,323,558 | 12,068,761 | - |
| Due to component units | 2,673,088 | 4,179,840 | 6,852,928 | - |
| Deposits and refunds | 24,358,117 | - | 24,358,117 | - |
| Unearned revenue | 3,196,357 | 15,511,990 | 18,708,347 | 12,227,905 |
| Settlement credit contingent liability | 25,000,000 | - | 25,000,000 | - |
| Net pension liability | 1,374,942,869 | 282,658,320 | 1,657,601,189 | 30,332,849 |
| Other liabilities | 28,702,034 | 26,247,963 | 54,949,997 | 196,047,311 |
| Long-term obligations: | | | | |
| Due within one year | 103,701,118 | 35,363,519 | 139,064,635 | 13,362,675 |
| Advance from primary government | - | - | - | 10,000,000 |
| Due in more than one year | 1,631,204,393 | 1,203,910,045 | 2,835,114,438 | 572,089,583 |
| Total liabilities | 3,361,222,963 | 1,725,233,180 | 5,086,456,143 | 903,026,745 |
| **Deferred Inflows of Resources** | 4,833,433 | 1,903,868 | 6,737,301 | 9,562,280 |
| **Net Position (Deficit)** | | | | |
| Net investment in capital assets | 1,111,259,232 | 407,668,088 | 1,518,927,320 | 607,174,258 |
| Restricted for: | | | | |
| Highway and street improvement | 54,448,243 | - | 54,448,243 | - |
| Construction code | 18,509,391 | - | 18,509,391 | - |
| Endowments and trust (expendable) | 687,258 | - | 687,258 | 13,291,398 |
| Endowments and trust (nonexpendable) | 1,005,096 | - | 1,005,096 | 788,213 |
| Capital projects and acquisitions | 13,714,763 | - | 13,714,763 | 189,565,671 |
| Debt service | 64,824,460 | - | 64,824,460 | - |
| Improvements and extensions | - | 48,871,608 | 48,871,608 | - |
| Budget stabilization | - | 10,933,000 | 10,933,000 | - |
| Pension | 186,046,059 | - | 186,046,059 | - |
| Grants | 15,326,037 | - | 15,326,037 | - |
| Local business growth | 478,084 | - | 478,084 | - |
| Police | 10,735,208 | - | 10,735,208 | - |
| Rubbish collection and disposal | 52,226,266 | - | 52,226,266 | - |
| Program activities | - | - | - | 5,184,747 |
| Unrestricted (deficit) | (1,880,824,756) | 696,163,192 | (1,184,661,604) | 34,099,038 |
| Total net position (deficit) | $  (351,562,659) | $  1,163,635,848 | $  812,073,189 | $  850,103,325 |

*Maher Ratio #7* (Investments / Accounts and contracts receivable - Net)

*Maher Ratio #6, #9* (Total assets)

*Maher Ratio #7* (Due within one year)

*Maher Ratio #9* (Due in more than one year)

*Maher Ratio #9* (Total liabilities)

*Maher Ratio #5* (Rubbish collection and disposal)

**FIGURE 8.A4** Sources of Maher's ratios: Statement of Net Position

Source: City of Detroit (2017)

## City of Detroit, Michigan

| Functions/Programs | Expenses | Charges for Services | Program Revenue Operating Grants and Contributions | Capital Grants and Contributions |
|---|---|---|---|---|
| Primary government: | | | | |
| Governmental activities: | | | | |
| Public protection | $ 643,746,962 | $ 87,794,040 | $ 22,238,229 | $ - |
| Health | 29,784,840 | 2,981,002 | 21,901,727 | - |
| Recreation and culture | 29,922,328 | 859,989 | 1,487,202 | - |
| Economic development | 42,562,725 | 669,987 | 41,532,543 | - |
| Housing supply and conditions | 9,810,694 | 2,386,191 | 4,247,081 | - |
| Physical environment | 116,733,180 | 33,804,805 | 79,425,797 | 3,187,539 |
| Transportation facilitation | 31,513,472 | 4,204,012 | 5,111,127 | - |
| Development and management | 325,937,109 | 46,510,771 | 5,180,541 | - |
| Interest on long-term debt | 91,611,017 | - | - | - |
| Total governmental activities | 1,321,622,327 | 179,210,797 | 181,124,247 | 3,187,539 |
| Business-type activities: | | | | |
| Water | 122,932,303 | 108,174,791 | - | 2,305,264 |
| Sewer | 314,993,258 | 273,687,927 | | |
| Transportation | 178,551,373 | 21,285,572 | 58,468,990 | 2,478,394 |
| Automobile parking | 10,257,721 | 14,795,766 | | |
| Airport | 2,504,453 | 701,032 | 14,071 | - |
| Public lighting authority | 16,328,382 | 13,381,653 | - | - |
| Total business-type activities | 645,567,490 | 432,026,741 | 58,483,061 | 4,783,658 |
| Total primary government | 1,967,189,817 | 611,237,538 | 239,607,308 | 7,971,197 |
| Component units: | | | | |
| Detroit Brownfield Redevelopment Authority | 1,820,080 | 196,265 | 248,000 | |
| Detroit Public Library | 26,055,387 | 328,459 | 1,651,728 | - |
| Detroit Transportation Corporation | 25,442,936 | 1,394,946 | 17,040,784 | - |
| Detroit Housing Commission | 100,048,517 | 84,578,638 | 3,481,833 | - |
| Downtown Development Authority | 33,245,196 | 284,569,046 | | |
| Eastern Market Corporation | 5,651,461 | 1,416,836 | 1,538,971 | |
| Economic Development Corporation | 7,705,600 | 6,275,507 | | |
| Local Development Finance Authority | 2,107,760 | - | | |
| Museum of African American History | 6,777,932 | 2,159,932 | 2,466,762 | |
| Detroit Land Bank Authority | 64,104,463 | - | 67,028,869 | |
| Eight Mile/Woodward Corridor Imp. Authority | 635,070 | | | |
| Detroit Employment Solutions Corporation | 40,814,432 | - | 42,502,773 | |
| Total component units | $ 317,008,867 | $ 380,903,629 | $ 136,956,720 | $ - |

Maher Ratio #2, #5

Maher Ratio #1, #3

Maher Ratio #3

**FIGURE 8.A5** Sources of Maher's ratios: Statement of Activities

Source: City of Detroit (2017)

| | Net (Expense) Revenue and Changes in Net Position | | | |
|---|---|---|---|---|
| | | Primary Government | | |
| | Governmental Activities | Business-type Activities | Totals | Component Units |
| | | | | |
| $ | (533,714,693) | $ — | $ (533,714,693) | $ — |
| | (4,902,111) | — | (4,902,111) | — |
| | (27,575,137) | — | (27,575,137) | — |
| | (360,195) | — | (360,195) | — |
| | (3,177,422) | — | (3,177,422) | — |
| | (315,039) | — | (315,039) | — |
| | (22,198,333) | — | (22,198,333) | — |
| | (274,245,797) | — | (274,245,797) | — |
| | (91,611,017) | — | (91,611,017) | — |
| | (958,099,744) | — | (958,099,744) | — |
| | — | (12,452,248) | (12,452,248) | — |
| | — | (41,305,331) | (41,305,331) | — |
| | — | (96,318,417) | (96,318,417) | — |
| | — | 4,538,045 | 4,538,045 | — |
| | — | (1,789,350) | (1,789,350) | — |
| | — | (2,946,729) | (2,946,729) | — |
| | — | (150,274,030) | (150,274,030) | — |
| | (958,099,744) | (150,274,030) | (1,108,373,774) | — |
| | — | — | — | (4,194,815) |
| | — | — | — | (24,075,200) |
| | — | — | — | (7,007,209) |
| | — | — | — | (11,988,076) |
| | — | — | — | 251,323,850 |
| | — | — | — | (2,695,654) |
| | — | — | — | (1,430,093) |
| | — | — | — | (2,107,760) |
| | — | — | — | (2,151,238) |
| | — | — | — | 2,924,406 |
| | — | — | — | (635,070) |
| | — | — | — | 1,888,341 |
| | — | — | — | 199,851,482 |
| | 248,296,337 | — | 248,296,337 | 70,624,592 |
| | 301,069,434 | — | 301,069,434 | — |
| | 27,068,555 | — | 27,068,555 | — |
| | 177,217,497 | — | 177,217,497 | — |
| | 10,362,346 | — | 10,362,346 | 2,989,869 |
| | 197,831,755 | — | 197,831,755 | — |
| | 3,609,115 | — | 3,609,115 | 356,140 |
| | — | — | — | 9,000,620 |
| | 15,849,922 | 539,854 | 16,389,776 | 896,508 |
| | 38,110,403 | 37,421,198 | 75,531,601 | 2,185,694 |
| | (185,285) | (1,622,362) | (1,807,647) | — |
| | 1,019,230,079 | 36,338,690 | 1,055,568,769 | 86,053,423 |
| | — | (157,954,520) | (157,954,520) | — |
| | (78,136,743) | 78,136,743 | | |
| | (17,006,408) | (193,753,117) | (210,759,525) | 285,904,905 |
| | (334,556,251) | 1,357,388,965 | 1,022,832,714 | 564,198,420 |
| $ | (361,562,659) | $ 1,163,635,848 | $ 812,073,189 | $ 850,103,325 |

Maher Ratio #3

Maher Ratio #1, #3

Maher Ratio #6

**FIGURE 8.A5** Continued

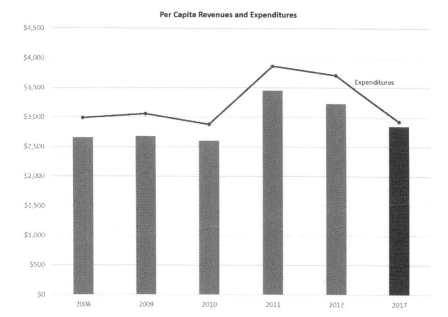

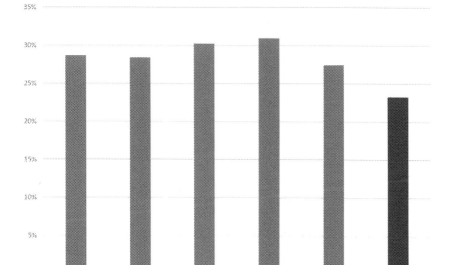

**FIGURE 8.A6**  Maher's ratios: Detroit, MI

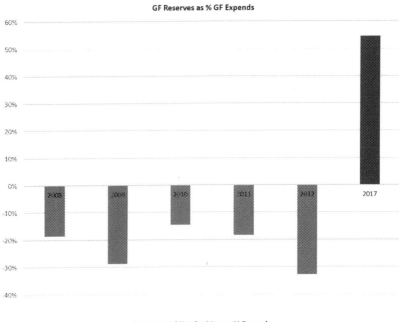

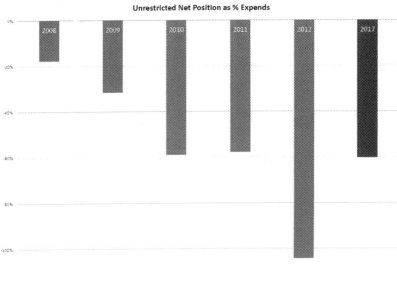

**FIGURE 8.A6** Continued

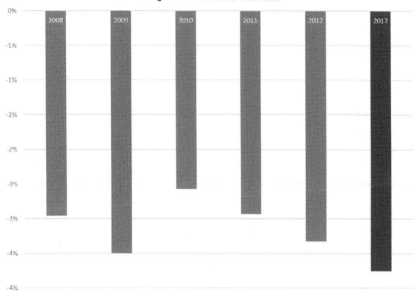

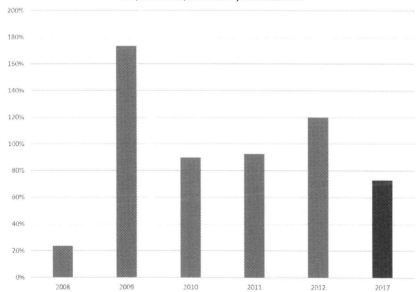

**FIGURE 8.A6** Continued

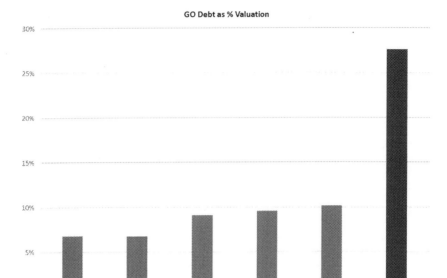

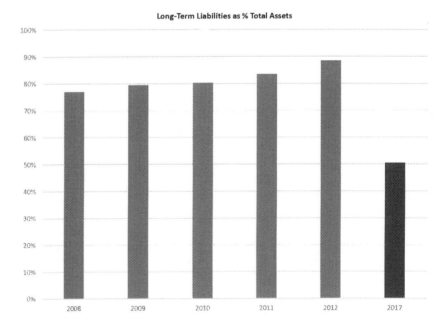

**FIGURE 8.A6** Continued

# 9

# PENSIONS

*Kenneth A. Kriz*

Governments are major employers. This seems like an obvious statement, but it carries major importance in terms of public finances given the American system of financing benefit programs like retirement savings and health care through systems of employer and employee contributions. Historically, public sector employers have given benefits to their employees that are relatively generous compared to private sector firms. However, starting in the early 2000s, concerns were raised about the cost of public pensions to taxpayers, the solvency of some public pension systems, and the propriety of the behavior of public officials making decisions about pension investments and governance.

Teaching about public pensions in an MPA program presents a combination of challenges and opportunities. One opportunity is that the topic is so relevant for many students. The troubles that the public sector is experiencing with maintaining pension system solvency have been well documented (Pew Charitable Trusts, 2020), such as the aggregation of contingent liabilities creating heavy debt burdens for future generations and questions about decisions made by pension trustees and public officials regarding investment in pension funds. This creates a sense of relevance for the topic. Further, many of the students in the class are or will be participants in public pension plans. This lends a sense of immediacy to the discussion. Typically, the most questions and discussion from students are during the public pension week in the public financial management course. The students are concerned not only about the policy implication of potential funding shortfalls, but also whether they will get the full amount of their benefits promised in their employment contracts. This illustrates typical misunderstandings around pension benefits as numerous courts have found that pension benefits, once granted, cannot be denied. The challenges with such misunderstandings are numerous, as I will discuss in the body of this chapter.

DOI: 10.4324/9781003240440-9

There is a strong need to develop understanding of how public pensions work. Aside from the solvency issues and participation in public pension plans, some students may wish to be trustees of public pension systems. There is a wide diversity of backgrounds in public pension trustees, with some evidence that plans with a larger percentage of trustees having finance education have better investment outcomes and are better funded (Hoang & Kriz, 2018).

This chapter discusses the subject context and structural placement of the public pension week within the curriculum, objectives for students, and how the topic relates to other parts of the program. Next, the chapter covers how to address the lack of finance preparation of MPA students in traditional programs. Also covered are the readings and materials used in the course, lecture structure and topics, and evaluation of students. Finally, there is a discussion of how the course might be organized differently with more time and students with more financial and economic backgrounds.

## Subject Context and Objectives

This chapter is written from the perspective of the pension as a topic in a course delivered in a traditional MPA program with a strong focus on educating a mix of in-service students (roughly 70–80% of students) who will continue in their current job in state or local government or nonprofit organizations, and pre-service students (20–30%). Like many MPA programs, the majority of students do not typically have a background in economics or finance. This mix of students and focuses leads to a need for a very broad but not particularly deep public finance education. Most MPA programs include a basic course in public budgeting that is very focused on institutional public budgeting and finance issues. Many of these courses only dedicate a portion of one week to pensions.

When they come to the public financial management class, students may have some understanding of the pension topic but tend to come to the class with numerous misunderstandings and gaps in their knowledge. Unfortunately, as this is the only financial management class in the curriculum, there is a need to address the topic material in the same course that combines elements of accounting, financial analysis, financial control, and short- and long-term financial management. With so much material needed to be delivered in one course, each topic receives only one week of coverage, pensions included. The approach is to give the students a lot of material in a short period of time and to not to go too deep into any one subject. There is also precursor material covered in a separate week that serves a dual purpose with another topic in the course. This is a less robust approach that would be preferred. The last section of this chapter discusses how the subject would be taught very differently if there was more time to deliver the material and better prepared students.

All of these factors lead us to try to balance a basic understanding of pension policy issues along with specific points of pension management in the course.

In this way, students will have a bridge to other courses in the program, and a potential capstone research topic. The MPA capstone project enables them to study various parts of public pension management and policy in more depth. The objectives for the pension management material are:

1.  Provide an understanding of the institutional and structural dimensions of pension management in the public sector.
2.  Define different types of pension systems and discuss briefly their strengths and weaknesses from different perspectives.
3.  Discuss the major decisions about plan benefits, plan funding, and plan investments that decision makers must make and best practices for making them.

## Precursors

The public financial management course is taught in a modular form. There are four modules in the semester-long course:

1.  Financial accounting;
2.  Financial analysis;
3.  Cost accounting/budgeting/financial control; and
4.  Long-term financial management (includes capital management, investment management and debt management).

The pensions material is in the fourth module. Because of the lack of preparation of students in basic concepts needed to address long-term financial management issues, the module begins with a week on basics of investment analysis. Then, there is a week on the next three topics in the following order: cash management, pension management, and capital and debt management. Two readings form the primary resources for the week on investment analysis. The first is a few pages from Finkler, Smith, and Calbrese's (2020) text, *Financial Management for Public, Health, and Not-for-Profit Organizations*, which is the primary textbook used in the class. Pages 176–186 are used, which cover the basics of the time value of money. The other resource is online, a set of modules covering *Key Investing Concepts*, published by the Financial Industry Regulatory Authority (FINRA, 2020). The FINRA materials cover important concepts like yield, risk, portfolio return and risk measures, diversification, and asset allocation. This material is important for pension as well as cash management and debt management. The material is also presented at the level where students in a generalist MPA program can understand and not get overwhelmed by mathematical presentation.

During the investment analysis week, the focus is on basic finance concepts. Calculations of the time value of money, individual asset risk and return, and portfolio risk and return are presented followed by a set of examples and exercises. For the time value of money material, these tend to be simple examples, like choosing between cash values and annuities when winning a lottery prize. Also, there is a motivating example of saving for retirement, presented as a two-part exercise (a present value calculation of how much will be needed at retirement and a future value calculation for how much is needed to accumulate that much). The asset allocation material starts by going over basics like the difference between an equity investment and a debt investment followed by introducing a discussion of "alternative investments" like real estate, commodities, private equity, venture capital, and hedge funds. Then a case study of an asset allocation study for a pension system is introduced. Lectures discuss how the pension system approached the asset allocation, preemptive allocations (not allowing certain asset classes), tradeoffs between portfolio return and risk, measures of return and risk in portfolios, and the role of risk preferences of members during discussions about asset allocations. If teaching in-class, the students participate in a role-playing exercise where they play the members of an investment committee. Students are given roles, such as being a board member elected by workers, an employer representative, and an outside member. They are given instructions about which stakeholders they nominally represent and the funding situation of the plan. Then they are presented with a set of hypothetical return and risk data as would be presented by a consultant, along with the consultant's recommendation. The students enjoy the role play, and during debriefs often discuss the dynamics they see in consideration of the hypothetical asset allocation decision.

## Readings and Materials

One of the issues with the students and the focus of most MPA program is the need for generalist-type readings and materials. The students are very sensitive to mathematical presentation and also to educational cost. So, we cannot use multiple textbooks in classes. Further, the material on pensions in most general public finance and financial management textbooks is very basic. I am currently using five short chapters from a book on public pensions by Baker, Logue, and Rader (2005, chapters 1-3, 8, 9). The chapters, which are relatively short, cover the following topics:

1. Broad overview of pension funds;
2. Defined benefit vs. defined contribution plans;
3. The economic functions of pension plans;
4. Plan design and funding issues;
5. Plan benefits and liability determination;
6. Plan contribution issues;
7. Investment policy;
8. Asset allocation, both strategic and tactical; and
9. Fund management and fund manager choice.

I have been using these readings since I began teaching and doing research on pensions in the mid-2000s. Peng (2009) is another book that covers similar topics and I have considered using chapters from that book instead. I have also thought about authoring an updated book as some of the topic areas have changed. For example, "hybrid" plans have developed over the last several years. These plans combine elements of defined benefit and defined contribution plans to produce a plan which is more financially sustainable from a plan sponsor perspective and which provides an adequate level of retirement security for workers (Pew Charitable Trusts, 2015).

Handouts are also used during the pensions week of the course. The two that I use are the Pew Charitable Trusts' (2020) nation-wide analysis of the funding status of plans and pages from an actuarial valuation done on one of the Illinois state pension plans, Teachers' Retirement System of the State of Illinois (TRS, 2021, pp. 1–24). These materials provide context and concrete examples of pension concepts, along with documentation of pension practice. The Pew Charitable Trust report covers the actuarial funding status of plans and captures key concepts about how the plan funding status is determined. The TRS report details actuarial funding calculations done by the plan's actuarial firm.

## Lecture Structure

### *Background and Definitions*

The lecture begins with a set of definitions. Figure 9.1 is used as an organizing and concept introduction tool. The approach is concrete to abstract and helps motivate the discussion. All pensions are a means to accumulate resources for use by workers in retirement. An analogy of personal savings during one's working life (the "accumulation phase") being put into a savings or investment account and then being withdrawn during retirement ("withdrawal phase") seems to anchor the idea of a pension for students. The concept is expanded out to include numerous workers, some of whom are in the accumulation phase and some in the withdrawal phase, resulting in a pension plan.

This becomes the focal point for my discussion of the different types of pensions. First is a talk about pay-as-you-go (PAYGO) pensions and the development of the earliest pension systems. While most of the talk in policy discussions these days revolves around defined benefit (DB), defined contributions (DC) or hybrid plans, PAYGO pension funding at one time was the dominant pension structure. For some, extremely poorly funded plans remain a possibility, such as with San Diego in the early 2000s (Summers & Christensen, 2014) and more recently with plans in Illinois such as East St. Louis (Lauterbach, 2019) and Harvey (Koeske, 2018). In the sense of Figure 9.1, there are no accounts in a PAYGO system, current contributions by workers and other government revenues are paid out to retirees. As long as worker contributions meet or exceed requirements to

# Basics of Pension Management

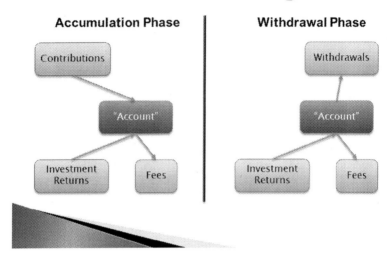

**FIGURE 9.1**  Basic structure of pensions

pay out benefits, PAYGO systems are viable. But when the ratio of retirees to workers grows, it becomes increasingly difficult to maintain the payouts. For that reason, many employer-based systems (and national retirement systems in other countries) are "prefunded," where at least a portion of payments are set aside, either held by the government employer in a fiduciary fund or at an investment management firm credited to the employee.

Next is the contrast between defined benefit plans (where the employer acts as a fiduciary on behalf of workers) and defined contribution plans (where the worker has more control but bears more risk), again concentrating on the framework from Figure 9.1. Table 9.1 presents them in terms of three distinct features. In a defined benefit plan, contributions are mandatory and carry some level of employer match (include examples of how the match can vary dramatically). In a defined contribution plan, if that plan is used as a primary retirement plan for an employer (under section 401(a) of IRS code), contributions are also mandatory and usually come with an employer match. However, there are other defined contribution plans (e.g., plans organized under 403(b) or 457 of IRS code) that are optional. In this case, employers may provide a small match to encourage worker saving, but unless they are part of a "hybrid" plan to be described later, employer match is not mandatory.

With respect to investments in the account, defined benefit plans allow for third-party control. This third-party control can be vested in a Board of Trustees, Investment Committee, or Plan/System Investment Consultant (at this point there is a discussion of the administration of a defined benefit pension plan, with the

**TABLE 9.1** Primary characteristics of pension plans

| Plan Type | Contributions & Employer Match | Control over Investments | Benefits |
|---|---|---|---|
| Defined Benefit | Contributions Required/ Employer Match | Third-party | Formula-based annuitization |
| Defined Contribution | Contributions Required or Optional/Employers Match for Required Contributions, May Match for Optional | Individual, from either a menu set by third-party or investments limited to one or a few providers | Controlled by beneficiary |

Plan or System Administrator and Staff, Board of Trustees, Investment Committee, Actuarial Committee, Plan or System Investment Consultant(s), Plan or System Actuary(ies), Plan or System Legal Counsel, and Investment Managers – some plans/systems also now employ a Medical Counsel for disability cases). As examples, the organizational charts and annual financial reports (CAFRs) from two city pension systems (Wichita and Omaha) are used to describe how the pension system works as a true system, with input, advice, consultation, and decisions from all actors.[1]

Defined contribution accounts typically are designed on the principle of constrained choice. A menu of investment options is developed by plan trustees, investment consultants, or investment management companies. Then participants are free to design their asset allocations within the constrained menu. Then there is an introduction of evidence from two studies on asset allocations. The results of Choi et al. (2002) suggest that uptake into optional plans and higher levels of mandatory plans that offer multiple levels of retirement savings are dependent on the number of options offered, and the results of Chen et al. (2013) suggests the vital role of choosing who sets the investment menu. The evidence is striking that plans who let certain types of investment managers decide on the investment menu have asset allocations of participants that favor that type of investment manager (e.g., letting an insurance company set the menu results in asset allocations that are much more heavily weighted toward "stable value" and "guaranteed investment contract" funds, which carry relatively high fees and produce strong benefits to insurance companies – they are major sources of liquidity).

Finally, there is a discussion of the differences in benefit determination. For defined benefit plans, there is the generic formula: Annual benefit = Years of credited service*multiplier*average annual wages. Also discussed is how various decisions can affect behavior of plan participants. For example, in some plans there is an issue with "spiking," where workers accrue many hours of overtime in plans where overtime is allowed in the calculation of average wages. Also discussed is how setting the number and period of years (or months in some plans) over which the average annual wages are calculated can change behavior (such as distinguishing plans with the average of the three highest years, three last years of employment, five highest years, five last years, etc.). Information on typical plan formulas using the Boston College Center for Retirement Research Public Plans Database (Center for Retirement Research, 2021) on benefit structures is then presented. Finally, there is the concept of "replacement rate," which indicates the adequacy of retirement benefits in a plan. This is an important policy indicator. Some work by the Urban Institute on measuring retirement security is used for discussion (see for example Kolasi & Johnson, 2019).

### Statistics and Pension Policy

The next part of the lecture is a discussion of broad statistics of pension plans. Unlike some topics, this is not done at the start of the lecture because much of the foundations and definitions must be established in order for students to understand the statistics in context. First discussed is national data on the number of plan participants and the splits between "active" (working participants) and total participants. This data is available from the U.S. Census Bureau's (2021) *Annual Survey of Public Pensions*. The ratio of total to active participants has widened with the start of retirement of the baby boomer generation. Then, the class discusses the implications of these statistics for plan funding. Data is presented on defined benefit and defined contribution plan assets. Then, the class moves back to a foundational piece, covering the way that the funding status of defined benefit pension plans is calculated. A brief discussion of actuarial methods emphasizes the roles of discounting (and the setting of the discount rate), selecting actuaries, and the types of analysis used. Figure 9.2 does a really good job of summarizing terms like funded ratio, unfunded actuarial accrued liability (UAAL), and normal cost.

Finally, as handouts, actuarial reports from city pension plans describe how the valuation was done and the implications of the valuation. Using statistics derived from the Public Plans Database, pension funding metrics over time are discussed. This allows the observation of how average funding rates have fallen and that there is evidence that this is driven in part by changes in the least well-funded plans. The evidence of increased dispersion of funding ratios is striking (for example, see Figure 9.3). This section closes by engaging in a discussion of pension policy, focusing on the levers that plans must close pension funding gaps. This pension policy discussion incorporates both a discussion of the technical elements and the political elements of pension policy, using material from pension reform projects done for the Pew Charitable Trusts.

### Investment Management – Defined Benefit Plans

I next discuss investment management. This is an area where, depending on their background, students can be very engaged. I start by discussing the three goals of

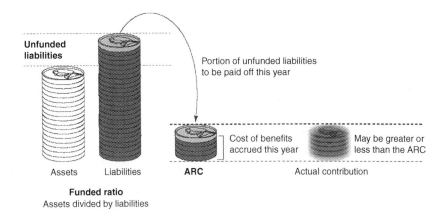

Assets = sum of past contributions from the state and local government plan sponsors, employees, and investment earnings that have not been paid out in benefits or administrative expenses.

Liabilities = current cost of all future benefits that have been accrued to date.

FIGURE 9.2 Relationship among the key measures of the funded status

Source: U.S. Government Accountability Office (2008, p. 11)

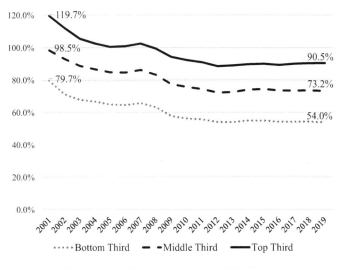

FIGURE 9.3 Average funded ratio of pension plans by 2019 funded status

Source: Center for Retirement Research (2021)

pension investment management. The first two are return maximization and risk minimization. I use the Markowitz portfolio optimization model – the familiar risk versus return tradeoff. I examine materials from the Index Fund Advisors (2021) website, they have a wealth of educational material for investors. I then discuss how the relationship between return and risk is affected by "holding periods" – how long an investment is held. I see that the rather stark tradeoff between risk and return in short time periods relaxes considerably when investments are held for longer periods of time (on this point, see Kriz & Chen, 2017). I then discuss the third goal, maintaining liquidity. The requirement to pay out benefits places a constraint in how much a plan can invest in non-liquid assets. With more mature plans (a higher ratio of retirees to workers), the liquidity constraint becomes more binding.

I then discuss the different asset classes that defined benefit pension plans can invest in. As some of this ground was covered in the fundamentals of investment analysis week, we simply review definitions. We then examine data on asset allocations using a dataset from Pensions & Investments (2021), which has more detailed asset class information than the Boston College or U.S. Census Bureau datasets. I then discuss constraints on asset allocation such as legal list requirements (where investments are limited to those on a list approved by a state government or regulatory body) and "prudent person" rules. I then engage the students in a discussion about the concept of fiduciary responsibility, which is highlighted in the readings. I discuss material from fiduciary training sessions offered to pension trustees.

Formulation of formal investment policies is the next topic. Defined benefit plans should have an investment policy that lays out strategies and tactical limits for a plan's investments. Typically, investment policies lay out the strategic asset allocation plus any rules for rebalancing such as ranges for asset classes (examples of ranges from plans are presented and discussed) and tactical decisions around rebalancing. I discuss how often rebalancing should be done, as well as how often to do formal asset allocation studies. Finally, I discuss plan investment consultants, and how they engage in these decisions.

The last areas I discuss in investment management are fund manager and asset custodian selection. Once a plan chooses its strategic asset allocation, then it must choose which investment managers will execute the investment plan. I talk about the role of the consultant in making manager selections, the process for selecting managers, and the reports that selection committees (or the investment committee as a whole) should review. I also review portfolio risk and return measures from the Investment Basics week and discuss which are most often used by plans and benchmarks for major asset classes. I then discuss manager monitoring, "watch list" procedures for managers that are underperforming, and reasons for removal of managers. I finish by discussing the plan custodian function, selecting a custodian, and briefly discuss securities lending (without getting into much detail).

## Defined Contribution Plans

In the fourth and final segment of the lecture, I review defined contribution pension plan policy and management. This is one of the most difficult portions of the lecture because of the variety of plans and approaches taken by different systems. With defined benefit plans, the structure and approach are similar, although particular strategies can differ. With defined contribution plans, there are many possible structures depending on whether the plan is a required or optional plan, whether the plan is administered by the employer or contracted to a third-party administrator, whether there is an employer match, and how investment options are decided and administered. So, I mostly discuss broad principles of the plans and what the students will need to know as managers.

I begin the discussion of the principles by discussing the way that the fiduciary role of a trustee and administrator in a defined contribution plan is different from those roles in a defined benefit plan. In a defined contribution plan, the plan participants make their own investment choices, and the employee and employer contributions are set by the employment contract (or union contract). Also, the fiduciary responsibilities of the plan's trustees are limited to overseeing the enrollment process, setting an appropriate menu of assets for participants to choose from, selecting and monitoring fund managers, and overseeing participant education and plan administration.

With regard to setting the investment menu of assets, I begin by discussing some generic strategies. One is to have the trustees select a menu with a few different options that are presented to participants. I demonstrate how some plan trustees choose them based on broad asset classes like the Equity Fund, Fixed Income Fund – the Nebraska State 457 Plan (State of Nebraska, 2021). Some plan trustees choose based on style factors like the Large-Cap Equity Fund, Core Bond Fund – the Minnesota State Deferred Compensation Plan (Minnesota State Retirement System, 2021). Others attempt to identify broad strategies or risk approaches like the Aggressive Fund, Conservative Fund, Income Fund – the newly redesigned State University Retirement System of Illinois 403(a) Fund embodies this approach (State University Retirement Systems, 2021). I discuss the benefits and limitations of each approach. Then I discuss the second broad way of developing investment choices, which is to offer a set of funds from one or more investment companies (Fidelity, TIAA, Vanguard, etc.). At this point I introduce the concept of behavioral finance, then discuss how lessons from studies of defined contribution investment decisions shapes best practices for setting investment menus, such as limiting the number of options that individuals have to choose from (on this point see Iyengar & Kamenica, 2010), presenting a full range of information so that participants do not rely too much on recent investment returns (Benartzi & Thaler, 1999; 2007), and the role of "target risk" and "target date" funds and how individuals can make systematic mistakes in their use (Benartzi & Thaler, 2007; Fox & Langer, 2005).

I also look at the role that consultants play in selecting investment menu options. One of the more important decisions with regard to the investment menu is the "default" option. Although this is an option that is supposed to be neutral with regard to risk and provide liquidity, in reality, the nature of the plan administrator and the plan consultant can result in choices which impart a definite investment strategy. I discuss the results of Chen et al. (2013) which suggest that plan administrator and consultant type may have a definite impact on default options and on participant asset allocation. For example, plans in the Chen sample that were administered or advised by an insurance company were more likely have a default option of a stable value (SV) fund or guaranteed investment contract (GIC – both products dominated by insurance companies) than other types of administrator/consultant pairs. Participants in those plans also had much higher asset allocations to SV or GIC funds.

I then discuss the related decisions of participant enrollment for optional plans and how much individuals will contribute to the plan. Once again, we examine the evidence offered from behavioral finance by pointing out that individuals often "leave money on the table" against their best interest (Choi et al., 2011). I discuss best practices suggested by the research, including opt-out defaults for participation (Madrian & Shea, 2001), contribution levels (Choi et al., 2002), increasing match, and limiting the number of fund options presented (Huberman, Iyengar, & Jiang, 2007).

I then discuss the role of participant education. Participants must be educated first on enrollment and initial asset allocation choices. Then, they need education on an ongoing basis regarding concepts like saving for retirement, rebalancing, and reallocation, which participants in defined contribution retirement plans do not do frequently enough (see Ameriks & Zeldes, 2004). Plans must provide periodic return and risk information as well as providing Securities and Exchange Commission required information disclosures. Most plans use either plan consultants or fund providers to provide information. Once again, the choice of who will provide information and disclosure is a key one. Individuals may be affected greatly by the provision of information that is biased or loaded. Plan trustees should review disclosures and information provision on a regular basis.

Next, I review material on monitoring of fund managers. There should be an ongoing process for regular monitoring of fund managers, along with the establishment and following of procedures regarding placing managers on watchlist, replacing them, or removing them from a watchlist. However, this does not appear to be the case in many places. I present results from Chen et al. (2013) who find that only one out of six case study plans had a robust monitoring and reporting procedure that was being followed. In four out of the six plans, the city employer played only a minor role in monitoring fund manager performance.

Our final discussion involves the ethics of serving as a pension trustee or administrator. I review the fiduciary responsibilities that the parties must observe (for defined benefit plans to the citizens of the jurisdiction, the employer, the workers, and the retirees within the system, for defined contribution plans primarily to the workers). I talk about practical ethical issues such as receiving gifts, meals, accommodations, and expenses at pension "conferences." I also discuss major ethical breaches that have occurred, and the roles of various parts of the government in ensuring ethical compliance.

## Evaluation of Student Learning

Students are evaluated through assignments at the end of each course module. The assignments are a combination of essay questions that ask the students to discuss theories and applications of the major concepts covered in readings and class sessions. For the pension material, the essay questions tend to either involve policy issues (such as the setting of actuarial rates of return and how it might affect plan solvency) or processes (such as the selection of a plan consultant). The assignments also contain exercises. For the pension week, this typically involves the presentation of information that the student must analyze and develop a memo or some other way to communicate a desired course of action. Indirectly, there are also problems involving the time value of money and calculation of risk and return measures that are on the assignment from the investment analysis week. A set of example questions is shown in Table 9.2. An associated answer key is provided in the appendix.

**TABLE 9.2** Sample assignment questions

1. (Essay/Short Answer) Read the 2017 valuation report for the Kansas Public Employees Retirement System (Beckham & Banister, 2018). Review the following sections and answer the following questions:

   a. What is the funded status of the plan at the end of 2016? What was the ARC for 2017?

   b. Explain why the funded status is different depending on whether the Market Value of Assets or the Actuarial Value of Assets is used.

   c. What have been the major challenges for plan funding? Why has the funded ratio of the plan declined since the early 2000s?

   d. What is the asset allocation of the plan's investments? Briefly describe the major categories of investments the plan holds, as you would explain them to a layperson.

   e. Describe the overall return performance of the plan's investments. Which type of investment has been the best performing compared to the policy index for that investment?

2. (Essay) Describe the relationship between the risk and the return on any long-term investment. Describe the types of analysis and/or measures that are used to assess the risk-to-return ratio of a long-term investment.

3. (Problem) You are trying to save $25,000 for a trip around the world. You want to go at the end of 10 years. Assuming that you think you can earn a 3% annual return on your savings, how much do you have to set aside each year in order to reach your goal?

4. (Essay/Application) Using the file [SHOWING INVESTMENT PERFORMANCE DATA], evaluate the investment performance of Peregrine Investment Management for the 7-year period ending August 2017. Then suggest other measures of investment performance that can be used to assess performance of this investment.

Note: Answer guide is provided in the appendix

## Alternative Structure

As discussed earlier, our choices regarding the placement of pension material in the curriculum and in the public financial management course, as well as how the material is delivered, is shaped strongly by the nature of our program and its students. If we had more time over which to deliver the material, the students were better prepared in terms of economics and finance, or both, we would choose to deliver the material at least as a half-semester course or a large portion of a full semester one. Fundamentals of investment analysis is a full semester course in many finance programs and deserves a minimum of three to four weeks to be covered in anything more than a cursory manner. Another four to five weeks could be spent on defined benefit pensions, with two to three of that devoted to structure and policy, one week on actuarial valuation, and two to three weeks on pension investing. A final three to four weeks could be devoted to defined contribution plans and hybrid plans. Pension reform is a topic that deserves much more coverage than we have time to provide.

## Note

1 Those wishing to obtain annual reports of pension systems can contact their local Finance Office or Treasurer's Office and ask. Many are online and can be found with simple Internet searches for "Annual Report XXX Pension System" where XXX is the jurisdiction. For example: www.wichita.gov/Finance/PensionDocuments/2019%20 Pension%20CAFR.pdf

## References

Ameriks, J., & Zeldes, S. R. (2004). *How do household portfolio shares vary with age?* Graduate School of Business, Columbia University.

Aubry, J. P., & Crawford, C. V. (2019). *Update on the funded status of state and local pension plans – FY 2018.* Center for Retirement Research.

Baker, A. J., Logue, D. E., & Rader, J. S. (2005). *Managing pension and retirement plans: A guide for employers, administrators, and other fiduciaries.* Oxford University Press.

Beckham, P. A., & Banister, B. A. (2018). Kansas public employees retirement system: Valuation report as of December 31, 2017. *Kansas Public Employees Retirement System.* Retrieved from www.kpers.org/valuationreport123117.pdf

Benartzi, S., & Thaler, R. H. (1999). Risk aversion or myopia? Choices in repeated gambles and retirement investments. *Management Science, 45*(3), 364–381.

Benartzi, S., & Thaler, R. H. (2007). Heuristics and biases in retirement savings behavior. *Journal of Economic Perspectives, 21*(3), 81–104.

Center for Retirement Research. (2021). *Public plans data.* Retrieved from https://crr.bc.edu/data/public-plans-database/

Chen, G., Ebdon, C., Kriz, K. A., & Laforge, O. M. (2013). The management of defined contribution pension plans in local government. *Public Budgeting & Finance, 33*(3), 75–95.

Choi, J. J., Laibson, D., & Madrian, B. C. (2011). $100 bills on the sidewalk: Suboptimal investment in 401(K) plans. *Review of Economics & Statistics, 93*(3), 748–763.

Choi, J. J., Laibson, D., Madrian, B. C., & Metrick, A. (2002). Defined contribution pensions: Plan rules, participant choices, and the path of least resistance. *Tax Policy and the Economy, 16,* 67–113.

Finkler, S. A., Smith, D. L., & Calabrese, T. D. (2020). *Financial management for public, health, and not-for-profit organizations* (6th ed.). CQ Press/SAGE.

Financial Industry Regulatory Authority. (2020). Key investing concepts. Retrieved from www.finra.org/investors/learn-to-invest/key-investing-concepts

Fox, C. R., & Langer, T. (2005). Biases in allocation under risk and uncertainty: Partition dependence, unit dependence, and procedure dependence. Retrieved from https://doi.org/10.2139/ssrn.757787

Hoang, T., & Kriz, K. A. (2018, October). Board structure and pension investment performance: Evidence from the common agency approach [Paper presentation]. Association for Budgeting and Financial Management Conference, Denver, CO.

Huberman, G., Iyengar, S., & Jiang, W. (2007). Defined contribution pension plans: Determinants of participation and contributions rates. *Journal of Financial Services Research, 31*(1), 1–32.

Index Fund Advisors, Inc. (2021). Fiduciary wealth services, DFA funds. Retrieved from www.ifa.com/

Iyengar, S. S., & Kamenica, E. (2010). Choice proliferation, simplicity seeking, and asset allocation. *Journal of Public Economics, 94*(7/8), 530–539.

Koeske, Z. (2018, July 24). Harvey reaches pension fund repayment agreement: State to cease withholding tax revenues. *Chicago Tribune.* Retrieved from www.chicagotribune.com/suburbs/daily-southtown/ct-sta-harvey-pension-agreement-st-0725-story.html

Kolasi, E., & Johnson, R. W. (2019). *The cost and adequacy of teacher pensions in Texas.* Urban Institute.

Kriz, K. A., & Chen, G. (2017). How well does the risk-free rate predict the future rate of return on investments? *Municipal Finance Journal, 38*(1), 57–72.

Lauterbach, C. (2019, September 23). Group wants Illinois to divert $2.2M for East St. Louis firefighter pensions. *Alton Telegraph.* Retrieved from www.thetelegraph.com/news/article/Group-wants-Illinois-to-divert-2-2M-for-East-St-14461318.php

Madrian, B. C., & Shea, D. F. (2001). The power of suggestion: Inertia in 401(k) participation and savings behavior. *Quarterly Journal of Economics, 116*(4), 1149–1187.

Minnesota State Retirement System. (2021). Minnesota deferred compensation plan overview. Retrieved from www.msrs.state.mn.us/about-mndcp

Pensions & Investments. (2021). *Data store.* Retrieved from www.pionline.com/data-store

Peng, J. (2009). *State and local pension fund management.* Taylor & Francis.

Pew Charitable Trusts. (2015). Hybrid public pension plans: A primer. Retrieved from www.pewtrusts.org/en/research-and-analysis/issue-briefs/2015/04/hybrid-public-pension-plans

Pew Charitable Trusts. (2020). The state pension funding gap: 2018. Retrieved from www.pewtrusts.org/en/research-and-analysis/issue-briefs/2020/06/the-state-pension-funding-gap-2018

State of Nebraska. (2021). Deferred compensation pension plan. Retrieved from https://npers.ne.gov/SelfService/public/planInformation/deferredCompensation/dcPlanInfo.jsp

State University Retirement Systems. (2021). Welcome to the SURS retirement savings plan. Retrieved from https://surs.org/welcome-surs-retirement-savings-plan

Summers, A. B., & Christensen, L. (2014). *Public pensions in San Diego: From "America's finest city" to "Enron-by-the-sea" (and back again?)* [Policy Study No. 440]. Reason Foundation.

Teachers' Retirement System of the State of Illinois. (2021). Valuation reports. Retrieved from www.trsil.org/financial/actuarial-reports/valuation-reports

U.S. Census Bureau (2021). Annual survey of public pensions (ASPP). Retrieved from www.census.gov/programs-surveys/aspp.html

U.S. Government Accountability Office. (2008). *State and local government retiree benefits: Current funded status of pension and health benefits* [Report No. GAO-08-223]. U.S. Government Accountability Office.

## Appendix: Answer Key to Sample Assignment Questions

Answers to the sample assignment questions provided in Table 9.2 are provided below in italic.

1. (Essay/Short Answer) Read the 2017 valuation report for the Kansas Public Employees Retirement System (Beckham & Banister, 2018). Review the following sections and answer the following questions:

   a. What is the funded status of the plan at the end of 2016? What was the ARC for 2017?

      *There are several plans. I would accept the KPERS system funded status reported in the table on page 80 (67% using the Actuarial Value of Assets or 65% using the Market Value of Assets), or the individual plan funded status reported in various tables over pages 89–96, as shown in Table 9.A1.*

      *The ARC (referred to in the report as the Actuarial Contribution Rate) appears in many places in the Actuarial section of the report. The correct figures provided in Table 9.A2.*

   b. Explain why the funded status is different depending on whether the Market Value of Assets or the Actuarial Value of Assets is used.

      *The Actuarial Value of Assets is calculated by "smoothing" the investment returns over several years. This has the effect of reducing volatility in the plan's valuations over time, as shown in the table on page 86 (in essence a "bad" investment year may be offset by a "good" following year). In any given year, then, the value of assets will differ based on this year's investment returns and those of previous years.*

**TABLE 9.A1**  Individual plan funded status

| Plan / Value of Assets | Actuarial Value of Assets | Market Value of Assets |
| --- | --- | --- |
| KPERS (State) | 79.0% | 76.5% |
| KPERS (School) | 60.2% | 58.3% |
| KPERS (State/School) | 64.5% | 62.5% |
| KPERS (Local) | 70.3% | 68.1% |
| KPERS (Total KPERS) | 65.8% | 63.7% |
| KPFRS | 73.4% | 71.1% |
| Judges | 93.9% | 91.0% |
| All Systems Combined | 66.8% | 64.8% |

**TABLE 9.A2** Actuarial contribution rate by plan

| Plan | Actuarial Contribution Rate (ARC) |
| --- | --- |
| KPERS(State) | 15.49% (6.0% Employee, 9.49% Employer) |
| KPERS(School) | 22.15% (6.0%, 16.15%) |
| KPERS(State/School) | 20.74% (6.0%, 14.74%) |
| KPERS(Local) | 14.89% (6.0%, 8.89%) |
| KPFRS | 29.28% (7.15%, 22.13%) |
| Judges | 24.29% (5.64%, 18.65%) |

c. What have been the major challenges for plan funding? Why has the funded ratio of the plan declined since the early 2000s?

*The table on page 88 has a nice recap of the items that have affected the UAAL. The major detractor increasing the UAAL has been the statutory cap on the growth of contributions, accounting for about half of the growth in the UAAL. Other large detractors have been assumption and method changes (assumption changes, changes in data/procedures, changes in cost method, amortization method), accounting for 47% of the growth in the UAAL, and lower than expected investment returns, accounting for just under 15% of UAAL growth.*

d. What is the asset allocation of the plan's investments? Briefly describe the major categories of investments the plan holds, as you would explain them to a layperson.

*The asset allocation is described on page 56 of the report. Students should do some web research to describe each of the asset classes.*

e. Describe the overall return performance of the plan's investments. Which type of investment has been the best performing compared to the policy index for that investment?

*Overall returns described on page 57 have the overall portfolio beating the policy index over 1-, 3-, 5-, and 10-year periods. Asset classes that beat their policy index (benchmark) over 10-year periods include International Equity, Fixed Income, and Real Return. Domestic Equity, Yield-Driven, and Real Estate returns have lagged their indices (Yield-Driven only has 3-year experience), while Alternative Investments have performed in line with their benchmark.*

2. (Essay) Describe the relationship between the risk and the return on any long-term investment. Describe the types of analysis and/or measures that are used to assess the risk-to-return ratio of a long-term investment.

*As discussed in lecture, there is a direct relationship between risk and return on any long-term investment. Analyses used to assess the risk-return tradeoff include efficient portfolio graphs (return on one axis and risk on the other), measures such as the alpha of the investment (return over the market return), beta (correlation between the investment return and the market return), Information Ratio, and Sharpe Ratio.*

3.   (Problem) You are trying to save $25,000 for a trip around the world. You want to go at the end of 10 years. Assuming that you think you can earn a 3% annual return on your savings, how much do you have to set aside each year in order to reach your goal?

*Assuming annual contributions, the amount to save each year would be $2,180.76. If you save monthly, the amount to save each month would be $178.90.*

4.   (Essay/Application) Using the file [SHOWING INVESTMENT PERFORMANCE DATA], evaluate the investment performance of Peregrine Investment Management for the 7-year period ending August 2017. Then suggest other measures of investment performance that can be used to assess performance of this investment.

*Peregrine's risk versus return profile on page 78 of the report (the first page of the .pdf file) puts it in the top right quadrant of the graph, indicating above average return and above average risk compared to its peers and to the indexes that it benchmarks against (the Russell 2000 Index and Russell 2000 Growth Index). It is below and to the right of a hypothetical "efficient frontier" as drawn below indicating that it could either earn a higher return for the amount of risk that it takes on, or decrease its risk dramatically if it wanted to earn a similar return.*

*At the bottom of page 79, we see the summary measures of performance for the Peregrine portfolio over the last seven years. The "Alpha" of the portfolio, as benchmarked to the Russell 2000 Growth index is 0.45 over that period, indicating that the fund has produced 45 basis points (0.45%) better performance than a passive set of investments that tracks the index, controlling for risk. So the fund is producing a good return for the plan. However, the "Sharpe Ratio" is 0.87, indicating that the extra performance is not enough to compensate the plan for the extra risk that this portfolio adds. We would ideally like to see a Sharpe Ratio greater than one.*

*The other metrics that would be good to have would be the "Beta" of the portfolio with the R2000 Growth Index, indicating how much risk the plan is exposed to in the form of market risk by investing in that segment of the market and "Information Ratio" indicating how much of the risk assumed by the plan is unique to the investments in the portfolio versus the overall market risk of the market segment.*

# 10

# NONPROFIT BUDGETING AND FINANCIAL MANAGEMENT

*Carol Ebdon*

More than 1.5 million nonprofit (or not-for-profit) organizations exist in the U.S., and they accounted for 5.6 percent of the national gross domestic product as of 2016 (National Center for Charitable Statistics, 2020). Our universities address this large sector in varying ways: some have specializations in this area with specific related courses, some have separate nonprofit management degrees, while others incorporate both public and nonprofit sectors in core courses or have little focus on nonprofits at all. Financial management is similar in many ways across government and nonprofit organizations, but there are some important differences and considerations. This chapter will offer suggestions for how to approach teaching nonprofit budgeting and financial management. My assumption here is that this will be used for courses that include both government and nonprofits, although this material can equally apply to courses that are solely focused on nonprofits.

Including nonprofit organizations when teaching financial management is relevant for several reasons. First, many of our students work for nonprofits, or are interested in a career in this sector. The Network of Schools of Public Policy, Affairs, and Administration (NASPAA, 2020), the organization that accredits MPA/MPP programs, reports that 26 percent of alumni from these programs are employed in nonprofits. Therefore, it is helpful for these students to better understand how to operate in the sector in which they work. Second, individuals tend to change jobs and work in different sectors over the course of their careers, so alumni of our programs are likely to move between nonprofit and government organizations. This makes it useful for them to be exposed to both public and nonprofit financial management.

Third, it is common for state and local governments to have significant relationships with nonprofit organizations in the provision of public services. This

DOI: 10.4324/9781003240440-10

occurs through grants, contracts, and networks/partnerships. MPA graduates who work in government will likely find themselves working with, monitoring, and having to make decisions about the fiscal capacity of nonprofit organizations to be involved in these activities. Understanding the environment and operations of nonprofits, then, is important even for students who may never work for a nonprofit.

Finally, graduates of our programs generally have a public service motivation. In addition to their paid employment, they are likely to serve on boards of nonprofit organizations throughout their careers. As board members, they have fiduciary responsibilities that require them to be familiar with, and carefully monitor, the organization's fiscal health. It is all too common for nonprofit board members to not ask important questions about finances because they do not understand the financial reports or know how to judge whether internal controls are in place. This can, and has, resulted in disastrous consequences for many organizations.

The competencies addressed when teaching nonprofit financial management are very similar to those related to the public sector. These may vary depending on the specific focus of the course (e.g., budgeting versus financial management). Learning outcomes for a budgeting or financial management course, for example, may include:

- Knowledge of budgeting and financial management practices;
- Developing analytical skills for decision-making and managing financial resources;
- Understanding how financial activities reflect the organization's mission, and are used to improve efficiency, effectiveness, and equity of services; and
- Enhancing skills to communicate complex information to stakeholders.

The next section discusses specific areas that an instructor may want to consider in incorporating nonprofit financial management into budgeting or financial management courses. Useful resources and possible course assignments are provided in the succeeding sections. Conclusions are in the final section of the chapter.

## Focus Areas for Teaching Nonprofit Financial Management

Much of what is taught in courses on government budgeting and financial management, as well as teaching approaches, also applies to nonprofits. My focus here, then, is on topical areas where there is divergence between the two sectors that you may want to address in your courses. These fall into seven categories: mission, organization structure, budget process, revenue sources and issues, financial reporting, financial analysis, and internal controls. I will discuss the importance and distinctions in each area.

## Mission

General-purpose governments provide a wide variety of services. Nonprofit organizations have a narrower focus. Nonprofits serve a wide gamut of purposes, such as arts and culture, education, human services, health care, labor unions, religious organizations, professional associations, and foundations. The Internal Revenue Service identifies 30 different types of tax-exempt nonprofit organizations (National Center for Charitable Statistics, 2020).

A nonprofit organization should have a clear mission statement that defines their purpose. The mission drives the operational decisions made by organization leaders, including those related to financial management. Fulfilling the mission requires financial resources; so careful planning for and monitoring of those resources are essential to success. Budgets, financial statements, requests for new programs, and grant applications should always be reviewed in light of the mission. Nonprofits in financial difficulties that do not plan well run the risk of "mission drift" by taking on grants or contracts to provide services that are not part of their mission. For example, a human services agency that is dedicated to providing recreational services to disabled children may receive funding to extend those services to adults or to children without disabilities. Leaders should carefully consider the consequences of those decisions on their mission. It is helpful to continually return to the topic of organizational mission throughout courses that include nonprofits.

## Organization Structure and Roles

Nonprofit organizations are governed by a board of trustees (or directors). Board responsibilities, structure, and operations are determined by a set of bylaws. Board sizes vary considerably, and term limits are often specified by the bylaws. Nonprofit board members usually do not receive compensation for their service. Boards set regular meeting schedules, but the frequency ranges from monthly to quarterly. Board members are often selected based on expertise in specific areas, such as financial management, law, fundraising, or the mission focus of the organization.

One definition of board members is that they are "the fiduciaries who steer the organization towards a sustainable future by adopting sound, ethical, and legal governance and financial management policies, as well as by making sure the nonprofit has adequate resources to advance its mission" (National Council of Nonprofits, 2021). Note the importance here of the fiduciary duty for financial management. It is the board's responsibility to make sure that financial resources are used to support the mission and are in line with the intentions of the donors. While each board member has this duty, and financial reports are presented regularly at board meetings for approval, boards typically have a finance committee and a treasurer or finance committee chair who takes the lead role in overseeing financial management. A separate audit committee may have responsibility for contracting with an external auditor for the annual financial statement review and overseeing internal controls.

Many nonprofits are all-volunteer organizations, such as parent-teacher associations or service clubs. In that case, the board is responsible for all activities of the organization; for example, the treasurer writes the checks. Others have paid staff, usually led by an executive director who is hired by the board. The executive director is responsible for the day-to-day operations of the organization to implement the strategic plan and mission developed in conjunction with the board. Small entities may have a part-time finance director or may even contract with an accounting firm for financial transactions. Larger nonprofits usually have a full-time chief financial officer (CFO) or finance director who oversees the financial operations and works closely with the board's finance committee.

In teaching, students can be asked to compare the organization structure of nonprofits with that of governments at the beginning of the semester, and also when addressing specific activities, such as the budget process and financial reporting. Useful resources include, for example, Weikart, Chen, and Sermier (2013), the National Council of Nonprofits, and Board Source.

## Budget Process

Budget processes for nonprofits are similar to those used by government, although there are generally no legal deadlines for the timing of budget submission and approval. In addition, nonprofit budgeting is not a public process, so is not as transparent as in the public sector. A nonprofit budget is not likely to be found on the organization's website, and public meetings are not held by the board.

Nonprofits do typically adopt annual operating budgets. Generally, the line-item format is used, although program budgets by responsibility/cost centers may also be presented. Depending on the size of the organization, the proposed budget may be developed in a bottom-up approach with individual program managers preparing estimates for their areas, or in a more centralized top-down method where the CFO works with the executive director to determine priorities and revenue/expense forecasts. The staff may work with the board president or treasurer as they are preparing the budget, particularly if there are serious fiscal challenges. In any event, the budget should be consistent with the strategic plan and mission. The board reviews and adopts the annual budget.

Formal capital budgets are not as common in nonprofit organizations as in governments. The staff and board may present information about capital plans to the board, especially if they are planning to undertake a capital campaign to fundraise for new capital assets. Coordinating capital and operating plans is important as one may have an effect on the other; purchasing additional vehicles will increase maintenance and operating costs, for example. One common difference between governments and nonprofits is in the budgetary treatment of capital spending. Governments tend to budget for capital on a cash basis. Nonprofits, on the other hand, typically report depreciation expense in the budget document and in financial reports throughout the year.

Many nonprofits have cash flow issues, especially if they have low levels of reserves. Revenues may equal or exceed expenses on an annual budget basis, but there may be times during the year when they are in danger of being unable to pay their bills due to timing flows of income versus spending. Some organizations utilize lines of credit with banks to deal with these situations and do this as a matter of routine. This is not a preferred solution, though, since it increases operating costs. Organizations with these issues should also prepare a cash flow budget for the year, which forecasts the timing of cash balances, income, and expenses by month or quarter. The staff and board can then work to try to mitigate potential issues; for example, by adjusting timing of purchases or moving up the schedule for major fundraising activities.

The budget process is more complex in government due to its political and public nature. Most of my time in classes is spent on the government process, with only a brief discussion of the distinctions on the nonprofit side. Nonprofit textbooks are useful for information on this topic; see, for example Finkler, Smith, and Calabrese (2020), Weikart, Chen, and Sermier (2013), and Dropkin, Halpin, and La Touche (2007).

## Revenue Sources and Issues

One area where nonprofits differ significantly from governments relates to revenues. In a budgeting or financial management course, I typically have a week devoted to nonprofit revenues. There are several areas that are helpful to address, including revenue sources, reserves, endowments, revenue diversification, crowding-out versus crowding-in of donations, commercialization, and the relationship between revenue sources and organizational benefits. For the most part, I use supplemental journal articles or book chapters for this purpose.

Nonprofits cannot levy taxes, which are the primary revenue source for most general-purpose governments. Public charities are the largest group of nonprofits, and include arts, culture, humanities, education, health care, and human services organizations. Fees for goods and services from private sources account for close to one-half of revenues for public charities (Finkler, Smith, & Calabrese, 2020); this is likely because hospitals and health care agencies receive about 60 percent of all revenues for this group (National Center for Charitable Statistics, 2019). Government funding through fees for goods and services accounts for approximately another 25 percent of revenues for public charities. The remaining roughly 25 percent of revenues are from contributions. In 2016, 72 percent of these were from individuals, 15 percent from foundations, 8 percent in the form of bequests, and 5 percent from corporations. Close to one-third of the donations went to religious organizations (Finkler, Smith, & Calabrese, 2020).

Nonprofits, like governments, are often encouraged to diversify their revenue streams to enhance flexibility and reduce vulnerability. However, diversification can also increase complexity and administrative costs, and potentially lead to mission drift in devoting resources to activities desired by donors even if they are unrelated to the organization's mission. The literature is mixed regarding the effects of diversification on nonprofit financial health. Hung and Hager (2019) provide a useful overview of existing studies and the theoretical arguments related to diversification. In their meta-analysis, they find a small, positive relationship between diversification and fiscal health.

A related topic is the extent to which government support for nonprofits affects private donations. On the one hand, government grants might "crowd-out" private funding, if they are viewed as substitutes by donors. On the other hand, they may have the opposite effect of leveraging, or "crowding-in," private dollars, because they can be seen as a signal of the nonprofit's quality and the importance of the mission; in addition, government grants may require matching funds that encourage private donations. The substantial literature on this topic has mixed findings. Lu (2016) is a useful summary of the theories and existing findings; this meta-analysis finds little relationship between government and private funding.

Another common research topic relates to the existence and use of reserve funds, which are considered important for "rainy days" to assist in financial sustainability. This is not easy for many organizations, especially small nonprofits that feel that they need to spend all of their income each year on vitally needed services. The rule of thumb is that nonprofits should have reserves equal to three to six months of expenses, although there is substantial variation in practice, with many having little or none at all (Calabrese, 2013). The actual effects of reserves are not clear. One study found that reserves do have a small effect in stabilizing finances during downturns, but that six months of reserves may be insufficient (Calabrese, 2018). Nonprofits have become painfully aware of the importance of reserve funds during the COVID-19 pandemic; for example, arts organizations dramatically reduced their performances/exhibits which decreased revenues to support ongoing expenses such as rent and salaries. A study conducted in spring 2020 found that nonprofit organizations that had lower levels of reserves were more likely to have to reduce staffing and operating hours at that stage in the pandemic (Kim & Mason, 2020).

Some nonprofit organizations also have endowments. Endowments are assets that are invested in order to provide a revenue stream for the organization (i.e., the principal is untouched while the investment earnings are used for operations). The endowments could be designated for specific purposes (e.g., scholarships in an educational institution). Endowments are prized, as they may offer long-term sustainability for important activities, but good investment management is critical for endowments (see, for example, Hooke, Yook, & Chu, 2019). One recent study using data reported to the IRS found that over 43 percent of the organizations reviewed had an endowment, the vast majority of which were held by institutions of higher education (Calabrese & Ely, 2017).

As noted above, fees from the sales of goods and services are a large share of nonprofit revenues. The increasing commercialization of nonprofits has been a controversial topic in the literature. Fees from some services may help to subsidize other important activities of the organization and enhance stability, such as a restaurant or gift shop in a museum. However, there are also concerns about the "marketization" of benevolence from this business-like model which can detract from serving populations most in need of services (see, for example, Eikenberry & Kluver, 2004). The work of Maier, Meyer, and Steinbereithner (2016) is a review of the literature in this area.

One way for nonprofits to think about the appropriateness of their revenue structure is to view it in the context of "benefit theory" (Young, 2018). In this framework, organizations are classified by the types of benefits they provide: private, group, public, or trade. Revenue sources should then match the benefits, according to this theory. For example, user fees are appropriate for private benefits, while governments should fund activities that benefit the public as a whole, and donations are appropriate for group and trade benefits. This typology can be helpful for organizations in developing revenue strategies.

I assign supplemental readings (such as those cited in this subsection) for students to understand nonprofit revenue issues and practices. For class discussions, I may ask students to review revenue sources of specific organizations to determine the level of diversification or the amount of reserves available. I often provide a list of possible fees and ask them to discuss in groups the extent to which the charge should cover the total cost of the good or service (e.g., Girl Scout cookies, Humane Society adoption fees, zoo admission, symphony concert tickets, or summer camps for disadvantaged youth). In a homework assignment, I may provide financial statements for an organization, along with the mission statement, and ask the students to apply the benefit theory to analyze how well the revenue sources match the benefits provided by the nonprofit.

## Financial Reporting

Financial reporting for nonprofits is less complicated than for governments because nonprofits do not use fund accounting in the same way. This reduces the number of statements in the annual financial report dramatically. Generally accepted accounting principles (GAAP) for nonprofit organizations are established by the Financial Accounting Standards Board (FASB), whereas government standards are governed by the Governmental Accounting Standards Board (GASB). Three of the financial statements used by nonprofits are similar to those used by other types of organizations (balance sheet, profit and loss statement, and cash flow statement). In addition, nonprofits also include an additional statement that provides more details related to expenses. Financial reporting guidance and standards can be found on websites of FASB (www.fasb.org), the American Institute of Certified Public Accountants (www.aicpa.org), and the National Council of Nonprofits (www.councilofnonprofits.org).

The *Statement of Financial Position* is the organization's "balance sheet." It includes the standard categories of assets, liabilities, and net assets. One difference from government reports is in the reporting of net assets. Nonprofits separate net assets into those "with donor restrictions" and those "without donor restrictions." A nonprofit may have funds that must be set aside for specific purposes based on donors' wishes, and endowments that may be permanently restricted. Net assets that are not restricted by donors are available for operating purposes, although some or all of these may be designated by the board for specific purposes. The information about the restrictions of net assets is valuable in allowing users to analyze fiscal health, as the net assets without donor restrictions could be used to keep the agency running if revenues were unavailable for a period of time.

The *Statement of Activities* is the profit and loss, or income, statement. As with other types of organizations, this includes the revenues, expenses, and changes in net assets for the given period. Nonprofits must detail changes for both funds with and without donor restrictions; this is commonly done by using separate columns. These distinctions enable the user to see which revenues during the period were restricted by the donors, and also where net assets were released from restrictions (e.g., if a donor contributed funding in a previous year to a library foundation for children's books, and the books were purchased in the reporting year, the net assets would be released from restriction and moved to the unrestricted category). In addition, expenses for nonprofits are organized by program services and supporting services. Program services include the various direct program activities, while supporting services are fundraising and management/general expenses. This distinction is useful for calculating the program services ratio (the portion of expenses that are used for programs versus overhead).

The *Statement of Cash Flows* is essentially the same as that used for government organizations. This statement focuses on the cash availability over the year and how the cash was used. Cash flows are separated into three categories of activities: operating, investing, and financing (debt-related).

Nonprofits also use an additional statement that is distinct from governments. This is the *Statement of Functional Expenses*. This statement is in matrix form and provides details of expenses by both programmatic purpose and line items (e.g., salaries, supplies, etc.). The same categories of functions are used as in the Statement of Activities (program services and support services). Disclosures are included in the notes that explain how costs are allocated between programs and support activities. This statement provides information for users related to how the organization spends its resources. For example, some organizations have been criticized for spending a large proportion of expenses on fundraising versus programs.

The financial statements also include notes, as is the case for organizations in other sectors. If the statements are audited, the auditor's letter is also included.

Nonprofits do not prepare anything similar to a Comprehensive Annual Financial Report in government, so no supplemental information is included with the financial statements, but they may have a separate Annual Report that they use for donors and the public to highlight their activities and outcomes during the year.

Nonprofit organizations are generally tax-exempt, but are required to file annual returns with the IRS, called the Form 990 (see www.irs.gov/charities-non-profits/form-990-resources-and-tools for detailed information). Organizations with annual receipts less than $50,000 file a simplified version. The Form 990 provides some information that is similar to the financial statements, but also includes other interesting data such as salaries of highest compensated employees, lobbying activities, source of large donations, as well as information pertaining to certain governance practices. Research studies of nonprofit finances often use the Form 990 data because it is readily available from the IRS. Form 990 data for many filing organizations can also be found at Guidestar (www.guidestar.org). Nonprofits are legally required to provide their Form 990 to anyone who requests it, which is not the case for the financial statements. The Form 990 data is not audited, so financial statements may be more appropriate for student analysis.

Some nonprofits do pay taxes, if they have operations that are unrelated to their mission that compete with private businesses. For example, a nonprofit museum located on a busy street may operate a restaurant that is easily accessible to the public who are not otherwise visiting the museum exhibits. In that case, the organization will file with the IRS and pay "unrelated business tax."

In budgeting courses that include both government and nonprofit organizations, it is difficult to find enough time to cover financial reporting in detail, particularly since there are substantial variations between the two sectors. When teaching financial management, the Finkler, Smith, and Calabrese (2020) textbook is useful its coverage of both governments and nonprofit financial reporting. It includes detailed case studies and clear, specific information about standards. In addition to this text, I generally use actual financial statements from local or national nonprofit organizations to help students understand the different statements and financial reporting concepts. I may ask them in discussions to look at two different but similar types of organizations and talk about two or three things that stand out to them. They may also be asked to look for specific things, such as information in notes related to how much of the fixed assets have been depreciated or the purpose of donor restricted net assets, or how the major program expenses match the mission.

## Financial Analysis

Students can learn to do analyses of the fiscal health of nonprofits in a similar fashion as the financial condition analysis for governments, using the data in the financial statements. The chapter in this book by Maher details the financial condition analysis methods; most of the ratios he discusses can also be used to analyze the fiscal health of nonprofits. Finkler, Smith, and Calabrese's (2020) book also provides details of financial analysis ratios. I will focus here on just a couple items specific to nonprofits. First, reserves are calculated as the amount of net assets that are not restricted (from the Statement of Financial Position), related to either the annual revenues or expenses (from the Statement of Activities). This can be used to determine the number of months the organization could continue to operate without revenues coming in. As noted earlier, the rule of thumb for nonprofits is that the reserves should be three to six months, but there is wide variation in actual practice (see Calabrese, 2013).

Second, the program ratio is a commonly cited measure for nonprofit organizations. This is the proportion of total expenses spent on program services (versus supporting services). In theory, we would want to see as many resources as possible used for direct program activities rather than overhead to maximize the organization's impact. Studies have found that donors often consider the program ratio in their funding decisions, and that donors think the ratio should be about 77 or 78 percent. The rule of thumb for this ratio varies, and charity rating agencies use different guidelines (Garven, Hofmann, & McSwain, 2016). Needs for overhead spending vary by type of nonprofit, though; for example, Charity Navigator (www.charitynavigator.org) notes that food banks should have lower administrative costs because they have large non-cash donations, while museums have expensive assets to maintain so would be expected to have lower program ratios. The focus on this ratio has been heavily criticized in recent years, as leading to a "starvation cycle" where funders have unrealistic expectations for low overhead but nonprofits feel compelled to continue increasing the program ratio (Lecy & Searing, 2015), either through misreporting expenses or reducing relative spending on supporting services (Garven, Hofmann, & McSwain, 2016; Lecy & Searing, 2015). This cycle can ultimately hurt the long-term sustainability of the organization.

As with governments, there are no clear answers regarding which ratios or financial information are most relevant in determining fiscal health. Studies use varying measures to assess the determinants and outcomes of fiscal health, and determinants of dissolution and recovery. Results are mixed across studies. Illustrative articles for classes, for example, include: Searing (2015), Prentice (2016a, 2016b), and Lu, Shon, and Zhang (2020).

Students should learn to conduct this type of analysis themselves, or to ask appropriate questions of staff or auditors when they serve in nonprofit leadership positions. Administrators and boards may find it useful to regularly track a few key ratios or measures. For example, an organization with cash flow issues may want to keep an eye on the quick ratio, or the number of months of cash on hand. The number of months of reserves is also considered important in many organizations. Calculating the operating ratio over time may be useful to observe the extent of annual surpluses/deficits, and debt ratios are also helpful measures for organizations with significant levels of debt.

### *Internal Controls*

Nonprofit organizations have been rocked by some major financial scandals over the years. Many nonprofits rely heavily on donations, and donors may be reluctant to contribute when they learn about an organization misusing its resources. Maintaining trust of the public is vital for the sector as a whole as well as individual organizations. In one study of nonprofit organizations experiencing a fraud, over 25 percent survived less than three years following the public awareness of the fraud (Archambeault & Webber, 2018).

Appropriate internal controls are therefore important. Best practices in this area are similar across all sectors. However, many nonprofits are quite small, and many are run entirely by volunteers with no paid staff. This can make it difficult to implement adequate controls. In addition, many small organizations do not have external audits of their financial statements. This makes it even more incumbent on the board (and staff leaders where they exist) to review the internal controls regularly and have strong policies in place. The importance of these controls is supported by a study that found that an independent voting board and the use of independent audits are the most important ways to prevent misuse of donations to benefit officers of the organization (LeClair, 2019). Independent Sector (www.independentsector.org) and Board Source (www.boardsource.org) have valuable resources related to internal control practices and policies.

I typically have one week or class session in a budgeting or financial management course devoted to internal controls. Finkler, Smith, and Calabrese (2020) and Weikart, Chen, and Sermier (2013) have chapters on this topic that include examples, discussion questions, and assignments/cases. In addition to reviewing internal control standards and best practices, I will often have students review textbook or real-world cases in class (and in a homework assignment) to discuss internal control issues and how to develop and implement policies to mitigate potential weaknesses.

This section has focused on financial management topics where nonprofits differ somewhat from government organizations, to help instructors in thinking about how they might address these areas in a course that includes both sectors. The next section provides suggestions for useful teaching resources.

## Resources

Textbooks are a challenge when trying to incorporate both nonprofits and governments in budgeting and financial management courses. One approach is to utilize books that are focused on governments, and then supplement with journal articles/book chapters to address nonprofits where appropriate (see my specific suggestions in the previous section). Another approach is to use books that cover both sectors. One example of this is the Finkler, Smith, and Calabrese (2020) book, *Financial Management for Public, Health, and Not-for-Profit Organizations*. This book is good for either a standalone nonprofit financial management course, or for a combined nonprofit/public sector financial management course. The text weaves examples, cases, and problems from governments, nonprofits, and health care organizations throughout the book.

For our required public and nonprofit budgeting course, I like to use two texts: one that addresses the public sector and one for nonprofits. For nonprofits, Weikart, Chen, and Sermier (2013) *Budgeting & Financial Management for Nonprofit Organizations* includes technical concepts and exercises (e.g., time-value-of-money decisions for capital budgeting, budget variance analysis, cost analysis, etc.). In addition, this book has a clear focus on the importance of the organization's mission that is related to most of the topics. It is several years old, so some of the information is out of date (for example, financial reporting standards have changed since this book was published), but the basic tools and focus are still relevant for budgeting purposes. Another option is Young's (2018) *Financing Nonprofits and Other Social Enterprises: A Benefits Approach.* This book utilizes the benefit theory (discussed earlier) to help students in understanding, analyzing, and developing revenue structures for nonprofits that relate to the benefits provided by the organizations.

In addition to books, there are many useful journal articles that can be used to supplement other course materials. I noted a number of these throughout the previous section. Two journals that often include budget and finance-related articles are: *Nonprofit and Voluntary Sector Quarterly* and *Nonprofit Management and Leadership*.

Online resources can also be valuable. Table 10.1 provides several sites that are particularly useful for faculty and students. The resources from these sites, for example, might be used for supplemental readings, or to provide trend data for lectures, or to find information related to specific nonprofit organizations that can be used in class or for assignments.

## Assignments

This section will discuss course assignments that include nonprofit finances. This generally includes three types of assignments: weekly discussions and activities, graded homework assignments, and a project. First, I try to give my students opportunities to practice using tools/concepts before they are required to use them for graded homework or projects. This is done through weekly discussions in fully online courses, and through small-group exercises in face-to-face classes. I select several nonprofit organizations each semester that post their financial statements online, and I use those as examples throughout the semester to allow students to analyze different items. Note that there is a certain amount of trial and error involved in finding financial statements. Larger nonprofits tend to include the statements on their websites (often in an "About Us" or "Governance" section). It is generally more difficult to find financial statements for smaller nonprofits on

**TABLE 10.1** Resources for teaching

| Resource | Description | Website |
|---|---|---|
| BoardSource | Provides information on best practices and other resources to strengthen nonprofit governance. | boardsource.org |
| Charity Navigator | Conducts ratings of nonprofits. | www.charitynavigator.org |
| Giving USA | Provides research on trends in charitable giving. | givingusa.org |
| Guidestar | Includes financial data for many nonprofits. | www.guidestar.org |
| Independent Sector | Is a membership organization for nonprofits, foundations, and corporate donors focused on policy that provides information on multiple topics. | independentsector.org |
| National Center for Charitable Statistics | Provides annual briefs on nonprofit finance and other trends and has data available for use by scholars. | nccs.urban.org |
| National Council of Nonprofits | Has a variety of resources and tools available for nonprofits. | www.councilofnon profits.org |

their website. Guidestar (www.guidestar.org) is a useful source for financial data, though, including financial statements for many organizations.

I often include organizations that may have some similarities in mission for interesting comparisons (e.g., Boy Scouts and Girl Scouts, YMCA and YWCA, or nonprofit zoos or museums). For example, in a week focused on revenues, students may determine where the money comes from in different organizations, and how that has changed over a period of time. In discussing expenses, they might review the Statement of Functional Expenses to see where the money goes, calculate the program ratio, and talk about how expenses align with the organization's mission. When discussing the benefit theory, students can analyze how the revenue sources align with who receives benefits from the organization. The same organizations can then be used to calculate ratios for financial statement analysis. This is particularly useful for online classes, where students can easily link to the organization website; they each focus on a different organization, or pair of organizations, and then similarities and differences become clear in the discussion.

Once the students have had the opportunity to practice using the concepts in the weekly classes, they are given graded homework assignments. In courses that include both government and nonprofit organizations, I try to balance the homework problems between the two sectors. For example, I may have two problems related to nonprofits and two for governments in one assignment. Some books, such as the Finkler, Smith, and Calabrese (2020) and Weikart, Chen, and Sermier (2013) texts, include good problems that can be used in homework assignments. I may also have them do similar analyses in the homework assignments as I do in the weekly class discussions, to ensure that they have learned the concepts. For example, I might have three sets of homework assignments in a financial management course, each worth about 20 percent of the total course grade. The first assignment might include problems that require students to develop an operating and/or cash budget, calculate break-even, and analyze and make recommendations related to make-or-buy decisions. A second assignment might include one problem from the Finkler, Smith, and Calabrese (2020) text that is a good case to analyze financial statements, and a second problem that requires students to find information and conduct analyses to compare and contrast specific items in financial statements of two similar actual organizations and then to draw conclusions and recommendations. The third homework might include problems related to capital budgeting decisions (e.g., Net Present Value or Net Present Cost exercises), budget variance analyses, preparation of aging schedules, and a case that requires students to make recommendations related to internal control policies.

All of the homework assignments are designed to determine how well the students have achieved the substantive learning objectives (knowledge of financial management practices, developing analytical skills for decision-making, and understanding the relationship of finances to organization mission, efficiency, effectiveness, and equity). My first assignment might primarily involve calculations, but the second and third include decision-making and recommendations, often in the form of memos, to test the final learning objective related to communication skills.

In my courses, I also generally have students do a project that involves a multi-year analysis of a specific organization of their choosing. This project is a major part of the course grade, typically 25–30 percent of the total, depending on whether it is an online course (in which I place more emphasis in grading on weekly discussions than I do in traditional face-to-face classes). This could be done either individually or as a group project. For courses including both government and nonprofit sectors, I allow students to use either type of organization for their project.

For a budget class, the project entails an overview of the organization, budget or actual trends in revenues and expenses, as well as sections on budget process/format, environmental factors affecting the budget, the use of performance data, and conclusions and recommendations related to the organization's budget. For a financial management class, students conduct a financial condition analysis (for more details regarding this type of project, see Chapter 8 or Maher, Ebdon, & Bartle, 2020). I usually have students do the project in stages. For example, they may be required to submit the financial data in tables/graphs first. This allows me to ensure that they have used data appropriately and make the correct calculations. When they have completed their initial analysis, they interview an appropriate leader in the organization to better understand and explain their findings, and they incorporate this information into the final paper which is written as if they were briefing a new budget, finance, or executive director and making recommendations. Students also present their findings to the class at the end of the semester.

Others on our faculty have used different approaches for class projects. For example, one budgeting class instructor has students conduct two projects: one, for governments, is similar to what I described above but a bit reduced in scope, while the other focuses on applying the benefit theory to a nonprofit organization of the student's choosing. Students usually appreciate the types of projects we use in these courses, which are an excellent way to assess how well the students have attained all of the learning objectives noted earlier in this section. We commonly receive comments, even years after they graduate, about how useful these assignments are for their careers.

## Conclusion

MPA and MPP programs have traditionally focused primarily on governments. Over time, though, we have seen the proliferation of nonprofit organizations with a concomitant interest in this area by our students, and the expansion of partnerships between government and nonprofit agencies. In addition, many of the students in our programs will likely serve on nonprofit boards throughout their career, even if their paid employment is not in this sector. For these reasons, many programs now cover, to varying degrees, topics related to nonprofit organizations in their curricula.

This chapter provides ideas and guidance for instructors who want to include nonprofit organizations when teaching budgeting and financial management courses. While there is significant overlap between government and nonprofits in these areas, there are also substantial differences. I have described specific topics where there are variations, to help in deciding where to incorporate nonprofits in courses that include both sectors. In addition, I have provided a number of possible resources for use in these courses, as well as suggestions for assignments. Students can then develop competencies in nonprofit financial management in conjunction with those related to government.

## References

Archambeault, D. S., & Webber, S. (2018). Fraud survival in nonprofit organizations: Empirical evidence. *Nonprofit Management and Leadership, 29*(1), 29–46.

Calabrese, T. D. (2013). Running on empty: The operating reserves of U.S. nonprofit organizations. *Nonprofit Management and Leadership, 23*(3), 281–302.

Calabrese, T. D. (2018). Do operating reserves stabilize spending by nonprofit organizations? *Nonprofit Management and Leadership, 28*(3), 295–311.

Calabrese, T. D., & Ely, T. L. (2017). Understanding and measuring endowment in public charities. *Nonprofit and Voluntary Sector Quarterly, 46*(4), 859–873.

Dropkin, M., Halpin, J., & La Touche, B. (2007). *The budget-building book for nonprofits.* Jossey-Bass.

Eikenberry, A. M., & Kluver, J. D. (2004). The marketization of the nonprofit sector: Civil society at risk? *Public Administration Review, 64*(2), 132–140.

Finkler, S. A., Smith, D. L., & Calabrese, T. D. (2020). *Financial management for public, health, and not-for-profit organizations* (6th ed.). CQ Press.

Garven, S. A., Hofmann, M. A., & McSwain, D. N. (2016). Playing the numbers game: Program ratio management in nonprofit organizations. *Nonprofit Management and Leadership, 26*(4), 401–416.

Hooke, J., Yook, K., & Chu, W. (2019). Top foundations' 10-year plunge into alternatives yields mixed results and high fees. *Nonprofit Management and Leadership, 29*(3), 449–460.

Hung, C., & Hager, M. A. (2019). The impact of revenue diversification on nonprofit financial health: A meta-analysis. *Nonprofit and Voluntary Sector Quarterly, 48*(1), 5–27.

Independent Sector. (October). Health of the U.S. nonprofit sector. Retrieved from https://independentsector.org/wp-content/uploads/2020/10/sector-health-report-101220.pdf

Kim, M., & Mason, D. P. (2020). Are you ready: Financial management, operating reserves, and the immediate impact of COVID-19 on nonprofits. *Nonprofit and Voluntary Sector Quarterly, 49*(6), 1191–1209.

LeClair, M. S. (2019). Malfeasance in the charitable sector: Determinants of "soft" corruption at nonprofit organizations. *Public Integrity, 21*(1), 54–68.

Lecy, J. D., & Searing, E. A. (2015). Anatomy of the nonprofit starvation cycle: An analysis of falling overhead ratios in the nonprofit sector. *Nonprofit and Voluntary Sector Quarterly, 44*(3), 539–563.

Lu, J. (2016). The philanthropic consequence of government grants to nonprofit organizations. *Nonprofit Management and Leadership, 26*(4), 381–400.

Lu, J., Shon, J., & Zhang, P. (2020). Understanding the dissolution of nonprofit organizations: A financial management perspective. *Nonprofit and Voluntary Sector Quarterly, 49*(1), 29–52.

Maher, C. S., Ebdon, C., & Bartle, J. R. (2020). Financial condition analysis: A key tool in the MPA curriculum. *Journal of Public Affairs Education, 26*(1), 4–10.

Maier, F., Meyer, M., & Steinbereithner, M. (2016). Nonprofit organizations becoming business-like: A systematic review. *Nonprofit and Voluntary Sector Quarterly, 45*(1), 64–86.

National Center for Charitable Statistics. (2020). The nonprofit sector in brief 2019. Retrieved from https://nccs.urban.org/publication/nonprofit-sector-brief-2019

National Council of Nonprofits (2021). Board roles and responsibilities. Retrieved from www.councilofnonprofits.org/tools-resources/board-roles-and-responsibilities

Network of Schools of Public Policy, Affairs, and Administration. (2020). Career resources employment facts. Retrieved from www.naspaa.org/resources/career-resources

Prentice, C. R. (2016a). Why so many measures of nonprofit financial performance? Analyzing and improving the use of financial measures in nonprofit research. *Nonprofit and Voluntary Sector Quarterly, 45*(4), 715–740.

Prentice, C. R. (2016b). Understanding nonprofit financial health: Exploring the effects of organizational and environmental variables. *Nonprofit and Voluntary Sector Quarterly, 45*(5), 888–909.

Searing, E. A. (2018). Determinants of the recovery of financially distressed nonprofits. *Nonprofit Management and Leadership, 28*(3), 313–328.

Weikart, L. A., Chen, G. G., & Sermier, E. (2013). *Budgeting & financial management for non-profit organizations.* CQ Press.

Young, D. R. (2018). *Financing nonprofits and other social enterprises: A benefits approach.* Edward Elgar Publishing.

# 11

# INCORPORATING SOCIAL EQUITY

*Bruce D. McDonald III and Sean McCandless*

Budgeting decisions have been described as the quintessential administrative decision (Bland & Overton, 2019). These decisions signify which public priorities matter because what gets funded gets done (Kettl, 2020; Mikesell, 2018). Still, despite the growing prevalence of social equity in public administration (Gooden, 2015a), budgeting remains under-examined in the context of social equity (Gooden, 2015b) despite budgeting's importance in considerations of what, where, why, and how to offer some sort of public service (or not) (Gerton & Mitchell, 2019; Glaeser, Resseger, & Tobio, 2015; McCandless & Guy, 2020). For instance, Gooden (2015b) examined the prevalence of articles focused on social equity in *Public Administration Review* and found that fewer than 5 percent of articles up to that time explicitly focused on equity. Of this small amount, only eight articles expressly focused on equity in budgeting and finance.

Despite the under-development in the academic literature of explicit connections between budgeting and social equity, there is growing recognition that social equity is important to budgeting decisions (Ali & Pirog, 2019; Cardenas & Ramirez, 2017; Jensen, Mortensen, & Serritzlew, 2019; Kavanagh & Kowalski, 2021). For one, it is becoming more common to see governments at all levels discussing how best to foster social equity, and the role budgeting plays in those processes (see City of Seattle, 2019). For another, academic programs in public administration and public affairs are increasingly expected to ensure that students are exposed to and competent in topics related to diversity, equity, and inclusion (DEI) (Berry-James et al., 2020; Stivers, 2019). Given these two dimensions, the field must be aware of and competent in the equity implications of equity and budgeting. As today's students are today's and tomorrow's administrators, it is incumbent on the field to ensure that anyone working in public service is competent in social equity (Gooden & Blessett, 2020).

DOI: 10.4324/9781003240440-11

While research on incorporating social equity perspectives into the budgeting process may be minimal, there has been a growing recognition that social equity must be incorporated into public budgeting and finance courses. The need to include social equity into the courses has been a topic of panels and presentations at several recent conferences, including the 2020 conference of the Network of Schools of Public Policy, Affairs, and Administration. Just as little research has been conducted exploring the relationship between public budgeting and social equity, too little has been explored on how to incorporate social equity perspectives into a public budgeting and finance course.

This chapter aims to help fill the void of teaching social equity by providing guidance on incorporating and effectively teaching social equity perspectives in a Master of Public Administration (MPA) course on public budgeting or financial management. To accomplish this goal, this chapter will first review the concept of social equity in public administration to provide a foundational understanding faculty can utilize in the classroom. The chapter then discusses the place of social equity in the budgeting process, followed by offering suggestions on how to incorporate a social equity perspective into budgeting and finance courses, including student learning outcomes. It concludes with a brief discussion of sample assignments that can promote the learning of public budgeting while incorporating the perspective into the learning process.

## Social Equity in Public Administration

To understand how social equity can best be incorporated into a public budgeting and finance course, it is helpful for faculty to understand what social equity is and what role it plays within public administration. Public administration is built upon four normative pillars, namely that public services should be created and delivered efficiently, effectively, economically, and equitably (Davis, Moldavanova, & Stazyk, 2020; Thomas, 2019). That is, public services should: be created and delivered through using resources as well as possible (efficiency); achieve the goals set out by policymakers (effectiveness); cost the right amount (economy); and be fair for all (social equity) (Johnson & Svara, 2015a, 2015b).

Social equity is most commonly and easily defined as fairness, due process, and justice (Guy & McCandless, 2012). The most widely used definition of social equity in public administration was created by the National Academy of Public Administration (NAPA):

> The fair, just and equitable management of all institutions serving the public directly or by contract, and the fair and equitable distribution of public services, and implementation of public policy, and the commitment to promote fairness, justice, and equity in the formation of public policy.
>
> *Johnson & Svara, 2015a, p. 19*

The logic behind including social equity as the fourth pillar of public administration is the recognition that the question of "Is a public service efficient, effective, and economical" misses an essential dimension of fairness if one does not also ask, "Efficient, effective, and economical for whom?" (Frederickson, 2010). Social equity is needed as a pillar because, historically, government institutions, in particular, have created, maintained, and exacerbated inequities based upon race, color, ethnicity, gender, gender identity, sexual orientation, class, and much more, as well as the many intersections between these. And as all of these institutions are funded through public money, questions of fairness in the budgeting process are essential (Mackey & McCandless, 2020).

Social equity consists of four primary dimensions: access, processes, quality, and outcomes. In other words, for public services to be socially equitable, they must be accessible, produced fairly, be of equal quality for all, and promote long-term benefits for all. *Access* refers to the reachability and obtainability of public services. Access (in)equities manifest in many ways, such as inaccessibility to buildings, technology, public transportation, education, to decision-makers themselves, and much more (Larson, 2020). *Processes* (or *procedural fairness*) refers to how fairly public services are produced and administered. Policing is a classic example of process (in)equities in that black persons, indigenous persons, and persons of color are stopped, searched, arrested, and killed in higher proportions by police than are white persons, thus raising questions about the fairness of policing processes (Headley, 2020). *Quality* refers to the condition, caliber, and degree of excellence of a public service. Common examples of concerns over quality inequities include questions about water quality, transportation, infrastructure, and even customer service interactions with government officials (Fenley, 2020). Finally, *outcomes* refer to the long-term consequences of administration and policy. Classic examples include how many historically marginalized groups experience inequities regarding access, processes, and quality with respect to a host of public programs— education, health care, job opportunities, and more—and, thus, experience fewer opportunities to benefit from these programs and, at times, may experience harm due to these programs (Johnson & Svara, 2015a, 2015b).

To better understand these four dimensions of social equity (which are critical for all public administrators to consider due to the reality that governments across the world, and the U.S. government, in particular, are responsible for creating, maintaining, and exacerbating systems of disadvantage and prejudice), it is essential to consider five broad questions (Gooden, 2015a). The questions begin by asking about the foundations of (un)fairness in U.S. public administration through to how public services can be made fairer for all.

First, any public administrator must understand the values upon which the U.S. system is based. The U.S. Constitution starts with the famous words: "We the People." Yet, what is the context of "We" (Gooden, 2015a)? To answer this question, one must look to what is enshrined and protected as political values regarding fairness. The Bill of Rights, for instance, enshrines many so-called *negative freedoms*, "negative" in that they limit what government can do. For instance, there are principles of the First Amendment (freedom of religion, speech, press, assembly, and petition of government for a redress of grievances), or the Fourth Amendment (prohibitions on unreasonable searches and seizures), or the Fifth (due process), and several others (McCandless & Guy, 2020).

Second, the question of the context of "We the People" leads to the question of how definitions of "We" have expanded, namely who was among "We the People" when the Constitution was drafted and ratified between 1787 and 1789 (Gooden, 2015a). At the founding of the U.S., only property-owning white men enjoyed full political rights. The definition of "We" has expanded rapidly since that time, most notably through amendments to the U.S. Constitution. For instance, the so-called Civil War Amendments—the 13th, 14th, and 15th passed in the aftermath of the U.S. Civil War—ushered in the first major expansions of political rights for historically marginalized populations. The 13th Amendment abolished slavery except as a punishment for crimes. The 14th Amendment applied the Bill of Rights to the states and provided for due process and equal protection of the laws at sub-national levels. The 15th Amendment expanded enfranchisement to all men. Later in 1920, the 19th Amendment expanded enfranchisement to women, although some sub-national governments had already extended suffrage long before. In the later 20th century, the 24th Amendment eliminated poll taxes, and the 26th Amendment expanded enfranchisement to citizens aged 18 and over. These expansions of enfranchisement and rights also come in tandem with expansions in legal protections, such as Title VII in the Civil Rights Act of 1964 that provided for the first-time explicit protections in employment against discrimination based upon race, color, sex, and more (Mackey & McCandless, 2020).

Third, despite all of these advancements, inequities continue to persist, meaning public administrators should always ask, "what is the extent of inequity?" (Gooden, 2015a). Inequities refer to disparities in access, processes, quality, and outcomes for historically marginalized groups. The list of areas in which inequities are evident are too extensive to document in this chapter, but they have been documented in nearly every domain in which public administration operates (Johnson & Svara, 2015b).

Fourth, if one is to understand the extent of inequities fully, one must also understand why inequities persist (Gooden, 2015a). This is a growing area of social equity research, but the evidence is rapidly growing that inequities persist due to multiple reasons and at multiple levels—individual, organizational, and systemic. *Individual administrators* could be prejudiced against particular historically marginalized populations and may not serve them in ways that are accessible, procedurally fair, of equal quality to other groups, and that promote long-term positives. *Organizational dynamics* within public agencies could lead to inequities. For instance, public service organizations often operate within and under principles of *de jure* (legal) discrimination (e.g., administrative policies and rules discriminate or that have organizational structures and dynamics that make it difficult for persons from historically marginalized populations to experience fairness) and *de facto* discrimination (e.g., administrative hostility toward social equity; poor demographic representation within the agency; HR policies that do not explicitly discriminate but that make it difficult for persons from historically marginalized groups to be recruited, hired, promoted, and supported within agencies). Additionally, inequities can be caused because of *systemic dynamics*, that is, discriminatory laws, societal prejudice, and entrenched power structures that make it difficult for persons from historically marginalized groups to express and exercise their voice (Gaynor, 2018; Gooden, 2014; Headley, 2020; McCandless, 2018; McCandless & Ronquillo, 2020; Wooldridge & Gooden, 2009).

Finally, these questions lead to the culminating question of social equity in public administration: How accountability for social equity is achieved (Gooden, 2015b). Gooden (2014) provides a useful tripartite framework for what accountability for social equity consists of. First, inequities must be *named*, or administrators must admit that inequities exist. Second, inequities must be *blamed*, or administrators must understand who and/or what is responsible for the inequity and to identify clearly how the inequity came about and what effects it has. Finally, inequities must be *claimed*, or administrators must take responsibility and engage in active steps to ameliorate inequities and foster fairness for all. Johnson and Svara (2015a; 2015b) provided numerous strategies to foster active steps. Similar to Gooden (2014), they assert that achieving accountability for social equity begins with agencies admitting the inequities that they create. This can be a contentious and difficult process because, historically, many agencies have been reluctant to accept such inequities (McCandless, 2018). However, from there, agencies must do several things, including making fairness a priority, measuring how fair they are and their progress at becoming fairer; reaching out to historically marginalized groups; and giving everyone a place at the table (Johnson & Svara, 2015b).

## Social Equity in Budgeting

The incorporation of social equity into public budgeting and finance may seem unusual at first. Afterall, the traditional perspective of the budget and finance role of a local government administrator follows the strict politics-administration dichotomy (Lee, Johnson, & Joyce, 2021). The staff is there to advise on the financials of the government, but the final decision of the budget and other policies is the responsibility of the elected officials. Within this perspective, the incorporation of a social equity perspective by the budgeting staff would involve moving their role from traditional advisor to policy advocate. While the politics-administration dichotomy is a useful heuristic for understanding the division of roles between the public administrator and the elected official, van Dorp and 't Hart (2019) remind us that the division is not quite so clean-cut in practice. Instead, administrators are often called upon by their employing governments to advise on any number of policy issues (see Ebinger, Veit, & Fromm, 2019; Lee & Park, 2020).

The incorporation of a social equity perspective can be traced to the New York Bureau of Municipal Research (henceforth referred to as the Bureau). The establishment of the Bureau in 1907, and indeed the advent of the MPA in the United States, was done on the premise of efficient citizenship (Stivers, 2000), or the idea that informed citizenship encourages administrators to act ethically and efficiently (Dahlberg, 1966). The Bureau believed that local governments, and elected officials in particular, were not representing the interests of all residents, with women, minorities, and immigrants often receiving little to no public services. Utilizing scientific management-based research and media campaigns, the Bureau believed that a government would be able to provide equal services to all residents and do so as cost-effectively as possible. The success of this approach, rooted in public budgeting, led to the spread of MPA programs around the country and the designing of budget processes for New York City, the state of New York, and the federal government (Dahlberg, 1966; Stivers, 2000). In essence, the Bureau's development of modern public budgeting places the roots of budgeting onto a social equity foundation.[1]

As the Bureau model expanded out of New York City, so did the establishment of budgeting as a central part of many administrators' duties. For instance, in the 1930s, Gulick (1937) famously described the major administrative functions as POSDCORB, or Planning, Organizing, Staffing, Directing, Coordinating, Reporting, and Budgeting. While a distinct pillar of social equity did not exist in Gulick's time, fairness issues, whether acknowledged or unacknowledged, are woven throughout all elements of POSDCORB (Frederickson, 2010).

Perhaps most centrally, budgeting decisions reflect priorities (Kettl, 2020). Since public administration has marginalized populations for centuries, the budgeting process goes hand in hand. While the Bureau played a pivotal role in developing public administration and public budgeting, the role that social equity plays in the process has been largely forgotten in recent decades. As a result, far fewer public resources have been spent improving access, processes, quality, and outcomes for historically marginalized groups. In many cases, public resources have funded policies outright against marginalized citizens' interests and well-being (Gooden, 2014). It is rare to see budgets explicitly focused on equity, but incorporating equity into budgeting decisions can impact when integrating equity perspectives in allocation decisions (Fabian, 2020). Some of these principles have been used in countries like Australia, the Philippines, and South Africa concerning recognizing *gender* inequities. Yet, few budgetary processes acknowledge the need to broadly factor in social equity principles (Bartle & Rubin, 2020).

Given the abandonment of social equity in the budgeting process, it is necessary to reintroduce social equity in budgeting terms. The previous section of this chapter defined social equity as fairness, due process, and justice (see Guy & McCandless, 2012). In budgetary terms, we understand this to be equal treatment

**FIGURE 11.1** The budget cycle

and consideration of how a budget or the financials of a policy or program affect all residents who live within the government's confines. It is also understood to include allocating resources to address community needs that have previously been unfunded or underfunded to return the impacted residents to an equal ground with the rest of the community.

It is helpful to think about the definition of social equity in budgeting terms and its incorporation into public budgeting and financial management by looking at the budget cycle. While every government develops a budgeting cycle that fits its own needs, the standard cycle follows four steps: executive preparation, legislative consideration, execution, and audit and evaluation. The progress of the budget throughout the cycle is represented by Figure 11.1. The majority of action by a public administrator to influence the budget and its outcomes comes in the first two stages. In the executive preparation stage, government departments and agencies can consider their needs and propose budgets and budget requests for consideration. And in the legislative consideration stage, the legislative body (i.e., city council or county commission) considers the budget requests they have received and listens to public feedback before voting on the final budget.

In these first two stages, the involvement of public administrators, and budget and finance staff, in particular, have the greatest opportunity to incorporate a social equity perspective. For example, in the executive preparation stage, budget and finance staff can ask agencies to consider the impact of their requests on all members of the community. What this looks like in practice may vary from one government to the next. The City of Seattle is an excellent example of a best practice in this area. The city effecting incorporates social equity into the budgeting process by requiring all budget requests reflect on which communities the request impacts and how the request can be made more fair (see City of Seattle, 2019).

The second stage of the budgeting process also provides an opportunity to incorporate the social equity perspective intentionally. A dominant aspect of legislative consideration is public hearings regarding budget proposals. While hearings are useful at gaining feedback from the community, they can also be used to encourage or discourage involvement by members of the community. This is particularly important as the hearing process is generally biased. The public that engages in the process is typically not representative of the whole population (Peeters, Goften, & Mexa, 2020). When the meetings are held, where they are held, and if child care will be provided for attendees all shape individuals' ability to attend. They can also be used to encourage or discourage the involvement of certain groups of residents in the budgeting process.

Adopting policies and engaging in practices that encourage broader involvement in the process suggests that the result will be a more equitable outcome.

Once social equity perspectives are incorporated into the executive preparation and legislative stages, the execution stage allows the government to carry out its programs and services. Ideally, if social equity is actively imposed on the first two stages, the execution should follow accordingly. Regardless, as the budget enters into audit and evaluation, budget and finance staff have the opportunity to review the equitableness of the budgeting process and how effective that process was in improving conditions within the community.

Many historically marginalized groups tend to be weary of public involvement due to the treatment they have received and thus are not likely to engage in the budgeting process independently (see Gilad & Dahan, 2020). Honest outreach efforts and community engagement can reduce the barrier that exists, but rebuilding a relationship with the communities can be slow. When involvement in budget hearings by disenfranchised communities does not occur, it becomes more critical for budget staff to address community imbalances in the budget during the executive stage. As a result, incorporating a social equity perspective into the budgeting process requires providing the opportunity for all to engage in the budget process, but intentional advising on the budget for equitable decision-making when engagement does not happen.

## Teaching Social Equity in Budgeting: Suggested Learning Outcomes

There are at least three takeaways from the discussion above. First, public administrators, including budgetary officers, are culpable in creating, maintaining, and expanding inequities. Second, everyone working in public administration has a responsibility to address these inequities and foster fairness for all. Third, given how fundamental budgeting is to public administration, budgeting courses must examine the equity dimensions.

Thus, we propose that budgeting courses can successfully incorporate social equity, specifically by classes being oriented around five learning outcomes (see Table 11.1). These learning outcomes are inspired by Gooden's (2014) *name, blame,* and *claim* framework: Budgeting students should be able to understand what equity is and *which* inequities occur (name); why inequities occur and

**TABLE 11.1** Suggested learning outcomes

At the end of this course, students should be able to:
• Define what equity is and how it is implicated in the budgetary process
• Articulate the roles governments have played in fostering inequities
• Align policy goals with budgetary changes
• Conduct social equity impact analyses on budgets
• Design budgetary policies and procedures to promote equity

public administration's culpability (blame); and how to remedy inequities (claim). These outcomes are meant to ensure that students understand the broad array of budgeting's social equity dimensions, from the basics of how equity is implicated in the budgetary process to design budgetary policies and procedures to promote equity.

We discuss more specific strategies to achieve these outcomes in the next section, but first, more context on the rationale of why a social equity perspective should be included in budgeting classes is needed. The most fundamental reason to incorporate social equity into budgeting courses is that social equity is a pillar of the field (and should be incorporated throughout the curriculum). All administrators, including and especially budgetary officers, need to be accountable for social equity. They have roles to play to ensure fairness is achieved for all (Gooden, 2015a).

Achieving accountability for social equity begins with agencies admitting the inequities that they have created (Gooden, 2014; Johnson & Svara, 2015b). This is a difficult task in which many competing interests within agencies are likely evident. Many policymakers and administrators may be reluctant to admit issues. Many may deny that inequities exist or at least assert that the agency does not cause them. Still, others may deny that the inequities are dire enough to warrant action (Mackey & McCandless, 2020; McCandless, 2018).

The approach to admitting issues taken by some city governments, including Seattle, can often go far beyond agency dynamics themselves. For one, political leaders are essential to any public agency establishing social equity goals. Political leaders set many of the priorities for agencies, and their desires to address social equity in and through public institutions are critical for any effort to foster social equity. For another, administrators themselves must "buy-in" to social equity as both a desirable and attainable goal for agencies. Not all persons working in public service agencies see social equity as either a desirable and/or attainable goal, making it important for agency leaders to establish organizational dynamics and work cultures that make the importance of social equity cornerstones of practice. As yet another consideration, community members and stakeholders help determine governments' priorities. When individual community members, community groups, and businesses demand social equity, it is more likely for governments to make social equity a priority (Mackey & McCandless, 2020).

Yet, achieving accountability for social equity requires steps beyond admitting issues. Policymakers and administrators must also center social equity in agencies through defining what is meant by equity, making considerations of fairness a priority, adopting strategies to better understand the causes and effects of inequities, measuring success, and reaching out to and incorporating historically marginalized communities throughout policy and administrative decisions (Gooden, 2014; Johnson & Svara, 2015b).

In terms of budgeting, this multi-part process often consists of conducting equity analyses, especially on differential impacts of budget requests regarding racial equity. Thus, in the next section, we discuss strategies instructors could use to achieve the outcomes listed in Table 11.1 and, in turn, help budgeting classes better prepare the next generation of administrators to bring equity lenses into everything they do, especially budgeting.

## Assignment Possibilities

At this point, we admit that many students may still picture equity principles as outside of the budgeting process. Like other aspects of public administration, some administrators may even see themselves operating under the politics-administration dichotomy, that is, that elected leaders establish the policies and administrators find ways of carrying them out. Some administrators, including budgetary officers, may see fostering awareness of and action on social equity as impinging on elected officials' work and outside the scope of their work. Thus, returning to Table 11.1, achieving the outcomes requires multiple strategies, such as wide-ranging discussions of equity in budgeting and "hands in the dough" classroom time, that is, the specific incorporation of and training in social equity impact analyses.

This section reviews assignment areas to incorporate and teach social equity lenses in the budgeting processes. The primary suggestions are summarized in Table 11.2, and, as seen therein, we broadly break down these pedagogical suggestions into two major categories: Assignments meant to help students understand social equity in the budgeting process and those meant to help students practice techniques to prioritize fairness. Throughout, we rely on the example of Seattle's Race and Social Justice Initiative (RSJI), "a citywide effort to end institutionalized racism and race-based disparities in City government" (Seattle Race and Social Justice Initiative, 2020), especially the racial equity toolkits and other sources developed as part of the RSJI (Seattle Race and Social Justice Initiative, 2012, 2015, 2019a, 2019b) as well as Nelson's and Brooks (2016) extended discussion of the RSJI toolkits.

### *Readings and Class Discussions*

As a reminder, in Table 11.1, we proposed that the first two suggested learning outcomes for incorporating social equity into a budgeting course are: a) defining

**TABLE 11.2** Pedagogical strategies to incorporate social equity into budgeting classes

| Topic | Potential Discussion Questions | Assignment Ideas |
|---|---|---|
| **Understanding Social Equity in the Budgeting Process** | 1. In what ways do budgets reflect public values and priorities?<br><br>2. In what ways have considerations of equity historically been factored into or not-factored into budgetary decisions?<br><br>3. Do budgetary officers have a social equity role, and if so, what are they? If not, whose responsibility is it to consider social equity in budgeting decisions? | Choose a local government and ask students to:<br><br>1. Identify at least one prevalent inequity in the community.<br><br>2. Determine the role of government in creating, maintaining, and exacerbating those inequities.<br><br>3. Discuss the degree to which the inequities were contingent on budgeting priorities. |
| **Prioritizing Fairness** | 1. Do research on your own local government, especially government websites. See if you can find information on how social equity is a priority of this government. Based upon what you find, to what extent is social equity a consideration for your local government? Why do you think that is?<br><br>2. What is an example of a specific funding decision that led to a social inequity or an improvement in social equity? How did this funding decision come about? | Choose a local government and ask students to conduct a racial equity impact analysis (see Nelson & Brooks, 2016). Students should:<br><br>1. Set outcomes.<br><br>2. Discuss how to involve stakeholders and analyze data.<br><br>3. Determine benefit and/or burden.<br><br>4. Advance opportunity or minimize harm.<br><br>5. Evaluate. Raise racial awareness. Be accountable.<br><br>6. Report back. |

what equity is and how it is implicated in the budgetary process; and b) articulating what roles governments have played in fostering inequities. We see these outcomes achieved largely through readings and course discussions that center social equity in the course.

Specifically, as shown in Table 11.2, in terms of teaching, centering equity in the budgeting classroom begins with a simple step—getting students to think of these issues in terms of the budgetary process. For instance, discussion questions could center on having students explore the degree to which budgets reflect public values and priorities, how considerations of equity are factored into budgeting decisions, and the social equity roles played by budgeting officers. Discussion around these questions could help elucidate how budgeting decisions are not simply value neutral, technical decisions but are the result of community-wide discourses on what does or does not matter to a community (Fischer, 2003). Further, as classroom replication of administrative work is essential to learning, a classroom exercise could consist of prompting students to examine a local community, perhaps their own. Students would study the inequity in that community, the role of government vis-à-vis that inequity, and also how budgeting decisions factored into creating, maintaining, and/or exacerbating that inequity.

While many working in budgeting will assert that budgeting officers act to carry out the will of elected officials (and this is mostly true), such discussion questions and assignments can situate budgeting within the large public service environment. In this environment, decisions are not neutral, and government actions can harm. Government harm is made possible because budgeting decisions allow both action and inaction on fostering equity or fostering inequity. Budgeting, as the quintessential administrative decision, is always implicated in social equity.

There are several ways in which social equity can be incorporated into the budgeting classroom. For instance, discussion questions could include asking students to discuss their local government and the extent to which social equity is or is not a consideration or to explore a specific funding decision that did, or did not, lead to a social inequality.

Further, budgeting instructors should ground coverage of social equity in budgeting in the broader public administration literature and how governments across the United States have defined equity. Thus, examining specific cities' equity approaches is a best practice to examine equity lenses, especially concerning budgeting, in action. One such case study is the City of Tacoma, Washington. In Tacoma, equity (fairness) is also associated with accessibility: "All residents are treated equitably and have access to services, facilities and financial stability" (City of Tacoma, 2020a). The City of Tacoma established numerous goals to help make their definition of equity realizable, including fostering representative bureaucracy, engaging in community outreach, providing equitable service delivery, supporting human rights and opportunities for people to achieve their full potential, and a general commitment to equity in policymaking (City of Tacoma, 2020b). Even further, the city has developed an equity index—"an interactive tool that highlights disparities within the city"—that establishes several key indicators, including dimensions like "[improving] access and proximity by residents to diverse income levels and race/ethnicity to community facilities, services, infrastructure, and employment," increasing digital access and equity, ensuring diverse representation at public meetings, increasing the number of households with livable wages, and more (City of Tacoma, 2020c).

By exploring how equity-minded cities like Tacoma center equity, students can explore tools about cities' disparities, linking present-day inequities to longstanding policies. Further, by understanding what is required for an equity lens to become policy—students can explore the budgeting dimensions of successful attempts to foster equity. For instance, Fabian (2020) notes how when "[a]pplying an equity lens, one of the most surprising realizations is that each and every program offered has an opportunity to be transformed, reimagined, and evolved to increase equity" and cites the City of Denver's approach to snow removal and how it enhanced services in neighborhoods previously identified in social equity impact analyses.

Other resources usable in classroom discussions are also available, which instructors could easily provide for students and review in class. For instance, the Government Alliance on Race and Equity [GARE] (2021) contains numerous tools and resources to implementing equity principles throughout government. Many of the resources articulate specific ways in which budgetary processes can and should be involved in promoting equity. As but one example, Nelson et al. (2015) provided a GARE resource guide to advance racial equity in government. This resource contextualizes the purpose and role of an equity lens in government and helps situate the need for social equity across government programs. Finally, as the chapter was being prepared for publication, Kavanagh and Kowalski (2021) published an article in *Government Finance Review* on social equity in budgeting from the perspective of the Government Finance Officers Association. This article takes a practitioner perspective and be useful reading for students to understand how budget staff have been working to improve equity.

### *Social Equity Impact Analyses: Racial Equity Toolkits*

Returning to Table 11.1, the next three learning outcomes for incorporating social equity into budgeting courses are: (1) aligning policy goals with budgetary changes; (2) conducting social equity impact analyses on budgets; and (3) designing budgetary policies and procedures to promote equity. As seen in Table 11.2, we see these outcomes largely fulfilled through budgeting classes incorporating social equity impact analyses, ideally centered on racial equity. These types of analyses are meant to understand how public priorities are shaped and how the creation and implementation of public services do, or do not, factor in social equity and the potential impacts on social equity programs could have.

Seattle's RSJI again provides a guideline for how to conduct this process. Seattle's city government required all agencies, including the budget office, to use a racial equity toolkit, of which a racial equity analysis was the central feature (see Seattle Race and Social Justice Initiative, 2015). This consists of a multi-part process (Seattle Race and Social Justice Initiative, 2012, 2019a). While instructors could find this toolkit directly through the RSJI, we recommend using the GARE resource provided by Nelson and Brooks (2016), who provide extensive details on each step of such analyses. We review the essential dimensions below.

First, outcomes must be established in that leaders communicate desired community outcomes for racial equity. In brief, this step requires that any government decision, including budgetary, must be clearly described with ideal end conditions as a result of the decision specified. As presented by Nelson and Brooks (2016), this step more specifically consists of administrators: (1) describing the policy, program, practice, or budget decision under consideration; (2) discussing and understanding the intended results in the community and outcomes in the organization; and (3) articulating who and what the proposal will impact, such as children and youth, criminal justice, education, the environment, workforce equity, and so forth (Nelson and Brooks 2016, p. 7). In the classroom, an instructor could accomplish this by choosing a specific example of a budgetary decision and ask students to discuss the three major elements above as if the proposal were just placed before them.

Second, administrators must involve stakeholders (i.e., gather information from community members and staff members on how a particular issue provides benefits for or burdens on the community) and analyze data (i.e., particularly to see if racial inequities are historically evident). More specifically, this step entails administrators, including budgetary officers, understanding the status quo better regarding inequities and how the status quo came about. Administrators must have access to demographic data, community indicators, performance measures, and also information on how communities have been factored in and consulted in previous policy and administrative discussions. When examining a proposal, administrators should be able to answer questions on whether the proposal will impact specific areas, which further necessitates having data on the racial demographics of those in that area. From there, administrators need to analyze existing data to examine the racial inequities and what might be the causes of those inequities. Further, any proposal should ideally come with performance-level data on programs and policies. Finally, administrators must determine if further data are needed. Relatedly, communities impacted by any policy or administrative decision should be engaged throughout the process—from the proposal and formulation of a policy through to evaluation. Administrators must identify communities impacted by a policy and reach out to and engage with those communities for feedback in proposals. While students will not be able to replicate these steps perfectly in the classroom, instructors can, after providing the budgetary proposal mentioned in the previous paragraph to students, do the following: (1) provide students with applicable demographic and community data and ask students to analyze data for existing racial inequities, or instructors could provide such analyses to students themselves; (2) assess the state and quality of performance-level data and any gaps; and (3) research how populations were incorporated into a decision or, at the very least, how they *should* be incorporated (Nelson & Brooks, 2016). As part of this third element, students could be prompted to review the City of Seattle's (2009) guidance on inclusive outreach and engagement, including its six community engagement strategies (pp. 8–9).

Third and fourth, administrators must: (1) determine benefits and/or burdens; and (2) advance opportunity or minimize harm. These steps consist of analyzing an issue to determine impacts on racial equity. At a minimum, this requires asking how a given policy, initiative, program, or budget issue will increase or decrease racial equity, whether through unintended consequences, benefits, and alignment with agency and community outcomes. This also consists of asking counterfactuals like asking what potential, unintended consequences may be, how proposals can be modified to promote equity, identifying new strategies needed to promote equity, partnering with communities, and aligning impacts with community outcomes. Relatedly, administrators must develop strategies to create further racial equity as well as minimizing harm from unintended consequences. This step requires addressing strategies' immediate and long-term impacts and ensuring that agencies partner with stakeholders to foster longitudinal and positive change. If policies and priorities need to be realigned, agencies should do so (Nelson & Brooks, 2016).

From a classroom perspective, this can be done by having students review the budget of a local government in the area and discuss how different projects and activities that are reported in the budget might improve social equity within the community or exasperate the issue. If the government broadcasts the budget sessions, then a recording of the sessions could be used to discuss the social equity effects of budget proposals that are brought up for discussion. As the access to transportation and quality infrastructure is often pointed to as an area where inequality exists (see Larson, 2020), a capital improvement plan can also be used. In this variation of the assignment, students would discuss the equitableness of both the projects on the community as a whole and the prioritization of the projects by the government.

Finally, administrators must evaluate, raise racial awareness, be accountable, and report back. This consists of tracking impacts, communicating with and involving stakeholders, and also documenting unresolved issues. This requires administrators to develop an implementation and evaluation plan that includes a timeline for addressing inequities, maintaining outreach, and establishing new partnerships. In the end, administrators must report back. This consists of sharing information learned from analyses as well as communicating unresolved issues. Ways to share analyses and report responses to make the findings as accessible as possible to showcase progress are essential (Nelson & Brooks, 2016). Students can be exposed to and gain experience with this in several ways. One such was the example assignment from the paragraph above on having students review and consider whether budget proposals are equitable. To give students the opportunity to experience raising racial awareness and being accountable, students should be encouraged to discuss ways that the inequity can be addressed when issues of inequity are found. This would include the development of an implementation plan and a timeline for addressing the issues, as well as a plan for evaluating their success at improving equitable outcomes. Furthermore, they can also discuss how the budget staff of the government can encourage (or at least contribute) to the improvement of equity in decision-making and government action.

## Modifying Classic Assignments

Finally, the suggested learning outcomes identified in Table 11.1 can be achieved through modifying existing, classic budgeting assignments. Simply, it is possible to add a social equity component to many of the existing assignments and projects utilized in public budgeting and finance courses.

Two common assignments are a fiscal review and assessment, which requires students to explore the budgetary and financial processes of a city or county, and a financial condition analysis, which requires students to determine the fiscal health of a government (see Maher, Ebdon, & Bartle, 2020; Mikesell, 2018). For both assignments, incorporating the perspective is fairly straightforward. For example, in a fiscal review and assessment, students are exploring the structure and nature of the budget and financial management processes of a public organization. As students research the organization of focus, they can also analyze whether any social equity concerns emerge. Particular questions that they could ask include:

- What social equity concerns emerge as a result of the organization's budget structure?
- What communities are being left out or over-represented?
- How can the organization's financial system be improved to better capture the community's needs and viewpoints as a whole?
- How can the organization's financial system be improved to better serve underrepresented constituents?

For a financial condition analysis, such as that designed by Maher, Ebdon, and Bartle (2020), students can be asked to consider how the financial condition of the local government being studied has influenced its ability to provide fair services. And, if equitable services are not being delivered, how the government can adjust its provision within the confines of its fiscal health.

While both of the assignments above incorporate a social equity viewpoint into existing assignments, a final assignment to possibly implement would be an applied project that requires students to understand and improve a local government's budget process. While improving the process, students would give particular attention to how social equity can be incorporated into the budget cycle and budget outcomes. Many local governments want to ensure their budget processes are equitable, but many also struggle with where to start and how to achieve the goal. This would allow for the project to be conducted as a service learning project (see Chapter 12 for a discussion on incorporating service learning into public budgeting and finance courses) or as a stand-alone exercise that draws on information from local governments in the area. In either case, students can explore the government's budgetary structure and processes throughout the semester as they are discussed in class. Either working alongside the government in the case of the service learning project or through independent research, students would consider the budget process being utilized, its efficiency and effectiveness, and then provide recommendations on how it can be improved to more fairly reflect the entire community. What those recommendations look like would vary significantly from one community to the next, but they would also provide useful guidance on achieving equity in budgeting in a way that also reflects the unique nature of the community. Support for this approach, both in terms of a classroom assignment and a solution for local governments, comes from the success of local governments who have adjusted their processes to incorporate equity. A number of local governments have been successful, but what the new process looks like varies from one location to the next as the nature of the communities and their needs likewise vary.

## Centering Social Equity in the Budgeting Classroom

While social equity has historically not been considered in the public budgetary processes, it is difficult to imagine an area of public administration education in which an understanding of equity is needed more. A growing body of evidence is emerging that for social equity to be achieved, public agencies must operate under visions and missions of eliminating inequities, especially racial inequities, in communities (Berry-James et al., 2020). In the case of programs like Seattle's RSJI, among others, such a vision must extend to all levels—individual, institutional, and structural—to eliminate inequities. Further, as it is becoming more common for city governments to require equity lenses in all budgeting decisions (see City of Tacoma, 2020a), MPA programs must ensure that all students are competent in understanding how equity is interwoven throughout all administrative processes. This includes understanding how budgeting is an incomparable tool to foster fairness for all.

Incorporating social equity in budgeting courses brings greater subtlety to budgeting concepts, and incorporating an equity lens is achievable and rewarding. Through the incorporation of five learning outcomes (Table 11.1) and assignments like racial equity impact analyses, the public administration budgeting classroom can be an unparalleled place for the budgetary officers of tomorrow to learn essential skills. As budgeting is the quintessential administrative decision, social equity will not be achieved without budgetary dimensions. And, as all administrators must be accountable for social equity in their communities, there is no better time than the present.

## Note

1 For more on the Bureau, their pursuit of social equity, and their role in budgeting, see Dahlberg (1966), McDonald (2010), and Stivers (2000).

# References

Ali, M. U., & Pirog, M. (2019). Social accountability and institutional change: The case of citizen oversight of police. *Public Administration Review, 79*(3), 311–426.

Bartle, J. R., & Rubin, M. M. (2020, September 28). *Gender equity in budgeting.* Retrieved from: https://gfrc.uic.edu/gender-equity-in-budgeting/

Berry-James, R. M., Blessett, B., Emas, R. McCandless, S., Nickels, A. E., Norman-Major, K., & Vinzant, P. (2020). Stepping up to the plate: Making social equity a priority in public administration's troubled times. *Journal of Public Affairs Education.* https://doi.org/10.1080/15236803.2020.1820289

Bland, R. L., & Overton, M. R. (2019). *A budgeting guide for local government.* ICMA.

Cardenas, S., & Ramirez de la Cruz, E. E. (2017). Controlling administrative discretion promotes social equity? Evidence from a natural experiment. *Public Administration Review, 77*(1), 80–89.

City of Seattle. (2009). *Inclusive outreach and public engagement guide.* Retrieved from: www.seattle.gov/Documents/Departments/Neighborhoods/PPatch/Inclusive-Outreach-and-Public-Engagement-Guide.pdf

City of Seattle. (2019). *Race and social justice initiative (RSJI).* Retrieved from: www.seattle.gov/rsji

City of Tacoma. (2020a). *Equity and empowerment framework.* Retrieved from: www.cityofta coma.org/government/city_departments/equity_and_human_rights/equity_and_empowerment_framework

City of Tacoma. (2020b). *Tacoma's strategic plan.* Retrieved from: www.cityoftacoma.org/tacoma_2025

City of Tacoma. (2020c). *Equity index.* Retrieved from: www.cityoftacoma.org/government/city_departments/equity_and_human_rights/equity_index

Dahlberg, J. S. (1966). *The New York Bureau of Municipal Research, pioneer in government administration.* New York University Press.

Davis, R. S., Moldavanova, A. V., & Stazyk, E. C. (2020). A tribute to H. George Frederickson—One of public administration's modern-day founding fathers. *Journal of Public Affairs Education, 26*(3), 256–263.

Ebinger, F., Veit, S., & Fromm, N. (2019). The partisan-professional dichotomy revisited: Politicization and decision-making of senior civil servants. *Public Administration, 97*(4), 861–876.

Fabian, C. (2020, September 14). *Budgeting with an equity lens.* Retrieved from: https://gfrc.uic.edu/budgeting-with-an-equity-lens/

Fay, D. L., Fryer, A. H., Meier, K. J., & Wilkins, V. (2020). Intersectionality and equity: Dynamic bureaucratic representation in higher education. *Public Administration.* https://doi.org/10.1111/padm.12691

Fenley, V. M. (2020). Layers of inequity: The challenge of homelessness. In M. E. Guy & S. A. McCandless (Eds.), *Achieving social equity: From problems to solutions* (pp. 67–81). Melvin & Leigh.

Fischer, F. (2003). *Reframing public policy: Discursive politics and deliberative practices.* Oxford University Press.

Frederickson, H. G. (2010). *Social equity and public administration: Origins, developments, and applications.* Routledge.

Gaynor, T. S. (2018). Social construction and the criminalization of identity: State-sanctioned oppression and an unethical administration. *Public Integrity, 20*(4), 358–369.

Gerton, T., & Mitchell, J. P. (2019). Grand challenges in public administration: Implications for public service education, training, and research. *Journal of Public Affairs Education*, *25*(4), 435–440.

Gilad, S., & Dahan, M. (2020). Representative bureaucracy and impartial policing. *Public Administration*. https://doi.org/10.1111/padm.12681

Glaeser, E. L., Resseger, M., & Tobio, K. (2015). Urban inequality. In N. J. Johnson & J. H. Svara (Eds.), *Justice for all: Promoting social equity in public administration* (pp. 76–99). Routledge.

Gooden, S. T. (2014). *Race and social equity: A nervous area of government.* Routledge.

Gooden, S. T. (2015a). From equality to social equity. In M. E. Guy & M. M. Rubin (Eds.), *Public administration evolving: From foundations to the future* (pp. 210–231). Routledge.

Gooden, S. T. (2015b). PAR's social equity footprint. *Public Administration Review*, *75*(3), 371–381.

Gooden, S. T., & Blessett, B. (2020). Cultural competency and social equity in public affairs programs. In B. D. McDonald & W. Hatcher (Eds.), *The public affairs faculty manual: A guide to the effective management of public affairs programs* (pp. 223–238). Routledge.

Government Alliance on Race & Equity. (2021). *Tools and resources.* Retrieved from: www.racialequityalliance.org/tools-resources/

Gulick, L. (1937). Notes on the theory or organization. In L. Gulick & L. Urwick (Eds.), *Papers on the science of administration* (pp. 3–13). Institute of Public Administration.

Guy, M. E., & McCandless, S. A. (2012). Social equity: Its legacy, its promise. *Public Administration Review*, *72*(s1), s5–s13.

Guy, M. E., & McCandless, S. A. (2020). In pursuit of social equity. In M. E. Guy & S. A. McCandless (Eds.), *Achieving social equity: From problems to solutions* (pp. 172–181). Melvin & Leigh.

Headley, A. M. (2020). Race, ethnicity, and social equity in policing. In M. E. Guy & S. A. McCandless (Eds.), *Achieving social equity: From problems to solutions* (pp. 82–97). Melvin & Leigh.

Jensen, J. L., Mortensen, P. B., & Serritzlew, S. (2019). A comparative distributional method for public administration illustrated using public budget data. *Journal of Public Administration Research & Theory*, *29*(3), 460–473.

Johnson, N. J., & Svara, J. H. (2015a). Social equity in American society and public administration. In N. J. Johnson & J. H. Svara (Eds.), *Justice for all: Promoting social equity in public administration* (pp. 3–25). Routledge.

Johnson, N. J., & Svara, J. H. (2015b). Toward a more perfect union: Moving forward with social equity. In N. J. Johnson & J. H. Svara (Eds.), *Justice for all: Promoting social equity in public administration* (pp. 265–290). Routledge.

Kavanagh, S., & Kowalski, J. (2021). The basics of equity in budgeting. *Government Finance Review*, *37*(1), 18–27.

Kettl, D. F. (2020). *Politics of the administrative process.* Sage Publishing.

Larson, S. J. (2020). How transit matters for social equity. In M. E. Guy & S. A. McCandless (eds.), *Achieving social equity: From problems to solutions* (pp. 98–111). Melvin & Leigh.

Lee, R. D., Johnson, R. W., & Joyce, P. G. (2021). *Public budgeting systems.* Jones & Bartlett Learning.

Lee, D. S., & Park, S. (2020). Bureaucratic responsiveness in times of political crisis: The case of presidential impeachment. *Public Administration*. https://doi.org/10.1111/padm.12701

Mackey, J., & McCandless, S. A. (2020). Social equity in public administration: A primer. In D. R. Slagle & A. M. Williams (Eds.), *Public affairs practicum* (pp. 157–188). Birkdale Publishers.

Maher, C. S., Ebdon, C., & Bartle, J. R. (2020). Financial condition analysis: A key tool in the MPA curriculum. *Journal of Public Affairs Education, 26*(1), 4–10.

McCandless, S. A. (2018). Improving community relations: How police strategies to improve accountability for social equity affect citizen perceptions. *Public Integrity, 20*(4), 370–385.

McCandless, S. A., & Guy, M. E. (2020). The social equity imperative. In M. E. Guy & S. A. McCandless (eds.), *Achieving social equity: From problems to solutions* (pp. 1–11). Melvin & Leigh.

McCandless, S. A., & Ronquillo, J. C. (2020). Social equity in professional codes of ethics. *Public Integrity, 22*(5), 470–484.

McDonald, B. D. (2010). The Bureau of Municipal Research and the development of a professional public service. *Administration & Society, 42*(7), 815–835.

Mikesell, J. L. (2018). *Fiscal administration: Analysis and applications for the public sector.* Cengage Learning.

Nelson, J., & Brooks, L. (2016). *Racial equity toolkit: An opportunity to operationalize equity.* Retrieved from: www.racialequityalliance.org/wp-content/uploads/2015/10/GARE-Racial_Equity_Toolkit.pdf

Nelson, J., Spokane, L., Ross, L., & Deng, N. (2015). *Advancing racial equity and transforming government: A resource guide to put ideas into action.* Retrieved from: https://racialequityalliance.org/wp-content/uploads/2015/02/GARE-Resource_Guide.pdf

Peeters, R., Goften, A., & Meza, O. (2020). Gaming the system: Responses to dissatisfaction with public services beyond exit and voice. *Public Administration.* https://doi.org/10.1111/padm.12680

Seattle Race and Social Justice Initiative. (2012). *Racial equity toolkit.* Retrieved from: www.seattle.gov/Documents/Departments/RSJI/RacialEquityToolkit_FINAL_August2012.pdf

Seattle Race and Social Justice Initiative. (2015). *Race & social justice initiative: Vision and Strategy 2015–2017.* Retrieved from: www.seattle.gov/Documents/Departments/RSJI/rsji-2015-2017-plan.pdf

Seattle Race and Social Justice Initiative. (2019a). *Condensed racial equity toolkit.* Retrieved from: www.seattle.gov/Documents/Departments/RSJI/Condensed%20Racial%20Equity%20Toolkit.pdf

Seattle Race and Social Justice Initiative. (2019b). *Race and social justice initiative: 2019–2021 strategy.* Retrieved from: www.seattle.gov/Documents/Departments/RSJI/18-21_RSJI_Strategic_Plan_4.6.19_FINAL.pdf

Seattle Race and Social Justice Initiative. (2020). *Race and social justice initiative (RSJI).* Retrieved from: www.seattle.gov/rsji

Starke, A., & Heckler, N. (2020). At the intersection of identities. In M. E. Guy & S. A. McCandless (Eds.), *Achieving social equity: From problems to solutions* (pp. 53–64). Melvin & Leigh.

Stivers, C. (2000). *Bureau men, settlement women: Constructing public administration in the progressive era.* University Press of Kansas.

Stivers, C. (2019). Forging new tools for new administrative houses: Comments on the symposium. *Journal of Public Affairs Education, 25*(2), 142–144.

Thomas, N. (2019). In the service of social equity: Leveraging the experiences of African American women professors. *Journal of Public Affairs Education, 25*(2), 185–206.

Van Dorp, E., & 't Hart, P. (2019). Navigating the dichotomy: The top public servant's craft. *Public Administration, 97*(4), 877–891.

Wooldridge, B., & Gooden, S. (2009). The epic of social equity: Evolution, essence, and emergence. *Administrative Theory & Praxis, 31*(2), 222–234.

Zeemering, E. (2020). Student public service value priorities. *Journal of Public Affairs Education, 26*(3), 358–379.

# 12

# CASE STUDIES AND SERVICE LEARNING IN PUBLIC BUDGETING AND FINANCE

*Meagan M. Jordan and Bruce D. McDonald III*

The majority of chapters in this book are focused on substantive content and how to best communicate that material in the classroom. To aid in that relay, the substantive chapters of this book provided some guidance on assignments that could be used in the classroom or as homework. This chapter intends to carry those discussions forward by introducing two core pedagogical tools and discussing how they can be used in the classroom to both relay the material, to prepare students to engage the material in a real and meaningful way, and to maximize learning outcomes.

The purpose of experiential learning techniques is to connect students to real-world problems and challenges so that they may gain experience applying course knowledge and skills (Svinicki & McKeachie, 2014). This chapter is focused on the use of two forms of experiential learning, case studies and service learning projects, in a public budgeting or financial management course. Case studies are stories that are developed to be used in the classroom to show the application of a theory or concept to a real-life situation (Hatcher, McDonald, & Brainard, 2018). They provide an opportunity for students to observe scenarios similar to what they can expect to encounter in their careers and compare their solutions to the solution taken by the public administrator in the case. Service learning, on the other hand, is a type of experiential learning where students provide a service to the community as a way for them to connect with the material by completing a project on behalf of a community client (Lebovits & Bharath, 2019). In the classroom, both case studies and service learning projects provide the opportunity to connect with the material on the highest levels of level, enhancing student learning outcomes (see Goodman, 2020).

Faculty members that have decided to use a case study or service learning project in a public budgeting and finance course are faced with the challenge of how

DOI: 10.4324/9781003240440-12

to do so successfully. For the unexperienced, finding case studies and implementing them into the course curriculum can be difficult and working with a community partner for a service learning project can be daunting. In this chapter, we aim to assist faculty members new to these pedagogical tools by providing guidance on how to implement the tools. To do so, this chapter discusses in more detail what case studies and service learning projects are and how they contribute to the learning process. We provide guidance on how to find a good case or project and discuss how they can be implemented in a class. Included in this discussion are the challenges that you may face when implementing the tools and how to overcome them. Finally, we provide examples of cases and projects that we have used in our own classes, including our notes on how we used the tools successfully.

## Using Case Studies

A case study is a story, whether fictional or based on real events, that relays a moral or principle (Hatcher, McDonald, & Brainard, 2018). The purpose of an effective case study is to place the student in the position to apply concepts and theories through a simulated scenario. Incorporating a case study approach to teaching public budgeting and financial management reminds the students of the public administration context of budgets and financial documents. Students will often understand a concept as explained in a textbook but not recognize the opportunity to apply the same concept in a real-life situation. Svinicki and McKeachie (2014) refer to this failure to transfer the book knowledge to practice as "situated learning." The case study provides the opportunity to practice such application, and to ensure relevance, the case must allow students to demonstrate their attainment of the learning objective. In addressing the given scenario, students have the opportunity to practice various skills like problem identification, decision-making, problem solving, and/or planning. The presentation of the solution also provides students with the opportunity to sharpen the critical skill of professional communication (Rivenbark, 2007). A post-case summary allows the instructor to emphasize how the case addressed the learning objectives and reading materials. The case studies serve the role of deepening comprehension via application. Therefore, case selection is critical.

### Case Selection

The quality and suitability of a case studies varies greatly. One that is "on topic" may not be of acceptable quality for the course. Hatcher, McDonald, & Brainard (2018) discuss the characteristics of writing a quality case study; however, these characteristics are also important for choosing a case study. An important criterion for selecting a case study is choosing a case that addresses at least one of the learning objectives. Particularly important with public finance case studies is the analytical component where students must synthesize and analyze financial data in order to make managerial decisions (Rivenbark, 2007). The case study is the opportunity for the student to demonstrate the ability to synthesize the information provided through instruction and the reading materials and apply that information to a specific scenario. The case study provides the opportunity to practice such application, and to ensure relevance, the case must allow students to demonstrate their attainment of the learning objective (Hatcher, McDonald, & Brainard, 2018).

Even while addressing the learning objective, cases may serve various roles in a course. Determining that role is a necessary step in case selection. The case may serve as a quick exercise during class time, a more in-depth discussion requiring pre-class preparation, or a more comprehensive case suitable as a major homework assignment. In fact, one case may serve all of these roles by varying complexity or the assumptions of the case scenario. The length of the case may seem like an obvious factor in determining the case's role in the class; however, more relevant is the breadth of the case in covering the learning objectives. For instance, a case that addresses a learning objective regarding budget preparation may also address budget reform, budget format, citizen participation in budgeting, and cutback budgeting. Ideally, students will experience an array of cases that call upon multiple managerial skills.

In addition to developing individual decision-making skills, case studies are useful for developing group decision-making skills. Cases that have multiple decision-making opportunities are most suitable for group decision-making. The requirement of producing one deliverable that represents the collective decision process is critical for developing those group skills. The instructor may even reconstitute the groups throughout the term to push students to adapt to different group dynamics. It is also appropriate to have a combination of individual cases and group cases within the course.

Other criteria for consideration involve case jurisdictional focus, like nonprofit, local government, state government, or federal government. Some cases may require an interaction of more than one jurisdiction. The decision is often influenced by the focus and careers of the academic programs; however, a variety is helpful for increasing breadth of knowledge. Selection criteria addresses "what"; however, the where to find the cases is a necessary determination. The easiest is a casebook; however, public budgeting and financial management casebooks are not common. There are general public administration casebooks that may not cover budget and finance. Cases within the required textbook for the course is another convenient option; but not available in every textbook.

Finally, there is creation of a case study. Committing to a case study approach to teaching budget and finance is sometimes easier said than done. What if you do not find a case that addresses the learning objectives for the module? Rivenbark (2007), in his review of his case study experiences in public financial management courses, emphasized the importance of creating or modifying cases to address public financial decision-making or the synthesis of public financial data.

Creating public finance cases has the benefits of relevance and timeliness. The surrounding jurisdictions (city, county, state) can turn into a case study, and the instructor has the flexibility of updating the financial data over time. Two great sources for creating cases are public financial data and the media, especially local news. There are often news stories about budget cuts, revenue policy changes, or financing a huge capital project. The financial data are found in annual financial reports and budget documents that are available on government websites. Some nonprofit financial data are available via Guidestar and other 990 tax form databases.

## Incorporating Case Studies into Public Budgeting and Financial Management Class

Regardless of the origins of the case, a successful case study contributes to the understanding of the course material and the attainment of the learning objectives. Instructors must identify the purpose of a case or its contribution to the course. A purpose statement as part of written instructions is helpful without revealing too much. Essentially, the purpose statement puts the case in context given the module's learning objectives.

Most courses using the case study approach tend to execute in one of two ways: discuss and emphasize key elements from the reading with lecture, notes, or discussion followed by case studies that apply the concepts; or go straight into a case analysis and emphasize reading materials as discuss the case solution. Both approaches require that students read the assigned materials in advance, the latter even more so than the former.

Asynchronous online case discussions may take multiple approaches. Creating small groups for discussion facilitates participation from each person. The ideal size may vary, but a size of 4–6 group members may promote sharing of the workload. One way to ensure each student participates in case analysis is to require each person in the group to write up an individual analysis and to require each student to provide feedback to group members. This allows each student to see different approaches to the case and make suggestions to each other. Another approach with group case discussions is to require the group to produce a single work product, like a policy memo. To reduce free-rider tendencies, a group evaluation or assessment where each member has to indicate the contribution of each specific group member, including a self-assessment.

With in-class or synchronously online case discussions, time management is critical. The case discussion(s) may occur after a lecture or in lieu of a lecture. After the lecture, case discussions serve to emphasize and apply what was discussed. This approach can be executed more than once in the same class—lecture and case followed by lecture and case. In lieu of a separate lecture, the instructor may use the entire class time as a series of case analyses or one large case analysis. The instructor may require students to demonstrate their knowledge of the assigned readings, and/

or instructor may choose to interject key points from the assigned readings. The case will either need to be short enough to read and analyze during class times or assigned as part of the reading before class. As with asynchronous classes group discussions are beneficial. With complex cases, some groups may be assigned to develop and execute certain positions. However, some cases are also conducive for open class discussion where the instructor asks individuals to report their solutions.

While many case studies are designed for use in a single class, a comprehensive case can be used over multiple class sessions (Rivenbark, 2007). Table 12.1 provides a demonstration of what a multi-class structure looks like. This format is easily adaptable for case size and class setting. For instance, for online instruction, the case introduction may take place on the syllabus as part of the case instructions or the assignment section of the online platform; then, the lecture notes and question and answer opportunities are used to provide the lecture and technical support. Finally, the case discussion may occur as an individual submission within group discussion board, individual submission as a homework assignment, or group submission on discussion board or homework assignment. Adaptation for in classroom or synchronous online classes may include using the second half or third of the class time to have students orally present their solutions individually or as a group after allowing time for deliberation.

The oral reporting of case analysis may create an environment of open disagreement. Ultimately, the instructor's role is to maintain the emphasis on the learning objectives with a recognition that the case may incorporate learning objectives addressed earlier in the course.

However, case parameters are not set in stone. At the instructor's discretion, it is appropriate and realistic to add challenges to the case discussions, that is, "what if" scenarios. "What if" scenarios are the perfect opportunity to bring in current events. For example, explain the change in your recommendation if the city's bond rating is lowered, the state enacts tax and expenditure limitations, or a disaster hits, causing a decline in tourism.

**TABLE 12.1**  Case cycle for a course

| Class | Activity | Purpose |
| --- | --- | --- |
| Class 1 | Introduce case | Present the critical problem faced by the public official and the objectives of the case. |
| Class 2 | Lecture and technical support | Lecture on financial management skills and related case topics and provide ongoing technical support. |
| Class 3 | Lecture and technical support | Lecture on financial management skills and related case topics and provide ongoing technical support. |
| Class 4 | Discuss case | Discuss how students analyzed the problem, including their recommendations for a solution. |

Source: Rivenbark (2007)

But what about the math? Students need reminders of the relationship between the math and the decision or alternatives presented. This reminder is particularly important for math phobic students. It is critical to start the discussion with everyone on the same page; therefore, it is usually necessary to ensure that everyone understands any and all calculated solutions. It is often necessary to include math-based exercises during the class or step-by-step examples online before the case study discussion is due. If it is possible for students to have different answers based on assumptions, then those assumptions must be reported as part of the discussion as well. The ability to discuss calculated solutions in terms of policy and decision-making is a critical skill used by public finance practitioners in communication with various stakeholders (i.e., department managers, legislative bodies, citizen). Varying presentation requirements broaden professional communication skills. Table 12.2 illustrates the various approaches to the presentation of a case study analysis and the appropriate course environment along with the accrued communication skills. For instance, an informal presentation of case analysis during a live class requires contemporaneous and persuasive demonstration of analytical decision-making.

One approach to elevating the realism and experience of a case study discussion is to bring in practitioners. For live classroom or synchronous online classes, practitioners are invited to the class for the discussion of an assigned case. Students have the opportunity to present their solutions to the practitioner and benefit from feedback. Asynchronous online courses may also incorporate practitioner input by having an online discussion of the case between instructor and practitioner recorded and posted on the platform. An example of incorporating practitioner input is with Stone's (1957) well-known "Seven Letters" case. This case illustrates the interactions between a city's department and central budget office over the course of seven letters. Because of the length and intricacies of the

**TABLE 12.2** Types of case study presentations

| Presentation Type | Course Environment | Communication Skills |
|---|---|---|
| Informal oral presentation | In class or synchronously online; quick deliberation | Contemporaneously speaking, persuasive speaking |
| Formal oral presentation | In class, synchronously and asynchronously online; deliberation in advance | PowerPoint presentation, persuasive speaking |
| Professional memo | In class, synchronously and asynchronously online; deliberation in advance | Concise professional writing |
| Professional report with executive summary | In class, synchronously and asynchronously online; deliberation in advance | Concise executive summary, visual aids (tables and/or figures), professional and technical writing |

case, students should receive the case in advance and prepare their answers to the questions provided and/or additional questions from the instructor. Having also read the case in advance, the invited local government budget analyst or budget director attends the case study section of class and observes the student presentation. Subsequently, the budget professional provides feedback as well as relating the case to his or her own experience.

## Overcoming Challenges of Case Study Discussions

Incorporating case studies may present challenges involving the students or the case content. As an experiential learning tool, it is critical that each student participates. Within any given discussion, there are often monopolizers and coasters. For whatever reason, monopolizers are the students that often dominate the discussion. Case instructions may include multiple criteria or questions. The instructor could require that the workload is divided. For grading group analyses, it is important to follow up with a group evaluation that requires the identification and assessment of each group member's role.

Coasters (or nonparticipants) often just need time to get in a word before the monopolizer. Cases that are provided in advance and require a written response by class time allow the coaster the opportunity to think through the solution in advance and participate in class, especially if called upon. Even during in-class individual case studies, having the students write their answers during class but before discussion allows the instructor to broaden the participation (Svinicki & McKeachie, 2014). Bottom line, the instructor sets the expectations of student conduct and participation in the case discussion. These expectations should be reinforced on the syllabus.

The content of the case may also present challenges. Sometimes the intricacies of a case may distract from the purpose. This may be particularly true for public budgeting and finance cases. If the case requires mathematical computation, it is easy to focus on producing the correct numerical answer. However, the number is merely a part of the answer. So, not only do students need sufficient time or space to calculate the answer, they must have time and space allotted to discussing (orally or in writing) the implications or decision-making regarding the calculation. For instance, a case that requires a revenue analysis is not sufficient without a memo or some discussion that explains the significance of the revenue analysis.

Another distraction created with case content is when there is extraneous or provocative information. Problem identification and problem solving require wading through an abundance of, and often superfluous, information. When there's a possible "controversial" or unpopular alternative, students may offer the infamous "devil's advocate" solution or suggest that all opinions or past work experiences are equally suitable solutions. While multiple solutions are common, especially regarding managerial decision-making, the optimal solutions are usually aligned with good managerial practices supported by public administration values, purpose, and goals of the authors of the assigned reading, and by the learning objectives. For instance, if students determine that an efficient way of reducing a department's budget is to terminate all senior staff by forcing retirement and early retirement on all employees over the age of 50, the instructor can discuss a possible legal ramification for age discrimination and the inefficiency of losing vast institutional knowledge, and then redirect the discussion back to problem solving within legal, ethical, and good managerial boundaries.

Resistance to solving or addressing the issues of a case may result in various avoidance techniques, such as changing the scenario, claiming a need for more information or too much information. A common attempt at changing the scenario is to change the timeline – that is, going back in time to prevent the problem. While discussing how the problem may have been avoided is an important exercise, most cases require a reactive and proactive rather than a retroactive viewpoint. In other words, address the problem now and in the future with changes in policy, programs, and/or personnel. And while students may desire more information to enhance realism, it is best to address that desire with the post analysis—"what if" discussion rather than over complicate the case study. As with all challenges to case discussion, emphasis on the learning objectives is key to a successful case discussion.

## Examples of Teaching Through Case Studies

The case study approach is a common method of instruction in public administration. This section provides two case studies along with suggestions for engaging student involvement while emphasizing learning objectives. As previously stated, the cases may have multiple acceptable solutions. Although the availability of ready-made case studies may be limited, public financial data is not; therefore, one of the cases illustrated below addresses using available government information.

### City Pool Funding Case

Scenario: You work as the Financial Director for the City of Wette. The City is constructing a swimming pool at the cost of $500,000. The board decided to finance the costs over a ten-year period and annual debt service will be $60,000 a year. Annual operating costs for the pool will be $100,000 (note: the current year's debt service is always a part of the operating cost). Although the city has 10,000 residents, it is anticipated that only 2,000 residents will use the pool regularly at an average of 20 visits a year per person. About 70 percent of all users (1400) are expected to be kids. About 20 percent of the adults and kids will qualify as low-income, and their ability to use the pool may depend on the fee charged. Your city is within ten miles of two other cities that have similar swimming pools. Their daily fees for visitors outside the city are $5.00 and $7.00. Their daily fees for their citizens are $1.50 and $2.00, respectively.

Teaching Note: The starting point for incorporating this case is to consider where it belongs in the course. This case fits nicely after or with readings that cover local government revenue sources and their characteristics, especially the user fees and charges. Second, students need to know the point-of-view from which to approach the case with a clearly stated role. If a ready-made case does not make this clear, the instructor can establish the student's point-of-view and role. The students must have a perspective from which to make their decisions. The learning objective for the module is that students understand and explain the characteristics of revenue characteristics and apply those characteristics to revenue policy decisions. The student's role is as Finance Director presenting alternatives to the City Manager and City Council. In the context of this role, students should:

- Provide multiple alternatives for the fee structure: fully covered by user fees, partially covered by user fees, fully covered by general fund revenue.
  - Each alternative must be presented with or without low-income consideration.
  - Each alternative must be presented with or without adult and children rates.
- Address the administration, equity, and economic effect of each presented rate structure.
- Make final recommendation for the daily rate and explain with justification for the decision.

After having covered in the course notes/lecture/readings "standards" of revenue policy (sometimes referred to as principles or characteristics of tax policy), students should be able to demonstrate their comprehension during this case analysis. This works as an individual homework assignment as well as an in-class or online group assignment.

## Citizen Budget Participation Case

Scenario: There have been complaints from several community activists that the city council regularly favors the affluent areas of the city for capital improvement projects and other maintenance issues (i.e., streets, parks, signage). Although some maintenance, like road repaving, is evenly distributed across each ward in the city, this even dollar distribution across the wards results in greater neglect in poorer wards. The wards that house much of the city's low-income and racial minorities have much older roads and other infrastructure. Most of the council members are offended by the accusation of bias and state that they listen to all citizens who voice their concerns at the council meetings. In addition, budget staff are leery about putting in the extra effort because of previous low citizen turnout to council meetings, and department heads are concerned about encouraging citizen demand that they cannot not meet.

As the new Budget Director, you recognize that city's website and budget document explain the budget process, however, neither the website or the budget document include a discussion of the citizen's role. As such, the citizen's role has been limited to showing up for the monthly city council meetings on the second Tuesday of the month at 5:30 pm when the council is addressing the budget for the next fiscal year. You are asked by the Finance Director to create a citizen participation program and policy that allow residents to bring up new infrastructure concerns and voice their views of the city's plans for future projects. In fact, you are instructed to create a comprehensive citizen participation policy that includes citizen review or input into all steps of the budget process—from budget creation to council consideration, implementation, and evaluation.

Teaching Note: This case clearly needs to be placed after the presentation of the material on the phases of the budget. The student's point-of-view here is the Budget Director. The learning objectives include understanding the phases of the budget processes and understanding the importance of transparency and citizen participation.

With this case, students can research the answer for the budget director using readings and other financial documentation available on government websites. While the previous Pool Funding case is presentable as a lengthy class exercise, this case is best provided to students in advance so that they may research city websites for methods of citizen engagement in budgeting. Most cities with websites have a budget section where they provide the ability to download the budget. If available, the budget section also provides additional information for citizens to use to familiarize themselves or participate in the budget process. This varies greatly by cities. Therefore, it is ideal for the instructor to point the students in the direction of at least one city with the information, while requiring the students to review five or ten cities. Deliverables may include both the summary of each city researched as well as the new citizen participation policy. The new policy must address: phases of the budget process, ward equity issues, and accessibility concerns. If assigned as a group project, then the groups could be required to research two additional cities per person to ensure that everyone has responsibilities (ideally, the group consists of three to five students). Again, this may also work as an individual homework assignment with each student required to research at least four other cities.

## Using Service Learning Projects

Service learning is a form of experiential education that involves the connection of students with community partners in order to carry out a project that addresses the partner's needs (Jacoby, 1996; Lebovits & Bharath, 2019). Service learning combines formal education with an internship or practitioner style of experience so that students can fully engage the course material while also developing the ability to apply the skills to a real-world situation. Often, service learning projects are proposed as a way to build civic engagement (Reinke, 2003), but they also promise to improve skills such as critical thinking, integrating theory and practice, and communication (Barth & Hamel, 2020; Jacoby, 1996; Reinke, 2003). In practice, service learning experiences are carefully chosen projects that provide a much needed service to a government agency or nonprofit organization that is overseen by course faculty and is conducted by students (Bacot, 2020). By moving assignments out of the classroom and into the field, service learning projects provide the opportunity to demonstrate mastery of learning objectives in a way that enhances both student growth and community need.

The projects intend to help students learn the course material, but they also teach the students how to use the material to solve real-life problems, such as what they will face in their own careers (Li, McDougle, & Gupta, 2020). This broader utility of service learning projects in the learning process highlights a key advantage of their use: service learning forces students to engage the material on a higher level of learning than what they would typically face in the classroom. In the designing of a course and its assignments, how students will engage and utilize the learned material should always be the primary concern (Goodman, 2020). One way to understand this is Bloom's "Taxonomy of Learning." According to the taxonomy, there are six different levels of learning by which students can gain knowledge (Armstrong, 2016). At the lowest level, students gain knowledge based on their ability to remember a set of information. As a student is taught material in the classroom, assignments are used to help elevate the level of learning. For example, a student may be able to define the budget process at the lowest level, but an assignment can be used that requires the student to explain the budget process to new city council members. As the student moves from defining to explaining, their level of knowledge increases. An overview of the taxonomy and its levels is provided in Figure 12.1.

## Bloom's taxonomy

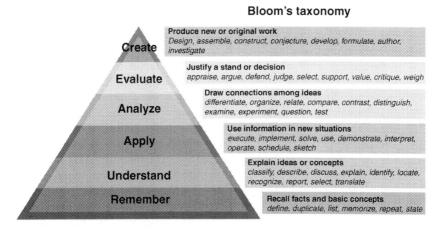

**FIGURE 12.1** Bloom's taxonomy of learning

Source: Armstrong (2016)

The benefit of service learning projects is that they require learning across all six levels. As students begin to work on the project, they will need to remember and understand basic principles of the course material, but they will also be forced apply the principles to the circumstance surrounding the project and analyze the situation or relevant data. Furthermore, they also must evaluate the project in order to fully understand the project and its issue. Up to this point, a financial condition analysis, such as that recommended by Maher, Ebdon, and Bartle (2020), covers the same levels of learning, as a financial condition analysis requires the analysis of data and the evaluation of the organizations position. A well-defined service learning project, however, takes one more step by requiring the students to create a solution that resolves the issue at hand. Ultimately, this suggests that a project may be the ideal assignment for a graduate class focused on application, such as a public budgeting or financial management course within a MPA program.

The use of service learning in MPA programs has a rich history. The establishment of the New York Bureau of Municipal Research's Training School centered around teaching students to be public administrators by doing work in the field (see Jin, 2020; McDonald, 2010; McDonald, Hatcher, & Abbott, 2021; Raadschelders et al., 2019). Dewey (1916) even advocated for a method of learning similar to service learning that connected practice experience with education (see also Barth & Hamel, 2020; Lebovits & Bharath, 2019). A number of programs in the field have even adopted service learning for their capstone courses as a way to evaluate student achievement and the meeting of NASPAA competencies (Berry-James et al., 2020; Lambright, 2008; Waldner & Hunter, 2008). Despite the benefit of service learning to the classroom, relatively few faculty, however, are using service learning projects to connect their individual classes with the community (Hatcher & McDonald, 2020).

## Incorporating Service Learning into Public Budgeting and Finance Classes

The value added that the projects provide particularly for public budgeting and finance courses cannot be understated. Not only to the projects provide the opportunity to engage the material at a higher level of learning, as previously discussed, but it also provides a direct connection between students and the organizations that might seek to employ them. Given the financial difficulty local governments have experienced in recent years (Flink & Molina, 2020; Liston-Heyes & Juillet, 2020), projects coming from public budgeting and finance courses have the possibility of making a real difference for the community, thereby solidifying the role of the MPA program in the community and helping to advance new student recruitment.

Once the decision to incorporate a service learning project into a public budgeting and finance course has been made, two key questions emerge: what makes a good service learning project and how do you find a suitable project? On the question of what makes a good service learning project, there are a few issues to consider. These are: appropriateness, feasibility, schedule, and organizational commitment. No matter how interested a faculty member is in adding a service component to a public budgeting and financial course, choosing a project for projects sake will do little to improve student learning outcomes. Rather, the focus of the project and the tasks associated with the project must align with the course being taught. This requirement may mean that early planning for a project needs to be done, but it also means that in some semesters, a project is not incorporated. In our experience, it may take at least a semester to line up the first project, though as the utility from engaging in a project is observed by the community, eager participants are likely to emerge on their own, reducing your lead time.

The feasibility of a project relates to whether the students will be able to satisfactorily complete the project. If the project is outside of the capacity of the students, then the project it setting the students up to fail. This may frustrate students, but it may also frustrate participating organizations and discourage others from participating. To balance out the possibility of failure, the role of the instructor of a course is to oversee the project and ensure its completion. If students are unable to complete the project for any reason, the faculty member should be prepared to step in to complete any missing details. Without such assurance, finding organizations to participate may be tricky, if not impossible. Of course, the need for the faculty member to step in should be avoided if at all possible, which makes finding a feasible project all the more important. What is feasible, however, is highly dependent on the students of the course and ultimately comes down to the faculty member of the course utilizing the project to judge.

Service learning projects need to be something that challenges the students, but they must also be doable within the allocated time, highlighting the importance of scheduling for project success. The semester-based orientation of most MPA programs establishes the general schedule of a project, but this must also work for the organization. Although scheduling may be a challenge for many courses, public budgeting and finance classes are uniquely suited for service learning projects. There are few real surprises in the budget offices of most local governments, rather the departments are in the habit of long-term planning, which allows for the incorporation of a project that meets the departments needs within the confines of the course schedule. Nonprofit organizations have less of a long-term plan, but many have needs, such as budgeting process reviews and financial plans that are required, but they lack the resources to complete them. The need for the projects often helps nonprofits overcome the issue of scheduling. Regardless, the schedule of the project and the expectations of the project are things that need to be agreed upon by the faculty member teaching the course and leadership within the organization in order to ensure all parties are on board.

The final issue on what makes a good service learning project is organizational commitment. When choosing a project, finding an organization that is excited to involve the students and is willing to make an investment into the project in order to see its success will lead to the greatest outcome. In this context, organizational commitment means that staff and leadership are willing and interested in meeting with students with some frequency, that they are willing to provide any and all data and information necessary to the students, and are committed to implementing the result of the project. In our experience, when commitment is high, organizations are just as interested in seeing students succeed as they are at receiving the final product.

The second question of how to find a suitable project is a concern in the management of any course or program (Schultz, 2019), but it is often easier than anticipated. The best places to find projects is within the alumni network of the respective MPA program. Alumni understand the experience of the MPA program and can understand where and how service learning fits within that experience. They are also able to connect the value for the students to the value for the organization in way that many cannot. Most MPA programs maintain an alumni board or program advisory board as part of their NASPAA accreditation, both of which provide direct connection to organization leadership who might have the need for a project to be conduct. Often, even if their own organizations do not need the work, they are able to help connect faculty with other organizations who could use the assistance. Alternatively, we have found success in finding suitable projects by working with our local United Way or the state's municipal league.

## Teaching with the Project

Once a service learning project is found, the faculty member must incorporate the project into the course. Generally speaking, there are two approaches for project incorporation: as a group project that is due at the end of the semester and as a fully immersed project where tasks are divided up throughout the semester and timed to coincide with class coverage of the relevant material. The choice of approach may be dependent on the nature of the students in the class as some students are better prepared for managing a large project on their own, whereas others may need more hand holding and planning for them to be successful. The choice may also be a function of the needs of the project that was chosen. If the full immersion approach is taken, then each aspect of the project should be laid out prior to starting the semester and then have the course material overlaid to ensure that the relevant material is discussed at a time that is suitable for the project. Course assignments are then created to contribute to the project or to use information related to the organization, even if not directly needed for the project, in order to create a cohesive class. If an end of semester approach is utilized, time should be factored into the course throughout the semester to allow students to work on the project and for the faculty to check in to ensure appropriate progress is being made.

Regardless of approach, student success in a service learning project is heavily tied to their understanding of the project, including the organization, the need, how the project meets the need, and what the final product should look like. These are also considerations that faculty should keep in mind when choosing a project as they are part of what the faculty member and the participating organization discuss and agree upon prior to the start of the project. To help relay this material to the class, we have found it helpful to take a two-step approach. In the first step, the idea and intent of the project is introduced and discussed with the students. Students are then encouraged to research the organization and conduct exploratory research on the project and similar projects. A member of leadership from the participating organization is invited to class during the next session to discuss the project at length and answer any questions that the students may have developed. At all times it is important for the faculty member to keep communication open with both the organization and the students to ensure the project is going according to plan and to thwart any complications before they emerge.

## Challenges to Service Learning

An advantage of traditional assignments for a course is that challenges can be anticipated and overcome. When incorporating a service learning project, challenges will always emerge, but what those challenges are and how they can be overcome is something that varies from one project to the next. Although it may not always be possible to anticipate what challenges will emerge, there are two challenges that occur more frequently, each of which can be prepared for and addressed should it emerge.

The first challenge of a service learning project is when a change happens with the partnering organization. This change may be a change in leadership, but it may also be a change in need. A change in leadership could result in a change in the level of commitment to the project while a change in need might lead to the organization encouraging students to conduct a different project than anticipated. Both of these can be prepared for prior to the start of the semester with the drafting of a brief memorandum of understanding between the faculty and the leadership of the organization. The memorandum should outline the nature of the project, what the project is expected to produce, the timeline of the project, and the nature of the organization's involvement in completing it. This helps to create a boundary for the project so that it can be completed as originally planned.

The second challenge relates to students. One of the frustrations of group projects is that the dynamic of student relationships can often complicate the process. Every faculty member has their own process for addressing student issues and they should be prepared to incorporate those processes should the need arise. Although students are encouraged to take the lead of the projects, with the faculty member serving in a guiding and assisting role, faculty should be prepared to take more of a hands-on approach if they view that the dynamic of the students is putting the project's completion at risk.

## Examples of Service Learning Projects

Implementing a service learning project for a public budgeting and finance course may feel overwhelming. To help aid in the creation of the project and its implementation, we want to provide two examples of what a project might entail and how it can overlap with a budget or financial management course. Both of the projects are based on our own experiences and both can be easily incorporated into a course. The first project is a budgeting project that requires the students to devise a plan for dealing with a budget cut for a local government agency. The second is a financial management project that requires students to explore the financial viability of the organization.

### *Budget Cut Project*

The budget cut project was implemented in a traditional public budgeting course in a MPA program and was performed on behalf of a local law enforcement agency. In preparation for the upcoming budget cycle, the elected officials had informed the agency that they would need to give all officers a 4 percent increase in salary, but the agency was not being provided additional funds to cover the increase. As a result, the agency would have to find the money for salary increases out of its own budget. Unsure of how to proceed with the budget cuts, the chief approached faculty in the MPA program seeking help, and, after some discussion, the agency agreed to being involved in the service learning project. The outcome of the project would be the budget choices that the chief would implement.

To carry out the project, the chief and their leadership agreed to make themselves available to the students during scheduled class hours. It was also agreed that any materials the students needed would likely be made available. After introducing the project to the class, the students were divided into three groups. Each group would explore the budget of the agency, it's processes, demands, and efficiency and develop a proposal for where the cuts could be implemented. Each week students were given some time to work on the project in class and class discussion often used the student's experience with the agency to highlight the relevant material for the week. For instance, in discussing the budget cycle, how the cycle is carried out for the agency was part of the class discussion. At the midpoint of the semester, each group made a presentation to the chief and their leadership team regarding their proposal for making the cut. The agency considered the options and chose the one that they felt aligned best with the organization's needs. For the remainder of the semester, groups work on developing whatever materials the agency needed to present the new budget for approval to the elected officials and to implement the new budget within the agency. This included detailed budgets, forecasts, presentations, and memos, depending on the nature of the project and the needs of the organization.

The addition of the project allowed for class discussions each week to follow the budgeting process, discuss the reality of budgeting, thus providing a connection between the theory of budgeting from course reading with the reality of the budgeting they were witnessing for the agency. For the students, it also provided a real-world experience that they were able to carry forward into their careers. The experience gained included directly working with staff, dealing with local government budgeting problems, and weighing the options while figuring out how to make cuts while minimizing the negative impact of the cuts. For the agency, the project solved a very real problem that they did not have an answer for. Where the experience of the service learning project has come in useful is that it has served as a case study type of project for students in subsequent semesters when a service learning project was unavailable.

It is worth noting that one of the advantages of service learning projects is that they may produce answers that had not previously been considered. In the case of the agency, the winning proposal was to balance the increase in salary with cuts in training, ammunition, repairs to patrol vehicles, and avoid any capital purchases. The plan was a controlled game of chicken, whereby students believed that the elected officials would not risk public safety, thus giving the agency an increase in its spending equivalent to the salary increases. The agency agreed and the elected officials ultimately caved to the pressure. The outcome is not what a faculty member would typically expect to see from such a project, but in this example, the agency chose the radical approach over more traditional budget cut plans.

## Financial Viability Project

The financial viability project was implemented in a MPA program's financial management course. The project was performed on behalf of a local nonprofit organization. The nonprofit organization had been suffering from declining revenue for several years, a problem that had been exasperated by the Great Recession. The organization provided a variety of services to the homeless population within the region, but the difficulty they experienced during the recession left many donors in the community unwilling to continue financing the organization as they were unsure of the ability of the organization to continue operating.

While looking for a service learning project for the financial management course, an alumnus of the MPA program who also sat on the board of the local United Way asked if a viability project would be suitable for the course. At the request of the United Way, the leadership of the nonprofit agreed to meet, and a plan was formed to help evaluate the financial position of the organization, audit its finances and financial practices, and develop a plan for rebuilding the organizations financial capacity. Leadership from the nonprofit organization agreed to participate in class discussions with students on a semi-regular basis, while also making their staff and records available to students during traditional business hours.

To incorporate the project into the course, all necessary tasks for the project were laid out and then matched with the weekly topics of the course. Individual assignments were then used to prepare the student for the work of the project, while the project itself was performed as a group, with group-based assignments due throughout the semester. For example, to prepare students for assessing the fiscal health of the organization, students learned about fiscal health in class and performed a homework assignment where they had to calculate and evaluate the fiscal health of a local governmental agency. This provided experience for the group's assessment of the nonprofit.

At the end of the semester, the students took the assignments they had completed as a group throughout the semester and posted them into a single report. The report was then polished and prepared for presentation to both the nonprofit organization and the United Way. Although the students found a number of concerns regarding financial practices within the organization, the United Way agreed to provide some funding to the nonprofit on the expectation that the recommended changes developed by the students be implemented. The transparency provided by the project and injected into the organization through the changes allowed for the nonprofit organization to take the plan and use it to fundraise the remaining revenue.

## Conclusion

One of the challenges faculty face when teaching data and processing heavy material is how to best relay the subject in way that students can grasp and understand. The field of education has developed a number of teaching philosophies to help in this regard, but ultimately the best teaching philosophy for a course is highly dependent upon a combination of student background, student characteristics, and course content. Given the applied nature of the field, case studies and service learning projects have emerged as a key pedagogical tool within public administration. As forms of experiential learning, case studies and service learning projects provide opportunities for students to engage course material by requiring them to act on a scenario as though they were in the careers.

Case studies and service learning projects require student engagement with the material at different depths, or levels, of learning. As many Master of Public Administration students are challenged by the course material in a public budgeting and finance course, the opportunity to engage with the material in a real and meaningful way can provide the connection that students need to achieve. As research indicates, both case studies and service learning projects provide the opportunity to connect with the material on the highest levels of level, enhancing the learning outcomes of our students.

In this chapter, we have sought to introduce the idea of using case studies and service learning projects in public budgeting and finance courses. While many faculty members may be familiar with the pedagogical tools, how to use them effectively can be tricky. Perhaps more importantly, the lack of experiences with the tools can dissuade faculty from working to incorporate them into their course.

Accordingly, our discussion centers on three aspects for each tool: what the tool is, how to teach with the tool, and how to find opportunities to use the tool. Although this chapter provides an overview of how to use case studies and service learning projects in a public budgeting and finance course, it is but an introduction. There are many resources that be accessed online, including articles and cases published in the *Journal of Public Affairs Education*, and the Network of Schools of Public Policy, Affairs, and Administration regularly holds training courses at its annual conference.

## References

Armstrong, P. (2016). *Bloom's taxonomy*. Vanderbilt University Center for Teaching.

Bacot, H. (2020). Community outreach and applied research centers. In B. D. McDonald & W. Hatcher (Eds.), *The public affairs faculty manual: A guide to the effective management of public affairs programs* (pp. 239–258). Routledge.

Barth, T. J., & Hamel, J. D. (2020). Understanding the degrees: MPA, MPP, versus MNM. In B. D. McDonald & W. Hatcher (Eds.), *The public affairs faculty manual: A guide to the effective management of public affairs programs* (pp. 11–32). Routledge.

Berry-James, R. M., Blessett, B., Emas, R., McCandless, S., Nickels, A. E., Norman-Major, K., & Vinzant, P. (2020). Stepping up to the plate: Making social equity a priority in public administration's troubled times. *Journal of Public Affairs Education*. https://doi.org/10.1080/15236803.2020.1820289

Dewey, J. (1916). *Democracy and education: An introduction to the philosophy of education*. Macmillan Press.

Flink, C., & Molina, A. L. (2020). Improving the performance of public organizations: Financial resources and the conditioning effect of clientele context. *Public Administration*. https://doi.org/10.1111/padm.12690

Goodman, D. (2020). Curriculum and instructional design. In B. D. McDonald & W. Hatcher (Eds.), *The public affairs faculty manual: A guide to the effective management of public affairs programs* (pp. 139–161). Routledge.

Hatcher, W., & McDonald, B. D. (2020). Managing your public affairs program. In B. D. McDonald & W. Hatcher (Eds.), *The public affairs faculty manual: A guide to the effective management of public affairs programs* (pp. 1–10). Routledge.

Hatcher, W., McDonald, B. D., & Brainard, L. A. (2018). How to write a case study for public affairs. *Journal of Public Affairs Education*, *24*(2), 274–285.

Jacoby, B. (1996). *Service-learning in higher education: Concepts and practices*. San Francisco, CA: Jossey-Bass.

Jin, M. H. (2020) Models of academic governance. In B. D. McDonald & W. Hatcher (Eds.), *The public affairs faculty manual: A guide to the effective management of public affairs programs* (pp. 33–47). Routledge.

Lambright, K. (2008). Lessons outside of the classroom: Examining the effectiveness of service learning projects at achieving learning objectives. *Journal of Public Affairs Education*, *14*(2), 205–217.

Lebovits, H., & Bharath, D. M. N. (2019). Service-learning as a tool to cultivate democratically minded students: A conceptual framework. *Journal of Public and Nonprofit Affairs*, *5*(3), 277–292.

Li, H., McDougle, L. M., & Gupta, A. (2020). Experiential philanthropy in China. *Journal of Public Affairs Education, 26*(2), 205–227.

Liston-Heyes, C., & Juillet, L. (2020). Burdens of transparency: An analysis of public sector internal auditing. *Public Administration, 98*(3), 659–674.

Maher, C. S., Ebdon, C., & Bartle, J. R. (2020). Financial condition analysis: A key tool in the MPA curriculum. *Journal of Public Affair Education, 26*(1), 4–10.

McDonald, B. D. (2010). The Bureau of Municipal Research and the development of a professional public service. *Administration and Society, 42*(7), 815–835.

McDonald, B. D., Hatcher, W., & Abbott, M. (2021). History of public administration education in the United States. In K. A. Bottom, P. Dunning, I. Elliot, & J. Diamond (Eds.), *Handbook on the teaching of public administration.* Edward Elgar Publishing.

Pautz, M. C., & Vogel, M. D. (2020). Investigating faculty motivation and its connection to faculty work-life balance: Engaging public service motivation to explore faculty motivation. *Journal of Public Affairs Education, 26*(4), 437–457.

Raadschelders, J., Whetsell, T., Dimand, A. M., & Kieninger, K. (2019). *Journal of Public Affairs Education* at 25: Topics, trends, and authors. *Journal of Public Affairs Education, 25*(1), 51–72.

Reinke, S. J. (2003). Making a difference: Does service-learning promote civic engagement in MPA students? *Journal of Public Affairs Education, 9*(3), 123–138.

Rivenbark, W. C. (2007). Using cases to teach financial management skills in MPA programs. *Journal of Public Affairs Education, 13*(2), 451–460.

Schultz, D. (2019). Yogi Berra and the art of public affair teaching. *Journal of Public Affairs Education, 25*(1), 18–22.

Stone, E. O. (1957). Seven letters: A case in public management. *Public Administration Review, 17*(2), 83–90.

Svinicki, M. D & McKeachie, W. J. (2014). *McKeachie's teaching tips: Strategies, research, and theory for college and university teachers.* Wadsworth.

Waldner, L. S., & Hunter, D. (2008). Client-based courses: Variations in service learning. *Journal of Public Affairs Education, 14*(2), 219–239.

# INDEX

*Note*: Page numbers in *italic* refer to figures, page numbers in **bold** refer to tables.

ABFM (Association for Budgeting
and Financial Management), public
budgeting mechanics 73
accountability 21–22; *see also* auditing
and internal controls; Government
Accountability Office (GAO)
153, 156, 158, 159–160, 161, 164;
Public Expenditure and Financial
Accountability (PEFA) 58–60; social
equity 235, 239–240
accounting cycle, financial management
114–115
annuities, capital budgeting and debt
financing 87, **88**
Apply Basic *Methods* Skillfully (REMIT
component) 75–107
assessment 21–22
Assess the *Environment* Thoroughly
(REMIT component) 75–107
assets, infrastructure asset disclosure for
governments that use the modified
approach for reporting infrastructure
assets 135
Association for Budgeting and Financial
Management (ABFM), public budgeting
mechanics 73
Association of Government Accountants
28
asynchronous online case discussions 255,
256, 257

audience for this book 2
auditing and internal controls 150–165;
assignment: auditor selection and
independence 160–161; assignment:
citizen engagement 161–162;
assignment: research papers/essay
questions 162; assignment: reviewing an
audit report 163–164; audit process
156–159; characteristics of audits
155–156; core competencies 151–152;
Generally Accepted Auditing Standards
(GAAS) 153–154, 157; Generally
Accepted Government Auditing
Standards (GAGAS) 153, 157;
Government Accountability Office
(GAO) 153, 156, 158, 159–160, 161,
164; information sources 153–155;
learning objectives 151–152; learning
outcomes 152; pedagogical strategies
152–160; student assessment 160–164;
teaching strategies 159–160; topics
in governmental and not- for- profit
auditing 155–156; websites 153–155

basic accounting equation, financial
management 115–116
basic governmental accounting equation,
financial management 116–117
behavioral responses, revenue policy
33–34

"benefit theory", nonprofit organizations 220

Bloomberg Terminal, capital budgeting and debt financing 82–84

Bloom's taxonomy of learning, service learning 262

Brown's 10-Point Test of Financial Condition, financial condition analysis 172–176, 182–188

Budgetary Comparison Schedules, financial management exercise 148

budgetary comparison schedules, Required Supplementary Information (RSI) 135

budgetary versus GAAP basis of accounting, financial management exercise 139

budget cut project, service learning 267–268

budget cycles 237, 267; COVID-19 24–25; disruption 25; elements 17–19; emerging issues and challenges 24–25; Government Finance Officers Association 25; interactions 24–25, 26–27; National Association of State Budget Officers 25; National League of Cities 25; public budgeting mechanics 51–66; research opportunities 10–11, 27; social equity 25, 237

budget decision-making, complexities and interrelationships 9–10

budgeting, social equity 235–240

budgeting and revenue issues and processes 17–19; see also public budgeting mechanics; changes in program needs 18; pension systems 16, 20; revenue receipts monitoring 18; revenue shortfalls actions 18

budget process, nonprofit organizations 217–218

budget simulation tools 22, 40, 159, 253

budget timelines of United States governments 53–64

Bureau of Municipal Research, social equity 236

buyer's utility maximizing choices, economic efficiency 37–38, 39

capital budgeting 19–20, 75–107; see also debt financing; annuities 87, **88**; Bloomberg Terminal 82–84; class activities 105–107; compound interest 86–87; cost of capital 94, **97**; debt disclosure document 102, **103**; debt

project assignment 94, **96**; educational applications 77–105; educational objectives and competencies 75–77; enterprise revenue bond analysis 103, **104**; excel functions **90**; financial structure and debt service analysis 98, **99**; fiscal impact analysis 90, **92–93**; fixed coupon and current year relationship 90, **94**; Life Cycle Cost Analysis (LCCA) 86–87; model financial plan 89, **91**; "Official Statement" (OS) 102, **103**; policies 77–81; REMIT (respect environment, methods interpreted transparently) 75–107; revenue bond financing **103**; revenue coverage capacity 94, **96**; secondary market pricing 98, **100**; state GO credit quality analysis 104, **105**; time value of money 76, 85–87, **89**, 94, 106n; valuing a bond with annual coupon 95, **98**

carbon tax on motor vehicles, student-led discussion of revenue policy debates 44

case studies 252–261, 269–270; asynchronous online case discussions 255, 256, 257; case cycle for a course 256; case selection 253–255; challenges 258–259; citizen budget participation case 260–261; city pool funding case 259–260; decision-making skills 254, 257, 258, 260; examples of teaching through case studies 259–261; incorporating case studies into public budgeting and financial management class 255–258; jurisdictional focus 254; learning objectives 253–254, 255–256, 259–261; types of case study presentations 257–258; using case studies 253–259

central bank see FED (Federal Reserve System)

citizen budget participation case, case study 260–261

city pool funding case, case study 259–260

collectability, revenue policy 34

Communicate *Transparently* (REMIT component) 75–107

communication and transparency of public financial information 21–22; written and oral communication skills 166–168

communication with decision makers, taxation 34–35

community relations, public budgeting mechanics 68, 69

complexities and interrelationships: budget decision-making 9–10; financial management 9–10

component units, financial management exercise 140

compound interest, capital budgeting and debt financing 86–87

Comprehensive Annual Financial Reports 109–110; financial condition analysis 169–171, 173, 179, 180

Congressional Budget Office 28

controls and auditing *see* auditing and internal controls

core competencies, auditing and internal controls 151–152

cost of capital, capital budgeting and debt financing 94, **97**

COVID-19: budget cycles 24–25; financial condition analysis 171; public budgeting mechanics 62, **65**

CSPAN 28

current or lagged revenue collections, fiscal capacity measurement 47

dark store assessment, student-led discussion of revenue policy debates 44

data and information 23–24

debt disclosure document, capital budgeting and debt financing 102, **103**

debt financing 19–20, 64, 75–107; *see also* capital budgeting; annuities 87, **88**; Bloomberg Terminal 82–84; class activities 105–107; compound interest 86–87; cost of capital 94, **97**; debt disclosure document 102, **103**; debt project assignment 94, **96**; educational applications 77–105; educational objectives and competencies 75–77; enterprise revenue bond analysis 103, **104**; excel functions **90**; financial structure and debt service analysis 98, **99**; fiscal impact analysis 90, **92**; fixed coupon and current year relationship 90, **94**; Life Cycle Cost Analysis (LCCA) 86–87; long-term debt 19–20; model debt plan 90–93, **95**; model financial plan 89, **91**; "Official Statement" (OS) 102, **103**; policies 77–81; REMIT (respect environment, methods interpreted transparently) 75–107; revenue bond financing **103**; revenue coverage capacity 94, **96**; secondary market pricing 98, **100**; state GO credit

quality analysis 104, **105**; time value of money 64, 85–87, **89**, 94, 106n; valuing a bond with annual coupon 95, **98**

debt project assignment, capital budgeting and debt financing 94, **96**

decision-making skills, case studies 254, 257, 258, 260

deferred resources, financial management exercise 140

defined benefit plans, pensions 200, 201–205

defined contribution plans, pensions 200–203, 205–207

definitions: major funds definition, financial management exercise 138, 140; pensions 200–203; social equity 232–233

disasters strategies, public budgeting mechanics 58, 62–63

duration of assets and liabilities, financial management exercise 140

e-commerce, student-led discussion of revenue policy debates 43–44

economic and political environment 15–17

economic efficiency 36–39; buyer's utility maximizing choices 37–38, 39; comparison of efficiency outcomes for different policy choices 39, **40**; marginal benefit/price ratio of consumer goods 36–39; revenue policy 36–39

educational objectives and competencies: 'REMIT', capital budgeting and debt financing 75–77

endowments, nonprofit organizations 219–220

enterprise revenue bond analysis, capital budgeting and debt financing 103, **104**

excel functions, capital budgeting and debt financing **90**

experiences, our teaching 2–3

experiential learning *see* case studies; service learning

FED (Federal Reserve System) 29; role 16

federal nondefense discretionary spending 12–13

federal revenues and expenditures 12–13

federal system 10–15

Fiduciary Fund, financial management exercise 141, *147*

fiduciary funds, fund financial statements 133

financial analysis, nonprofit organizations 222–223

financial condition analysis 166–180; Brown's 10-Point Test of Financial Condition 172–176, 182–188; Comprehensive Annual Financial Reports 169–171, 173, 179, 180; conditions for consideration 171–172; COVID-19 171; elements of financial condition 168–169; Financial Trend Monitoring System (FTMS) 168; Government Accounting Standards Board (GASB) 169–171; governmental fund statement 172–176; Government Finance Officers Association (GFAO) 168–169; government-wide financial statements 176–178; International City/County Management Association's (ICMA) 168–169, 172; Maher's ratios 189, 190, 192–195; Management Discussion and Analysis (MD&A) 169–171; nonprofit organizations 222–223; program competency: to lead and manage in public governance 167; tools 172–178; written and oral communication skills 166–167

Financial Industry Regulatory Authority (FINRA), pensions 198–199

financial management 109–149; *see also* financial reporting; accounting cycle 114–115; basic accounting equation 115–116; basic governmental accounting equation 116–117; complexities and interrelationships 9–10; Comprehensive Annual Financial Reports 109–110; Generally Accepted Accounting Principles (GAAP) 113–114; Government Accounting Standards Board (GASB) 113–114; learning objectives 110; Management Discussion and Analysis (MD&A) 110, 113; measurement focus and basis of accounting (MFBA) standards 112–113; Required Statistical Information (RSI) 110

financial management exercises: Budgetary Comparison Schedules 148; budgetary versus GAAP basis of accounting 139; component units 140; deferred resources 140; duration of assets and liabilities 140; Fiduciary Fund 141, *147*; governmental fund 140–141; major funds definition 138, 140; Management Discussion and Analysis (MD&A) 148; Proprietary Fund 141, *142–146*; Reconciliation 141–148; types of fund financial statements 140

financial reporting 117–138; *see also* financial management; basic financial statements 117–118; fund financial statements 125–133; Government Accounting Standards Board (GASB) 111; government-wide financial statements 118–125; nonprofit organizations 220–222; principles of governmental accounting and financial reporting 111–113; reconciliation between government-wide financial statements and fund financial statements 133–134; Required Supplementary Information (RSI) 134–136; Statement of Activities 123–125; Statement of Net Position 120–123

financial statements *see* financial reporting

financial structure and debt service analysis, capital budgeting and debt financing 98, **99**

Financial Trend Monitoring System (FTMS), financial condition analysis 168

financial viability project, service learning 268–269

FINRA (Financial Industry Regulatory Authority), pensions 198–199

fiscal capacity measurement 46–50; current or lagged revenue collections 47; gross regional product 48; personal income per capita 47–49; Representative Tax System (RTS) 49–50; Total Taxable Resources (TTR) 48

fiscal disparity assignment 46–50

fiscal effort of subnational governments 46–50

fiscal impact analysis, capital budgeting and debt financing 90, **92–93**

fiscal stress test, student-led discussion of revenue policy debates 43

fiscal year dates, public budgeting mechanics 53–64

fixed coupon and current year relationship, capital budgeting and debt financing 90, **94**

FTMS (Financial Trend Monitoring System), financial condition analysis 168

fund financial statements 125–133; fiduciary funds 133; governmental fund 126–130; proprietary fund 130–133;

reconciliation between government-wide financial statements and fund financial statements 133–134

GAAP *see* Generally Accepted Accounting Principles
GAAS (Generally Accepted Auditing Standards), auditing and internal controls 153–154, 157
GAGAS (Generally Accepted Government Auditing Standards), auditing and internal controls 153, 157
GAO (Government Accountability Office), auditing and internal controls 153, 156, 158, 159–160, 161, 164
GARE (Government Alliance on Race and Equity), social equity 243
GASB *see* Government Accounting Standards Board
Generally Accepted Accounting Principles (GAAP) 21; financial management 113–114; role in the accounting process 113–114
Generally Accepted Auditing Standards (GAAS), auditing and internal controls 153–154, 157
Generally Accepted Government Auditing Standards (GAGAS), auditing and internal controls 153, 157
GFAO (Government Finance Officers Association), financial condition analysis 168–169
governance, public budgeting mechanics 58–60
Government Accountability Office (GAO), auditing and internal controls 153, 156, 158, 159–160, 161, 164
Government Accounting Standards Board (GASB): basic financial statements 117–118; basic governmental accounting equation 116; fiduciary funds 133; financial condition analysis 169–171; financial management 113–114; financial reporting 111; fund financial statements 126; governmental fund statement 127; government-wide financial statements 120; major funds definition 138; Required Supplementary Information (RSI) 134–136; role in the accounting process 113–114; source of studies 28
governmental fund: financial management exercise 140–141; fund financial statements 126–130

governmental fund statement 129, 134; financial condition analysis 172–176
Government Alliance on Race and Equity (GARE), social equity 243
government budget equation 60–61
Government Finance Officers Association 28; budget cycles 25
Government Finance Officers Association (GFAO), financial condition analysis 168–169
government regulation 12
government's role 10–15
government-wide financial statements: financial condition analysis 176–178; financial reporting 118–125; reconciliation between government-wide financial statements and fund financial statements 133–134
gross regional product, fiscal capacity measurement 48

IBM Center for The Business of Government, public budgeting mechanics 62, **63**, 74
ICMA *see* International City/County Management Association
income tax, student-led discussion of revenue policy debates 43
information and data 23–24
interdisciplinary roots, public finance 10–11
internal controls: *see also* auditing and internal controls; nonprofit organizations 224
International City/County Management Association (ICMA) 28; financial condition analysis 168–169, 172; Financial Trend Monitoring System (FTMS) 168
*Interpret* Results Fairly (REMIT component) 75–107
interrelationships and complexities: budget decision-making 9–10; financial management 9–10
investment management: defined benefit plans 203–205; pensions 203–207

jurisdictional focus, case studies 254

knowledge-building techniques, public budgeting mechanics 68–73

LCCA (Life Cycle Cost Analysis), capital budgeting and debt financing 86–87

learning objectives: auditing and internal controls 151–152; case studies 253–254, 255–256, 259–261; financial management 110; public budgeting mechanics 52–53

learning outcomes: auditing and internal controls 152; nonprofit organizations 215; social equity 238–241; student learning objectives 52–53

legacy issues 19–20

Legislative Services Agency (LSA), student-led discussion of revenue policy debates 44–45

Life Cycle Cost Analysis (LCCA), capital budgeting and debt financing 86–87

long-term debt 19–20

macroeconomic stabilization, revenue policy 32

Maher's ratios, financial condition analysis 189, 190, 192–195

major funds definition, financial management exercise 138, 140

Management Discussion and Analysis (MD&A) 110, 113; financial condition analysis 169–171; financial management exercise 148; Required Supplementary Information (RSI) 135

marginal benefit/price ratio of consumer goods, economic efficiency 36–39

marijuana tax, student-led discussion of revenue policy debates 43

market failure 11–12

Master of Public Administration (MPA) programs 1–7; experiences, our teaching 2–3; pedagogical challenges 3–4; service learning 263–265, 268–269

MD&A see Management Discussion and Analysis

measurement focus and basis of accounting (MFBA) standards 112–113

Medicaid 12–14

Medicare 12–14

MFBA (measurement focus and basis of accounting) standards 112–113

model debt plan, debt financing 90–93, **95**

model financial plan, capital budgeting and debt financing 89, **91**

MPA programs see Master of Public Administration programs

NASBO see National Association of State Budget Officers

NASPAA see Network of Schools of Public Policy, Analysis, and Administration

National Association of State Budget Officers (NASBO) 28; budget cycles 25; public budgeting mechanics 60, 61

National Conference of State Legislatures 28

National League of Cities 29; budget cycles 25

need for teaching 1–2

Network of Schools of Public Policy, Analysis, and Administration (NASPAA); nonprofit organizations 214; public budgeting mechanics 52, 73, 265

nonprofit organizations 214–228; assignments 225–228; "benefit theory" 220; budget process 217–218; endowments 219–220; financial analysis 222–223; financial condition analysis 222–223; financial reporting 220–222; focus areas for teaching nonprofit financial management 215–224; internal controls 224; learning outcomes 215; mission 216; Network of Schools of Public Policy, Analysis, and Administration (NASPAA) 214; operating ratio 223; organization structure and roles 216–217; private donations 219; program ratio 223; quick ratio 223; reserve funds 219; resources 224–225; resources for teaching 225, **226**; revenue sources and issues 218–220; Statement of Activities 221; Statement of Cash Flows 221; Statement of Financial Position 221; Statement of Functional Expenses 221; statistics 214; taxation 222

Office of Management and Budget 29

"Official Statement" (OS), capital budgeting and debt financing 102, **103**

operating ratio, nonprofit organizations 223

pay-as-you-go (PAYGO) pensions 200–201

pedagogical challenges 3–4

pedagogical content, revenue policy 36–45

pedagogical strategies: auditing and internal controls 152–160; social equity 240–242

PEFA (Public Expenditure and Financial Accountability), public budgeting mechanics 58–60

pensions 196–213; alternative program structure 209; background 200–203; basic structure of pensions 201; benefit determination 202–203; defined benefit plans 200, 201–205; defined contribution plans 200–203, 205–207; definitions 200–203; evaluation of student learning 208; Financial Industry Regulatory Authority (FINRA) 198–199; handouts 200; investment management 203–207; lecture structure 200–207; misunderstandings 196, 197; pay-as-you-go (PAYGO) pensions 200–201; pension systems 16, 20; precursors 198–199; primary characteristics 201, **202**; readings and materials 199–200; sample assignment questions 208; sample assignment questions (answer keys) 211–213; statistics and pension policy 203; subject context and objectives 197–198; time value of money 198–199

personal income per capita, fiscal capacity measurement 47–49

philosophy teaching, public budgeting mechanics 68–73

political and economic environment 15–17

POSDCORB (Planning, Organizing, Staffing, Directing, Coordinating, Reporting, and Budgeting), social equity 236

pre-populated tax forms, student-led discussion of revenue policy debates 44

private donations, nonprofit organizations 219

program evaluation 21

program ratio, nonprofit organizations 223

property tax exemptions, student-led discussion of revenue policy debates 44

Proprietary Fund, financial management exercise 141, *142–146*

proprietary fund, fund financial statements 130–133

public administration, social equity 232–235

public budgeting mechanics 51–74; *see also* budgeting and revenue issues and processes; Association for Budgeting and Financial Management (ABFM) 73; budget cycles 51–66; budgeting in

a pandemic 62, **65**; budget timelines of United States governments 53–64; community relations *68, 69*; COVID-19 62, **65**; development 58–62; disasters strategies 58, 62–63; essential knowledge 53–68; fiscal year dates 53–64; governance 58–60; government budget equation 60–61; IBM Center for The Business of Government 62, **63**, 74; knowledge-building techniques 68–73; learning objectives 52–53; National Association of State Budget Officers (NASBO) 60, 61; Network of Schools of Public Policy, Analysis, and Administration (NASPAA) 52, 73, 265; philosophy teaching 68–73; public budgeting: theories and practice **71–72**; Public Expenditure and Financial Accountability (PEFA) 58–60; strategies 60, 62–63; variability 51–52

public confidence 21–22

Public Expenditure and Financial Accountability (PEFA), public budgeting mechanics 58–60

quick ratio, nonprofit organizations 223

racial equity toolkits, social equity 243–245

Reconciliation, financial management exercise 141–148

regulation, government 12

REMIT (respect environment, methods interpreted transparently), capital budgeting and debt financing 75–107

reporting, financial *see* financial reporting

Representative Tax System (RTS), fiscal capacity measurement 49–50

Required Statistical Information (RSI) 110

Required Supplementary Information (RSI): budgetary comparison schedules 135; financial reporting 134–136; infrastructure asset disclosure for governments that use the modified approach for reporting infrastructure assets 135; Management Discussion and Analysis (MD&A) 135; other RSI 136

research opportunities, budget cycles 10–11, 27

reserve funds, nonprofit organizations 219

*Respect* the Rules Completely (REMIT component) 75–107

revenue 30–50; *see also* budgeting and revenue issues and processes; federal

revenues and expenditures 12–13; revenue receipts monitoring 18; taxation 30
revenue bond financing, capital budgeting and debt financing **103**
revenue coverage capacity: capital budgeting and debt financing 94, **96**; debt financing 94, **96**
revenue policy 31–35; *see also* student-led discussion of revenue policy debates; behavioral responses 33–34; collectability 34; criteria 32–34; economic efficiency 36–39; evaluation of instruments 32–34; goals 31–32; macroeconomic stabilization 32; objectives 31–35; pedagogical content 36–45; suggested approach 35–36; taxation 32–34; technical skills assignment 36; transparency 34
revenue sources and issues, nonprofit organizations 218–220
road mileage tax, student-led discussion of revenue policy debates 43
RSI *see* Required Statistical Information; Required Supplementary Information

secondary market pricing, capital budgeting and debt financing 98, **100**
service learning 252–253, 261–270; Bloom's taxonomy of learning 262; budget cut project 267–268; challenges 266; examples of service learning projects 267–269; financial viability project 268–269; incorporating service learning into public budgeting and finance classes 263–265; MPA programs 263–265, 268–269; projects 261–266; teaching with the project 265–266
social equity 26, 231–247; accountability 235, 239–240; assignment possibilities 240–247; budget cycles 25, 26, 237; budgeting 235–240; Bureau of Municipal Research 236; centering social equity in the budgeting classroom 247; definitions 232–233; dimensions 233–235; Government Alliance on Race and Equity (GARE) 243; impact analyses 243–245; importance 231–232; incorporating into the budgeting classroom 242; inequities 233–235; learning outcomes 238–241; modifying classic assignments 246–247; pedagogical strategies 240–242; POSDCORB (Planning, Organizing, Staffing, Directing, Coordinating, Reporting, and Budgeting) 236; public administration 232–235; racial equity toolkits 243–245; readings and class discussions 240–243; resources for teaching 243; U.S. Constitution 233–235
state and local government finances 14–15
state GO credit quality analysis, capital budgeting and debt financing 104, **105**
Statement of Activities: financial reporting 123–125; nonprofit organizations 221
Statement of Cash Flows, nonprofit organizations 221
Statement of Financial Position, nonprofit organizations 221
Statement of Functional Expenses, nonprofit organizations 221
Statement of Net Position, financial reporting 120–123
strategies: disasters 58, 62–63; public budgeting mechanics 60, 62–63
student-led discussion of revenue policy debates 39–45; carbon tax on motor vehicles 44; dark store assessment 44; deliverables 41–42; description for students 40; e-commerce 43–44; examples of topics 42–45; fiscal stress test 43; grade/rubric 42; guidelines for the report 41; income tax 43; Legislative Services Agency (LSA) 44–45; marijuana tax 43; pre-populated tax forms 44; property tax exemptions 44; revenue policy 39–45; road mileage tax 43; tax incremental financing (TIF) 42–43; wheel tax 43
synopsis of chapters 4–6

taxation: *see also* revenue; revenue policy; communication with decision makers 34–35; nonprofit organizations 222; pre-populated tax forms 44; revenue 30; revenue policy 32–34
tax incremental financing (TIF), student-led discussion of revenue policy debates 42–43
technical skills assignment, revenue policy 36
TIF (tax incremental financing), student-led discussion of revenue policy debates 42–43

time value of money: capital budgeting 76, 85–87, **89**, 94, 106n; debt financing 64, 85–87, **89**, 94, 106n; pensions 198–199
Total Taxable Resources (TTR), fiscal capacity measurement 48
transparency 21–22; revenue policy 34
TTR (Total Taxable Resources), fiscal capacity measurement 48
types of fund financial statements, financial management exercise 140

unknowable data 23–24
U.S. Census – Government Finances 29
U.S. Constitution, social equity 233–235

U.S. Department of Commerce 29
U.S. Federal Reserve *see* FED (Federal Reserve System)
U.S. Government Accountability Office 29

valuing a bond with annual coupon, capital budgeting and debt financing 95, **98**

websites, auditing and internal controls 153–155
wheel tax, student-led discussion of revenue policy debates 43
written and oral communication skills 166–168

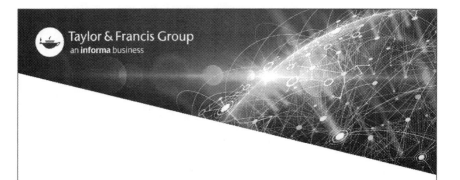

Printed in the United States
by Baker & Taylor Publisher Services